Steep

Steep

The Precipitous Rise of the Tea Party

EDITED BY
Lawrence Rosenthal
Christine Trost

UNIVERSITY OF CALIFORNIA PRESS
Berkeley · Los Angeles · London

University of California Press, one of the most distinguished university presses in the United States, enriches
lives around the world by advancing scholarship in the
humanities, social sciences, and natural sciences. Its activities are supported by the UC Press Foundation and by
philanthropic contributions from individuals and institutions. For more information, visit www.ucpress.edu.

University of California Press
Berkeley and Los Angeles, California

University of California Press, Ltd.
London, England

Library of Congress Cataloging-in-Publication Data

Steep : the precipitous rise of the Tea Party / edited by
Lawrence Rosenthal, Christine Trost.
      p. cm.
    Includes index.
    ISBN 978-0-520-27422-8 (cloth)—ISBN 978-0-520-
27423-5 (pbk.)
  1. Tea Party movement. I. Rosenthal, Lawrence,
1949- II. Trost, Christine.
    JK2391.T43S74 2012
    320.520973—dc23
                                        2012007436

19 18 17 16 15 14 13 12
10 9 8 7 6 5 4 3 2 1

In keeping with a commitment to support environ-
mentally responsible and sustainable printing practices,
UC Press has printed this book on Rolland Enviro100,
a 100% post-consumer fiber paper that is FSC certified,
deinked, processed chlorine-free, and manufactured with
renewable biogas energy. It is acid-free and EcoLogo
certified.

Contents

List of Illustrations

FIGURES

The Rise of the Tea Party

CHRISTINE TROST AND LAWRENCE ROSENTHAL

Nobody predicted the Tea Party.

In the wake of Barack Obama's inauguration as president in 2009, the Tea Party's emergence on the American scene was stunning. True, hints of the Tea Party had surfaced at Republican rallies during the 2008 presidential campaign, especially when vice presidential candidate Sarah Palin appeared. But the passion of those mobilized by the Tea Party movement, their anger, and their very numbers—this was a bolt from the blue.

To understand the shock of the Tea Party's emergence, it helps to recall the political environment of late 2008 and early 2009. The conservative movement, mostly in power and mostly defining the terms of American political debate since 1980, seemed to have run aground, perhaps fatally. After eight years under the most conservative president in memory—six of which included a Republican majority in Congress—things had not only gone wrong socially, economically, and even in foreign affairs; they had gone catastrophically wrong.

George W. Bush's tagline, "compassionate conservative," plus innovations such as the White House Office of Faith-Based and Community Initiatives that Bush established through an executive order in January 2001, had promised a novel but serious approach to addressing American social problems. A new chapter in the left-right debate in this country had begun, including a more robust dialogue on church-state relations and the efficacy of private versus public safety nets. But any credibility the administration had earned as the country's domestic steward was swept away with the winds and floods of Hurricane Katrina in late August 2005. As Americans watched one of our major cities felled as we had never seen or imagined before, the fecklessness, if not indifference, of the Bush government stood out in tragic relief.

With respect to the economy, Bush's policy of tax cuts (to say nothing of massive military expenditures) had not only turned financial surplus into severe national debt, it had created a yawning divide between rich and poor with a dwindling middle class that seemed to render the country less and less like the one most Americans had grown up in.[1] While this could be covered up rhetorically, the financial crisis that hit in the fall of 2008 could not. Suddenly—and it was sudden—the administration announced that the country's financial system was on the verge of collapse. The word *depression,* as in the Great Depression, made a startling reappearance. Not since the 1930s had there been an economic emergency anything like this. John McCain unilaterally suspended his presidential campaign to deal with it. Only the oldest generation of Americans had any experience of the Great Depression. Never, in the lifetimes of the rest of us, had the word been pulled out of mothballs to chronicle what was upon us as a nation. Never had we seen the extraordinary financial bailout measures the administration pushed through Congress to avoid what government officials promised would be "total financial collapse."

Bush's foreign policy had been dominated by the war his administration launched in Iraq in March 2003. But everything the administration had said about the war—its cost, its duration, the reasons for starting it, and even a stagy early declaration of victory—had turned out to be wrong. The photographs out of Abu Ghraib had shamed American armed forces and the politicians who had sent them. And, while it was rarely mentioned in polite company, this country's most disastrous foreign attack on its own soil (on September 11, 2001) had taken place on the administration's watch.

In the 2008 presidential election, John McCain, the Republican candidate chosen by his party to succeed George Bush, was not merely beaten by a Democrat; he was beaten by an African American. This was not only a triumph of the Democratic Party, but it also seemed a historic moment—*transformative,* as the catchword went—an eclipse of conservatism that had liberals both here and abroad dreaming of a second coming of the New Deal.

McCain had run with almost no mention of the Bush administration. In the election's aftermath, some voices aimed to save the good name of conservatism by arguing that it was Bush's incompetence, not conservative ideology, that had brought on the disasters.[2] Others argued that Bush had not been conservative enough, or even that he had never been a true conservative.[3] But these seemed minority voices. A more general mood suggested that American conservatism, after its thirty-year run in power, was an ideology worn out. Its electoral chances were spent. In a changing American demographic environment, Republicans were perhaps doomed to be a rump or regional party.[4] Intellectually, its ideas were exhausted. As Sam Tanenhaus put it in his book title of early 2010, we were watching "The Death of Conservatism."[5]

The Tea Party upended this gathering conventional wisdom with a vengeance. Any notion of the right fading into the sunset dissolved overnight. Instead, the right, or at least a subset of the right, was louder than ever, swiftly becoming the outstanding political phenomenon of the Obama presidency. In breathtakingly short order, American conservatism not only failed to fade away, not only regrouped, but also moved decisively farther to the right. The Tea Party resurrected themes that mainstream conservatism had rejected as too radical forty years earlier. And it managed to mobilize either in action or in sympathy at least a Perot-sized[6] chunk of the American electorate.

From the beginning, the Tea Party sparked no end of debate. Traditional print media, talk radio, network and cable television, and copious blogs opined endlessly about the Tea Party. The movement[7] enjoyed a special relationship with one national television network, Fox News, which spared no effort in helping organize and publicize Tea Party events. Fox News treated issues that Tea Party militants raised as prominent news items and, Glenn Beck, especially, pugnaciously instructed the Tea Party in the enemy they faced (largely American liberalism) and the tenets they, the Tea Partiers, stood for as the "real Americans."

In all the journalism and all the opinionating, it remained difficult to put a finger on just what the Tea Party was and is. The national debate seemed more productive at reinforcing people's attitudes about the Tea Party than challenging them with well-argued and well-grounded studies. In October 2010, the Center for Right-Wing Studies at the University of California at Berkeley organized a major academic conference to bring rigorous scholarly analysis to bear on the Tea Party movement. Assembling historians, political scientists, sociologists, and experts on the right in American politics, the conference was a major response to the vital need for scholarship on the Tea Party.

Steep: The Precipitous Rise of the Tea Party is an outgrowth and updating of the findings presented at the Berkeley conference. We have organized the volume with several fundamental questions in mind that we think go to the heart of an informed and profound understanding of the Tea Party.

We ask first, what kind of movement is the Tea Party? Is it unique? Or have we seen its like before? For example, there are striking similarities between 2009 and 1993, the year Bill Clinton took office as president of the United States. In both years, a Democrat assuming the presidency evoked a response from the right that, in its essence, did not regard the new president as legitimate. Both responses had their extremes—their "don't-tread-on-me" sides—but both reached well up into established Republican Party politics. Is the Tea Party simply an iteration of a surge of radicalism on the right when a Democrat is in the White House in an age habituated to conservative power? Or does the movement draw upon older traditions and strains in American history and society? It is a commonplace, for instance, that observers today call the Tea Party a populist movement. Is the Tea Party simply today's version of that recurring American chestnut?

Part I of this book, "What Manner of Movement?," addresses this question. In the first two chapters, the question of populism and the Tea Party becomes a touchstone for debate and for lucid articulation of the forerunners and implications of Tea Party demands. In his chapter, "The Tea Party in Historical Perspective: A Conservative Response to a Crisis of Political Economy," Charles Postel argues against the populist nature of the Tea Party, by closely comparing it to the history of American populism. He directs us instead to America's conservative tradition as the appropriate historical backdrop of the Tea Party. In the course of his argument, the significance of the John Birch Society and the complexities of the issues of elites and resentment are illuminated.

In contrast, in "Reframing Populist Resentments in the Tea Party Movement," Chip Berlet locates the Tea Party's rhetoric in a tradition of "right-wing populism." In particular, a variant of populism called "producerism" links the Tea Party to a crucial historical tradition. Berlet's analysis also points to the contradiction within the Tea Party movement between its populist and libertarian tendencies.

Devin Burghart's chapter, "View from the Top: Report on Six National Tea Party Organizations" (Chapter 3), is informed by a view of the Tea Party that emphasizes its historical kinship to nationalist movements. Identifying the six leading nationally based Tea Party organizations, Burghart presents a detailed account of the emergence and activities of these groups over the Tea Party's first couple of years. He explores the internal organization of these groups as well as spelling out their relationship with corporations, political action committees, and each other.

Finally, in his chapter, "Astroturf versus Grass Roots: Scenes from Early Tea Party Mobilization" (Chapter 4), Clarence Y. H. Lo takes on the much-disputed question of whether the Tea Party is a top-down production manipulated by long-standing conservative powers, or a bottom-up organic shock wave. In the process, Lo gives us a dramatic behind-the-scenes look at how the Tea Party actually got started and how its extraordinary momentum snowballed.

What is the relationship of class, race, and gender to the rise and successes of the Tea Party? We take up these issues in Part II of the book, "'The Real Americans': Motivation and Identity." Racist depictions of President Obama, for example, pop up not infrequently at Tea Party rallies and in written and electronic materials. Fused with the movement's nearly all-white membership, this has led to the charge of racism that has dogged the movement. But many Tea Party leaders are adamant about and attempt to enforce the nonracist character of the movement. And yet, as Michelle Alexander has shown with respect to the prison system, if "color-blindness" has come to mask novel iterations of the racialization of American society, is this also at play in the rise of the Tea Party?[8]

And what about the anger? The hints of anger in the 2008 Republican vice presidential rallies—the hurling of epithets like "Socialism!" and "Muslim!"—grew into the furious "Obamacare" showdowns in town hall meetings across the country in the summer of 2009. The equation of Obama, Democrats, and liberals generally with the most villainous political figures of the twentieth century became commonplace. What was behind such rage? Was this just an exaggeration of the standard resentment against "liberal elites" that had galled voters on the right for decades? Or had this resentment come to combine with another note in the Tea Party refrain: the note of dispossession? For Tea Partiers, elites weren't merely telling them how to run their lives anymore; these elites were now taking from them what they saw as rightly, and uniquely, theirs. Is the Tea Party worldview defined by perceiving not only benefits, like Medicare and Social Security, as zero-sum commodities, but also rights and freedoms? Does extending rights or benefits to those without them also mean taking them away from those who possess them? Is this how to make sense of the Tea Party notion that Obama's social policies are an attack on their liberty?[9]

In her chapter, "The Tea Party: A 'White Citizenship' Movement?" (Chapter 5), Lisa Disch challenges conventional liberal views of Tea Party supporters around race and fiscal conservatism. In Disch's view, despite rhetorically attacking liberalism, Tea Partiers are actually in-group defenders of a powerful inheritance of liberal welfare policy that, from its origins in the New Deal, has built in "color-blind" white privilege. As exemplified in its defense of Social Security and Medicare and virulent opposition to Obama's health care reform, Tea Party anger and race antagonism are reactions to demands to extend this racialized inheritance to out-group others.

Joseph Lowndes' chapter, "The Past and Future of Race in the Tea Party Movement" (Chapter 6), highlights how the place of race in conservative politics has been reshaped since the era of the Southern strategy that first brought the conservative movement to power. Then, an image like Ronald Reagan's "welfare queens" was an attack at once against the black underclass below and their perceived enablers among "liberal elites" above. For the Tea Party, the threats have now coalesced into a single engulfing threat from above, symbolized in the figure of President Barack Obama. The response has been a furious attack on the state.

At local and national levels, women play important lead roles in the Tea Party. Indeed, Sarah Palin and Michele Bachmann were the movement's most favored nationally known politicians in its first years. Is there something about this historical moment that makes right-wing politics and roll-up-the-sleeves activism more compelling than ever to American women? In "Of Mama Grizzlies and Politics: Women and the Tea Party" (Chapter 7), Melissa Deckman presents a detailed analysis of the extreme fiscal conservatism that distinguishes Tea Party women from other women voters, including Republican women, and the greater religiosity that distinguishes them from Tea Party men. A politics rooted in motherhood has accorded women in the Tea Party an end run to leadership roles that had historically been closed to them in the Republican Party.

The Tea Party has brought the dual meaning of the word *party* into relief as perhaps rarely before. A party can be an event. The Boston Tea Party, which gives the movement its name, was an event. Or it can be an association behaving as a defined actor, like a political party. "Tea Party candidates," "Tea Party leaders," and "Tea Party demonstrations"—all these seem like the trappings of a political party. Yet even as it claims a unique identity as a political party, much of the Tea Party's politicking takes place within the Republican Party. Is this the face of an emerging political party? If so, does its relationship to Fox News herald a new, postmodern model of the political party?[10]

Or is it an insurgency within the Republican Party? If it is, can the Tea Party hold itself together in the face of its own internal contradictions? For example, while the whole movement seems on board with a fairly radical version of free-market economics, two of its crucial constituencies, the religious right and libertarians, represent profoundly contradictory positions on how to philosophically ground these views: the libertarians on the basis of their Ayn Randian version of pure reason[11]; the religious right in their reading of the Bible.[12]

As an insurgency in the Republican Party, the Tea Party certainly scored early victories. By 2010, the Tea Party was able to challenge established Republicans in primaries and to elect dozens of members of the House along with a few Republican senators. Indeed, it had become the quasi-official arbiter of the conservative bona fides of Republican candidates. Is the historical function of the Tea Party to move the Republican Party farther to the right, to a new, more extreme, or more pure, conservatism than even the Bush administration espoused? In this, does the Tea Party's influence resemble that of the religious right's overhaul of the GOP in the 1980s and '90s?

These questions are taken up in Part III of this volume, "New on the Bloc: Political Impact." Alan I. Abramowitz uses survey data to identify Tea Party supporters and specify their distinctive characteristics in his chapter, "Grand Old Tea Party: Partisan Polarization and the Rise of the Tea Party Movement" (Chapter 8). Abramowitz finds that Republicans in the past two decades have generally become more ideologically conservative, disdainful of Democrats, and politically active—and that the Republicans who have moved most radically in these directions disproportionately make up the activists and supporters of the Tea Party movement. Tea Party activism and the movement's appeal to conservative Republicans suggest that the Tea Party's role in vetting Republican candidates will endure at least as long as Barack Obama or, to a lesser extent, any other Democrat remains in the White House.

Martin Cohen offers an arresting analysis of the Tea Party's likely effect on the Republican Party in "The Future of the Tea Party: Scoring an Invitation to the Republican Party" (Chapter 9). Cohen explores the criteria needed for movement newcomers to have an effect on the established parties, and then analyzes the success of the religious right in inserting itself into the Republican Party. The religious right model is then juxtaposed to the Tea Party, and Cohen explores the necessary transformations the Tea Party would have to make to duplicate the religious right's success.

In "The Tea Party and Religious Right Movements: Frenemies with Benefits" (Chapter 10), Peter Montgomery directly takes up the question of the relations between the religious right and the Tea Party. In its split between libertarianism and social conservatism, the Tea Party is writing a new chapter in the history of the division between fiscal conservatism and social issues like abortion and gay marriage that has long been a point of antagonism between the religious right and the establishment Republican Party. Montgomery shows how new lines of ideological thinking, such as an emphasis on "American exceptionalism" and "socialism," allow the religious right and the Tea Party to support the same goals based on divergent premises. Besides ideological overlap, key individuals and local and national connections help bridge this gap, though now, once in Congress, Tea Party representatives have taken this contradiction to a new level.

Together, these chapters raise a larger question that informs the analysis in this book: Is there something about the Tea Party phenomenon that is illustrative of right-wing movements generally? Are there some qualities, some dynamics, or some motivations that uniquely fit the right? For the work of the Center for Right-Wing Studies, this is a crucial question. Founded in 2009 to foster interdisciplinary research on right-wing movements of the twentieth and twenty-first centuries, the Center takes as its premise that in fact there is something unique, *sui generis*, about right-wing movements. This distinction enables study of the right to stand on its own as an independent field of inquiry.

If the Tea Party is to teach us something about right-wing movements generally, the question of identity is likely to prove of central importance in getting us there. Paola Bacchetta and Margaret Power have observed: "If there is anything that actually distinguishes both the center and the far right from other political tendencies, it is the right's reliance on some form of internal or external Other."[13] To define the "other" is at once, by contrast, to define oneself. It is a statement of one's own identity, or a movement's identity. As Bacchetta and Power imply, identity formation on the left and center is more inward looking, the prime mover is the self, not the other. It is not a stretch to conceive of a movement on the left defining itself on its own terms before defining its adversaries. This is inconceivable on the right.

In the study of social movements, contemporary sociology has moved the place of identity from a secondary phenomenon—something that emerges among a movement's membership after mobilization around interests has taken place—to a position of primacy. With the path-breaking work of Alberto Melucci, identity is now seen as primary, the first step in the process of movement formation, a sense and a sentiment of who we are among movement members that precedes the articulation of interests and ideology.[14] Does study of the Tea Party confirm and perhaps deepen our understanding of social movements that arise out of the other-oriented nature of right identity?

As many observers have already pointed out, the correlation between the emergence of the Tea Party and the ascension of Barack Obama to the U.S. presidency is unmistakable.[15] Perhaps nothing better expresses Obama's "otherness" than the conviction of 45 percent of Tea Partiers as late as April 2011 that Barack Obama was not born in the United States.[16] Sarah Palin has popularized the Tea Party's sense of self as the "real Americans." The Tea Party's very definition of the other, Obama, is precisely that he is not American. Is this definition of otherness fungible? Is what Obama represents politically—liberal ideology, those "elites"—are these political views and actors themselves not "American" in the eyes of the "real Americans"? For the Tea Party, finally, do all liberals come from Kenya? Before turning to these questions in the chapters that follow, we provide a brief overview of the swift and steep rise of the Tea Party.

ORIGINS: THE EMERGENCE OF THE TEA PARTY

The Tea Party burst onto the American political scene in the spring of 2009. Set within a broader context of globalization and fears of American decline, the Tea Party emerged out of a unique economic and political moment marked by the aftermath of a near financial meltdown—the likes of which had not been seen since the Great Depression—and the first African American to assume the presidency. Outrage over the Obama administration's response to the economic crisis (which included a second bank bailout, massive loans for two major auto companies, and more than $750 billion in stimulus funds to restart the economy), and questions about the legitimacy of Obama's presidency (raised by "birthers" who deny that Obama is a U.S.-born citizen) provided key ingredients for the political brew known as the Tea Party.

Most accounts trace the origins of the Tea Party to CNBC on-air editor Rick Santelli's rant on the floor of the Chicago Mercantile Exchange on February 19, 2009.[17] Commenting on the Homeowners Affordability and Stability Plan, which was designed to provide relief to mortgage holders and signed into law by President Obama on February 17, Santelli accused Obama of "promoting bad behavior" by proposing to "subsidize the losers' mortgages." Turning to the traders on the floor, Santelli shouted, "This is America! How many of you people want to pay for your neighbor's mortgage that has an extra bathroom and can't pay their bills? Raise their [sic] hand!" Met with cheers, Santelli continued, "President Obama, are you listening?" He concluded, "It's time for another tea party. What we are doing in this country will make Thomas Jefferson and Benjamin Franklin roll over in their graves."[18]

Though some have questioned whether Santelli's rant was staged and even coordinated with right-wing groups,[19] none dispute its role in providing a spark that helped to mobilize antitax and antigovernment organizations and protesters during the spring of 2009. In the days immediately following Santelli's outburst, FreedomWorks, a conservative Washington-based advocacy group led by former Republican House Majority Leader Dick Armey, put Rick Santelli's picture on its website and asked "Are you with Rick? We are." After contacting supporters around the country to ask if they were willing to organize a Tea Party, FreedomWorks staffers announced the launch of a twenty-five-city nationwide Tea Party tour "where taxpayers angry that their hard-earned money is being usurped by the government for irresponsible bailouts, can show President Obama and congressional Democrats that their push towards outright socialism will not stand."[20] In the weeks following, locally based protests opposing taxes and government spending sprang up in Cincinnati, Ohio, Green Bay, Wisconsin, and Harrisburg, Pennsylvania, among other cities and towns across the country.[21]

Even before Santelli's screed, local activists had begun to channel their anger into organizing antigovernment protests. On February 1, 2009, members of FedUpUSA[22] called upon Americans to send tea bags to members of Congress to protest using taxpayer dollars to bail out Wall Street.[23] In Seattle, Washington, Keli Carender, a teacher, actress, and blogger known as Liberty Belle, organized a "Porkulus" protest against Obama's proposed $787 billion stimulus package on Presidents' Day (February 16). Carender's rally reportedly drew only 120 people, but one week later at a second rally organized by Carender, the number of attendees was more than double. And on April 15, 1,200 people gathered for Carender's "Tax Day Tea Party," one of hundreds like it held in cities and towns across the country.[24] Spurred on by Fox News coverage[25] and assisted by FreedomWorks and Americans for Prosperity (another DC-based conservative advocacy group founded by oil tycoon and billionaire David Koch), these "TEA [Taxed Enough Already] Party" rallies drew anywhere from a handful to thousands of participants.[26]

By mid-April, at least six Tea Party factions national in scope could be identified. Three emerged out of already established groups (FreedomWorks, ResistNet, and the Our Country Deserves Better PAC, which spawned Tea Party Express), and three were new to the political scene (1776 Tea Party, Tea Party Patriots, and Tea Party Nation).[27] Over the summer of 2009, these organizations, in addition to many other local groups, set their sights on mobilizing conservative Americans around a new object of fury—the health care overhaul proposed by the Obama administration. Using social networking tools, and in some cases tapping into the local Republican Party apparatus, Tea Party organizers targeted congressional town hall meetings designed to discuss the proposed changes in health care with constituents. Angry, and sometimes threatening, activists shouted down members of Congress for supporting "socialized medicine" and its government-sponsored "death panels," disrupting the meetings and leaving long-serving (mostly Democratic) officeholders stunned.[28]

The summer of 2009 health-care protests culminated in a "Taxpayer March on Washington" held on Saturday, September 12. The final stop in a 34-city, 7,000-mile bus tour sponsored by Tea Party Express that began in Sacramento, California, two weeks earlier, the march was organized by a loose coalition of national groups (including FreedomWorks, ResistNet, Tea Party Patriots, and Glenn Beck's 9/12 Project) and was highly publicized by Fox News and conservative talk radio hosts. After marching down Pennsylvania Avenue, tens of thousands of protesters converged on the steps of the Capitol where they were addressed by conservative activists as well as Republican congressional leaders eager to harness the energy and votes of what was beginning to resemble a fledgling social movement.

Those in attendance included self-described libertarians, independents, and conservatives animated not only by their opposition to "Obamacare," but by anger over what they perceived to be excessive government spending and taxation, government interference with personal freedoms, such as gun ownership, and a belief that Obama is leading the country toward socialism. The themes of anger and distrust were reflected in the handmade signs the protesters carried: "I'm Not Your ATM," "We came unarmed from Montana and Utah . . . this time!," and the now iconic mass-produced poster of Obama made up to look like the Joker from *The Dark Knight* with the caption "Socialism."[29] As one marcher explained, "It was finally an opportunity to get involved. It's been boiling over. . . . It's not just about health care. It's about so much more than that."[30]

The first major political victory claimed by the Tea Party came in January 2010, when Republican Scott Brown defeated Democrat Martha Coakley in a special election for the Massachusetts Senate seat held by the late Teddy Kennedy. Given little chance of winning in this deep blue state, Brown promised to deny the sixtieth vote needed in the Senate to advance Obama's health care plan. This position won him the endorsement of Tea Party supporters across the nation, who sent small donations and made get-out-the-vote calls for his campaign. According to news reports, Tea Party groups raised and spent over $200,000 in support of Brown, including paying for last-minute TV ads that promoted Brown as "the nation's best chance to stop this harmful legislation."[31] Observers across the political spectrum viewed Brown's unexpected win as an indicator of the political force of antiestablishment anger and a sign of things to come.[32]

In the spring of 2010, Tea Party Nation (TPN), a for-profit corporation formed in 2009 by a local Republican activist and former Tennessee Assistant District Attorney Judson Phillips and his wife Sherry, organized a national conference in Nashville.[33] The purpose of the meeting was to bring Tea Party activists together for networking, training, and strategy sessions. Having booked former Alaska Governor Sarah Palin as the keynote speaker, conference organizers expected to draw large crowds. However, concerns over the hefty price tag ($549 per ticket, plus hotel and airfare) and the for-profit nature of Tea Party Nation turned away many potential participants and caused convention sponsors to pull out. Eric Odom, executive director of the American Liberty Alliance and an organizer of the April 2009 tax day rallies, explained, "When we look at the $500 price tag for the event and the fact that many of the original leaders in the group left over similar issues, it's hard for us not to assume the worst."[34] Other sponsors left over concerns that the Republican National Committee was hijacking the event. When Philip Glass, national director of the National Precinct Alliance, announced that his group was withdrawing its support from the conference, he explained: "We are very concerned about the appearance of TPN profiteering and exploitation of the grass-roots movement" by "Republican National Committee-related groups," such as Tea Party Express and FreedomWorks.[35] Glass continued, "At best it creates the appearance of an RNC hijacking; at worst it is one."[36]

While some Tea Partiers worked to form a national coalition free of RNC influence, others pursued a strategy of transforming the Republican Party from within by pushing it farther to the right. Rather than form a separate third party, whose candidates would face an uphill battle to win in a two-party dominated system, Tea Party activists such as Eric Odom advised, "Use the Republican Party to your advantage. Move in and take it over." Christie Carden, who organizes a Tea Party group in Huntsville, Alabama, explained, "We don't need another party. We just need to use the vehicles for political change that are already there."[37] By March 2010, at least fifty-eight Tea Party-identified candidates were running for House seats, Senate seats, or governorships in twenty-five states.[38] Over the next six months, the Republican Party saw its veterans turned out of office in primary after primary against Tea Party-aligned candidates, leading the conservative Daily Caller to exclaim, "It's official: the Tea Party takeover of the Republican Party is in full effect."[39] A *New York Times* analysis of 2010 House and Senate races showed that by mid-October, Tea Party-identified candidates, all Republicans, were running in the general election for 129 House and 9 Senate seats.[40] Although most of these races were in solidly Democratic districts, enough were viewed as competitive to give Tea Party supporters hope of wielding significant influence in the new Congress.

The results of the 2010 midterm elections were mixed. Tea Party-identified candidates, many of whom were first-time candidates, won a large number of seats in the House, adding to the new Republican majority and contributing to the GOP's historic pickup of sixty-three seats.[41] Voters elected several Tea Party favorites to the Senate, including Kentucky's Rand Paul and Florida's Marco Rubio,[42] but they also rejected other Tea Party candidates (Delaware's Christine O'Donnell, Nevada's Sharron Angle, and Colorado's Ken Buck), costing the Republican Party key seats it should have won. By early spring 2011, Tea Party leaders had already initiated a new round of organizing designed to coordinate their efforts[43] and avoid costly vote splitting in the 2012 primaries.[44]

Armed with a new Republican majority, newly elected House Speaker John Boehner opened the 112th Congress with both symbolic and substantive changes to the House rules that aligned with Tea Party concerns. In addition to mandating the reading of the Constitution aloud from the House floor on the first day of the session,[45] every member was now required to cite the constitutional authority needed to enact their proposed bills (a leading demand of the "Contract From America," a manifesto issued by the Tea Party in the weeks leading up to the midterm elections). Additionally, any proposed spending increases were to be directly offset with cuts elsewhere.[46] But while rule changes came easily, legislative victories were harder to achieve. Instead of dismantling "Obamacare" and passing a balanced budget amendment, two key demands of Tea Party supporters, the new Congress has been marked by legislative stalemate, repeated episodes of a near government shutdown brought on by the failure to pass a 2011 budget and averted at the last moment with temporary spending bills, and a nasty fight over raising the debt ceiling in August 2011 that brought the federal government to the brink of default (too late to avert a downgrading of the government's AAA credit rating by Moody's).[47] While Tea Party freshmen succeeded in changing the terms of national debate to an almost singular focus on debt and the need for spending cuts, less clear is the extent to which this will translate into legislative and political successes.[48]

More than two years after its emergence onto the American political scene, it is still difficult to gauge the size and scope of this movement. Although Tea Party supporters share certain characteristics in common (overwhelmingly white, male, very conservative, and frequent Republican voters[49]), they also vary in terms of their level of involvement and political goals. Burghart and Zeskind's 2010 analysis distinguishes three categories of Tea Party supporters based on their level of "agreement and commitment": sympathizers, which national opinion polls place at anywhere from 16 to 18 percent of the adult population; activists, which Burghart and Zeskind estimate to be a couple million supporters who attend meetings and local and national protests; and core supporters, made up of approximately "250,000 members in all fifty states who have signed up on the websites of the six national organizational networks that form the core of this movement."[50]

What little evidence there is suggests a large, fragmented and mostly uncoordinated group of organizations driven by different motivations and agendas. In an attempt to understand the network of individuals and organizations that make up the Tea Party, reporters from *The Washington Post* set out to contact and survey leaders of every Tea Party group in the nation in the fall of 2010. After identifying 1,400 possible groups, *Post* reporters were able to verify and interview leaders of nearly 650 of these groups.[51] Most groups had fewer than 50 members (only 39 groups had more than 1,000 members), and the median amount of money each group raised in 2010 was $800. Most local leaders (86 percent) said that their members were new to politics, suggesting a potentially significant political force of hundreds of thousands of first-time activists. But the survey also found very little coordination between groups at the national level,[52] and there was no agreement on what the political aim of the Tea Party should be. Indeed, a majority (57 percent) of those interviewed said they want to "operate as a network of independent political organizations," while 24 percent said they would like to "take over leadership of the Republican Party," and only 4 percent said they would like to form a separate political party.[53] Moreover, a vast majority (70 percent) of the organizations surveyed were not engaged in political campaigning, and for the 29 percent of organizations that were campaigning, most (70 percent) of their activity was limited to planning get-out-the-vote efforts for Election Day.

Although respondents were nearly unified in their concern about the economy (99 percent), mistrust of government (92 percent), opposition to Obama/the Democratic Party's policies (87 percent), and even dissatisfaction with mainstream Republican Party leaders (87 percent), there was very little agreement among groups on "the single most important issue."[54] Joe Lisante, founder of Miami County Liberty, a Tea Party group based near Dayton, Ohio, described the decentralized nature and distinctly local flavor of Tea Party groups in Ohio: "Some of the groups want to take on prayer in school. Some of them want to take on voter education. Some want to be endorsing candidates. But there is no particular person, at least in the state of Ohio, who is the president of the Tea Party; it just doesn't exist. That's a disadvantage for us because we can't move quickly on things. We can't always agree."[55]

The 2012 presidential race offers an opportunity for a national candidate to emerge and unite Tea Party supporters around a single platform. It may also lead to a war within the Republican Party as establishment candidates, such as former Massachusetts Governor Mitt Romney, face off against a succession of Tea Party favorites like Representative Michele Bachmann, Texas Governor Rick Perry, and former Senator Rick Santorum, whose social conservatism appeals to many in the base, but may be viewed as too extreme to win over general voters. By 2011, polls showed a significant decline in the Tea Party's favorability rating among the general public (from 38 percent in November 2010 to 32 percent in April 2011 to 28 percent in September 2011). Even more significantly, by April 2011, nearly half of all Americans (47 percent) viewed the Tea Party unfavorably, more than twice as many as held this view in January 2010, and on par with the unfavorability ratings of both the Democratic and Republican parties.[56] Are such poll numbers a sign that the Tea Party has peaked and is about to fade from American memory, joining the likes of Ross Perot's Reform Party and other failed attempts to alter the American political landscape? Or will Tea Party leaders rally their supporters and build a social movement that appeals to a broad constituency while pushing the country farther to the right? Only time will tell, but the chapters in this volume suggest that the Tea Party has already taken on characteristics of a social movement, with viable paths for expanding its base in the months and years ahead.

NOTES

1. On the debt: "With no fanfare and little notice, the national debt has grown by more than $4 trillion during George W. Bush's presidency. It's the biggest increase under any president in U.S. history." Mark Knoller, "Bush Administration Adds $4 Trillion to National Debt," CBSNews.com, September 29, 2008, http://www.cbsnews.com/8301-500803_162-4486228-500803.html.

On job creation: "The Bush administration created about three million jobs (net) over its eight years, a fraction of the 23 million jobs created under President Bill Clinton's administration and only slightly better than President George H. W. Bush did in his four years in office. . . . The current President Bush, once taking account [sic] how long he's been in office, shows the worst track record for job creation since the government began keeping records [1939]." Sudeep Reddy, "Bush on Jobs: The Worst Track Record on Record," *Wall Street Journal*, Real Time Economics blog, January 9, 2009, http://blogs.wsj.com/economics/2009/01/09/bush-on-jobs-the-worst-track-record-on-record/.

2. A striking example was the neoconservative defense of the ideas behind the invasion of Iraq, chalking up the disaster that ensued to the incompetence of the Bush government. A typical lament, from Kenneth Adelman, who had predicted a "cakewalk" in Iraq: ". . . I feel that the incompetence of the Bush team means that most everything we ever stood for now also lies in ruins." Quoted in David Rose, "Neo Culpa," *Vanity Fair*, January 2007, http://www.vanityfair.com/politics/features/2007/01/neocons200701.

3. Pajamas Media posted a notable piece of video from 2007, in which George Bush's successor as governor of Texas, Rick Perry, criticizes Bush as having never been a fiscal conservative, neither as president nor, earlier, as governor. Pajamas Media, "Flashback: Rick Perry Says George W. Bush Was 'Never Ever a Fiscal Conservative,'" http://pajamasmedia.com/tatler/2011/06/10/flashback-rick-perry-says-george-w-bush-was-never-ever-a-fiscal-conservative/.

4. "We're all concerned about the fact that the very wealthy and the very poor, the most and least educated, and a majority of minority voters, seem to have more or less stopped paying attention to us, and we should be concerned that, as a result of all this, the Republican Party seems to be slipping into a position of being more of a regional party than a national one." Mitch McConnell, Senate Majority Leader (R-KY), January 29, 2009. Quoted in Charles Blow, "Whither the Republicans?" *New York Times,* January 31, 2009.

5. Sam Tanenhaus, *The Death of Conservatism* (New York: Random House, 2009).

6. Ross Perot received 19 percent of the popular vote in his 1992 third-party candidacy for president against Bill Clinton and George H. W. Bush.

7. We refer to the Tea Party as a "movement" throughout this volume rather than as an emergent political party or an extra-party mobilization. As succeeding chapters will demonstrate, the hallmarks of the Tea Party accord with definitions of "social movement" that span the sociological literature. The "collective behavior" tradition (as exemplified in Neil J. Smelser's *Theory of Collective Behavior* [New York: Free Press, 1962]) defines a social movement as a phenomenon made up of large numbers of people who are mobilized by organizations, often informally affiliated with one another, to pursue common ideological goals or to resist the imposition of others. In Chapter 3, Devin Burghart provides a discussion of the network of national organizations engaged in mobilizing Tea Party supporters around shared goals. In the 1970s, the "collective behavior" model of social movements was superseded by resource mobilization theory, which emphasizes the importance of resources in determining the development and success of social movements. In Chapter 4, Clarence Lo offers an analysis of the various resources Tea Party leaders drew upon in the initial stages of the movement to facilitate its development. Finally, new social movement theory, which emerged in the late 1980s, emphasizes the role of identity and "the other" in the emergence of social movements. These themes are echoed in Tea Party supporters' excessive focus on Barack Obama's citizenship and in their conviction of embodying the "real Americans."

8. Michelle Alexander, *The New Jim Crow: Mass Incarceration in the Age of Colorblindness* (New York: The New Press, 2010).

9. See Dick Armey's *Give Us Liberty: A Tea Party Manifesto* (New York: William Morrow, 2010).

10. Historically, successful political parties have grown up in connection with institutions in civil society—for example, labor parties and the union movement, or Christian Democratic parties and the church's parish infrastructure. If a postmodern version of this connection is that between a television network and a political party, this has been played out in Italy since Silvio Berlusconi first entered politics in 1994 and spent much of the successive eighteen years as prime minister. See, for example, Alexander Stille, "The Corrupt Reign of Emperor Silvio," *The New York Review of Books,* April 8, 2010; and Paul Ginsborg, *Silvio Berlusconi: Television, Power and Patrimony* (London: Verso, 2004).

11. See Jennifer Burns, *Goddess of the Market: Ayn Rand and the American Right* (New York: Oxford University Press, 2009).

12. Currently, the most significant actor attempting to ground free-market ideology in Christian theology is David Barton. See Peter Montgomery's chapter in this volume (Chapter 10).

13. Paola Bacchetta and Margaret Power, "Introduction," in *Right-Wing Women: From Conservatives to Extremists around the World*, eds. Paola Bacchetta and Margaret Power (New York: Routledge, 2002), 4.

14. See, for example, these two seminal articles: Alberto Melucci, "The Symbolic Challenge of Contemporary Movements," *Social Research* 52 (1985): 789–816; and Melucci, "Getting Involved: Identity and Mobilization in Social Movements," *International Social Movement Research* 1 (1988): 329–48.

15. See Abramowitz, Chapter 8 in this volume.

16. Stephanie Condon, "Poll: One in Four Americans Think Obama Was Not Born in the U.S.," CBS News Political Hotsheet, April 21, 2011. Accessed October 12, 2011, http://www.cbsnews.com/8301-503544_162-20056061-503544.html.

17. Some trace the Tea Party's roots to an earlier moment. Devin Burghart and Leonard Zeskind write that even before Barack Obama was inaugurated, "the Libertarian Party of Illinois began formulating a concept they called the Boston Tea Party Chicago," which they advertised using the Libertarian Party of Illinois's Yahoo and "meetup" groups, the Ron Paul Meetup and Campaign for Liberty groups, and other national antitax groups. Indeed, Dave Brady, a member of the Libertarian Party of Illinois claimed, "we gave Rick Santelli the idea for the Tax Day Tea Parties." Quoted in Devin Burghart and Leonard Zeskind, *Tea Party Nationalism: A Critical Examination of the Tea Party Movement* (Kansas City, MO; Institute for Research and Education on Human Rights, 2010), 15, http://www.irehr.org/the-report. Matt Taibbi also traces the origins of the Tea Party label to an earlier political moment. Taibbi writes that Ron Paul's 2008 presidential campaign rallies were called "Tea Parties": "The pre-Obama 'Tea Parties' were therefore peopled by young anti-war types and libertarian intellectuals who were as turned off by George W. Bush and Karl Rove as they were by liberals and Democrats. The failure of the Republican Party to invite the elder Paul into the tent of power did not mean, however, that it didn't see the utility of borrowing his insurgent rhetoric and parts of his platform for Tea Party 2.0. This second-generation Tea Party came into being a month after Barack Obama moved into the Oval Office, when CNBC windbag Rick Santelli went on air to denounce one of Obama's bailout programs and called for 'tea parties' to protest." From Matt Taibbi, "The Truth about the Tea Party," *Rolling Stone*, September 28, 2010.

18. Santelli's rant can be seen here: http://www.youtube.com/watch?v=bEZB4taSEoA.

19. Brian Stelter, "Reporter Says Outburst Was Spontaneous," *New York Times*, March 3, 2009, B10.

20. From the FreedomWorks website (March 3, 2009), quoted in Burghart and Zeskind, *Tea Party Nationalism*, 17.

21. Liz Robbins, "Protesters Air Views on Government Spending at Tax Day Tea Parties across U.S.," *New York Times*, April 16, 2009, A16.

22. FedUpUSA was formed by a group of investors outraged over government bailouts for Wall Street. The FedUpUSA website states: "The American People cannot be heard until they truly understand how they're being robbed blind by the Wall Street bankers" who pay for the reelection "of those who will ensure legislation to facilitate their thievery." Accessed at http://fedupsua .org/about-us/. Although initially supportive of the Tea Party movement that emerged in the Spring of 2009, Karl Denninger, one of the founders of FedUpUSA, posted a blog in October 2010 denouncing the Tea Party: "Tea Party my ass. This was nothing other than the Republican Party stealing the anger of a population that was fed up with the Republican Party's own theft of their tax money at gunpoint to bail out the robbers of Wall Street and fraudulently redirecting it back toward electing the very people who stole all the ****ing money!" From Daniel Tencer, "Tea Party 'Founder': Palin, Gingrich a 'Joke,'" The Raw Story, October 20, 2010, http://www.rawstory.com/ rs/2010/10/tea-party-founder-slams-tea-party/.

23. Burghart and Zeskind, Tea Party Nationalism, 15.

24. Kate Zernike, "Unlikely Activist Who Got to the Tea Party Early," New York Times, February 27, 2010; Liz Robbins, "Protesters Air Views on Government Spending at Tax Day Tea Parties Across U.S.," New York Times, April 16, 2009. Burghart and Zeskind write that in the weeks following the Tax Day protests, Carender would travel to Washington, DC, to participate in training provided by FreedomWorks. From Burghart and Zeskind, Tea Party Nationalism, 16.

25. In the days leading up to April 15, Fox News ran more than 100 promos about its coverage of the Tax Day Tea Party events, and it dispatched four of its leading hosts (Glenn Beck, Sean Hannity, Tobin Smith, and Neil Cavuto) to different parts of the country to provide all-day coverage on the day of the event. In one promo, then Fox News host Glenn Beck invited viewers to "Bring your kids and experience history" with him in Alamo, New Mexico, where he would be covering the tax day protests. From David Carr, "Cable Wars Are Killing Objectivity," New York Times, April 20, 2009, B1.

26. Liz Robbins, "Protesters Air Views on Government Spending at Tax Day Tea Parties across U.S.," New York Times, April 16, 2009, A16; Dana Milbank, "Obama Is Just Not Their Cup of Tea," The Washington Post, April 16, 2009, A02.

27. Burghart and Zeskind, Tea Party Nationalism, 17.

28. Disruption seemed to be an intentional strategy promoted by some of the organizers. A strategy memo circulated by the Tea Party Patriots' website instructed, "Pack the hall. Yell out and challenge the Rep's statements early. Get him [sic] off his prepared script and agenda. Stand up and shout and sit right back down." Quoted in Ian Urbina, "Beyond the Beltway, Health Debate Turns Hostile," New York Times, August 8, 2009, A1. See also David Herszenhorn and Sheryl Gay Stolberg, "Health Plan Opponents Make Their Voices Heard," New York Times, August 4, 2009, A12; and Ian Urbina and Katharine Seelye, "Senator Goes Face to Face with Dissent," New York Times, August 12, 2009, A1.

29. Dan Eggen and Perry Bacon Jr., "GOP Sees Protest as an Opportunity," The Washington Post, September 12, 2009, A01; Emma Brown, James

Hohmann, and Perry Bacon Jr., "Lashing Out at the Capitol: Tens of Thousands Protest Obama Initiatives and Government Spending," *The Washington Post*, September 13, 2009, A01.

30. Brown et al., "Lashing Out at the Capitol."

31. Steve LeBlanc, "Senate Race in Mass. Draws Millions to Pay for Ads," Associated Press Online, Sec. Political News, January 17, 2010.

32. Ed Hornick, "Independents' Anger in Massachusetts a Sign of Things To Come," CNN.com, January 21, 2010.

33. Burghart and Zeskind, *Tea Party Nationalism,* 33.

34. Kate Zernike, "Disputes among Tea Party Groups Are Taking a Toll on February Convention," *New York Times*, January 26, 2010, 12.

35. Kate Zernike reports that FreedomWorks was not a convention sponsor, and Burghart and Zeskind write that FreedomWorks "did not support the Tea Party Nation Convention." According to FreedomWorks staff person Adam Brandon, "A number of people in Nashville might be focused on social issues, like being anti-gay, or being anti-immigration and that is not a good way of building a movement. We want to focus on what we have in common, which is opposition to big government and taxes." Quoted in Burghart and Zeskind, *Tea Party Nationalism,* 36.

36. Other national Tea Party groups withheld their support from the convention entirely, underscoring the fragmented quality and exposing the fractures of this so-called movement. Burghart and Zeskind point out that, in spite of having a significant number of supporters in Tennessee, Mark Meckler, a Tea Party Patriot cofounder, described the Nashville event as the "usurpation of a grassroots movement." Burghart and Zeskind write that "the high cost of registration and Palin's speaking fee [rumored to be over $100,000] was later cited as one of the reasons why a second convention was soon organized in Tennessee by an alternative coalition of Tea Party groups." According to Burghart and Zeskind, in spite of these problems, the conference was well attended. In Burghart and Zeskind, *Tea Party Nationalism,* 37.

37. Quoted in Peter Katel, "Tea Party Movement," *CQ Researcher,* 20, no. 11 (2010), 259.

38. Peter Katel, "Tea Party Movement," *CQ Researcher,* 20, no. 11 (2010), 244.

39. Quoted in Patrik Jonsson, "'Tea Party' Is Polarizing, but Has Many 'Closet Admirers,' Poll Finds," *The Christian Science Monitor*, September 15, 2010.

40. The *New York Times*'s report defined Tea Party candidates as "those who had entered politics through the movement or who are receiving significant support from local Tea Party groups and who share the ideology of the movement." In Kate Zernike, "Tea Party Set to Win Enough Races for Wide Influence," *New York Times*, October 14, 2010.

41. The new class of freshman members included eighty-nine Republicans, nearly half of whom were elected with Tea Party support. In Walter Rodgers, "Will Congress's Tea Party Class Go Native in Washington?," *The Christian Science Monitor*, January 3, 2011.

42. Ron Johnson (Wisconsin), Mike Lee (Utah), and Pat Toomey (Pennsylvania) also ran under the Tea Party banner and were elected.

43. For example, in January 2011, leaders of more than seventy Tea Party groups met in Sharpsville, Indiana, called upon U.S. Senator Richard Lugar to resign, and agreed to join forces to support a still-to-be-determined primary challenger to Senator Lugar, a self-described conservative Republican who has held the seat since 1977. Other U.S. senators targeted by Tea Party groups include Maine's moderate Olympia Snowe and Utah's conservative Orrin Hatch. In Kate Zernike, "Tea Party Gets Early Start on G.O.P. Targets for 2012," *New York Times*, January 29, 2011.

44. In 2010, vote splitting in U.S. Senate primaries in Illinois and Indiana and in congressional races in Virginia allowed establishment candidates to defeat candidates favored by Tea Party supporters with less than 40 percent of the vote. In Kate Zernike, "Tea Party Gets Early Start on G.O.P. Targets for 2012."

45. Congressional leaders decided to read an abridged version of the Constitution, one that left out references to slaves as "three-fifths of all other Persons" and repealed amendments, such as the Eighteenth Amendment (on Prohibition). In Jennifer Steinhauer, "Constitution Has Its Day (More or Less) in House," *New York Times*, January 7, 2011, A15.

46. There were a few exceptions to these rules: "[T]he rules would allow future tax cuts to be enacted without offsetting spending reductions, and would permit repeal of health care legislation, which was estimated to save the government more than $140 billion over 10 years, without any requirement that those revenue losses be made up elsewhere." From Carl Hulse, "Taking Control, G.O.P. Overhauls Rules in House," *New York Times*, January 6, 2011, A1.

47. One-third of the House's Republican freshmen voted against the debt ceiling compromise.

48. Jennifer Steinhauer, "For Republican Freshmen, the Power of No," *New York Times*, July 30, 2011, A17.

49. See Abramowitz, Chapter 8 in this volume.

50. Burghart and Zeskind, *Tea Party Nationalism*, 8.

51. *Post* reporters called Tea Party group leaders up to six times, before giving up, concluding, "It is unclear whether they are just hard to reach or don't exist." From Amy Gardner, "Gauging the Scope of the Tea Party Movement in America," *The Washington Post*, October 24, 2010.

52. Of the groups' main political activities, 87 percent are directed mostly at the local level, 42 percent of the groups said they did not work with any national organization, and "there was no broad agreement on which national figure best represents the groups": "No one" was the most popular response (34 percent), with Sarah Palin (14 percent) coming in second, followed by Glenn Beck (7 percent), Jim DeMint (6 percent), Ron Paul (6 percent), and Michele Bachmann (4 percent). From *Washington Post*, "An Up-Close Look at the Tea Party and Its Role in the Midterm Elections," Tea Party Canvass, accessed on March 23, 2011, http://www.washingtonpost.com/wp-srv/special/politics/tea-party-canvass/.

53. Fifteen percent answered, "Don't know." From *Washington Post*, "An Up-Close Look at the Tea Party and Its Role in the Midterm Elections."

54. "Government spending/deficit" (24 percent) and "size of government" (20 percent) received the most support, followed by "other" with 16 percent. Other single most important issues included "protecting the Constitution" (11 percent), voter education (8 percent), "economy/unemployment" (5 percent), "taxes" (4 percent), Tenth Amendment /states rights (2 percent), and immigration (1 percent). From *Washington Post*, "An Up-Close Look at the Tea Party and Its Role in the Midterm Elections."

55. Amy Gardner, "Gauging the Scope of the Tea Party Movement in America," *The Washington Post*, October 24, 2010.

56. Linda Feldmann, "New Polls Make Tea Party Leaders Ask: Are We in Trouble?," *The Christian Science Monitor*, March 30, 2011; and Zeke Miller, "Tea Party More Disliked Than Ever," *Business Insider*, September 27, 2011, http://articles.businessinsider.com/2011-09-27/politics/30207187_1_approval-rating-favorability-rating-wrong-direction.

PART ONE

What Manner of Movement?

CHAPTER 1

The Tea Party in Historical Perspective

A Conservative Response to a Crisis of Political Economy

CHARLES POSTEL

On February 19, 2009, Rick Santelli, an entertainer and financial commentator on CNBC cable news unleashed his now famous scream against the Obama administration's economic policies. In the months leading up to this episode, presidents Bush and Obama had provided hundreds of billions of dollars under the Troubled Asset Relief Program to the Bank of America, Citibank, and other giants of American finance. But what pushed Santelli over the edge was word that the Obama administration might provide mortgage relief to distressed homeowners. Fox News proceeded to explain what had happened: The Association of Community Organizations for Reform Now (ACORN) had conned the American taxpayers into subsidizing mortgages for people that Santelli defined as "losers," that is, mainly new homeowners that managed their money badly and did not deserve to own a home in the first place. ACORN, with the aid of its liberal supporters in Congress, had brought the American economy to its knees. Fox News and its viewers had had enough. The Tea Party movement burst onto the national stage on Tax Day 2009.

In the midst of the most severe financial and economic crisis in over seventy years, the Tea Party has been able to tap deep veins of resentment and anger over potential shifts in the post-World War II political economy. Since the Second World War, mainly white homeowners—beneficiaries of federal subsidies for mortgages and suburban development—had counted on rising home values to anchor their economic security. As home values tumbled in 2008 and 2009, the federal government contemplated coming to the aid of distressed home-owners, including African Americans, Latinos, and other minorities historically excluded from the web of federal support. Although such aid was never forthcoming, the mere suggestion provoked a storm of opposition. The ensuing debates about health care reform poured gasoline on the fire. At a time of declining retirement portfolios, rising health care costs, and fears about the viability of Social Security and Medicare, the administration's efforts to extend a health safety net to the forty million Americans without protection appeared as a bitter betrayal of those who already had such protections.

Santelli's scream also provides clues as to the historical context of the Tea Party. It sounded an alarm with deep resonance in conservative politics in America, and especially with the far right that has been locked in a trial of strength for the control of the Republican Party since the 1940s. The Tea Party has tapped into fear and anger over potential shifts in political economy to form a grassroots movement following in the historical traditions of the anti–New Deal American Liberty League, Joseph McCarthy and the witch hunts, Robert Welch and the John Birch Society, and Barry Goldwater and the right-wing Republicans of the early Cold War.

"POPULIST RAGE"?

Since the Tea Party emerged on the national scene, its members have made great efforts to maintain the public appearance of being a movement without leaders, without a defined ideology, and without history.[1] Much of this effort has an instrumental value in terms of Republican Party politics. And much of it has been facilitated by the media's treating the Tea Party phenomenon as an enigma best explained by the term *populism*. Indeed, much of the print, online, and televised media has discovered that the country has entered a season of "populist" discontent, where angry folk wielding sharpened pitchforks threaten to storm the gates of power. A striking example of this commentary is the cover of *Newsweek* from March 2009. Under the title, "The Thinking Man's Guide to Populist Rage," the cover is a photo of an angry mob brandishing torches. The photo, of course, is not of populists, but comes from the 1931 movie *Frankenstein*.[2]

In reality, the depiction of populism as an out-of-control or Frankenstein mob is a crude caricature of the original Populists.

According to today's pundits, the Populists represented the reactive, unthinking politics of blind rage, the politics of the gut instead of the head. But this has no connection to the historical Populism of the 1890s, a vast movement of rural education; nor to the process whereby millions of Populist men and women, as C. Vann Woodward put it, started to "think as well as to throb"[3]; nor to the central Populist premise that if ordinary citizens gained knowledge of the workings of political economy, they could shape a more equitable and just society.[4]

Numerous commentators have presented the Tea Party as the latest incarnation or twist in the evolution of American populism.[5] The key idea here is taken from the work of Richard Hofstadter. Over fifty years ago in his extraordinarily influential work, *The Age of Reform*, Hofstadter suggested that the right-wing and intolerant followers of Joseph McCarthy were the historical heirs of the farmer and labor Populists of the 1890s. Presumably, Populism represented an irrational and highly malleable ideology that had gone sour and turned into bitter and paranoid right-wing extremism.[6]

The problem in Hofstadter's analysis is that it did not happen. The political scientist Michael Rogin tested Hofstadter's theory in his 1967 work *The Intellectuals and McCarthy*. What Rogin confirmed was that, yes, there were Populists in Wisconsin in the 1890s. And, yes, there were followers of Joseph McCarthy in Wisconsin in the 1950s. But beyond the fact that they were both in Wisconsin, there were few ideological, political, sociological, or demographic connections between Populism and McCarthyism.[7] Walter Nugent, C. Vann Woodward, and other scholars confirmed much the same thing.[8] Nonetheless, the notion stuck, and Hofstadter's thesis continues to cast a shadow over the national discussion about the Tea Party and its historical meaning. Perhaps it is a losing proposition to protest the indiscriminate use of the word *populism*. But the present employment of the term obscures more than it clarifies about the historical roots of the Tea Party.

The purpose of this distinction is not to idealize the original farmer Populists. To paraphrase Linda Gordon's question about the Progressive movement, if the Populists were advising us today, should we listen?[9] Populism of the 1890s was a democratic movement for economic justice. But there were also currents within the Populist movement that were authoritarian, exploitative, patriarchal, and white nationalist. From that perspective, it makes sense that a spectrum of political phenomena has been described as left- or right-wing populism. But the Tea Party suggests the limits of the usefulness of the term. In this time of crisis of political economy, where is the populism in a movement that demands hard money and to revert to the gold standard? That seeks to repeal the Sixteenth Amendment and the graduated income tax? That seeks to repeal the Seventeenth Amendment and the direct election of senators? That seeks to remove funding from public education? That seeks to lift regulations on bank and corporate giants? In short, where is the populism in a movement that seeks to repeal everything that the original Populists stood for?

The political theorist Margaret Canovan observes that populism takes different forms and shapes in different times and countries. In the late nineteenth-century United States, for example, the farmer-labor People's Party, otherwise known as the Populist Party, emerged soon after the formation of the Narodnik movement among Russian intellectuals. As Canovan aptly points out, the most important connection between the two was the quite accidental translation of the Russian word *narodnik* into the English *populism*. Although they may have shared a common name, the American and Russian variants of populist were distinct and incompatible species. The American form, according to Canovan, was a variety of farmer-labor redistributive politics that had some relation to social democracy. The Eastern European form often appeared as peasant traditionalism. And in Western Europe today, we have right-wing movements driven by xenophobia that are often described as populist. So in that sense, *populism* is an elastic term that covers a wide array of phenomena.[10]

In the U.S. historical context, the Populism of the 1890s was the ancestor of forces that would influence American politics deep into the twentieth century. Populism tilled the soil of rural socialism in Kansas, Oklahoma, and other rural bases of the Socialist Party in the new century's first decades.[11] As Elizabeth Sanders has persuasively demonstrated, the Populist farm and labor movements led to the emergence of the reform or progressive wings of both the Democratic and Republican parties that would enact the reforms of the Progressive Era, and whose influence would reverberate through the New Deal.[12] Huey Long's campaign to "Share the Wealth" also reflected the Populist tradition, despite Long's autocratic methods of running Louisiana as his private fiefdom.[13] In the postwar period, Lyndon Baines Johnson pursued his vision of the Great Society, a vision that he inherited from his grandfather, Sam Johnson, who was a bona fide Populist politician among the cotton farmers of central Texas.[14] Perhaps George Wallace also inherited something of the Populist tradition in that, along with his racist demagogy, he also accepted elements of redistributive social justice (at least among white people) that the Populists had introduced into Alabama politics.

It is difficult, however, to trace Populist ancestry in the Tea Party because it belongs to a different branch on the tree of American politics. While pundits and media analysts may describe the Tea Party as populist, the Tea Partiers call themselves conservatives. And to examine their historical roots, we have to look at the traditions of the conservative movement. Since the 1990s, Alan Brinkley, Heather Thompson, Leo Ribuffo, and other historians have challenged their colleagues to take more seriously the study of the conservative movement. A great deal has been learned, and that historiography has the greatest bearing on the Tea Party phenomenon.[15]

THE CONSERVATIVE TRADITION

In the 1930s, America's business leaders sharply divided over Franklin Roosevelt's New Deal. Some corporate executives expressed gratitude to Roosevelt for what he had done to save capitalism and accepted the advent of the New Deal political economy. But a critical group of business leaders vehemently rejected the new order. They viewed the administration's efforts towards the legalization of industrial trade unions and the initiation of a federal social safety net as grave threats to American freedom. They called Roosevelt a socialist, a fascist, a dictator, and a tyrant. In 1934, led by the DuPont brothers of the DuPont chemical company, business and political elites organized the American Liberty League with the stated aim of restoring constitutional government and reversing the power grab of the New Deal. The Liberty League boasted that it was entirely nonpartisan since it was led by Republicans as well as disaffected Democrats such as one-time presidential candidate Al Smith. The Liberty League also understood the political necessity of presenting itself as an organization of ordinary citizens motivated by their commitment to constitutional principles. Roosevelt, nonetheless, successfully attacked the Liberty League and similar opponents as "economic royalists" seeking to protect the power and wealth of the few. And the Liberty League failed to gain political traction.[16]

In the 1940s and '50s, the right wing of the Republican Party, led by Senators Robert Taft of Ohio and Joseph McCarthy of Wisconsin, took up where the Liberty League left off. Much of their wrath was directed at New York Governor Thomas Dewey, California Governor Earl

Warren, and other moderates who reflected the reform traditions of an earlier Republican Progressivism, and who accepted much of the New Deal order. Taft sought the recriminalization of trade union activism, a goal that was partly realized with the Taft-Hartley Act of 1947. And McCarthy made dark charges of treason against both the Democratic administration of Harry Truman and the administration of the moderate Republican Dwight Eisenhower.

In 1958, business executives from the National Association of Manufacturers came together to form the John Birch Society (JBS). Led by the candy manufacturer Robert Welch, the JBS sought to liberate America from the slavery of trade unions, labor regulations, minimum wages, the Social Security Act, and other instruments of "collectivism" and "socialist tyranny." The JBS attacked the civil rights movement as part of the "communist conspiracy." And Welch branded President Eisenhower, who had served as the commander of the Allied forces in Europe during World War II, as a communist dupe in a plot to subjugate America under "one-world government." The JBS took its paranoia to extremes, as when it famously uncovered the hand of the communist menace in municipal plans to fluoridate public water supplies.

However weird its claims, it would be a mistake to underestimate the historical role of the John Birch Society. In its heyday, the JBS was a broad grassroots movement. It probably had over 100,000 members, but those were the relatively dedicated activists who formed the semi-secret cells of the JBS organization. Its influence spread further. The JBS organized in local chambers of commerce, parent-teacher associations, churches, and within the Republican Party. In conservative middle-class suburbs, housewives organized luncheons to do their part to free America from "socialist tyranny" and "one-world government." Indeed, the mobilization of women activists within conservative networks represented a signal success of the JBS. By the early 1960s, the JBS had its greatest strength in such Sunbelt states as Texas, California, and Arizona. It had sufficient grassroots support on a national scale to help secure the nomination of Senator Barry Goldwater (R-AZ) as the Republican candidate for president in 1964. In his famous acceptance speech at the Republican convention at the Cow Palace in San Francisco, when Goldwater declared that "[e]xtremism in defense of liberty is no vice," he was paying tribute to the JBS foot soldiers who had made his nomination possible.[17]

At the time, commentators on the national television networks and other media painted John Birch Society members as "extremists."

New York Governor Nelson Rockefeller and other moderate Republican leaders agreed. Significantly, William Buckley, Jr., the dean of the rising conservative movement, viewed Robert Welch as a liability to their common cause. In Buckley's estimation, when Welch painted moderates and liberals such as Eisenhower and Kennedy as "communists," he only undermined the anticommunist struggle.[18] Buckley and his allies demanded Welch's excommunication from the conservative flock, and the JBS faded from its prominent place in public life.[19]

But the John Birch Society is in the midst of a revival. In 2008, Ron Paul, a Texas congressperson who is a Tea Party favorite and a campaigner for the Republican nomination for president in 2012, delivered the keynote address at the society's fiftieth anniversary celebration.[20] In 2010, the JBS cosponsored the CPAC conference, a national gathering of conservatives.[21] On September 16, 2010, Sharron Angle, the Tea Party candidate in Nevada for the U.S. Senate, took time out from her campaign to address a "United Freedom Rally" in Salt Lake City, sponsored nationally by the John Birch Society and the National Center for Constitutional Studies. The event also had the support of local Birch societies and 9/12 groups inspired by the radio and television host Glenn Beck.[22] The National Center for Constitutional Studies was founded by the late Cleon Skousen, a close political ally of Welch who was if anything yet more paranoid and extreme in his views. Glenn Beck, who many Tea Partiers consider their intellectual guide, promotes the books of Cleon Skousen on his radio and television shows; Senator Mike Lee (R-UT) and other Tea Party politicians are devotees of Skousen's work; and local Tea Party study groups have made Skousen's book *The 5000 Year Leap* required reading.[23]

The disciples of Welch, Skousen, and other far right conservatives are hard at work within the Tea Party movement. Whether this is through direct organizing efforts, or through a more diffuse influence by way of conservative media and conservative corporate advocacy, this Cold War era right-wing tradition has shaped the ideology of the Tea Party. The slogans, the ideological frameworks, and the style of the Tea Party echo the earlier movements: The denunciation of a moderate sitting president as a socialist tyrant; the warnings of government treachery in the face of America's enemies (today's Islamic radicalism as yesterday's Soviet Union); the fetishism about restoring the Constitution (read highly selectively); the equation of graduated tax rates, estate taxes, and similar redistributive measures with communism; the demonization of inflation and the demand to dissolve the Federal Reserve and return to the gold standard; and the appeal to resist "one-world government"—all of these were characteristic of far right politics in the midst of the Cold War passions of the past. And today they are given play by Glenn Beck, Fox News, and on Tea Party websites and placards. The same demands and rhetoric have also made their way into the speeches of Republican politicians and into Republican state platforms from Maine to Texas.[24]

The extent to which this reflects the organizational revival of the JBS and related movements is unclear. Moreover, other traditions and influences are at work within the Tea Party movement. This includes varieties of Christian conservatism and apocalyptic fears of sexual perversion and moral decline. It includes nativism and xenophobia, as expressed in "birther" fears of Obama as Manchurian candidate, Islamaphobic fears of "jihadi mosques," and anti-immigrant fears of "anchor babies." And it includes white nationalism and racial fears of ACORN, the New Black Panther Party, and other bogeymen.

Yet, despite its heterogeneity, the Tea Party movement has maintained a degree of political coherence. It has done so by focusing on the corporate conservative agenda of fighting the "socialist" takeover: defeating health care reform, lowering taxes on the wealthy, lifting corporate regulations, and restricting union rights. Partly, this focus can be explained by the role that corporate advocacy organizations such as FreedomWorks and Americans for Prosperity (AFP) play in the training of Tea Party activists and in the financing of their operations. And partly, it is due to the fact that much of the Tea Party movement has embraced an ideological framework that has its ancestry in the John Birch Society and related elements of the Cold War far right. Indeed, these two explanations are not mutually exclusive. The AFP, for example, is funded by the brothers David and Charles Koch. Multibillionaire owners of the petrochemical conglomerate Koch Industries, the brothers aggressively pursue the conservative vision of their father, who was a founding member the John Birch Society.[25]

THE PROBLEM OF ELITES

Observers often emphasize the role of resentment toward elites in fueling the rage of the Tea Party. But this is not nearly as straightforward as it is usually presented. The first problem is that at least since the Jeffersonian "revolution" of 1800, and the extension of the white male franchise, political groups seeking to make their way into power by winning votes have done so in the name of the people overturning the misrule of whoever is on top. In the nineteenth century, this meant that a requirement of a successful election campaign was a claim—often false—of being a common "man of the plain people," and preferably one who was born in a log cabin. In the twentieth century, political candidates perfected appeals to "the forgotten man" or "the middle class." President Nixon spoke in the name of "the silent majority," and his Vice President Spiro Agnew savaged Nixon's antiwar critics as "an effete corps of impudent snobs." The Tea Party has unleashed its own arsenal of insults in this grand tradition of American political combat.

Michael Kazin has described this pattern of appealing to the common people against various elites as a "populist persuasion," a flexible rhetorical mode with deep historical roots in pre-Civil War "producerism."[26] According to this concept, nineteenth-century farmer, labor, and other movements viewed those engaged in productive labor as standing on higher moral ground than either the unproductive poor or the unproductive wealthy elites. As useful as this concept might be to describe the rhetorical strategies of a number of labor and reform movements in American history, its explanatory power has its limits for historical analysis. The Populists of the 1890s, for example, at times employed such rhetorical strategies, but they were much more deeply invested in the "business politics" of economic interest than in the "moral politics" of "producerism."[27] Chip Berlet's use of *producerism* (Chapter 2 in this volume) is problematic in that the Tea Party sends only occasional barbs toward the corporate executives, bankers, and lobbyists, who in the past were the systematic targets of "producerist" movements. Instead, today's Tea Party usually celebrates the corporate elites as heroes of the market. At the same time, Tea Party views about the poor and poverty follow in a different historical tradition, echoing the arguments of William Graham Sumner and other academic and corporate Social Darwinists of the late nineteenth century, who believed that any social policy to protect the poor or address the gaping social inequalities of the Gilded Age violated the allegedly natural order of laissez-faire economics.[28]

The Tea Party's moral center is the market and the supposed freedom of the marketplace, and the movement has shown relatively little interest in producerist-related questions of work or the moral value of labor. Americans for Tax Reform, directed by conservative power broker and Tea Party hero Grover Norquist, has a special project called the Alliance for Worker Freedom. The project is devoted to outlawing public-sector unions, expanding antiunion right-to-work laws, and gutting regulations that protect the pay, benefits, and safety of construction workers, airline employees, and other workers.[29] New Tea Party governors and legislatures in Wisconsin, Ohio, Indiana, and elsewhere have vigorously pursued much of this agenda at the state level. This is a version of worker freedom that harkens back to the nineteenth-century corporate notions of freedom of contract, whereby employees had the freedom to enter into individual contracts with their employers without the interference of government regulation of the workday or trade union contracts. In other words, this conservative corporate vision places no particular value on labor beyond what the market dictates.

Here it must be underscored that Norquist and the Tea Party only oppose some types of government intervention in the labor market. Their support for right-to-work laws and bans on public-sector collective bargaining are part of a wider web of federal and state laws and regulations that restrict the rights of workers to take collective action in the face of the collective action of their employers. In this regard, the conservative movement has consistently supported state intervention in the market. More broadly, although the Tea Partiers deify the free market, that does not mean that they want corporations to be free of governmental support. Except for some hesitation on the libertarian edge of their movement, conservatives embrace the system of federal and state contracts, subsidies, and regulations that make corporations— from military suppliers to drug companies—so profitable.

However, there are features of the Tea Party that pertain to elites and elitism that deserve a closer look. One way to make sense of the complex relationship that the Tea Party has to the elite centers of power in this country is to recognize that they pick and choose whom to like or not like. They may denounce experts (mainly scientists toiling in university and government agency laboratories) who claim that human activity is responsible for global warming, but they embrace the climate change skeptics of the highly elite corporate advocacy groups, such as the U.S. Chamber of Commerce or Americans for Prosperity.

The Tea Partiers may denounce academic elites, but at their back they have the Heritage Foundation, the Cato Institute, and a host of corporate think tanks and foundations that provide right-wing opinion makers with resources and access to power, the likes of which few academics can even dream. They may denounce what they call the elite "lamestream" media, such as the New York Times, while Rupert Murdoch and his News Corporation—the most powerful media corporation on the planet, which owns The Wall Street Journal, the largest circulation newspaper in the United States (and read closely by corporate elites), as well as Fox News—serve as essential vehicles of Tea Party advocacy. They may denounce Washington insiders, but Dick Armey, the former House majority leader, directs FreedomWorks, a powerful corporate lobby that provides invaluable service to the Tea Party.[30] Or how about the courts? Here, too, the same pattern applies, with the interesting twist that they even have Virginia Thomas, the wife of Supreme Court Justice Clarence Thomas, directing Liberty Central, another corporate Tea Party lobby.[31] In short, the Tea Partiers resent elites with whom they disagree, and like elites with whom they agree and who sustain their cause.

This reality complicates the idea of the Tea Party representing middle-class sectors fearing elites above and the poor below. Over half a century ago, Richard Hofstadter wrote that the status anxiety of the squeezed middle was the source of Populism and other "softheaded" and irrational movements.[32] And this notion remains current in the social sciences. But Hofstadter was wrong about the Populists, who mobilized on the basis of pressing and real economic interests rather than on the flights of irrationality suggested by the status anxiety concept. Similarly, the Tea Party members are no less hardheaded and realistic about pursuing economic goals. And, although the majority of Tea Party supporters belong to the middle class, for a variety of reasons they have calculated that their interests lie with the multimillionaires and billionaires. In that sense, when Samuel "Joe the Plumber" Wurzelbacher told then presidential candidate Obama that he feared that restoring taxes on the wealthy was "kind of" socialistic and at odds with the American dream, he anticipated broader concerns of the Tea Party.[33] According to the type of market fundamentalism advocated by the Tea Party, what is good for Koch Industries is what is good for America. And that is why, for example, Tea Party activists view any shifts in the tax structure or energy policy that may not be favorable to the oil, gas, and coal billionaires as a threat to their own prosperity and well-being.

For Tea Party activists, the market faces lurking danger from the political arena, where voting majorities may seek to mediate corporate power or otherwise infringe on the sanctity of the marketplace. This sheds light on another dimension of the problem of elites and elitism. One of the most esoteric of the Tea Party demands is the repeal of the Seventeenth Amendment. In the 1890s, the Populists issued the demand for the direct election of senators because they viewed the state legislatures as dens of corruption, and they considered the system whereby legislative bosses chose U.S. senators to be a violation of democratic principles. The adoption of the Seventeenth Amendment in 1913 placed the selection of senators in the hands of voters. But this has not sat well with conservatives. For Robert Welch and his acolytes, expanded democracy was what was wrong with America. The John Birch Society continues to stress that the United States is "a republic," where the properly suited represent the people, and is not "a democracy," subject to the undue influence of the populace.[34] According to Cleon Skousen, the Seventeenth Amendment left senators vulnerable to the "popular pressure" of the voting public.[35] The Tea Party politicians now advocating Seventeenth Amendment repeal are doing so for the same reasons. Texas Governor Rick Perry explains that the Seventeenth Amendment, enacted in "a fit of populist rage," is one of the key Progressive Era changes that put the country on the wrong path by violating the principle that "better senators" are produced when they are "the elect of the elected."[36] Not surprisingly, taking voting rights from voters has not translated well on the campaign trail. Alaska Tea Party candidate Joe Miller, for example, decided to play down his support for scrapping the Seventeenth Amendment while out appealing to voters to elect him to the U.S. Senate.[37] Nonetheless, resentments and fears of the voting mob are very much alive within the Tea Party movement.

In this regard, the Tea Party slogan "Take back our country!" is not merely metaphorical. It has the practical meaning that people within the Tea Party view the election of 2008 as illegitimate. Here, too, Fox News has provided the essential narrative: Voters who lacked the education and intelligence to know better were led to the polls like sheep to vote for the demagogue and false savior Obama. Community organizations like ACORN and the New Black Panther Party facilitated voter fraud and voter intimidation in America's inner cities, where felons, aliens, and racialist thugs tipped the scales of the elections. It does not matter that such claims about voter fraud and voter intimidation amount to fantasy, because they reflect morbid fears of what many within the Tea Party perceive as racially dangerous populations. Meanwhile, in practical terms, the Tea Party influence in more than a dozen states has resulted in legislation to rescind motor voter laws, expand felony disqualification lists, add new residency and identification requirements, and impose other hurdles that make it more difficult to vote. The Brennan Center for Justice estimates that as many as five million eligible voters, mainly among minorities, the young, and the poor, could find it significantly harder to cast ballots as a result of these new laws.[38] At the same time, many within the Tea Party are demanding a revision of the Fourteenth Amendment, which established birthright citizenship for all people born in the United States, with the aim of barring citizenship and voting rights from a section of immigrant Americans.[39] At the end of the nineteenth century, the conservative backlash against the Populist revolt produced poll taxes, literacy tests, and widespread disfranchisement of black as well as a section of poor white voters. Today, it is Tea Party anger that, in the same spirit if not with the same thoroughness, is directed at restricting the franchise and democracy.

THE PROBLEM OF GOVERNMENT

Making sense of Tea Party anger against government is similarly fraught with complexity. The rage against "big government" is usually directed at the federal branch of government, and posed in terms of the violated rights of the states. When Tea Partiers refer to constitutional principles, usually at the top of their list stands the Tenth Amendment, which they read as providing states with the right to ignore or "nullify" federal legislation. Tea Party political figures from Mississippi to Alaska make declarations about "nullification" in regard to the new health care legislation and other measures taken in Washington with which they disagree.[40] Historically, the banner of states' rights has most often been raised by those on the conservative side of American political conflict: from the defenders of slavery and white supremacy in the nineteenth century, to the opponents of labor rights and civil rights in the twentieth century. But this history also shows that states' rights cut multiple ways and are more instrumental than the usual generalizations about these matters allow.

In the political crisis of the 1850s, the federal government was in the hands of people that the southern slave owners viewed as reliable friends. That is why the southern defenders of slavery, who are most closely associated in memory with states' rights, had no objection when the Fugitive Slave Act expanded federal power over the states for the purpose of the capture and return of escaped slaves. Similarly, when the Supreme Court in the *Dred Scott* decision of 1857 ruled that African Americans had no rights under the Constitution and that the territories could not restrict slavery, southern slave owners nodded in agreement with the ruling. But in the free states, *Dred Scott* provoked fears of expanding federal powers in support of slavery. Abraham Lincoln, in his 1858 "House Divided" speech, famously warned that the next Supreme Court ruling could make Illinois a slave state. The election of Lincoln in 1860, however, raised the fury about states' rights to full throttle. The source of the anger in the slave-owning South was that Lincoln and the Republicans now controlled a federal power that had the potential ability to interfere with the institution of slavery. Of course, Lincoln denied any such intention. But the fear and rage that he might and could in the future is what drove the South into secession and the Civil War.[41]

Today's conservatives often support expanded federal power on their side of the equation. Most Tea Party activists would welcome a strengthened federal hand in the restriction of abortion, for example, or in the prohibition of homosexual marriages. After 9/11, when the George W. Bush administration expanded federal police powers, only a few libertarians in the conservative camp protested federal overreach. The same goes for the Bush administration's attempts to override California's climate change law, or the medical marijuana laws several states adopted. But with the election of Barack Obama, the angry banner of states' rights flies again. A self-identified African American sits in the Oval Office, and Obama might or could alter the framework of federal policy to address the gaping social inequities that afflict national minorities and other constituencies that helped get him elected. So far, the Obama administration has lived up to its promise of cautious and moderate change. But federal health care legislation only confirmed the worst fears about "redistribution" that has fueled the conservative rage against the federal government on Fox News and conservative websites.

In reality, despite simplistic rhetoric, Tea Partiers often express a complex approach to the federal government. This approach might be best summed up by the slogan "Keep the Government Out of My Medicare" that appeared in rallies against health care reform. Although this slogan was the butt of jokes on late-night television, it is a good expression of what is at stake in the antigovernment anger of the Tea Party. Because Social Security and Medicare violate conservative *ideology*, activists within the Tea Party call for dismantling these government programs. And this demand has made it into the Republican state platforms in Texas and elsewhere.[42]

But older Americans, who also happen to make up an essential Tea Party constituency, tend to support Social Security and Medicare. Therefore, *politically*, the defense of these government programs has been a key element in Tea Party mobilization. The logic works like this: Obama is expanding federal health protections to new constituencies, many of them nonwhite and younger. This, the Tea Partiers argue, undermines federal protections for those who already have them. As argued by Representative Michele Bachmann (R-MN), a leader of the Tea Party caucus in Congress, health care reform threatens to take money from Medicare for seniors "to pay for younger people."[43] The budget proposed by Representative Paul Ryan (R-WI) and embraced by the Tea Party and the Republicans in Congress reflects this same logic. Starting in 2022, the Ryan budget would provide only vouchers for private insurance to new beneficiaries, but would protect traditional Medicare for people who already have it.

The inconsistency here is not the point, any more than the inconsistencies in the use and misuse of states' rights. But it confirms the value of Lisa Disch's (Chapter 5 in this volume) insight about the Tea Party operating within the framework of rights and privileges defined by the New Deal. Mainly older and whiter Americans provide the Tea Party with its strongest base of support.[44] This is the same demographic that gained the most during the post–World War II decades when "affirmative action was white," and the Federal Housing Administration and the GI Bill used taxpayer funds to put millions of white Americans through college and into homes in segregated suburbs.[45] The Tea Party hit a nerve among this older and whiter population at a moment when the threat of new racial politics and new stakeholders in line for federal support compounded the stress of shrinking retirement portfolios and a collapsing housing market.

This is not the first time that threatened changes in the rules of government support have stoked antigovernment anger. The Sagebrush Rebellion that fueled anti-Washington fires during the Reagan years represents a key precedent. For decades, the federal government has provided the extractive industries in the mainly western states with extensive subsidies and services, making states such as Arizona and Alaska the hands-down winners in the high-stakes game of federal largesse. Yet, in the 1980s, ranchers, loggers, miners, and other entrepreneurs in the western states launched bitter and angry protests against the Bureau of Land Management, the Environmental Protection Agency, and other federal institutions. Enraged Sagebrush rebels loudly challenged federal authority, and in Alaska, they even burned an airplane owned by the National Park Service. And some conservative Alaskans, including Todd Palin, joined the Alaskan Independence Party that periodically threatens secession from the United States.[46]

The underlying logic of the rebellion, however, was driven by the *dependency* of ranchers, loggers, miners, and oil drillers on Washington and its bureaucratic agencies. The federal government owns the lands they exploit; maintains the roads, water projects, and other services that make exploitation profitable; and provides the farm subsidies and other bureaucratic support that keep many ranches and rural businesses in business. Indeed, at the height of their antigovernment fever, Sagebrush rebels continued to lobby for expanded federal water projects and other subsidies. What aroused the wrath of the rebels was that other stakeholders— environmentalists, and tourist and recreation industries, as well as Indians—were also shaping federal policy.[47] In other words, this was not a conflict over the pros and cons of federal power, but over who would gain most from federal support and protection. Significantly, today's anti-Washington agitation has the most strength in those states that receive the most in federal expenditures, including the extractive West where the old Sagebrush rebels have found a comfortable place in the new Tea Party.

THE PROBLEM OF RACE

Finally, to understand the present Tea Party rage, it needs to be kept in mind that racial and ethnic resentments have repeatedly served to fan the flames of antigovernment passions. In the 1940s, '50s, and '60s, federal support for African American civil rights provoked a fierce response from southern segregationists. To protest Truman's order to integrate the armed forces, Strom Thurmond broke with the Democratic Party and in 1948 ran for president as the candidate of the avowedly segregationist States' Rights Party. In 1963, in the face of federal civil rights enforcement, Alabama Governor George Wallace "tossed the gauntlet" at the feet of government tyranny and vowed "segregation today, segregation tomorrow, segregation forever." Meanwhile, Robert Welch, Barry Goldwater, and other conservative leaders launched their own parallel attack on federal civil rights action that they viewed as the tyrannical expansion of federal power. Although Welch denied being motivated by racial animus, the JBS received wide support among segregationists for its campaign to impeach Supreme Court Chief Justice Earl Warren. Similarly, in his 1964 campaign, Goldwater received the support of Strom Thurmond, George Wallace, and the other segregationist leaders. The white supremacist bigots and the Cold War era conservatives distrusted and often disliked each other. Yet, in the name of a common battle against federal tyranny, they joined together to ride the wave of white resistance to racial equality.[48]

Today, the racial and cultural fears and resentments of many Americans focus on immigrants and especially Muslims. This makes President Obama a large target as the son of an immigrant with a Muslim name. Tea Party leaders, much like Welch and Goldwater in the past, claim to eschew racism. Yet, again much in the Welch-Goldwater mold, they hope to ride the racist tide by exploiting fears about the so-called "Ground Zero mosque" or stoking xenophobic speculations about Obama's birth certificate. Nonetheless, in the ideological world of the Tea Party, such matters pale in significance as compared to the larger questions that they group under the rubric of "redistribution of wealth" and "reparations." Many Tea Partiers fear that the Obama administration—with a president self-identifying as an African American and with voting constituencies of poor people of color—represents at its core the politics of "reparations." Whether it is health care or taxes, they see Obama as redistributing wealth at the expense of older and whiter Americans.

Rick Santelli's scream that launched the Tea Party carried this implicit message. And Dinesh D'Souza spelled it out explicitly in a widely distributed article in *Forbes* magazine titled, "How Obama Thinks." A conservative commentator, D'Souza has been a sharp critic of affirmative action, which he sees as a form of discrimination against white people. He has linked this critique into a wider thesis that white people face the imminent threat of having their property stolen in the name of redress of past racial wrongs. In that light, according to D'Souza, the president is far worse than a mere socialist; he is an anticolonialist seeking a global system of reparations by punishing the white nations and shifting wealth and power to the former colonies. When it comes to health care, for example, Obama is not interested in socializing health care but in "decolonizing" it, using mandatory medical insurance as a means of payback against the perceived wrongs of the past.[49] For D'Souza, as with much of the Tea Party movement, the very possibility that Obama might have the desire and ability to pursue a redistributive policy at the expense of white Americans is what makes him such an odious threat.

Playing on such fears has a long tradition in American politics. At the conclusion of the Civil War, a shattered country faced a crisis of reconstruction. One of the most pressing problems was addressing the humanitarian catastrophe facing the four million freed people who emerged from slavery often with little more than the rags on their backs. Congress established the Freedmen's Bureau, which among other things distributed blankets and foodstuffs to those facing exposure and hunger. This congressional action provoked a backlash of white rage, not only in the former Confederacy but also in the North. It did not matter that the Homestead Act of 1862 distributed millions of acres of federal lands to white settlers, and the great railroad corporations received federal subsidies including more millions of acres of public lands. It did not matter that the federal government reversed the small experiments it had undertaken to provide the former slaves with land.[50] Just the idea that Congress would provide humanitarian relief to the former slaves provoked furious opposition. Northern Democrats, whose reputation had been shaken as the opposition party during the war, seized on the popular anger by denouncing the Freedmen's Bureau as "[a]n agency to keep the Negro in idleness at the expense of the white man."[51]

Today, the financial and economic crisis has opened deep wounds. The crisis has hit African American and Latino communities and the urban poor with devastating force, including Depression–era levels of unemployment. Yet, the deepest wounds are left to fester, as efforts to address them are overwhelmed by the rage on the Tea Party right. Rick Santelli's scream at the very possibility that the government might aid the "losers" in this crisis has for the time being set the terms of the debate about who the winners and losers will be in shifting sands of the postwar political economy.

CONCLUSION

Over the last three decades, the United States has been conducting a remarkable experiment in market fundamentalism. Even before the inauguration of Ronald Reagan, leading politicians, both Republicans and Democrats, accepted the terms of this experiment: dismantling economic regulations, reducing taxes on corporations and the wealthiest citizens, and otherwise expanding the power of the market in the expectation that this would bring about an era of unlimited economic growth and prosperity. Not surprisingly, this experiment made wealthy Americans much wealthier, and gave hope of such wealth to many others. Meanwhile, middle-class incomes stagnated, and the ranks of the poor grew apace. By 2008, the divisions between the rich and the poor and the inequitable division of wealth matched levels unseen since before the Great Depression.[52]

On September 15, 2008, Lehman Brothers, the financial services giant, filed for bankruptcy, as the financial sector teetered on the edge of collapse. On October 23, 2008, Alan Greenspan, the former chair of the Federal Reserve and leading architect of the market fundamentalist experiment, testified on Capitol Hill that he was in "a state of shocked-disbelief" that unregulated financial institutions had failed to regulate themselves. As Greenspan bluntly put it, "the whole intellectual edifice" that had justified deregulating the financial sector, an edifice that his Federal Reserve had contributed so much to building, had now "collapsed."[53] Less than two weeks after Greenspan's confession, Americans went to the polls and elected a president who promised to restore responsibility in governance and rein in the excesses of an unregulated financial market. Yet, one month after President Obama's inauguration, Rick Santelli's scream marked the beginning of a resurgence of a militant right-wing political mobilization demanding the further liberation of the market from regulation, taxes, and what remains of America's social safety net.

The rise of the Tea Party movement may appear to be historically incongruous given the causal relationship between the worst economic meltdown since the Great Depression and the conservative market fundamentalist policies that preceded the meltdown. Indeed, by that measure, the right-wing rage expressed in the Tea Party is not just out of place, but downright irrational. And in that spirit, analysts and commentators have dusted off Richard Hofstadter's old guesswork about the "populist" irrationality of the distressed middle strata.

But by other measures, the Tea Party can be understood as a mobilization in the hardheaded pursuit of self-interest. It needs to be kept in mind that the experiment in market fundamentalism made millions of Americans richer, and gave hope to others that they could be part of that group. In that sense, the Tea Party can be understood as a militant defense of that experiment (no matter the destruction that it precipitated). At a deeper level, the Tea Party embodies the concerns of mainly older, white Americans, the demographic that benefited most from the New Deal state, and that feels the ground shifting underfoot. Health care reform reflects the challenges of new stakeholders. And the demographic realities of immigration and nonwhite population growth fuels dread of potential changes in the political economy—fears brought to a boil with the election of Obama.

During the Cold War, the John Birch Society and other corporate conservative groups tapped into apocalyptic fears of communism to build a mass right-wing movement. In the present moment of fear and resentment, similar corporate conservatives are hard at work. Borrowing a great deal from the Cold War far right, and with the careful nurturing of corporate foundations and Fox News, the Tea Party represents a mass conservative response to the current crisis of political economy. The speed with which the Tea Party organized, and its rapid capture of much of one of the nation's two main political parties, shows the volatility of the political environment in the wake of the Great Recession. There is no predicting the outcome here. But there are already signs of the Tea Party losing its initial momentum. And there is no reason to rule out that the same economic and political volatility that initially gave the Tea Party strength will also prove its undoing.

NOTES

1. Tea Party leaders have adopted as their organizational handbook a study of decentralized and amorphous networks: Ori Brafman and Rod A. Beckstrom's *The Starfish and the Spider: The Unstoppable Power of Leaderless Organizations* (New York: Portfolio Hardcover, 2006). See Kenneth P. Vogel, "The New Tea Party Bible," Politico, July 31, 2010.

2. *Newsweek*, March 22, 2009.

3. C. Vann Woodward, *Tom Watson: Agrarian Rebel* (New York: Oxford University Press, 1938, reprint 1970), 138.

4. Charles Postel, "Knowledge and Power," in *The Populist Vision* (New York: Oxford University Press, 2007), 26–45.

5. David Broder, "Sarah Palin Displays Her Pitch-Perfect Populism," *Washington Post*, February 11, 2010; George Will, "Sarah Palin and the Mutual Loathing Society," *Washington Post*, February 18, 2010; and Ben McGrath, "The Movement: The Rise of Tea Party Activism," *The New Yorker*, February 1, 2010.

6. Richard Hofstadter, *The Age of Reform* (New York: Vintage, 1955), 12–22, 46–47.

7. Michael P. Rogin, *The Intellectuals and McCarthy: The Radical Specter* (Cambridge, MA: MIT Press, 1967).

8. C. Vann Woodward, "The Populist Heritage and the Intellectual," in *The Burden of Southern History* (Baton Rouge: Louisiana State University Press, [1960] 1977), 141–66; Walter K. Nugent, *The Tolerant Populists: Kansas Populism and Nativism* (Chicago: University of Chicago Press, 1963).

9. Linda Gordon, "If the Progressives Were Advising Us Today, Should We Listen?" *Journal of the Gilded Age and Progressive Era* 1, no. 2 (2002): 109–21.

10. Margaret Canovan, *Populism* (New York: Houghton Mifflin Harcourt Press, 1981), 3–16.

11. James R. Green, *Grass-Roots Socialism: Radical Movements in the Southwest, 1895–1943* (Baton Rouge: Louisiana State University Press, 1978).

12. Elizabeth Sanders, *Roots of Reform: Farmers, Workers, and the American State, 1877–1917* (Chicago: University of Chicago Press, 1999).

13. Alan Brinkley, *Voices of Protest: Huey Long, Father Coughlin, and the Great Depression* (New York: Vintage, 1983).

14. Robert A. Caro, *The Path to Power: The Years of Lyndon Johnson*, vol. 1 (New York: Vintage, 1990).

15. Alan Brinkley, "The Problem of American Conservativism," *American Historical Review* 99, no. 2 (1994): 409–29; Heather Thompson, "Rescuing the Right," *Reviews in American History* 30, no. 2 (2002): 322–32; Leo P. Ribuffo, "The Discovery and Rediscovery of American Conservatism Broadly Conceived," *Magazine of History* 17, no. 2 (2003): 5–10.

16. Kim Phillips-Fein, *Invisible Hands: The Making of the Conservative Movement from the New Deal to Reagan* (New York: W. W. Norton and Company, 2009), 3–25.

17. Lisa McGirr, *Suburban Warriors: The Origins of the New American Right* (Princeton, NJ: Princeton University Press, 2002).

18. William F. Buckley, Jr., "Goldwater, the John Birch Society, and Me," *Commentary*, March 2008, 52–54.

19. Rick Perlstein, *Before the Storm: Barry Goldwater and the Unmaking of the American Consensus* (New York: Hill and Wang, 2001), 110–19, 154–56.

20. Brian Farmer, "Ron Paul Addresses John Birch Society," *The New American*, October 8, 2008, www.thenewamerican.com/usnews/constitution/409.

21. William E. Jasper, "CPAC: 'Conservatism' at the Crossroads," *The New American*, February 24, 2010, www.thenewamerican.com/index.php/usnews/politics/3013-cpac-qconservatismq-at-the-crossroads.

22. Ann Turner, "Utah's United Freedom Conference," *The New American*, September 20, 2010, www.thenewamerican.com/index.php/usnews/constitution/4642-utahs-freedom-conference.

23. Jeffrey Rosen, "Radical Constitutionalism," *New York Times*, November 26, 2010.

24. See www.mainegop.com/PlatformMission.aspx; www.hrc.org/documents/2010_RPT_PLATFORM.pdf.

25. Sean Wilentz, "Confounding Fathers, the Tea Party's Cold War Roots," *The New Yorker*, October 18, 2010; and Stacy Singer, "David Koch Intends to Cure Cancer in His Lifetime and Remake American Politics," *The Palm Beach Post*, February 18, 2012.

26. Michael Kazin, *The Populist Persuasion: An American History* (New York: Basic Books, 1995).

27. Bruce Palmer, *"Man Over Money": The Southern Populist Critique of American Capitalism* (Chapel Hill: University of North Carolina Press, 1980); Postel, "Business Politics," *Populist Vision*, 137–72.

28. William Graham Sumner, *What Social Classes Owe to Each Other* (New York: Harper & Brothers, 1883).

29. See www.workerfreedom.org/.

30. Dick Armey and Matt Kibbe, *Give Us Liberty: A Tea Party Manifesto* (New York: Harper Collins, 2010).

31. Jackie Calmes, "Activism of Thomas's Wife Could Raise Judicial Issues," *New York Times*, October 8, 2010.

32. Hofstadter, *The Age of Reform*, 93, 164.

33. Larry Rohter, "Plumber from Ohio Is Thrust into Spotlight," *New York Times*, October 15, 2008.

34. "John Birch," The John Birch Society, http://jbs.org/component/content/article/1006-quick-hits/6557-republics-and-democracies.

35. W. Cleon Skousen, *The Five Thousand Year Leap* (Malta, Idaho: National Center for Constitutional Studies, [1981] 2009), 163.

36. Rick Perry, *Fed Up! Our Fight to Save America from Washington* (New York: Little Brown and Company, 2010), 38, 41–43.

37. Chris Freiberg, "Alaska U.S. Senate Candidate Joe Miller Explains His Positions at Fairbanks Town Hall Meeting," *Fairbanks Daily News-Miner*, October 4, 2010; and "Joe Miller Responds to 17th Amendment Controversy," *Fairbanks Daily News-Miner*, October 6, 2010.

38. Matt Simpson, "The REAL Voting Problem in Texas," *The Liberty* (blog), American Civil Liberties Union of Texas website, March 15, 2011, www.aclutx.org/blog/?cat=26; and Wendy R. Weiser and Lawrence Norden, "Voting Law Changes in 2012," Brennan Center for Justice at New York University School of Law, 2012, accessed February 27, 2012, www.brennancenter.org/content/resource/voting_law_changes_in_2012/#summ.

39. Marc Lacey, "Birthright Citizenship Looms as Next Immigration Battle," *New York Times*, January 4, 2011; and Simmi Auja, "Immigration Hard-Liners to Lead Judiciary?" Politico, October 26, 2011.

40. A number of Tea Party groups describe themselves as "Tenthers," and have adopted names such as the "Tenth Amendment Center," the "Virginia 10th Amendment Coalition," the "10th Amendment Foundation," and so forth.

41. Eric Foner, *The Fiery Trial: Abraham Lincoln and American Slavery* (New York: W. W. Norton & Co., 2010).

42. "2010 State Republican Party Platform," accessed October 8, 2011, http://tcgop.org/wp-content/uploads/2010/06/2010_RPT_PLATFORM.pdf.

43. Glenn Kessler, "Fact Checking the GOP Debate: $500 Billion in Cuts to Medicare?" *Washington Post*, June 15, 2011.

44. Theda Skocpol and Vanessa Williamson, *The Tea Party and the Remaking of Republican Conservatism* (New York: Oxford University Press, 2012), 23–26.

45. Ira Katznelson, *When Affirmative Action Was White: An Untold History of Racial Inequality in Twentieth-Century America* (New York: W.W. Norton & Company, 2005).

46. "Press Release with Corrections from the AIP Chairman, Lynette Clark," Alaskan Independence Party website, www.akip.org/090308.html.

47. James Morton Turner, "'The Specter of Environmentalism': Wilderness, Environmental Politics, and the Evolution of the New Right," *Journal of American History* 96, no. 1 (2009): 123–49.

48. Perlstein, *Before the Storm*, 431–32.

49. Dinesh D'Souza, "How Obama Thinks," *Forbes*, September 27, 2010.

50. Eric Foner, *Reconstruction: America's Unfinished Revolution, 1863–1877* (New York: Harper Perennial Modern Classics, 1988).

51. In the Pennsylvania gubernatorial election of 1866, the Democratic candidate ran on a platform of opposition to federal relief for the former slaves, with the campaign poster reading: "The Freedman's Bureau! An agency to keep the Negro in idleness at the expense of the white man." Broadside Collection, Library of Congress Rare Books and Special Collections.

52. Congressional Budget Office, *Trends in the Distribution of Household Income Between 1979 and 2007* (Washington, DC: Congress of the United States, October 2011).

53. Edmund L. Andrews, "Greenspan Concedes Error on Regulation," *New York Times*, October 23, 2008.

CHAPTER 2

Reframing Populist Resentments in the Tea Party Movement

CHIP BERLET

Radical-in-Chief: Barack Obama and the Untold Story of American Socialism

—Title of a book by Stanley Kurtz of *National Review* (2010)

Change We Can Believe In.

—Obama 2008 presidential campaign slogan

"Change" is a word we hear over and over. By "change" these groups mean Socialism.

—Gary Allen with Larry Abraham,
None Dare Call It Conspiracy (1971)

The signs, slogans, stories, and claims of the Tea Party movement are often incomprehensible to many observers. A frequent response is to describe the Tea Party movement participants as stupid, ignorant, or crazy. What else could explain the "extremist" idea that Obama is both Hitler and Stalin? Who but a "wing nut" on the "lunatic fringe" would claim that government reform of health care could result in a bureaucrat unplugging grandma from her life support system in a hospital?

The underlying frames and narratives that produce these seemingly absurd tropes popular in the Tea Party movement are actually quite common in conservative, economic libertarian, and Christian evangelical households—and they have been for decades. This chapter argues that the Tea Party movement is a form of right-wing populism that uses a "producerist" narrative, and that this model has reappeared periodically in right-wing movements throughout U.S. history. The signs and statements at Tea Party demonstrations might reflect garbled prose, but the ideas have a clear textual pedigree.[1]

In reviewing the frames and narratives of the Tea Party movement, it becomes clear that the Tea Party (and the gravitation of the Republican Party toward its obvious energy and activism) marks the return of previously marginalized theories and policy positions of the ultraconservative and conspiracist John Birch Society (JBS), which was founded in the late 1950s. These theories and positions are now emerging in the public square as a major viewpoint. In this regard, Chapter 1 in this volume by Charles Postel establishes the importance of the JBS for understanding the Tea Party movement, with an excellent overview that needs no repeating here.

However, whereas Postel argues that the Tea Party is not an example of right-wing populism, I argue that the Tea Party uses the historic rhetoric, tropes, and frames of right-wing populism, especially the narrative called "producerism," to advance its agenda. In right-wing producerist movements, activists tend to perceive their political adversaries through the lens of fear-based dualism (self versus other; us versus them) and demonization of the "other." They claim their opponents threaten the very existence of the nation. In the Tea Party movement, these views are intertwined with long-standing right-wing conspiracy theories about liberal betrayal. In an effort to mobilize its members, the Tea Party movement largely has adopted fear-based frames and narratives in which liberal and left ideological opponents are demonized and scapegoated as consciously or unconsciously destroying the America of liberty and freedom.[2]

MOBILIZING RESENTMENT

Much popular and journalistic work on the nature of the Tea Party movement uses outdated social science models based on what is known variously as the pluralist school, classical theory, or centrist-extremist theory. This set of theories tends to view people who joined social movements of the left or right as psychologically dysfunctional and a threat to democracy. In 1967, political scientist Michael Paul Rogin challenged the notion that right-wing movements—whether populist or elitist—reflected dysfunctional outbursts of irrational "extremism."

Other scholars joined this critique,[3] and since then numerous scholars have produced a substantial body of work detailing the mobilization and recruitment mechanisms of right-wing movements, the mainstream demographics of their members,[4] and how these movements interact with political parties and elections. The flawed claims of the pluralist school, nonetheless, continue to dominate public debates.

Sara Diamond, a protégé of Rogin, defines right-wing politics as supporting "the state in its capacity as enforcer of order and [opposing] the state as distributor of wealth and power downward and more equitably in society."[5] Rory McVeigh has demonstrated that right-wing movements tend to defend preexisting power and privilege in three arenas: political, economic, and social status.[6] We see this process today in the Tea Party movement. It is hardly irrational. Jean Hardisty calls this process "mobilizing resentment."[7]

People who join social movements are average folks with grievances. They join with others to resolve their grievances. To accomplish this they mobilize resources, exploit opportunities that open up in the political system, develop their own internal culture, and create perceptual frames, clever slogans, and parable-like stories to achieve their aims.[8]

Sociologists talk about "framing" as an ongoing process in which social movement leaders illustrate a power struggle by narrowing the subject to a specific point of view or perspective easily understood by followers.[9] A narrative is simply a story told inside a movement that is sometimes shared with the public. These stories serve as parables, with the plot and story line revealing heroes and villains. Movement participants learn lessons about expected ideas and actions valued by the movement as a whole. These become internalized and live on as if they are "common sense."[10] Narrative stories can be told in ways that defend or challenge the status quo.[11] Successful movements find a way to achieve their ideological goals by skillfully deploying their frames and narratives.[12]

The Tea Party movement is the latest instance of a campaign the political right launched in the 1930s to roll back the social welfare policies of the Roosevelt administration. This campaign has always been a loose-knit coalition of large corporate interests, small business owners, economic libertarians, antiunion activists, conservative Christians, and moral traditionalists. They all share a general antipathy to collectivism. Their opposition to taxes, however, is selective. For example, they tend to support funding for the military and law enforcement, but tend to oppose government programs that weave a social safety net.

Similar themes were stressed by the anticommunist movement of the 1950s and 1960s; in the mobilization against the civil rights movement in the 1960s; in the ultraconservative Goldwater campaign of 1964; in the Nixon administration's Southern Strategy to gain white voters in the South; and in the patriot and armed citizens' militia movements of the 1990s.

Ask Tea Party activists where they get their news and political information and they mention Glenn Beck, Lou Dobbs, Fox News, AM talk radio, and Internet sites such as Free Republic and World Net Daily, all of which function as information silos that reinforce their beliefs.[13] Examining Tea Party rhetoric reveals three distinct story lines of why Obama must be stopped: (1) Obama and political liberalism are greasing the skids to collectivist, socialist, and/or totalitarian rule; (2) the Obama administration and its liberal allies are naïve dupes, or puppets, of clever leftist elites and socialist ideologues; and (3) leftists, liberals, and Democrats are the aboveground apparatus for an age-old, vast left-wing conspiracy to create a one-world government on behalf of secret elites who control everything. Whether these conspiracies track back to Marx or Satan is open to debate.

When Obama took office, he brought with him a laundry list of policies his supporters favored. These included revising labor laws and passing the pro-union card check legislation; comprehensive immigration reform; health care reform; ending wars in the Middle East; combating global climate change; expanding gay rights; and preserving the right of a woman to choose abortion. There were preexisting conservative groups and constituencies that opposed all these plans in 2008. While demonizing and conspiracist rhetoric did not have to be part of their conservative rhetorical strategy, by 2010, influential Republican and conservative strategists were employing hyperbolic demonization, relying on alarmist demagoguery, and tolerating the spread of conspiracy theories in their campaign to block President Obama's policy agenda.[14] As David Weigel observes, the "tea party will succeed, if it hasn't already, in making one of America's political parties more devoted to supply-side, pro-war-on-terror, anti-spending principles. But it is pushing on an open door."[15]

LIBERTARIANS AND POPULISTS

The Tea Party movement in 2010 was still in a process of developing its frames, narratives, and issue boundaries. Ideologically it is still in tension internally, with an awkward collage of ideological positions piled together from several preexisting formations on the right. Often there is overlap, and many of these sectors have previously cooperated. Today, hobbling the Obama administration is the movement's shared goal, but it is based on different worldviews with different story lines that motivate action. For example, while libertarians suggest abortion is a private matter that should be immune from government intervention, the Christian right thinks abortion is sinful and murder of an unborn child. But the libertarians also don't think the government should fund abortions because libertarians oppose government-run health care. Therefore, despite strategic differences, both Christian right activists and libertarians can work together on a tactical project to oppose the abortion policies of the Obama administration.

The Tea Party's use of the rhetoric of right-wing populism to build a mass movement against Obama has, to some extent, already been shown in cases of similar movements of contemporary European populism.[16] Hans-Georg Betz has found that right-wing populist movements in Europe share a common theme of xenophobia and racist scapegoating of immigrants and asylum seekers.[17] Politicians in these movements tend especially to attract men, people employed in the private sector, and younger voters. Two demographic groups emerge: economic libertarians who are in the upper middle class or are small entrepreneurs, and lower-middle-class and wage workers attracted to xenophobia and ethnocentric nationalism.[18]

Douglas R. Holmes looks at attempts by what he calls European "integralists" to exploit resentment and alienation. He highlights Jean-Marie Le Pen as skillfully mixing left and right elements from populism, expressionism, and pluralism.[19] Ray Taras studies how "in western Europe the rise of xenophobia is nearly synonymous with the anti-immigrant backlash," especially against non-Europeans and "people who are not racially Caucasian or religiously Judeo-Christian."[20] Taras traces the development of "phobias" built around ethnic hierarchies in which prejudice against immigrants—especially asylum seekers—is notably high. He sees great anxiety produced by the transition from Old Europe to New Europe.[21]

In many ways these are the same themes and constituencies that make up the Tea Party movement in the United States. One difference though is that there is a significantly larger population of evangelical and fundamentalist Protestants in the United States as compared to right-wing populist movements in Europe. Many adopt libertarian or free-market ideas as a legacy of early Calvinism.[22] This individualistic form of free enterprise was influential in the formation of the United States.[23] Conservative evangelicals have adapted this libertarianism into a form of political economy analysis called "Christian economics," which is seen as compatible with a concern over moral traditionalist forms of patriarchy and heterosexism.[24]

TEA PARTY FRAMING

Among the top agenda items of the Tea Party nationally is the repeal of "Obamacare," by which Tea Partiers mean the reform of health care financing signed into law by the Obama administration. To illustrate the Tea Party's ideological treatment of this and other issues, and especially the Tea Party's capacity to fold libertarian views into populist rhetoric, consider how Big Sky Tea Party Association of Montana presented these issues one day in early October 2010.

To understand Obamacare, the Big Sky Tea Party directs its readers to the book *Liberty and Tyranny: A Conservative Manifesto* by Mark Levin, and the article "Max Baucus, Health Care Reform, and the 'Mal-Distribution of Income'" by Mark Whittington.[25] According to Levin, "Roosevelt and a relatively small band of Cronies, most of whom came from academia and the labor movement and worked their will in the halls of the bureaucracy and Congress—usually out of public view—had wanted to include government-run universal health care as part of Social Security." Levin suggests this was "too politically ambitious even for an overwhelmingly Democratic Congress," but the crafty strategists "knew if they persisted incrementally, however, manipulating public information and perceptions and adding more and more people to Social Security's rolls, over time they would achieve their ends."[26]

This view casts liberal public policy objectives as part of a shadowy conspiracy of collectivist elites, intellectuals, and labor bosses: a soft version of claims the John Birch Society made. Levin's analysis avoids overt conspiracism and reflects the basic themes of economic libertarianism, but it can be read by a conspiracy theorist to support that view as well.

Mark Whittington, in "Max Baucus, Health Care Reform, and the 'Mal-Distribution of Income,'" charges that the "effects of President Obama's redistributionist policies will not fall heaviest on the super rich, the Wall Street fat cats, the 'economic royalists' against whom Democrats have inveighed since the dark days of Franklin Roosevelt.

They have their wealth and can afford battalions of accountants and tax attorneys to protect it." According to Whittington:

> The effort to address the "mal-distribution of income" will fall on those who are trying to create wealth, the small businessmen and women. These are people who are operating hair and nail salons, ethnic restaurants, auto repair shops, small entrepreneurial technology companies, and a myriad of other small businesses with which they hope to grab a portion of the American dream. President Obama has targeted them, imposing health insurance mandates and taxes that will cripple them.[27]

Either way, the hardworking and productive middle-class Tea Party activist is beset by government programs that line the pockets of the parasites above and below on the socioeconomic ladder.

Sex education in the public schools was highlighted the day I browsed the website of the Big Sky Tea Party Association. There was a link to a news article from the *Billings Gazette,* which reported that a "Helena mother says the final adoption of a highly controversial proposed health curriculum will cause her and her children 'irreparable harm.'" The calendar of Tea Party events listed one general meeting and three meetings about sex education and the new health curriculum. The Action Alerts also featured the sex education controversy, and linked to a Fox News segment covering the local issue in Montana.

Jim Walker, the chairman of the Big Sky Tea Party board in October 2010, announced the group's opposition to the curriculum developed by the national Association for Supervision and Curriculum Development (ASCD). Walker falsely implied it was part of a plan coordinated by the United Nations through the U.S. federal government that would erode U.S. sovereignty. According to Walker, the curriculum was consistent with the "United Nations' established philosophies with an emphasis on development of 'global citizens' while intentionally diminishing the importance of national heritage." He concluded, "the Big Sky Tea Party urges the citizens of the Helena area to use your power of the vote to begin systematically replacing the existing board members with candidates that will uphold traditional American and Montana rights, values, and sovereignty."[28]

The idea that the United Nations is part of the conspiracy for global conquest resulting in the building of a New World Order is a core premise of the John Birch Society and a handful of other conspiracist groups on the political right. So is the idea that sex education, abortion, and gay rights are part of that conspiracy.

For further information, the Big Sky Tea Party site sends users to the website of World Net Daily and also to Glenn Beck. The link to World Net Daily leads to the book *The Manchurian President* by Aaron Klein with Brenda J. Elliott.[29] Klein and Elliott suggest that Obama was groomed for the presidency by a nest of subversive socialists, communists, and other dangerous radicals based in the Hyde Park neighborhood of Chicago. The book is published by WND Books, a division of World Net Daily. Klein is a senior staff reporter for World Net Daily and runs an anti-Obama conspiracy theory website.[30] The Glenn Beck program features manic blackboard chalk talks charting the vast leftist conspiracy in endless and often erroneous or guilt-by-association detail.[31] The Big Sky Tea Party website contains a reading list that includes the book *Common Sense* by Glenn Beck.[32]

At the top of the reading list, however, is *The 5000 Year Leap* by W. Cleon Skousen, which Glenn Beck tells his audience is the most important book in his life.[33] Skousen worked closely with the John Birch Society, which promoted his ideas. In his book, Skousen presents the 28 basic principles of the founders that he claims made America leap ahead in a short 200 years in a way that outdistanced all the previous progress of the prior 5,000 years. The list is a blend of libertarian, free-market, and Christian right lore, including:

- Without religion the government of a free people cannot be maintained.
- The highest level of prosperity occurs when there is a free-market economy and a minimum of government regulations.
- Only limited and carefully defined powers should be delegated to government, all others being retained by the people.
- The burden of debt is as destructive to human freedom as subjugation by conquest.
- The United States has a manifest destiny to eventually become a glorious example of God's law under a restored Constitution that will inspire the entire human race.

RIGHT-WING VERSIONS OF POPULISM

Should the term *populism* be limited to study of the United States People's Party, the "prairie radicals," and other populist formations launched in the late 1800s in North America, or is there a heuristic value in a broader generic usage? Postel (Chapter 1 in this volume) suggests that it is not proper to use the term *populism* to describe the Tea Party movement, arguing that they are essentially conservative and not populist. Burghart and his colleague at the Institute for Research and Education on Human Rights, Leonard Zeskind, have argued that it is wrong to use the term *populism* to describe right-wing movements including the Tea Party.[34]

This type of debate occurs in other areas of study. For example, should the term *fascism* be limited to the interwar movements and regimes primarily in Italy and Germany, or is there an appropriate broader generic usage? In both cases, I respect those who want a more limited usage, but since the 1980s, numerous scholars have been productively using the broader generic terms for both *populism* and *fascism* as useful analytical lenses.

Historian Lawrence Goodwyn described the People's Party mass movement as "the flowering of the largest democratic mass movement in American history."[35] In many ways Goodwyn's observation is valid; but as with other scholars who emphasize the positive aspects of late 1800s populism, it is too narrow a field of vision.[36] Goodwyn and his compatriots were confronting the earlier "pluralist school," scholars such as Richard Hofstadter, Daniel Bell, Seymour Martin Lipset, and others who emphasized the negative in People's Party populism, lumping it together with a number of other mass movements as threatening the stability of democratic civil society.[37]

In 1981, Margaret Canovan overhauled the study of populism. She agreed that the U.S. People's Party "combined farmers' radicalism and populist democracy"; but she observed, "like its rivals, Goodwyn's interpretation has a political axe to grind."[38] Canovan called for an approach that neither demonized nor romanticized populist mass social movements.[39] She observes there are only two universal elements across a variety of populist movements. They embody "some kind of exaltation of and appeal to 'the people,' and all are in one sense or another antielitist."[40] That, however, is just part of her complex definitional exercise. Canovan identified two main branches of populism worldwide—agrarian and political—and mapped out seven disparate subcategories in a typology:

Agrarian Populism:

- Commodity farmer movements with radical economic agendas such as the People's Party of the late 1800s in the United States
- Subsistence peasant movements such as the East European Green Rising

- Intellectuals who wistfully romanticize hardworking farmers and peasants and build radical agrarian movements like the Russian narodniki

Political Populism:

- Populist democracy, including calls for more political participation, including the use of the popular referendum
- Politicians' populism marked by nonideological appeals for "the people" to build a unified coalition
- Reactionary populism such as the white backlash harvested by George Wallace
- Populist dictatorship such as that established by Perón in Argentina[41]

There are "a great many interconnections" among the seven forms of populism, says Canovan, and many "actual populist phenomena—perhaps most—belong in more than one category." She adds, "given the contradictions" between some of the categories, "none ever could satisfy all the conditions at once."[42]

Michael Kazin showed how right-wing ideologues had picked up the legacy of populist rhetoric and used it to attract white voters in the 1960s.[43] In *Right-Wing Populism in America*, Matthew N. Lyons and I expanded on Canovan and Kazin.[44] We contend that while many right-wing movements are conservative, some are both conservative and populist—at least in how they frame issues and use rhetoric. We also pointed out the fundamental place occupied by reacting against the "other" in right-wing populism. These movements are motivated or defined centrally by a backlash against liberation movements, social reform, or revolution. This does not mean that right-wing populism's goals are only defensive or reactive, but rather that the movement's growth is fueled in a central way by fears of the left and its political gains.[45]

The late nineteenth-century populist movement had many progressive features. As Lyons notes, "It promoted forms of mass democratic participation; popularized anti-monopolism and trust-busting sentiments, put the brakes on the greediest corporate pillagers and the concentration of economic power; demanded accountability of elected officials; formed cooperatives that promoted humane working relationships and economic justice; and set the stage for substantial reforms in the economic system."[46]

This earlier iteration of populism, however, also embraced themes from several historic currents that have had rightist (and often negative) consequences in mass movements. These are:

- *Producerism*—the idea that the real Americans are hardworking people who create goods and wealth while fighting against parasites at the top and bottom of society. There may be promotion of scapegoating and blurring of issues of class and economic justice, and a history of assuming that proper citizenship is defined by white males.

- *Antielitism*—a suspicion of politicians, powerful people, the wealthy, and high culture. This sometimes leads to conspiracist allegations about control of the world by secret elites, especially the scapegoating of Jews as sinister and powerful manipulators of the economy or media.

- *Anti-intellectualism*—a distrust and dismissal of professor types. Rational debate can be undercut by discarding logic and factual evidence in favor of following the emotional appeals of demagogues.

- *Majoritarianism*—the notion that the will of the majority of people has absolute primacy in matters of governance, which leads to sacrificing rights for minorities, especially people of color.

- *Moralism*—evangelical-style campaigns rooted in Protestant revivalism. These sometimes lead to authoritarian and theocratic attempts to impose orthodoxy, especially relating to gender.

- *Americanism*—a form of patriotic nationalism that often promotes ethnocentric, nativist, or xenophobic fears that immigrants bring alien ideas and customs that damage civil society.[47]

RIGHT-WING VERSIONS OF PRODUCERISM

The mass base of the Tea Party—the predominantly white middle class—is in a precarious position. Barbara Ehrenreich, a sociologist as well as a popular writer, analyzed this in her book *Fear of Falling: The Inner Life of the Middle Class*.[48] Lisa Disch (Chapter 5 in this volume) also looks at the role "fear, anger and resentment play in Tea Party mobilization," especially among middle-class whites who cast the government as the problem for proliferating social welfare programs.

These government programs are seen as benefiting the undeserving (and thus parasitic) poor—often stereotyped as people of color. This tension helps interpolate a key component of contemporary right-wing populism: a right-wing form of producerism—the idea that the middle class is being squeezed into the poorhouse by parasitic forces above and below them on the socioeconomic ladder.[49] Past right-wing populist movements have been accompanied by at least the *perception* (and sometimes the reality) that economic security was being threatened. This was the case with the Ku Klux Klan of the 1920s[50] and the patriot and armed citizens militia movements of the 1990s.[51]

Postel's observations on the attitude of Tea Partiers toward corporate power (Chapter 1 in this volume) miss a good part of the story when he states that "Tea Parties send only occasional barbs towards the corporate executives, bankers, and lobbyists [and] usually celebrate the corporate elites as heroes of the free market." In fact, grassroots Tea Party activists routinely condemn the financial manipulators, "banksters," and treacherous liberal collectivists led by President Obama, who they claim are plotting to subvert the "free market."[52] At the same time as they praise the "productive" corporate elites, they condemn the "parasitic" corporate elites—a hallmark of right-wing populist producerism.

Looked at in this light, the Tea Party's scapegoating becomes more significant than in Postel's account. In *Right-Wing Populism in America*, Matthew Lyons and I argued that the rhetorical style of right-wing populism and producerism serves to shift the blame away from long-term solutions toward handy scapegoats who are chimeric "bad" elites and their supposed allies among the lazy, sinful, and subversive parasites located in the lower margins of society.[53] This tends to reinforce existing racial and gender hierarchies and protect the interests of organized wealth.

At least since the 1960s, right-wing ideologues and organizers have popularized the concept of producerism using a racialized subtext.[54] For example, conservative activists Gary Allen and Larry Abraham used a producerist framework built around a conspiracy theory in *None Dare Call It Conspiracy* to explain the success of the communist conspiracy in penetrating America. They claimed this involved the use of the "Communist tactic of pressure from above and pressure from below":

> The pressure from above comes from secret, ostensible respectable Comrades in the government and Establishment, forming with the radicalized [leftist] mobs in the streets below, a giant pincer around middle-class society. The street rioters are pawns, shills, puppets, and dupes for an oligarchy of elitist

conspirators working above to turn America's limited government into an unlimited government with total control over our lives and property.[55]

In 1975, from a rationalist (rather than conspiracist) perspective, conservative ideologue and longtime publisher of *National Review* William Rusher picked up the producerist refrain as part of an ongoing discussion among conservatives on whether it made more sense to start a third political party or to try to take over the Republican Party. Rusher charged that a

> new economic division pits the producers—businessmen, manufacturers, hard-hats, blue-collar workers, and farmers—against the new and powerful class of nonproducers comprised of a liberal verbalist elite (the dominant media, the major foundations and research institutions, the educational establishment, the federal and state bureaucracies) and a semipermanent welfare constituency, all coexisting happily in a state of mutually sustaining symbiosis.[56]

Social science has come to an understanding of the populist producerist narrative in small steps. Among the first to notice a resurgence of producerism was Donald I. Warren, a biographer of 1930s populist radio firebrand Father Charles Coughlin.[57] While writing a book on Coughlin in the 1970s, Warren "began to see George Wallace, as well as Charles Coughlin, presenting a kind of distinct politics that combined left and right: a concern with the elite exploiting the middle class, and a concern with ethnic minorities sometimes seeming to gain power, with the middle class more or less squeezed in the middle."[58] Warren called these folks "Middle American radicals." The title of Warren's 1976 book, *The Radical Center: Middle Americans and the Politics of Alienation*, captures the essence of what many scholars today call right-wing populism.

Michael Barkun, a scholar who studies apocalyptic and conspiracist movements, puts the emergence of the Tea Party in the context of a middle-class squeeze that has been decades in the making, noting that income "inequality has been rising for nearly 30 years, but was masked for most of that time by the availability of easy credit and rising home values that allowed people to use their houses as ATMs."[59] After the recession hit, with "credit constricted and home prices collapsing, the reality of income inequality began to sink in" for a lot of people. Attention was focused on the "bailouts," which became "the symbol of the perceived inequitable distribution of wealth." In fact, says Barkun, the "reality has been there for a long time. But the perception is new, a product of the crisis of the last three years, and that perception is shared by both the employed and the jobless."[60]

CONCLUSION

The use of demonization and scapegoating in the contemporary political scene by opponents of the Obama administration clustered around the Tea Party movement is neither unique nor marginal. It is not evidence of psychological dysfunction or lack of education. Nor is it evidence of a vast right-wing conspiracy manipulating an army of ignorant and crazy protestors. It is, instead, evidence of the recurrence in the United States of the master frame of right-wing populist movements that use a "producerist" narrative about hardworking people having their wallets stolen by malicious elites and lazy, sinful, and subversive freeloaders. All this has happened before and in this iteration, the resentment, anxiety, anger, and fear are propelled by economic issues as well as by relatively recent tectonic shifts in racial and gender dynamics.

Right-wing populist producerism allows a set of conservative elites to bash their elite rivals who have at least slightly more egalitarian and redistributive notions of the role of government. Meanwhile, the heroic "producers" in the white middle class frequently fester in frustration. All too often these producers begin to beat up the unproductive scapegoats below them on the socioeconomic ladder.

Populism is complicated, and it remains undertheorized. Nonetheless, there is plenty of current and historic evidence to identify the Tea Party movement as a predominantly white right-wing populist movement that uses conspiratorial, xenophobic, and reactionary rhetoric to reframe and mobilize resentment based on race, gender, and class. The overheated rhetoric about Obama, liberals, and socialists destroying the "American way of life" is a form of demonization used in many social and political struggles, but it is central to right-wing populist producerism.

The economic distress in populist movements can be measurably real, realistically anticipated, or a sense of relative deprivation that is a blend of concrete and imaginary fears. Status anxiety may just be in our head, but that does not mean it is not real in terms of our political or social movement activism. If we want to understand and explain the actions of today's Tea Partiers, we would do well to remember the core sociological maxim: "If people define situations as real, they are real in their consequences."[61]

NOTES

1. This paper draws ideas and snippets of text from studies that have previously appeared in print, especially the theoretical concepts that appear in Chip Berlet and Matthew N. Lyons, *Right-Wing Populism in America: Too Close for Comfort* (New York: Guilford, 2000). Preliminary work on the Tea Party movement was presented in papers delivered at the 2010 annual meeting of the American Sociological Association and the 2011 annual meeting of the American Sociological Association; at the Brandeis University Center for American and European Studies (2010); and at the Global Studies Association of North America (2010).

2. David Neiwert, *The Eliminationists: How Hate Talk Radicalized the American Right* (Sausalito, CA: PoliPointPress, 2009); John Amato and David Neiwert, *Over the Cliff: How Obama's Election Drove the American Right Insane* (Sausalito, CA: PoliPointPress, 2010); Alexander Zaitchik, *Common Nonsense: Glenn Beck and the Triumph of Ignorance* (Hoboken, NJ: Wiley, 2010); Will Bunch, *The Backlash: Right-Wing Radicals, High-Def Hucksters, and Paranoid Politics in the Age of Obama* (New York: Harper, 2010). The demonization of an adversary involves well-established psychological processes. See Robert J. Lifton, *Thought Reform and the Psychology of Totalism* (Chapel Hill: University of North Carolina Press, [1961] 1989); Lisa Noël, *Intolerance: A General Survey* (Montreal, Canada: McGill–Queen's University Press, 1994); Bob Altemeyer, *The Authoritarian Specter* (Cambridge, MA: Harvard University Press, 1996); Elisabeth Young-Bruehl, *The Anatomy of Prejudices* (Cambridge, MA: Harvard University Press, 1996); and Evan R. Harrington, "The Social Psychology of Hatred," *Journal of Hate Studies* 3, no. 1 (2006): 49–82, http://web02.gonzaga.edu/againsthate/journal3/GHS110.pdf.

3. See Michael Paul Rogin, *The Intellectuals and McCarthy: The Radical Specter* (Cambridge, MA: MIT Press, 1967), 261–82; Richard O. Curry and Thomas M. Brown, "Introduction," in *Conspiracy: The Fear of Subversion in American History*, ed. Richard O. Curry and Thomas M. Brown (New York: Holt, Rinehart and Winston, 1972), vii–xi; Leo P. Ribuffo, *The Old Christian Right: The Protestant Far Right from the Great Depression to the Cold War* (Philadelphia, PA: Temple University Press, 1983), 237–57; Margaret Canovan, *Populism* (New York: Harcourt Brace Jovanovich, 1981), 46–51, 179–90; Jerome L. Himmelstein, *To The Right: The Transformation of American Conservatism* (Berkeley: University of California Press, 1990), 1–5, 72–76, 152–64; William B. Hixson Jr., *Search for the American Right Wing: An Analysis of the Social Science Record, 1955–1987* (Princeton, NJ: Princeton University Press, 1992), 10–48, 77–123, 273–92; Sara Diamond, *Roads to Dominion: Right-Wing Movements and Political Power in the United States* (New York: Guilford, 1995), 5–6, 40–41; and Michael Kazin, *The Populist Persuasion: An American History* (New York: Basic Books, 1995), 190–93.

4. Several studies refute claims made by pluralists about the demographics and social base of the "radical right." See Rogin, *The Intellectuals and McCarthy*; Fred W. Grupp Jr., "The Political Perspectives of Birch Society Members," in *The American Right Wing: Readings in Political Behavior*,

ed. Robert A. Schoenberger (New York: Holt, Rinehart and Winston, 1969), 83–118; James McEvoy III, "Conservatism or Extremism: Goldwater Supporters in the 1964 Presidential Election," in *The American Right Wing: Readings in Political Behavior*, ed. Robert A. Schoenberger (New York: Holt, Rinehart and Winston, 1969), 241–79; Charles Jeffrey Kraft, *A Preliminary Socio-Economic and State Demographic Profile of the John Birch Society* (Cambridge, MA: Political Research Associates, 1992); and Sara Diamond, "How 'Radical' Is the Christian Right?" *The Humanist* 54, no. 2 (1994): 32–34, ("Watch on the Right" column).

5. Diamond, *Roads to Dominion: Right-Wing Movements and Political Power in the United States*, 9.

6. Rory McVeigh, "Structured Ignorance and Organized Racism in the United States," *Social Forces* 82 (2004): 895–936.

7. Jean V. Hardisty, *Mobilizing Resentment: Conservative Resurgence from the John Birch Society to the Promise Keepers* (Boston, MA: Beacon, 1999).

8. William A. Gamson, *The Strategy of Social Protest*, 2nd ed. (Belmont, CA: Wadsworth Publishing, [1975] 1990); John D. McCarthy and Mayer N. Zald, "Resource Mobilization and Social Movements: A Partial Theory," *American Journal of Sociology* 82 (1977): 1212–41; Doug McAdam, *Political Process and the Development of Black Insurgency, 1930–1970* (Chicago: University of Chicago Press, [1982] 1985); and Jeff Goodwin and James M. Jasper, *Rethinking Social Movements: Structure, Meaning, and Emotion* (Lanham, MD: Rowman and Littlefield, 2004).

9. Erving Goffman, *Frame Analysis: An Essay on the Organization of Experience* (Cambridge, MA: Harvard University Press, 1974); McCarthy and Zald, "Resource Mobilization and Social Movements: A Partial Theory"; David A. Snow, E. Burke Rochford Jr., Steven K. Worden, and Robert D. Benford, "Frame Alignment Processes, Micromobilization, and Movement Participation," *American Sociological Review* 51 (1986): 464–81 (reprinted in *Social Movements: Perspectives and Issues*, ed. by Steven M. Buechler and F. Kurt Cylke Jr. [Mountain View, CA: Mayfield Publishing, 1997], 211–28); David A. Snow and Robert D. Benford, "Master Frames and Cycles of Protest," in *Frontiers in Social Movement Theory*, ed. Aldon D. Morris and Carol McClurg Mueller (New Haven, Connecticut: Yale University Press, 1992), 133–55; and William A. Gamson and Charlotte Ryan, "Thinking about Elephants: Toward a Dialogue with George Lakoff," *The Public Eye* magazine 19, no. 2 (2006): 1, 13–16, accessed on May 1, 2011, www.publiceye.org/movement/handouts/Thinking%20about%20Elephants.pdf.

10. Francesca Polletta, "Contending Stories: Narrative in Social Movements," *Qualitative Sociology* 21, no. 4 (1998): 419–46; and Joseph E. Davis, ed., *Stories of Change: Narrative and Social Movements* (Albany, NY: State University of New York Press, 2002).

11. Patricia Ewick and Susan S. Silbey, "Subversive Stories and Hegemonic Tales: Toward a Sociology of Narrative," *Law and Society Review* 29, no. 2 (1995): 197–226.

12. Pamela E. Oliver and Hank Johnston, "What a Good Idea! Frames and Ideologies in Social Movement Research," *Mobilization: An International*

Journal 5, no. 1 (2000): 37–54; and David A. Snow and Robert D. Benford, "Clarifying the Relationship between Framing and Ideology in the Study of Social Movements: A Comment on Oliver and Johnston," *Mobilization: An International Journal* 5, no. 1 (2000): 55–60.

13. Amato and Neiwert, *Over the Cliff: How Obama's Election Drove the American Right Insane*. Also based on author interviews with Tea Party supporters in several states between 2009 and 2011.

14. Matthew Rothschild of the *Progressive Magazine* has been pointing out this trend in his column "McCarthyism Watch" since an article he wrote in 2002 on the infringement of civil liberties in the United States. See Matthew Rothschild, "McCarthyism Watch," *The Progressive Magazine* website, ongoing online series of articles on civil liberties by the editor, accessed on May 1, 2011, www.progressive.org/list/mccarthy. It appears that this trend toward countersubversion panics and political witch hunts is an extension of hyperbolic fears of Muslim terrorism that emerged after 9/11 terror attacks. As early as 1978, historian and civil liberties attorney Frank Donner warned that the term *terrorism* would replace *communism* in the rhetorical arsenal of conservative conspiracists. See Frank Donner, "The Terrorist as Scapegoat," *The Nation*, May 20, 1978, 590–94.

15. David Weigel, "Five Myths about the 'Tea Party,'" WashingtonPost. com, August 8, 2010, accessed on May 1, 2011, www.washingtonpost.com/wp–dyn/content/article/2010/08/05/AR2010080506105.html.

16. In Europe, references to right-wing populism in scholarly studies are common; see for example, Hans-Georg Betz, *Radical Right-Wing Populism in Western Europe* (New York: St. Martin's Press, 1994); Hans-Georg Betz and Stefan Immerfall, eds., *The New Politics of the Right: Neo-Populist Parties and Movements in Established Democracies* (New York: St. Martin's Press, 1998); and Mabel Berezin, *Illiberal Politics in Neoliberal Times: Culture, Security and Populism in the New Europe* (New York: Cambridge University Press, 2009).

17. Betz, *Radical Right-Wing Populism in Western Europe*.

18. Betz, *Radical Right-Wing Populism in Western Europe*, 106–08, 174.

19. Douglas R. Holmes, *Integral Europe: Fast-Capitalism, Multiculturalism, Neofascism* (Princeton, NJ: Princeton University Press, 2000), 6–9, 13, 58.

20. Ray Taras, *Europe Old and New: Transnationalism, Belonging, Xenophobia* (Lanham, MD: Rowman and Littlefield, 2009), 93.

21. Taras, *Europe Old and New*, 83–172.

22. Max Weber, *The Protestant Ethic and the Spirit of Capitalism*, trans. Talcott Parsons (New York: Routledge, [1930] 1999).

23. Nathan O. Hatch, *The Democratization of American Christianity* (New Haven, Connecticut: Yale University Press, 1989); Philip Greven, *Spare the Child: The Religious Roots of Punishment and the Psychological Impact of Physical Abuse* (New York: Knopf, 1991); George Lakoff, *Moral Politics: How Liberals and Conservatives Think* (Chicago: University of Chicago, [1996] 2002); and Edmund S. Morgan, *The Puritan Family* (New York: Harper, [1942] 1966).

24. Linda Kintz, *Between Jesus and the Market: The Emotions that Matter in Right-Wing America* (Durham, NC: Duke University Press, 1997).

25. Mark Levin, *Liberty and Tyranny: A Conservative Manifesto* (New York: Threshold Editions, 2009); and Mark Whittington, "Max Baucus, Health Care Reform, and the 'Mal-Distribution of Income,'" March 26, 2010, accessed on May 1, 2011, www.associatedcontent.com/article/2828802/max_baucus_health_care_reform_and_the.html?cat=5.

26. Levin, *Liberty and Tyranny*, 100–01.

27. Whittington, "Max Baucus, Health Care Reform, and the 'Mal-Distribution of Income.'"

28. Jim Walker, "Tea Party Urges Board to Throw Out Draft Health Curriculum," *Helena Independent Record*, September 30, 2010, accessed on May 1, 2011, http://helenair.com/news/opinion/readers_alley/article_6db16e34-cc54-11df-9fc7-001cc4c002e0.html.

29. Aaron Klein with Brenda J. Elliott, *The Manchurian President: Barack Obama's Ties to Communists, Socialists and other Anti-American Extremists* (Washington, DC: WND Books, 2010).

30. Chip Berlet, "The Roots of Anti-Obama Rhetoric," in *Race in the Age of Obama* (Research in Race and Ethnic Relations), ed. Donald Cunnigen and Marino A. Bruce (Emerald Group Publishing Limited, 2010), 301–19.

31. Zaitchik, *Common Nonsense: Glenn Beck and the Triumph of Ignorance*.

32. Glenn Beck, *Glenn Beck's Common Sense: The Case against an Out-of-Control Government, Inspired by Thomas Paine* (New York: Threshold Editions, 2009).

33. W. Cleon Skousen, *The 5000 Year Leap: A Miracle that Changed the World* (Malta, Idaho: National Center for Constitutional Studies, [1981] 2009); and Zaitchik, *Common Nonsense: Glenn Beck and the Triumph of Ignorance*.

34. Leonard Zeskind, *It's Not Populism: America's New Populist Party a Fraud by Racists and Anti-Semites* (Atlanta, GA: National Anti-Klan Network, 1984).

35. Lawrence Goodwyn, *The Populist Moment: A Short History of the Agrarian Revolt in America* (Oxford: Oxford University Press, 1978), vii.

36. Canovan, *Populism*, 294, 551.

37. Rogin, *The Intellectuals and McCarthy*; Hixson, *Search for the American Right Wing: An Analysis of the Social Science Record, 1955–1987*; and Berlet and Lyons, *Right-Wing Populism in America*, 1–18.

38. Canovan, *Populism*, 293, 51.

39. Since Canovan's book was published, a number of scholars have produced studies of populist movements that neither demonize nor romanticize the reality of populist mass movements on the left or right. See Robert C. McMath Jr., *American Populism: A Social History 1877–1898* (New York: Hill and Wang; Farrar, Straus and Giroux, 1993); Jeffrey Ostler, *Prairie Populism: The Fate of Agrarian Radicalism in Kansas, Nebraska, and Iowa, 1880–1892* (Lawrence, Kansas: University Press of Kansas, 1993); Kazin, *The Populist Persuasion*; Catherine McNicol Stock, *Rural Radicals: Righteous Rage in the American Grain* (Ithaca, NY: Cornell University Press, 1996); and Charles Postel, *The Populist Vision* (New York: Oxford University Press, 2007). In *The Populist Persuasion,* Kazin sees both the positive and the negative. He traces "two different but not exclusive strains of vision and protest" in the

original U.S. populist movement: the revivalist "pietistic impulse issuing from the Protestant Reformation" and the "secular faith of the Enlightenment, the belief that ordinary people could think and act rationally, more rationally, in fact, than their ancestral overlords" (10–11).

40. Canovan, *Populism*, 294.

41. Canovan, *Populism*, 13, 128–38.

42. Canovan, *Populism*, 289.

43. Kazin, *The Populist Persuasion*, 23–24.

44. Berlet and Lyons, *Right-Wing Populism in America*.

45. Berlet and Lyons, *Right-Wing Populism in America*, 5.

46. Matthew N. Lyons, unpublished working paper for draft chapter in Berlet and Lyons, *Right-Wing Populism in America*.

47. These elements are culled from the work of John Higham, *Strangers in the Land: Patterns of American Nativism 1860–1925* (New York: Atheneum, [1955] 1972); Richard Hofstadter, *The Paranoid Style in American Politics, and Other Essays* (New York: Knopf, 1965); Canovan, *Populism*; David H. Bennett, *The Party of Fear: The American Far Right from Nativism to the Militia Movement*, revised and updated (New York: Vintage Books, [1988] 1995); Kazin, *The Populist Persuasion: An American History*; and Stock, *Rural Radicals: Righteous Rage in the American Grain*. Portions of this section are adapted from Berlet and Lyons, *Right-Wing Populism in America: Too Close for Comfort*.

48. Barbara Ehrenreich, *Fear of Falling: The Inner Life of the Middle Class* (New York: Harper Perennial, 1990).

49. For a chart on how right-wing populist producerism works, other explanatory materials, and a more detailed response to Postel, see www.publiceye.org/right_wing_populism/producerism.html.

50. McVeigh, "Structured Ignorance and Organized Racism in the United States."

51. Nella Van Dyke and Sarah A. Soule, "Structural Social Change and the Mobilizing Effect of Threat: Explaining Levels of Patriot and Militia Organizing in the United States," *Social Problems* 49, no. 4 (2002): 497–520; and Deborah Kaplan, "Republic of Rage: A Look Inside the Patriot Movement," paper presented at the annual meeting of the American Sociological Association, San Francisco, CA, August 1998.

52. Berlet, "The Roots of Anti-Obama Rhetoric."

53. Berlet and Lyons, *Right-Wing Populism in America*.

54. Kazin, *The Populist Persuasion*; and Berlet and Lyons, *Right-Wing Populism in America*.

55. Gary Allen with Larry Abraham, *None Dare Call It Conspiracy* (Rossmoor, California/Seal Beach, California: Concord Press, [1971] 1972), 24. A copy of Allen and Abraham's diagram of producerism (which indicates "Rothschild," "Rockefeller," and "C. F. R. Elite" applying pressure from above and "S. D. S.," "Panthers," "Yippees," "Y. S. A.," and "Common Cause" applying pressure from below) can be found at www.researchforprogress.us/producerism/.

56. William Rusher, *The Making of the New Majority Party* (Ottawa, IL: Greenhill Publications, 1975), 14.

57. Donald I. Warren, *The Radical Center: Middle Americans and the Politics of Alienation* (Notre Dame, IN: University of Notre Dame Press, 1976); and Donald I. Warren, *Radio Priest: Charles Coughlin, The Father of Hate Radio* (New York: The Free Press, 1996).

58. Donald I. Warren, interview by Brian Lamb, "Book Notes" program on C-SPAN, based on Warren's book *Radio Priest: Charles Coughlin, The Father of Hate Radio*, September 8, 1996. Text based on radio transcript, accessed on May 1, 2011, www.booknotes.org/FullPage.aspx?SID=73853-1.

59. Personal email correspondence with Michael Barkun, based on listserv discussion, 2010.

60. Personal email correspondence with Michael Barkun, based on listserv discussion, 2010.

61. William I. Thomas and Dorothy S. Thomas, *The Child in America* (New York: Alfred A. Knopf, 1928). Excerpt republished as "Situations Defined as Real are Real in Their Consequences," in *Social Psychology through Symbolic Interaction*, edited by Gregory P. Stone and Harvey A. Faberman (Waltham, MA: Ginn Blaisdell/Xerox, 1970), 154–55.

CHAPTER 3

View from the Top

Report on Six National Tea Party Organizations

DEVIN BURGHART

The Tea Party has unleashed a still inchoate political movement by angry Americans who believe their country, their nation, has been taken from them. And they want it back. They are overwhelmingly white and middle-class, and their oft-repeated call to "Take America Back" is an explicitly nationalist refrain. It is sometimes coupled with the assertion that there are "real Americans," as opposed to others who they believe are driving the country into a socialist ditch.

Supporting the Tea Party movement is a multimillion dollar complex that includes for-profit corporations, nonparty nonprofit organizations, and political action committees. Collectively, they have erased the advantage that Democrats once enjoyed in the arena of Internet fundraising and web-based mobilization. They have resuscitated the ultraconservative wing of American political life, created a stiff pole of opinion within Republican Party ranks, and had a significant impact on shaping debate over policy making at all levels of government.

The findings of our 2010 Special Report, *Tea Party Nationalism: A Critical Examination of the Size, Scope and Focus of the Tea Party Movement and Its National Factions*, contravene many of the Tea Party's self-invented myths, particularly their supposedly sole concentration on budget deficits, taxes, and the power of the federal government.[1] Instead, we found Tea Party ranks to be permeated with concerns about race and national identity and other so-called social issues. In these ranks, an abiding obsession with Barack Obama's birth certificate is often a stand-in for the belief that the first black president of the United States is not a "real American." Rather than strict adherence to the Constitution, many Tea Partiers would prefer to extirpate significant elements of it, including the Fourteenth, Sixteenth, and Seventeenth Amendments.

The Tea Party phenomenon exists at three levels of agreement and commitment. Several national opinion polls point to support for the Tea Party running at approximately 16 to 18 percent of the adult population, which would put the number of sympathizers in the tens of millions. That would be the outermost ring of support. At the next level is a larger, less-defined group of a couple of million activists who go to meetings, buy the literature, and attend the many local and national protests. At the core of this movement are more than 330,000 members in all fifty states who have signed up on the websites of the movement's six national organizational networks.

Updating our initial report, *Tea Party Nationalism*, this chapter provides a description of the six national organizational networks at the core of the Tea Party movement: FreedomWorks, 1776 Tea Party, Tea Party Nation, Tea Party Patriots, Patriot Action Network (formerly known as ResistNet), and Tea Party Express. It documents the corporate structures and leaderships, finances, and membership concentrations of each faction.[2] An understanding of the movement's structure provides a view into the larger politics that motivate each faction and the Tea Party movement generally.[3]

The nucleus of what would become the six different national Tea Party factions formed in the first weeks and months of 2009. Some of the groups already existed (FreedomWorks, ResistNet, and the Our Country Deserves Better PAC). Others formed almost immediately (1776 Tea Party on February 20; Tea Party Patriots on March 10; and Tea Party Nation on April 6). Throughout the summer, Tea Party momentum continued to build as the national factions stoked the anger and fear that raged in local health care protests and town hall meetings. The turning point for the Tea Party was the September 12, 2009, FreedomWorks-hosted rally in Washington, DC. Planning the massive event gave Tea Party groups an opportunity to work together. Hundreds of thousands of Tea Partiers met in the streets, broke bread together, shared their stories and their anger, and made connections with one another. Before the last portable toilets were removed from the Capitol Mall, the Tea Party had turned from periodic protests into a full-fledged social movement.

Analysis of membership data shows that the core organizations are continuing to grow.[4] The Tea Party movement is not going away, and members can be expected to have a continuing impact on public policy debate in the future. It should not be expected, however, for the Tea Party movement to have the same organizational configurations well into an indefinite future. Already, a sorting-out process has taken place regarding the importance of race and culture war issues, and a rebranding process is also underway in the aftermath of the 2010 congressional elections.

FREEDOMWORKS TEA PARTY

FreedomWorks is the organization most often credited for helping give birth to the Tea Party movement. After the 2008 election, FreedomWorks set out to develop an insurgency that would separate conservatives from the legacy of the failed Bush administration. It wanted to find alternatives to the grassroots organizing previously done by Democratic Party activists. The emergence of the Tea Party proved to be just what FreedomWorks needed.

FreedomWorks was born out of one of the organizational splinters created by a disagreement within a conservative think tank known as Citizens for a Sound Economy (CSE) in 2003. One side of this conflict formed Americans for Prosperity. When CSE's remnants merged with a group called Empower America in 2004, FreedomWorks was created. Its advocacy agenda has included support for Social Security privatization, tax cuts for the wealthiest Americans, caps on lawsuit damages, deregulation, and free trade. A recipient of sizable industry funding, FreedomWorks also has opposed efforts to address global climate change.

In the anger that the Tea Party theme captured, FreedomWorks would find the street activists they felt they had been missing. On February 9, 2009, FreedomWorks contacted a Florida activist, one who had attended an earlier FreedomWorks training session, and recommended that she organize a protest in response to President Obama's visit to Fort Myers.[5] FreedomWorks staff members also called local supporters across the country, asking if they were willing to organize a local Tea Party. Then FreedomWorks quickly announced the launch of a nationwide Tea Party tour.[6] A week later, on February 27, the first official "Tea Party" took place, organized primarily by the Sam Adams Alliance, FreedomWorks, and Americans for Prosperity.

When compared to other national Tea Party organizations, the FreedomWorks Tea Party has the largest structure of support. The

FreedomWorks corporate complex includes both a foundation and a (c)4 membership organization. In 2008, the (c)4 raised and spent more than four million dollars. The foundation took in more than three million dollars that year, and spent about $100,000 more than it received. As of February 2010, FreedomWorks boasted a staff of thirteen professionals, including state directors in North Carolina, Georgia, and Florida. Former House Majority Leader Dick Armey chairs FreedomWorks. In 2008 he received $300,000 in compensation from the foundation, and another $250,000 from the related membership organization.[7]

Commentators have cited the presence of FreedomWorks inside the Tea Party as proof that the Tea Party is an "Astroturf" phenomenon—a sleight-of-hand effort manufactured by inside-the-Beltway organizations to concoct the appearance of grassroots support.[8] This suspicion is not completely unfounded. In 2004, for example, when President George W. Bush was pushing for Social Security privatization, the administration heaped praise upon someone described as a "regular single mom." This person turned out to be the FreedomWorks Iowa state director, according to the *New York Times* investigative story on the incident.[9] Similarly, in 2008, the *Wall Street Journal* exposed FreedomWorks' role in creating the grassroots-looking angryrenter.com website that campaigned against federal insurance to help refinance troubled mortgages.[10]

Nevertheless, it would be a mistake to conflate FreedomWorks's corporate machinations with the grassroots insurgency of the Tea Party. FreedomWorks's Tea Party membership was the second smallest of the national factions, with 15,044 online members as of August 1, 2010. But thanks to new outreach initiatives, including the launch of the new FreedomConnect social network, and reaping the benefits of the 2010 electoral successes of Tea Party candidates, FreedomWorks's membership skyrocketed to 94,308 as of June 1, 2011, giving FreedomWorks the second largest online Tea Party membership.[11]

After the initial burst of activity in early 2009, FreedomWorks created a website containing ideas for slogans on signs, a sample press release, and a map of local events.[12] In a video interview, Brendan Steinhauser, FreedomWorks's director of federal and state campaigns, described FreedomWorks's role with local Tea Party groups:

> Usually what happens is an organizer from anywhere in the country will contact me and say I'd like to organize a Tea Party and do something in my city. So what we do is we help resource them with ideas for signs, locations, for media outreach, and we try to give them this list of things to do so that they can make sure their event is successful. A lot of that just entails paying attention to

details, like signing up people when they come, and sending email reminders, and following up with phone calls and things like that. And we've seen a lot of success. There are a lot of people out there that have never done this before but they are having successful events by sort of following this recipe.[13]

In fact, FreedomWorks played an important role from the beginning, coordinating Tea Party efforts, as well as offering training and technical support to new Tea Party organizations. They provided online and phone consultations on how to organize a local group, how to hold rallies, and how to protest at town hall meetings.[14] FreedomWorks also facilitated intramovement communication. They sponsored a weekly Tea Party conference call with activists from around the country, where activists got to know one another.[15] FreedomWorks's staff even provided technical support to other national Tea Party factions.[16]

During this early stage, in anticipation of battles to come, FreedomWorks provided organizers with information on health care and climate change legislation.[17] By August 2009, even before the heat of the town halls, Dick Armey announced that "his organization's members are ready to sabotage immigration reform, a cap-and-trade proposal, and other Democratic legislative priorities that are likely to stir the conservative base."[18] On August 18, FreedomWorks joined with the Our Country Deserves Better PAC and six other organizations to launch a sixteen-day national Tea Party bus tour that would become the Tea Party Express.[19]

FreedomWorks then turned the organization's attention to a planned September 12, 2009 march in Washington.[20] Before the big rally, the group offered a two-day grassroots training session that attracted more than 2,000 local activists. That number was up ten times from the two hundred people who had attended a similar session the year before.[21]

Attendance numbers for the September 12, 2009 Tea Party rally in Washington, DC remain in dispute. Estimates range between 60,000 to over one million, depending on who is doing the counting. There is no disagreement over the importance of the rally, nor over the range of organizations that supported it. While FreedomWorks hosted the event, Tea Party sponsors included Tea Party Express, ResistNet, Tea Party Nation, and Tea Party Patriots. Also sponsoring this march were established DC lobbies, such as Club for Growth, Americans for Tax Reform, and National Taxpayers Union, and other organizations and websites with one foot inside the Tea Party (Campaign for Liberty, the website Smart Girl Politics, the Leadership Institute, Free Republic, and American Liberty Alliance).

In January 2010, FreedomWorks began focusing its Tea Party activism on the 2010 elections. Dubbed as "the first leadership summit of the Tea Party era," more than sixty leaders from two-dozen states gathered in DC under its auspices. The meeting developed 2010 midterm election plans, and gave FreedomWorks the opportunity to roll out its list of sixty-five targeted congressional races. A workshop taught effective television techniques and how to master social media. Another session was entitled, "What You Can and Can't Say: How To Stay out of Jail This Year."[22] FreedomWorks announced plans to fund opposition research, direct mail, door-to-door, and get-out-the-vote efforts with the hope of electing "ideologically pure conservatives," according to one of its staff personnel.[23]

After the January summit, several Tea Party groups released the Declaration of Tea Party Independence (though the spokespeople refused to release a list of the initial organizations involved in crafting the document).[24] The five-page manifesto declared war against "the Democrat Party" and moderate Republicans. And it announced: "We are the Tea Party Movement of America and we believe in American Exceptionalism."[25] The document tried to distance Tea Party doctrine from social issues promoted by the religious right. The only three points of unity in the declaration were "fiscal responsibility, constitutionally limited government, and free markets." According to the declaration, "[t]his threefold purpose is the source of our unity in the Tea Party Movement."[26]

FreedomWorks maintains a particularly close working relationship with Tea Party Patriots, which sports the FreedomWorks logo as one of several organizations promoted on its website's homepage. FreedomWorks staffer Tom Gaitens runs the Tea Party Patriots Listserv.[27] And Tea Party Patriots board member Diana Reimer has also been listed as a FreedomWorks volunteer.[28] Tea Party Patriots participated in the January 2010 sessions in DC, and the two organizations have collaborated on local events, such as the April 15, 2010 Atlanta Tax Day Tea Party.[29] Relationships with the other Tea Party factions, however, are not as cozy. Despite its partnership with Glenn Beck, FreedomWorks has been the loudest voice opposing inclusion of culture war "social issues" into the Tea Party platform.

The rest of 2010 was focused on turning street mobilizations into electoral gains. FreedomWorks endorsed sixty-one congressional candidates in the November 2010 general election (nine Senate and fifty-two House candidates). In the Senate races, five FreedomWorks–endorsed candidates won; four lost. In House races, twenty-eight

FreedomWorks–endorsed candidates won; twenty-four lost. Overall, FreedomWorks–endorsed candidates were successful in thirty-three of the sixty-one races, a winning percentage of roughly 54 percent.[30]

In 2011, FreedomWorks again shifted focus, turning from electoral politics to state-level issue campaigns such as the elimination of collective bargaining for public-sector unionized employees and support for school voucher programs.

1776 TEA PARTY

The 1776 Tea Party, also known as TeaParty.org, is the national faction most directly connected to the anti-immigrant movement. Its corporate headquarters are in Woodlake, Texas, north of the Houston area, where a Texas certificate of formation nonprofit corporation was filed in February 2009. Its staff positions are situated in California. With 12,458 online members as of June 1, 2011, the 1776 Tea Party is the smallest of the national Tea Party factions. Nevertheless, that number is nearly double the membership from August 1, 2010, when online membership was just 6,987.

The 1776 Tea Party describes itself as "a Christian political organization that will bridge the gap of all parties, in particular Democratic and Republican Parties. It will welcome all peoples and ideological perspectives, with the intent to streamline government and adhere to the Constitutional Rights addressed in the U.S. Constitution, and by God above." In striking contrast to this inclusive tone, the 1776 Tea Party has adopted a deliberately confrontational posture. One of its leaders argued, "Most of the other TP's [Tea Parties] are afraid to make such a powerful stand. We tell the world we have Core Beliefs! We don't step on toes, we step on necks! . . ."[31]

The organization's platform includes points on immigration issues as well as taxes and federal budgets: "Illegal Aliens Are Here Illegally. Pro-Domestic Employment Is Indispensable. . . . Gun Ownership Is Sacred. Government Must Be Downsized. National Budget Must Be Balanced. Deficit Spending Will End. Bail-Out and Stimulus Plans Are Illegal. . . . English as Core Language Is Required. Traditional Family Values are Encouraged. Common Sense Constitutional Conservative Self-Governance."[32]

The 1776 Tea Party's founding president was Dale Robertson, a former naval officer who served with the Marines. On February 27, 2009, Robertson attended a Tea Party event in Houston with a sign reading,

"Congress = Slaveowner, Taxpayer = Niggar."[33] He also sent out racist fund-raising emails depicting President Obama as a pimp.[34] Robertson also has a history of promoting anti-Semites on his "Tea Party Hour" radio program. Both incidents increased the negative publicity surrounding the 1776 Tea Party, but its notoriety did not stop two leaders of an anti-immigrant vigilante group, the Minuteman Project, from stepping in to run the organization.

On June 8, 2009, Robertson sent out a press release claiming that financial hardship would soon force him to sell the teaparty.org website domain to the highest bidder on eBay.[35] At that point, Stephen Eichler and Tim Bueler stepped in. Eichler was the Minuteman Project's executive director and Bueler was its media director at the time.

Eichler and Bueler's path to the 1776 Tea Party corresponded with a sharp decline in the Minuteman Project's organizational fortunes. The nativist group had been fractured in 2007 by a series of lawsuits and countersuits in which the Minuteman Project leaders sued each other for fraud, defamation, and business tort.[36] A second step in the Minuteman Project's decline occurred after one of its "border operations directors," Shawna Forde, was arrested and later convicted of the murder of Raul Flores and his nine-year-old daughter Brisenia in Arizona.[37] The murders were part of a plot to secure funds for the Minuteman Project's border war, and police records indicate that Eichler was one of the last people Forde spoke to before she was arrested.[38] As scrutiny of the Minutemen increased dramatically, the organization continued to lose members and money.

Despite this chain of events, Eichler claimed, "We are seeing a substantial increase of groups wanting to be Minuteman Project chapters, not to mention our growing relationship with Tea Party and 9/12 organizations."[39] Actually, while the Minuteman Project's fortunes plummeted, Eichler and Bueler were in the process of affiliating with Robertson's 1776 Tea Party. According to records filed with the Texas secretary of state, Eichler and Bueler formally became corporate directors of the 1776 Tea Party on October 28, 2009, Eichler as treasurer and Bueler as secretary. Robertson is president of the Texas nonprofit corporation. Although Robertson remained the public face of the 1776 Tea Party, much of the day-to-day operations and the public relations shifted to Eichler, who became the 1776 Tea Party executive director, and to Bueler, who became media director. To complete the transformation from Minutemen to Tea Partiers, the teaparty.org website was redesigned in May 2010, to look strikingly similar to that of the Minuteman Project. The group helped pull nativism deep into the Tea Party ranks.

Dale Robertson's grandstanding as "a founder of the Tea Party movement," combined with the negative attention attached to his group, has created some distance between the 1776 Tea Party and the other factions. While the group has been notoriously marred by racist incidents, it is not the only Tea Party faction with problems in this regard.

PATRIOT ACTION NETWORK (FORMERLY RESISTNET TEA PARTY)

One of the noticeable changes inside the Tea Party movement since its inception is the rebranding of some of the groups after they have faced scrutiny. Case in point: With nary a word to loyal members, the ResistNet Tea Party faction started the process of quietly changing the name of the group to the Patriot Action Network at the end of 2010.[40] The change is primarily cosmetic—a change of the website address, the logo, and the "About Us" page. Otherwise, the content has stayed the same. The web makeover is part of a post-election rebranding strategy that the group's parent company has used before. The company has a history of changing names.

According to its website, "Patriot Action Network is the nation's largest conservative social action network, serving hundreds of thousands of citizens every month. We are united by our passion for reestablishing Constitution-based liberty and limited government through dialogue, debate, legislation, and elections." Note the change in tone. Before the rebranding, the website claimed, "ResistNet is a place where citizens can resist—in a peaceful, patriotic way—the efforts to move our nation away from our heritage of individual liberties toward a 'brave new world' of collectivism. ResistNet is designed to give citizens a new level of networking resources to organize the Patriotic Resistance."

The Patriot Action Network, and ResistNet before it, is part of a for-profit organization. The corporate structure that envelops the Patriot Action Network is similar to that of Russian nesting dolls. It is a for-profit project of Grassfire Nation, a division of Grassroots Action, which is a for-profit, Internet activism services organization privately held by Steve Elliott.[41] To further complicate the structure, Grassroots Action, Inc. is more a virtual rather than traditional bricks-and-mortar organization. Elliott lives in Virginia, but the company's business address is in the small town of Maxwell, Iowa (population 793), because Elliott uses web developers who are based there.[42] In addition to its for-profit side, to which ResistNet belongs, Grassfire also has a 501(c)4 nonprofit corporation,

Grassfire.org Alliance, with its corporate headquarters in Iowa. The 501(c)4 was created in 2004, and had total revenue of $1,415,667 in 2008.[43] Elliott served as president and was paid $61,000 for the year.

Grassfire has grown through the use of Internet petition campaigns, using a model once employed by MoveOn.org. The nature of these petition campaigns points to a political base with a set of concerns much broader than simply taxes and budgets. Its first petition, which was sent to 200 friends on September 15, 2000, supported the Boy Scouts' anti-gay stance. Within forty-five days, more than 140,000 people had signed it.[44] Petitions included calls to save traditional marriage, "stand for the unborn," oppose partial birth abortion, stop Internet porn, make "God Bless America" the national hymn, support the Pledge of Allegiance, and support Judge Roy Moore's fight to place the Ten Commandments in his Alabama courtroom.[45] Grassfire also started several petitions opposing meaningful immigration reform. By June 2010, Grassfire had developed a contact database of 3,713,521 people (including 2,608,818 phone numbers and 1,211,259 opt-in email names).[46]

After the 2008 election, Grassfire's email blasts warned that "what President-elect Obama and the Pelosi-Reid Congress have in store has the potential to rapidly move America to the socialist Left." People were asked to sign up with Grassfire.org and join the resistance. On December 15, 2008, Elliott registered the ResistNet.com website domain, and soon after, it was officially launched as the "Home of the Patriotic Resistance." This new website argued that, "Resisting is just the first step. That is why we propose a three-phased recovery for conservatives: Resist, Rebuild, and Restore. We believe that resisting will create newfound unity among conservatives."[47]

Soon after, Darla Dawald joined this social network, and during January 2009, she organized a team of volunteers to promote Tea Parties at every state capitol. By early February, Dawald had a paid position as national director of ResistNet.com. Indeed, ResistNet's leadership team is all women, unlike other male-dominated Tea Party factions.[48] (Of course, ResistNet is a project owned primarily by Steve Elliott, who ultimately calls the shots.)

Perhaps due to post-rebranding confusion, the Patriot Action Network (PAN) has slipped from the second largest national Tea Party faction to the third. As of June 1, 2011, online membership in the Patriot Action Network sat at 88,048, up slightly from the 81,248 online members on August 1, 2010. ResistNet listed 142 different local

Tea Party chapters in 34 states, and has worked at one time or another with all the national Tea Party factions.

As exhaustively documented in Tea Party Nationalism, more than any other national Tea Party faction, the sprawling ResistNet online social network was a gathering spot for nativists, militia types, birthers, white nationalists, and Islamophobes. Despite the rebranding efforts, the Patriot Action Network has not shied away from far-right organizations. In January 2011, for instance, PAN was a cosponsor of the "Nullify Now!" national conference in Phoenix, Arizona. The conference, which encouraged states to ignore federal laws, was also sponsored by the conspiracy-mongering John Birch Society and the Oath Keepers, a group that encourages law enforcement officers and military personnel to disobey orders that conflict with their conspiracy theories.

TEA PARTY NATION

Tea Party Nation (TPN) spans the Tea Party spectrum from the mainstream to the margins that loudly insist on culture war concerns and birtherism. The Tea Party Nation faction was organized by Judson Phillips, a Nashville attorney, and his wife Sherry Phillips. Judson Phillips is a local Republican activist and former assistant district attorney. In 2010, his private practice specialized in drunk driving and personal injury cases. In 1999, Judson Phillips filed for Chapter 7 personal bankruptcy, according to public records. He also has had three federal tax liens against him, totaling more than $22,000. Phillips claims the tax liens have been paid off.[49]

TPN describes itself as a "user-driven group of like-minded people who desire our God-given Individual Freedoms which were written out by the Founding Fathers. We believe in Limited Government, Free Speech, the 2nd Amendment, our Military, Secure Borders, and our Country!"[50] It has become an unapologetic conduit for both Christian nationalism and explicit white nationalism. "I'm not trying [to] attract moderates. Moderates are just those who have no core beliefs," explained Judson Phillips.[51]

The birth of Tea Party Nation was similar to that of several of the other factions. Phillips helped organize a Tea Party rally in Nashville on February 27, 2009. That event attracted several hundred people. Several became volunteers in the operation. On April 6, Phillips registered the TeaPartyNation.com domain name. Phillips and his volunteers organized April 15 Tax Day Tea Party protests in Nashville, where about

10,000 people attended, and in nearby Franklin, Tennessee, drawing an additional 4,000. The success of these events provided the impetus to officially go national. Tea Party Nation ranks fourth among national Tea Party networks, with 40,991 online members as of June 1, 2011, up from 31,402 members on August 1, 2010.

Early disputes revealed a fault line within the Tea Party over money handling and the movement's relationship to Republican Party structures. According to Kevin Smith, a volunteer who served as the group's founding webmaster, Phillips gave the impression that the newly formed organization was going to be a nonprofit effort. Nevertheless, on April 21, 2009, Phillips formally filed records with the Tennessee secretary of state, registering Tea Party Nation, Inc. as a for-profit corporation.[52] This action led to the first internal clash, and webmaster Smith resigned in protest on April 24, 2009. Smith attacked the direction the organization was taking, writing, "It's become clear to me that Judson and his for-profit Tea Party Nation Corporation are at the forefront of the GOP's process of hijacking the tea party movement. What began as cries for true liberty and a public showing of frustration with the big government policies of both Democrats and Republicans has now been co-opted by mainstream Republican demagogues determined to use this as their 2010 election platform."[53]

After casting aside other volunteers, Phillips turned to a select group of seven to handle Tea Party Nation's activities: his wife Sherry Phillips; his sister-in-law Pam Farnsworth; president of the Chicago-based Surge USA, Bruce Donnelly; founder of Upper Deck sports cards, Bill Hemrick; and Hemrick's business partner Jason Lukowitz.[54] The group organized the Tea Party Nation convention.

The high point for Tea Party Nation was the heavily hyped national convention in Nashville in February 2010, featuring Sarah Palin (and nearly as many reporters as participants).[55] The attention lavished on the convention and the decision to include birther, nativist, and Christian nationalist speakers at the event created consternation and antipathy in other Tea Party camps, leaving Phillips and TPN with fewer allies.

Tea Party Nation spent much of the spring and summer of 2010 planning, and then cancelling, two different Tea Party conventions in Las Vegas. The reason for failure: lack of registrants willing to pay the steep convention fees.

Despite the failures, TPN quickly pivoted to the 2010 elections. Previously steering clear of endorsements, Tea Party Nation founder Judson Phillips chose to endorse eight candidates in the 2010 elections.

The one Senate candidate endorsed by Tea Party Nation lost, as did five of the seven candidates endorsed in House races.

After the election, Tea Party Nation sought to seize the moment. Phillips convinced 180 Tea Party groups, leaders, and activists to sign a letter to the Republican leadership demanding that they include culture war staples, such as opposition to gay marriage, anti-immigration policies, and opposition to abortion, in the party's 2011 legislative agenda: "We, the undersigned, are leaders of mainstream Tea Party groups. We are the people that helped get conservatives elected on November 2. While we do not speak for this movement as a whole, we are a large cross-section of this movement and we want to tell you what this movement wants."[56] They added, "We, the members of the mainstream Tea Party movement have a lot of expectations for you in this Congress. We realize the limitations you face. But we also realize the tools you have at your disposal. America is a conservative country. We expect conservative leadership from our country."[57]

Phillips continued to relentlessly push for inclusion of culture war issues in the Tea Party agenda. On November 27, Phillips wrote, "The Tea Party movement is made up of both fiscal conservatives and social conservatives. There is no bright line that defines or separates the two groups. The two groups are not mutually exclusive nor are they antagonistic. . . . History cannot be denied. When fiscal and social conservatives unite, we win. Any group that seeks to divide the two needs to be viewed with suspicion because when the two are separated, we end up with bad, losing candidates."[58] His declarations were met with fierce attacks from other factions, particularly Tea Party Patriots.

At the same time, Phillips was pushing the envelope beyond the religion-based culture war concerns he had staked out in this letter to Republicans. He further embraced the birthers, supported restricting the voting rights of non–property owners and gutting the Fourteenth Amendment, and even moved his faction closer toward full-fledged white nationalism. On March 29, 2011, Tea Party Nation sent out an email to TPN members entitled, "Destroy the Family, You Destroy the Country!" The email featured an article by Rich Swier, a Tea Party Nation member and a contributing editor to the anti-Muslim group Family Security Matters. Swier mourned the falling birthrate of native-born Americans, and warned that "American culture" will soon perish since the "White Anglo-Saxon Protestant (WASP) population is headed for extinction."[59] This notion of white dispossession has been a staple of white supremacists organizing since the early 1970s. The theme was echoed in Pat

Buchanan's 2002 book, *The Death of the West*, and now Judson Phillips and Tea Party Nation appear intent upon carrying this idea forward.

TEA PARTY PATRIOTS

The Tea Party Patriots website was registered on March 10, 2009. Its credo contained a statement of faith in the Founding Fathers and private property: "The Tea Party Patriots stand with our founders, as heirs to the republic, to claim our rights and duties which preserve their legacy and our own. We hold, as did the founders, that there exists an inherent benefit to our country when private property and prosperity are secured by natural law and the rights of the individual."[60] In June 2009, Tea Party Patriots self-identified as a 501(c)4 nonprofit organization, though as of February 2011, it still had not filed with the IRS.[61] In January 2010, Tea Party Patriots Inc. PAC registered with the Federal Election Commission. As of June 1, 2011, however, the PAC had neither raised nor spent any significant amount of money.[62]

Of all the Tea Party factions, Tea Party Patriots can rightly make the claim that it is the most grassroots. In October 2010, online membership in the main Tea Party Patriots site was 139,216, up from 115,311 registered members on August 1, 2010.[63] The organization relies on a social networking site for members to join. This networking site had 86,116 members registered as of June 1, 2011, up from 74,779 as of August 1, 2010. There were also more than 2,900 local Tea Party chapters listed on the Tea Party Patriots website, up from 2,200 in August 2010.

Despite its size, Tea Party Patriots' budget has been considerably smaller than the budgets of FreedomWorks, Tea Party Express, and ResistNet.[64] Tea Party Patriots' financial information for the fiscal year ending May 31, 2010, showed total contributions of $538,009 and total expenses of $400,596 ($342,559 to program service, and $58,037 to administration and management).[65]

The original Tea Party Patriots' national coordinators, as listed on the group's Facebook page, were Jenny Beth Martin, Mark Meckler, and Amy Kremer. Jenny Beth Martin, a 39-year-old from Atlanta, Georgia, once worked as a Republican consultant.[66] Her route to the Tea Party includes a bumpy collision with tax collectors. According to court documents, Martin and her husband owed over $680,000 in tax debt, including over a half million dollars to the Internal Revenue Service, when the pair filed for bankruptcy in August 2008.[67] Though the Martins' financial woes occurred entirely under the administration of Republican George W. Bush, the Tea Party Patriots' vitriol is targeted squarely at President Obama. In 2010 Martin was pulling down around $6,000 a month working as CEO of Tea Party Patriots.[68] Her husband served as treasurer of the organization, and her cousin was listed as a Tea Party Patriots employee.[69]

Mark Meckler, 48, a punk rock DJ turned business attorney, lives in southern California. In 2007, Meckler developed an Internet firm, Opt-In Movement, which aimed to build email lists on behalf of political candidates. The firm aspired to work for GOP candidates and causes, including FreedomWorks. Meckler was also paid by a California Republican business group to gather petition signatures for an anti–public employee union ballot initiative.[70]

Amy Kremer, of Roswell, Georgia, was the third original Tea Party Patriot national coordinator. Kremer organized Georgia Tea Partiers, and also helped to coordinate with other local groups across the country during the first round of nationwide protests. Kremer worked as a Tea Party Patriots organizer until she became director of grassroots and coalitions at Tea Party Express.

After successfully working with the other Tea Party factions on the September 2009 march in Washington, DC, Tea Party Patriots had its first significant conflict with another national group when Kremer jumped over to Tea Party Express. Tea Party Patriots formally removed her from its leadership with a letter from its board on October 15,[71] then filed a lawsuit against Kremer, and on November 10, was granted an injunction preventing her from using the Patriots' name.[72] At that point, the two organizations stopped cooperating with each other.

As new local groups continued to pop up, they gravitated to Tea Party Patriots, and the national network grew rapidly. The greatest strength and greatest potential liability to the Tea Party Patriots is the network of more than 2,900 local chapters across the country that they have cultivated. This massive network gives Tea Party Patriots enhanced stature and political power. Yet at the same time, a continuing infestation of those local chapters by other far-right groups and ideas has led many chapters to veer from the tightly scripted national messaging on "fiscal responsibility, constitutionally limited government, and free markets." For instance:

- A local Texas Tea Party Patriots chapter is run by a former member of the Knights of the Ku Klux Klan.

- A Tea Party Patriots–sponsored Tennessee statewide convention featured Islamophobic speakers and calls for a repeal of the Seventeenth Amendment.

- The Idaho Tea Party Patriots' state coordinator organized an event featuring anti-Semitic illustrations, the John Birch Society, birthers, and militia-style conspiracies about the Federal Reserve.
- Several local Tea Party Patriots chapters have sponsored speaking engagements by militia figure Richard Mack.
- In Maryland, a Tea Party Patriots chapter is run by the nativist group Help Save Maryland.
- Local Tea Party Patriots meetings have even featured exhortations to political violence.

Tea Party Patriots has refused to acknowledge, let alone deal with, any of these problematic elements inside their local chapters, despite a policy that "TPP does not condone and will not tolerate discrimination of any kind."

After claiming to be a nonprofit organization prohibited from partisan political activity, Tea Party Patriots chose not to endorse candidates in the 2010 electoral cycle. Instead, the organization focused on building up its donor list, compelling local groups to part with their membership rosters with the lure of grants that have not materialized.[73] The growing tension over national fund-raising and other moves by the leadership have soured relationships between the national group and some local chapters.

Despite the growing disunity in the ranks, TPP was able to attract over 2,500 people to its February 2011 convention in Phoenix, Arizona. In addition to speeches by several potential Republican presidential candidates, the event highlighted a new voter suppression campaign and a debate about Tea Party tax policy.

TEA PARTY EXPRESS

Tea Party Express, more than any other faction, has driven Tea Party electoral politics. The organization was created in 2009, by a preexisting conservative operation, Our Country Deserves Better Political Action Committee (OCDB PAC). Tea Party Express has conducted cross-country publicity-driven bus tours, as well as raised funds in support of Republican candidates.[74] It is not a membership organization and is not attempting to build or support local groups, which distinguishes it from other national factions. Its initial chairman, Mark Williams, has repeatedly crossed the line from civil discourse into vicious rants and explicit racism. Further, its leadership has clashed repeatedly with other Tea Party organizations, and has been the most marked by public controversy.

The Our Country Deserves Better PAC was formed in July 2008, by Howard Kaloogian and Sal Russo, "to champion the Reaganesque conservatism of lower taxes, smaller government, strong national defense, and respect for the strength of the family as the core of a strong America."[75] Kaloogian, who serves as chairman of OCDB PAC, is a former Republican California state assemblyman. In 2006, Kaloogian ran unsuccessfully for Congress in spite of having a well-funded campaign, due to his opposition to the ban on assault weapons that garnered the support of Larry Pratt's Gun Owners of America Political Victory Fund. (Pratt was one of the founding figures in the militia movement of the mid-1990s.)[76] Sal Russo, a California Republican political consultant who ran Kaloogian's unsuccessful congressional campaign, serves as OCDB PAC's "chief strategist."[77] Russo is a principal of Russo Marsh & Rogers, a public relations firm that also does business under the names Kings Media Group and Russo Marsh & Associates, Inc. The firm was hired by the California Republican Party in 1996 to help pass Proposition 209, the anti–affirmative action ballot measure. And it has been involved in a number of other GOP-affiliated campaigns.[78]

In April 2009, OCDB PAC's coordinator Joe Wierzbicki circulated a memo outlining the project that would become the Tea Party Express. The memo suggested an initial gap between the Express group and other budding Tea Parties. "This will be a very sensitive matter that we will need to discuss in the coming days," Wierzbicki wrote. "We have to be very, very careful about discussing amongst ourselves anyone we include 'outside of the family' because quite frankly, we are not only NOT part of the political establishment or conservative establishment, but we are also sadly not currently a part of the 'tea party' establishment. . . ."[79]

The initial vice chairman of OCDB PAC and chairman of the Tea Party Express was Mark Williams, a radio talk-show host and a past director of the National Association of Talk Show Hosts. According to Williams, Tea Parties are "gatherings of people who believe in America and while maybe not knowing the Constitution verbatim nonetheless are still well schooled on its spirit, and they are gathering to Take Back America, One Tea Party at a Time."[80] Williams has referred to President Obama as a Nazi, a half-white racist, a half-black racist, and an Indonesian Muslim turned welfare fraud.[81] He has stated, "it is time for not just Republicans but all Americans to regroup and stage our own coup. That's right, '*coup*.'"[82] After his racist remarks about the National Association for the Advancement of Colored People (NAACP) were challenged, Williams abruptly announced that he was stepping down as chairman of the Tea Party Express on June 19, 2010.

Amy Kremer took over for Mark Williams as the chair of Tea Party Express. She had previously served as its director of grassroots and coalitions. As discussed previously, before joining Tea Party Express she had been a staff member of a different faction, Tea Party Patriots. Recruiting Kremer away from Tea Party Patriots exacerbated tensions that existed between the two organizations. Tea Party Patriots sued Kremer, and a Georgia judge decided that the defendant had to return control of the organization's website, relinquish the use of the mailing lists, and not take advantage of any inside information she might have gained while working with Tea Party Patriots.[83]

Although Kremer has adamantly dismissed charges of racism in the Tea Party movement, she was quick to defend a July 2009 email featuring a racist caricature of President Obama that Dr. David McKalip sent to fellow Tea Partiers.[84] Kremer's blog, "Southern Belle Politics," is filled with calumny for the president, including repetition of the (false) charge that he is not a natural-born American: "There are many reasons that I don't like Barack Obama, including his health care plan, tax policies, and his big government and socialist programs that will be initiated through his massive tax and spend policies. However, more importantly than the reasons listed above, I truly do not think Barack Obama is eligible to be President of this great country. If he is eligible and really doesn't have anything to hide, then why not just produce the vault copy of his birth certificate and put the issue to rest?"[85]

Another defender of the Tea Party is Lloyd Marcus, a "spokesperson" for OCDB PAC and a peripatetic pop-up figure at Tea Party events, who has consistently challenged the charge that racists exist within the Tea Party's ranks, including the period when Mark Williams served as head of Tea Party Express.[86] Marcus, who is from Deltona, Florida, describes himself as a "(black) Unhyphenated American, singer/songwriter, entertainer, author, artist, and Tea Party patriot." The African American entertainer supported the reelection of George W. Bush in 2004. He is also president of the National Association for the Advancement of Conservative People of Color (which later changed its name to the National Association for the Advancement of Conservative People of ALL Colors). The group is focused on ridiculing and opposing the NAACP, the oldest and largest civil rights organization in the country. According to Federal Election Commission (FEC) records, Marcus received over $21,000 in consulting fees from OCDB PAC between March 2009 and May 2010.

Unlike the other groups, Tea Party Express was designed at the beginning as a campaign vehicle to attack "politically vulnerable" electoral candidates. Wierzbicki's 2009 memo explains to potential donors how OCDB PAC and Tea Party Express would establish bus tours to "defeat Harry Reid," "defeat Chris Dodd," and "defeat Arlen Specter." In addition, Wierzbicki proposed renting the mailing lists of other right-wing groups, including Newsmax, Human Events, Townhall, WorldNetDaily, and others, to kick-start the Tea Party Express efforts.[87] Expenditure reports filed with the FEC confirm that the organization has paid $187,340 to NewsMax Media, $93,800 to Human Events, and $36,206 to TownHall.com.[88] The need to "buttress our 'authenticity'" by using locals was also discussed in the memo.

The first Tea Party Express bus tour started in Sacramento on August 28, 2009. The tour crisscrossed the country, holding events in several cities in Nevada and Texas, as well as in multiple places in the Midwest and mid-South before arriving in Washington, DC for the September 12 "March on Washington." These rallies gathered support for the Tea Party movement generally, as well as finding new contributors to the political action committee. In October, after that first tour was completed, the group officially filed with the FEC to change the name of the PAC to the "Our Country Deserves Better PAC—TeaPartyExpress.org" (OCDB PAC—TPE).

A second tour, entitled "Tea Party Express II: Countdown to Judgment Day," kicked off in San Diego on October 25, and again included multiple stops in Nevada and the West before heading South through Texas, Louisiana, Mississippi, Alabama, and Georgia. It concluded in Orlando, Florida, on November 12.

As the second bus tour concluded, the attention of OCDB PAC—TPE turned to a special election in Massachusetts to fill the Senate seat left open by the death of Ted Kennedy in August. Hoping to make the election a referendum against health care reform, the PAC pumped $348,670 in independent expenditures into the campaign of Scott Brown, a relatively unknown Republican state senator. On January 20, 2010, Brown defeated Democrat Martha Coakley. Whatever the reason for Brown's election, to Tea Partiers, this was the "Scott heard 'round the world,'" and Tea Party Express was quick to take credit for the victory.

Tea Party Express was expected to participate in a convention held by Tea Party Nation in February 2010, but pulled out. This created a bit of a rift between the two groups. Just two weeks later, Tea Party Express held a rally at the annual Conservative Political Action Conference convention in Washington, DC. The Conservative Political Action Conference (CPAC) is an annual conference for conservative activists and politicians. Tea Party groups played a significant role at the 2010 CPAC conference, including staging a rally near the Tea Party Express bus. Also in attendance at the 2010 CPAC convention were representatives of the far-right, conspiracy-mongering John Birch Society—the first time in the thirty-seven-year history of the conference that the John Birch Society was a conference sponsor.[89]

A third round of the bus tour was launched on March 27, 2010, with a big rally in Searchlight, Nevada (Harry Reid's hometown). Tea Party Express III visited towns in Nevada, trying to drum up opposition to Senator Reid, before winding across the country. Along the way, the Tea Party Express announced the endorsement of additional candidates, including Minnesota Congresswoman Michele Bachmann. The tour concluded again in Washington, DC, on April 15, to coincide with the Tax Day 2010 Tea Party protests.

On April 15, Tea Party Express announced its endorsement of Sharron Angle in the Republican U.S. Senate primary in Nevada. On April 25, the organization rolled out two television ads and a radio spot in support of Angle,[90] and on May 11, it ran a full-page newspaper ad in support of Angle.[91] On May 16, TeaPartyExpress.com announced it would raise a Tea Party Express $150,000 "Money Bomb" in support of Sharron Angle.[92] Within a week, the organization was more than halfway there, raising $80,910.[93] Sharron Angle came from behind to win the June 9 primary.

Tea Party Express, and its parent company, the Our Country Deserves Better PAC, lack an online social network presence like the rest of the Tea Party factions. As a political action committee, the group has donors who give money, not members who can just sign up. This difference makes it difficult to draw direct comparisons to the other factions. We do know that the Our Country Deserves Better PAC collected $7,684,925 in contributions during the 2010 election cycle, reporting 4,052 donors of more than $200 to the Federal Election Commission.[94] According to FEC records, in 2010, the PAC spent $7,720,942, including $2,772,405 in independent campaign expenditures.

Tea Party Express made 117 candidate endorsements in the 2010 electoral cycle (15 in Senate races and 102 in House races). In the Senate races, 9 Tea Party Express candidates won, 6 lost. In House races, 62 won, 40 lost. Overall, Tea Party Express candidates won nearly 61 percent of their campaigns.

CONCLUSION

As the 2011 state legislative sessions wound down, Tea Party attentions pivoted to the 2012 elections. Tea Party groups began seeking a prominent role in shaping the Republican side of presidential electoral politics. In February 2011, several likely Republican candidates appeared at the Tea Party Patriots convention to try and win over the Tea Party faithful. Multiple Tea Party candidates threw their hats into the ring, including Michele Bachmann, the head of the House Tea Party Caucus. At the same time, other candidates were openly opposed by different Tea Party factions. FreedomWorks decided that it did not like GOP presidential frontrunner, Mitt Romney, and launched an opposition campaign. Despite a potential conflict of interest, the Tea Party Express sought to enhance both its power and legitimacy by officially partnering with cable television network CNN to host a Republican presidential primary debate in September 2011. Beyond the presidential election, national Tea Party factions are working to expand their electoral footprint by supporting Tea Party–aligned candidates in congressional, state, and local races in 2012.

Also in preparation for the 2012 electoral battle, several of the national Tea Party factions made voter suppression a significant part of their work in 2011, including supporting stricter state voter identification laws and conducting workshops on "voter fraud." None of the other national factions have adopted Tea Party Nation's Judson Phillips' idea of restricting voting rights to property owners, but the harsh identification requirements made have much the same impact by deterring participation of people of low income and communities of color.

Looking ahead, it is unclear as to whether the firewall keeping the far right out of the Tea Parties will erode completely. FreedomWorks and Tea Party Patriots, the two factions most vocally opposed to "social issues" in the Tea Party agenda, are doing what seemed unthinkable and letting the John Birch Society into the Tea Party fold. And whatever separation existed between culture war concerns and the Tea Party agenda is quickly vanishing, particularly among local Tea Party groups.

The Tea Party movement is still an inchoate and unstable ideological configuration. Just as during the first two years of Tea Party movement development, we can expect more changes in the future. Significant changes in movement size and structure are likely again, and more sorting out will occur, particularly as the movement shifts and adapts to the results of the 2012 election.

APPENDIX: METHODOLOGY OF TEA PARTY FACTION DATA COLLECTION AND ANALYSIS

During the past two years, we have employed a variety of investigative reporting techniques to study the Tea Parties to keep up with the expanding and ever-changing dynamic of the movement:

- We read through the Tea Party literature—from movement-produced books like *The Official Tea Party Handbook* and *Taking America Back One Tea Party at a Time,* to electronic publications including emails, electronic newsletters, articles, blog posts, and tweets written by Tea Partiers. We also watched many hours of online video of Tea Party events. For firsthand accounts, we and our research assistants attended Tea Party rallies, conventions, and meetings from Washington, DC to Washington State. We also talked with numerous Tea Party activists.

- To follow the money trail, we dug through government documents and databases, including corporate filings, IRS forms, court cases, campaign finance reports, and unemployment statistics. We utilized computer-assisted reporting to collect additional data and help make sense of it all.

- We also did a thorough scan of secondary sources, including the exceptional reporting that is already available on the Tea Parties. We also analyzed the considerable amount of polling that's been conducted on the Tea Parties.

Membership Data

The membership data in this essay was derived from a collection of online directories on the major national Tea Party faction websites: Tea Party Nation, Tea Party Patriots, 1776 Tea Party (also known as TeaParty .org), FreedomWorks Tea Party, and ResistNet Tea Party. The data for the sixth national Tea Party formation mentioned in this chapter, the

Tea Party Express, was drawn from filings with the Federal Election Commission (FEC).

The data provides a partial picture of the Tea Party activist base. It is important to note that there may be many more individuals who are not listed in these social networking directories—who either chose not to register, who have registered on some other site (such as one or more of the many local Tea Party sites), or who do not have sufficient computer skills.

An automated process allowed for the copying and compiling of the website membership data into a local SQL database.

Records retrieved from all five Tea Party faction sources generally included name, city, state, country, and gender. Some records were incomplete—missing city, state, country, gender, and so on. Incomplete records were included in the overall numbers, not in areas where data was missing. We also downloaded the contribution records from FEC.gov for Our Country Deserves Better PAC—TeaPartyExpress.com for the same period and imported those records.

From the initial captured material, we worked with the data to eliminate duplicates and extraneous data. We also normalized the data, making sure that column names were the same, and that state and abbreviations were consistent. We then imported that data into a main SQL database.

Once we had a completed Tea Party membership data set, we then geo-coded the set using the city and state information. That information was later used to map the location of membership using Tableau Public.

After the importation process, we ran specific queries to work specifically with Tea Party member data and to extract the information we needed. Those queries included Tea Party members by state, Tea Party members by city, Tea Party members by faction, Tea Party membership by city versus local unemployment rate, and Tea Party membership totals by city as a percentage of the city population.

Tea Party Chapter Data

The data on Tea Party chapters was also collected using a process similar to how membership information was compiled. Due to poor site layout, one site required manual data entry of the group data.

The data was placed into a separate Tea Party chapter database. We used the same process as we did with Tea Party membership data to clean and normalize the Tea Party chapter data. We also geo-coded the data to be able to map the chapter locations.

NOTES

1. As much of this essay is drawn directly from the Institute for Research and Education on Human Rights Special Report, *Tea Party Nationalism: A Critical Examination of the Size, Scope and Focus of the Tea Party Movement and Its National Factions*, I want to give a special acknowledgment to my coauthor, editor, colleague, mentor, and friend, Leonard Zeskind. This work would not be possible without his vision, insight, patience, and leadership.

2. See the Appendix at the end of this chapter for details on the methods used for data collection and analysis.

3. All of the local groups that are not affiliated with one national network or the other are outside the scope of this essay. Similarly beyond the reach of this chapter are the many ancillary organizations that have contributed to the movement since its inception, including Ron Paul's Campaign for Liberty, Americans for Prosperity, National Precinct Alliance, and the John Birch Society. Nor did we include an analysis of the various national 9/12 groups. The 9/12 formations lack the same sort of national structure present in the Tea Party movement. The national 9/12 formations are important peripheral forces, but as organizational actors, they do not appear to play a notable role in the internal movement infrastructure. Moreover, much of the 9/12 group momentum was co-opted by the Tea Party movement.

4. Interactive maps, which provide a graphic overview of the size and scope of the Tea Party organizations, including the geographic location of their members, are available at www.teapartynationalism.com.

5. Alex Brant-Zawadzki and Dawn Teo, "Anatomy of the Tea Party Movement: FreedomWorks," Huffington Post website, December 11, 2009, www.huffingtonpost.com/alex-brantzawadzki/anatomy-of-the-tea-party_b_380575.html.

6. Rob Jordan, "FreedomWorks Launches Nationwide 'Tea Party' Tour," FreedomWorks website, March 9, 2009, www.freedomworks.org/publications/freedomworks-launches-nationwide-%E2%80%9Ctea-party%E2%80%9D-tour.

7. FreedomWorks Foundation Inc., IRS Form 990, 2008; FreedomWorks, Inc., IRS Form 990, 2008.

8. Paul Krugman, "Tea Parties Forever," *New York Times*, April 12, 2009, www.nytimes.com/2009/04/13/opinion/13krugman.html; and Paul Krugman, "Armey of Darkness," on *The Conscience of a Liberal* (blog), *New York Times* website, April 11, 2009, http://krugman.blogs.nytimes.com/2009/04/11/armey-of-darkness/.

9. Edmund L. Andrews, "Clamor Grows in the Privatization Debate," *New York Times*, December 14, 2004, www.nytimes.com/2004/12/17/politics/17mom.htm.

10. Michael M. Phillips, "Mortgage Bailout Infuriates Tenants (and Steve Forbes): 'Angry Renter' Web Site Has Grass-Roots Look, But This Turf is Fake," *Wall Street Journal*, May 16, 2008, http://online.wsj.com/article/SB121090164137297527.html?mod=hpp_us_pageone.

11. FreedomWorks, FreedomConnector website, http://connect.freedomworks.org, accessed May 25, 2011.

12. "Jeff Frazee Interviews Brendan Steinhauser of FreedomWorks to Discuss the Tax Day Coalition," YouTube video, March 30, 2009, www.youtube.com/watch?v=yHDFWViHL70.

13. "Jeff Frazee Interviews Brendan Steinhauser."

14. See the FreedomWorks website, IamWithRick.com, for examples of all of these.

15. "Jeff Frazee Interviews Brendan Steinhauser."

16. "Jeff Frazee Interviews Brendan Steinhauser."

17. Jackie Kucinich, "Anti-Tax Groups Reprise Tea Parties," *Roll Call*, June 24, 2009, www.freedomworks.org/news/anti-tax-groups-reprise-tea-parties.

18. Matthew Murray, "Armey Says FreedomWorks Ready to Mobilize Beyond Health Debate," *Roll Call*, August 18, 2009, www.freedomworks.org/news/armey-says-freedomworks-ready-to-mobilize-beyond-h.

19. Jake Sherman, "Conservatives Plan New Round of Tea Parties," on *Washington Wire* (blog), *Wall Street Journal* website, August 18, 2009, www.freedomworks.org/news/conservatives-plan-new-round-of-tea-parties.

20. Rebecca Sinderbrand, "FreedomWorks, Tea Party Patriots Head for the Hill," *CNN Political Ticker* (blog), September 3, 2009, www.freedomworks.org/news/freedomworks-tea-party-patriots-head-for-the-hill.

21. Sinderbrand, "FreedomWorks, Tea Party Patriots Head for the Hill."

22. Alex Pappas, "Tea Party Leaders Release List of Targeted Races at FreedomWorks Summit," *The Daily Caller*, January 25, 2010, www.freedomworks.org/news/tea-party-leaders-release-list-of-targeted-races-a.

23. Kathleen Hennessy, "Still a Disorganized 'Tea Party,'" *Los Angeles Times*, January 25, 2010, www.freedomworks.org/news/still-a-disorganized-tea-party.

24. Alex Pappas, "Tea Party Activists Circulate 'Declaration of Independence' and Distance Selves from Republicans," *The Daily Caller*, February 24, 2010, dailycaller.com/2010/02/24/tea-party-activists-circulate-declaration-of-independence-and-distance-selves-from-republicans/#ixzzoqzlLXlW8.

25. "Declaration of Tea Party Independence" document, *The Daily Caller*, February 24, 2010, dailycaller.com/2010/02/24/tea-party-activists-circulate-declaration-of-independence-and-distance-selves-from-republicans/#ixzzoqzlLXlW8.

26. "Declaration of Tea Party Independence" document.

27. Brian Beutler, "Industry-Backed Anti-Health Care Reform Group: Yeah, We're Packing and Disrupting the Health Care Town Halls," *Talking Points Memo* (blog), August 4, 2009, http://tpmdc.talkingpointsmemo.com/2009/08/anti-health-care-reform-group-yeah-were-packing-and-disrupting-the-health-care-town-halls.php.

28. Kate Zernike, "With No Jobs, Plenty of Time for Tea Party," *New York Times*, March 27, 2010, www.nytimes.com/2010/03/28/us/politics/28teaparty.html?_r=1.

29. "April 15th Tax Day Tea Party," Georgia Tea Party Patriots website, March 7, 2010, http://georgiateapartypatriots.com/wordpress/?p=142.

30. Researchers at Brigham Young University conducted a study of the impact of Tea Party endorsements on the 2010 midterm elections. They found that while endorsements by Tea Party groups did not produce dramatic results

in the general election overall, FreedomWorks's endorsements were shown to have an effect: "Of the Tea Party groups that backed candidates in the general election, only FreedomWorks endorsements were associated with a statistically significant increase in votes for the Republican candidates. The Republican candidate's vote share increased by a little more than two percentage points when a FreedomWorks endorsement was involved" (p. 305). The researchers credit FreedomWorks's strategy of supporting Republican candidates in swing districts for this result: "FreedomWorks was more strategic in its choice of candidates than some other Tea Party–affiliated groups. . . . While other endorsers embraced a more scattershot approach, FreedomWorks went hunting 'where the ducks were.' And in those swing districts, the hunting turned out to be good: A FreedomWorks endorsement was correlated with better performance from the Republican candidate" (p. 306). See Christopher F. Karpowitz, J. Quin Monson, Kelly D. Patterson, and Jeremy C. Pope, "Tea Time in America? The Impact of the Tea Party Movement on the 2010 Midterm Elections," *PS: Political Science and Politics* (April 2011): 303–09.

31. Steve Eichler, "We Agree On Most Points! Fight On!" TeaParty.org social networking site, May 16, 2010, http://teapartyorg.ning.com/profiles/blogs/we-agree-on-most-points-fight?xg_source=activity.

32. Eichler, "We Agree On Most Points! Fight On!"

33. David Weigel, "'N-Word' Sign Dogs Would-Be Tea Party Leader," *The Washington Independent,* January 4, 2010, washingtonindependent .com/73036/n-word-sign-dogs-would-be-tea-party-leader.

34. Zachary Roth, "Tea Party Fundraising Email Shows Obama as Pimp," *Talking Points Memo* (blog), January 28, 2010, tpmmuckraker.talkingpointsmemo .com/2010/01/tea_party_fundraising_email_shows_obama_as_pimp.php.

35. Dale Robertson, "TEAPARTY.ORG for Sale—Tea Party Founder Loses Home," PRWeb, June 8, 2009, www.prweb.com/releases/2009/06/prweb2510974.htm.

36. The term *nativist* was invented in the 1850s to describe the program of the antiforeign, anti-Catholic political party commonly referred to as the Know-Nothings. In his book *Strangers in the Land: Patterns of American Nativism, 1860–1925* (New Brunswick, NJ: Rutgers University Press, 1992), John Higham defined nativism as "intense opposition to an internal minority on the ground of its foreign (i.e., un-American) connections" (p. 4). For more on the various lawsuits, see Frank Mickadeit, "Gilchrist and Foes Declare Victory," *Orange County Register,* May 17, 2010, www.ocregister.com/articles/gilchrist-249195-courtney-jury.html; Frank Mickadeit, "Gilchrist Wins Court Fight," *Orange County Register,* February 7, 2010, www.ocregister .com/articles/gilchrist-233048-courtney-board.html; Frank Mickadeit, "Gilchrist Foes Fight the Odds," *Orange County Register,* January 18, 2010, www. ocregister.com/articles/gilchrist-229695-courtney-stewart.html; Frank Mickadeit, "Minuteman Leader Gilchrist Loses Another Biggie in Court," *Orange County Register,* August 7, 2008, www.ocregister.com/articles/gilchrist-202875-coe -lula.html; "Jim Gilchrist Files Another Suit against Ex-Minutemen Cohorts," *Orange County Register,* April 18, 2008, www.ocregister.com/articles/gilchrist-196210-immigration-emotional.html; and Martin Wisckol, "Gilchrist

Abandons Lawsuit," *Orange County Register*, April 24, 2007, www.ocregister
.com/news/gilchrist-3217-minuteman-project.html.

37. Stephen Lemons, "Shawna Forde, Alleged Kid Killer, Extremist, Phoenix Tea Party Attendee, and Ghost of Tea Parties Future," *Feathered Bastard* (blog), *Phoenix New Times*, June 22, 2009, http://blogs.phoenixnewtimes.com/bastard/2009/06/right_wing_extremist_shawna_fo.php. Shawna Forde was an early Tea Partier. She attended the April 15, 2009 Tea Party rally in Phoenix. "This is the time for all Americans to join organizations and REVOLT!!!" Forde blogged from the Tea Party rally. "Refuse to be part of a system only designed to enslave you and your children. Times will get worse before they get worse. *Say no to illegal immigration* Lock and Load, Shawna Forde."

38. Scott North, "No Boundaries: Shawna Forde and the Minutemen Movement," *Everett Herald*, October 25, 2009, www.heraldnet.com/article/20091025/NEWS01/710259945&newso1ad=1; and Daniel Newhauser, "Minutemen Regroup after Shootings," *Green Valley News and Sun*, June 20, 2009, www.gvnews.com/news/article_deaf7954-b631-5dbf-8c16-b97394cfaff1.html.

39. "Legal Victories for Jim Gilchrist's Minuteman Project Continue," Minuteman Express News, Minuteman Project website, September 2009, http://web.archive.org/web/20110727203945/http://minutemanproject.com/newsmanager/templates/light.aspx?articleid=1108&zoneid=1.

40. Devin Burghart, "ResistNet Re-Branding," Institute for Research and Education on Human Rights Tea Party Nationalism website, December 15, 2010, www.irehr.org/issue-areas/tea-party-nationalism/tea-party-news-and-analysis/item/352-resistnet-re-branding.

41. "What is Grassfire Nation?" Grassfire.com website, accessed August 9, 2010, www.grassfire.com/faq.shtm.

42. Amy Lorentzen, "Web Groups Claim Victory in Bill Defeat," AP News, June 30, 2007, www.thefreelibrary.com/_/print/PrintArticle.aspx?id=1611367799. According to the Grassroots Action website, www.grassrootsaction.com/, its clients have included Focus on the Family Action, the National Republican Congressional Committee, and Reclaiming America.

43. Figure available from Grassfire.org Alliance, IRS Form 990, 2008, www2.guidestar.org/ReportNonProfit.aspx?ein=20-0440372&name=grassfire-org-alliance#. According to its 990 filing, Grassfire.org Alliance Inc. was formed in 2004. In Colorado only, the nonprofit fund-raising status of Grassfire.org Alliance was suspended in January 2010, according to the Colorado Secretary of State website summary page for Grassfire.org Alliance Inc., accessed August 1, 2010, www.sos.state.co.us/ccsa/ViewSummary.do?ceId=38928.

44. "Frequently Asked Questions (FAQ)," Grassfire.net website, December 21, 2002, accessed on August 5, 2010, http://web.archive.org/web/20021221164825/www.grassfire.net/images/myGrassfire/faq.asp.

45. "Petition to Support the Public Display of the Ten Commandments in Our Communities," Grassfire.net website, October 2, 2002, accessed on August 5, 2010, http://web.archive.org/web/20021002223641/www.grassfire.net/mygrassfire.asp?rid=.

46. NextMark, Inc., "Grassroots Action Masterfile (Formerly Known as Grassfire.net Masterfile) Mailing List" NextMark Mailing List Finder website,

accessed August 1, 2010, http://lists.nextmark.com/market;jsessionid=C2198A 3CCA36582397BCACC2B41FCBD6?page=order/online/datacard&id=74913.

47. People for the American Way, "The Emerging Right-Wing 'Resistance,'" Right Wing Watch website, November 19, 2008, www.rightwingwatch.org/ content/emerging-right-wing-resistance.

48. Darla Dawald, "Key Contacts on ResistNet.com, Home of the Patriotic Resistance," ResistNet website, December 20, 2009, www.resistnet.com/notes/ Key_Contacts.

49. Domenico Montanaro, "Tea Partying for Profit?" First Read blog on MSNBC.com, January 15, 2010, http://firstread.msnbc.msn.com/_news/ 2010/01/15/4431927-tea-partying-for-profit.

50. "Welcome to Tea Party Nation!!!" Tea Party Nation website homepage, undated, accessed August 1, 2010, http://www.teapartynation.com/.

51. Judson Phillips, "Tea Party Battles Racism Allegations," Live Q&A transcript, *Washington Post*, May 5, 2010, www.washingtonpost.com/wp-dyn/ content/discussion/2010/05/05/DI2010050502168.html.

52. Kevin Smith, "On the Backs of Tennessee's Middle Class (or, The Story Behind Tea Party Nation's Dishonest Beginnings)," *media res* (blog), January 12, 2010, http://ksmith.in/inmediasres/2010/01/12/on-the-backs-of-tennessees -middle-class-or-the-story-behind-tea-party-nations-dishonest-beginnings/; and "Entity Detail: 00600840: Corporation For-Profit—Domestic. Tea Party Nation Corporation," Tennessee Department of State website, April 21, 2009, http://tnbear.tn.gov/ECommerce/Common/FilingDetail.aspx?FilingNum =000600840.

53. "Tea Party Convention Loses Sponsor Following 'Whistleblower' Blog Post," *Politics* (blog), *Nashville Post*, January 13, 2010, http://politics.nashvillepost .com/2010/01/13/key-sponsor-drops-out-of-tea-party-convention-after-accusation- against-organizer-surface/.

54. Melissa Clouthier, "Tea Party Nation's Judson Phillips: 'I Want to Make a Million from This Movement,'" MelissaClouthier.com website, January 15, 2010, www.melissaclouthier.com/2010/01/15/tea-party-nations-judson-phillips -i-want-to-make-a-million-from-this-movement/.

55. For a detailed description of the convention, see Devin Burghart, "Revival and Revolt: Inside the Tea Party Nation Convention," Institute for Research and Education on Human Rights website, February 11, 2010, http:// irehr.org/race-racism-a-white-nationalism/10-analysis/52-revival-and-revolt -inside-the-tea-party-nation-convention.

56. Judson Phillips, "Letter to the GOP Leadership," Tea Party Nation website, November 22, 2010, www.teapartynation.com/forum/topics/ letter-to-the-gop-leadership.

57. Phillips, "Letter to the GOP Leadership."

58. Judson Phillips, "Social Issues and the Tea Party," Tea Party Nation website, November 27, 2010, www.teapartynation.com/forum/topics/ social-issues-and-the-tea.

59. Rich Swier, "Destroy the Family, You Destroy the Country!" Tea Party Nation website, March 28, 2011, www.teapartynation.com/profiles/blogs/ destroy-the-family-you-destroy.

60. Tea Party Patriots, "Tea Party Patriots Mission Statement and Core Values," Tea Party Patriots website, undated, accessed August 1, 2010, www .teapartypatriots.org/Mission.aspx.

61. Stephanie Mencimer, "Tea Party Patriots Investigated: Don't Ask, Don't Tell," Mother Jones website, February 15, 2011, motherjones.com/ politics/2011/02/tea-party-patriots-investigated-part-two.

62. In fact, as of July 31, 2010, the PAC had not raised or spent anything for the 2009–2010 election cycle. "Tea Party Patriots Inc. PAC: Committee [C00473660] Summary Reports—2009–2010 Cycle," Federal Election Commission website, accessed September 4, 2010, http://query.nictusa.com/ cgi-bin/cancomsrs/?_10+C00473660.

63. In November 2010, Tea Party Patriots altered its main website, making it impossible to continue to calculate individual membership.

64. As a for-profit entity, Tea Party Nation does not make its revenue or expenditures available to the public. Hence, it is impossible to gauge how they would compare to other factions.

65. "Summary Page: Tea Party Patriots, Inc.," Colorado Secretary of State Licensing Center website, accessed August 1, 2010, www.sos.state.co.us/ccsa/ ViewSummary.do?ceId=62632.

66. Tea Party Patriots' national coordinating group grew to include Debbie Dooley, Mike Gaske, Kellen Giuda, Ryan Hecker, Sally Oljar, Diana Reimer, Billie Tucker, and Dawn Wildman. Zachary Roth, "Top Tea Partier, Husband, Owed IRS Half a Million Dollars," *Talking Points Memo* (blog), October 8, 2009, http://tpmmuckraker.talkingpointsmemo.com/2009/10/top_tea_partier _husband_owed_irs_half_a_million_do.php; and Oren Dorell, "Tax Revolt a Recipe for Tea Parties," *USA Today,* April 13, 2009, www.usatoday.com/ news/washington/2009-04-12-teaparties12_N.htm.

67. Prior to the bankruptcy, the couple lived in a five-bedroom house in a Woodstock, Georgia, subdivision. The couple had purchased twin Lincoln Navigator SUVs, contracted a yard service, purchased an expensive club membership, and more. For details, see Mark Davis, "Jenny Beth Martin: The Head Tea Party Patriot," *Atlanta Journal-Constitution*, May 9, 2010, http://www .ajc.com/news/georgia-politics-elections/jenny-beth-martin-the-522344.html; bankruptcy details found in Ford Motor Credit Company, LLC. A Delaware Limited Liability Company v. Lee Sanders Martin, IV, Jennifer Elisabeth Martin, and Robert B. Silliman, as Trustee, Chapter 7, No. 08-76980-CRM, United States Bankruptcy Court, Northern District of Georgia, December 5, 2008; and Voluntary Petition, No. 08-76980-crm, United States Bankruptcy Court, Northern District of Georgia, August 29, 2008.

68. Davis, "Jenny Beth Martin: The Head Tea Party Patriot."

69. Stephanie Mencimer, "Tea Party Patriots Investigated: The Tax-Dodging Treasurer," Mother Jones website, February 16, 2011, motherjones. com/politics/2011/02/tea-party-patriots-investigated-part-3.

70. Zachary Roth, "Top Tea Party Leader Was Paid by GOP Biz Group's Campaign," *Talking Points Memo* (blog), March 3, 2010, http://tpmmuckraker .talkingpointsmemo.com/2010/03/top_tea_party_leader_being_paid_by_gop _biz_group.php#more.

71. Jenny Beth Martin, letter to Amy Kremer, October 15, 2009.

72. Tea Party Patriots, Inc. v. Amy Kremer, Civil Action No. 09-1-10603-42, Superior Court of Cobb County State of Georgia, November 10, 2009.

73. Stephanie Mencimer, "Tea Party Patriots Investigated: 'They Use and Abuse You,'" Mother Jones website, February 14, 2011, motherjones.com/politics/2011/02/tea-party-patriots-investigated.

74. The bus tour for which the Tea Party Express became known was actually a tactic recycled from the Our Country Deserves Better 2008 "Stop Obama Bus Tour." Mark Williams, *Taking Back America One Tea Party at a Time* (MarkTalk.com, 2010, electronic edition, 156). After Obama won the presidency, OCDB continued to support Sarah Palin, including running pro-Palin advertisements. Palin later returned the favor by headlining two events on the Tea Party Express III tour.

75. "About Us," Our Country Deserves Better PAC website, undated, accessed August 1, 2010, www.ourcountrydeservesbetter.com/about-us.

76. "Staunch Gun Rights Defender Vying for Open Congressional Seat," Gun Owners of America Political Victory Fund email alert, www.calguns.net/calgunforum/showthread.php?t=25125]], December 1, 2005. Kaloogian was exposed during this campaign for using a photo of Istanbul and claiming it was a picture of Baghdad. See Dana Milbank, "Baghdad on the Bosporus," *Washington Post* online, March 30, 2006, www.washingtonpost.com/wp-dyn/content/article/2006/03/29/AR2006032902277.html.

77. "Principals," Russo Marsh and Rogers website, undated, accessed July 1, 2010, www.rmrwest.com/index.php/RMRWest/Principals/.

78. "Agency Experience," Russo Marsh and Rogers website, undated, accessed July 1, 2010, http://www.rmrwest.com/index.php/RMRWest/Experience/. Kaloogian led the successful 2003 effort to recall California Governor Gray Davis. He and Russo also produced a series of TV ads that claimed Iraq actually had weapons of mass destruction, launched an "I love Gitmo" campaign to support U.S. detention policies, and organized protests against antiwar demonstrators. See "'I Love GITMO' Campaign Launched by Move America Forward," Move America Forward website, June 17, 2005, www.moveamericaforward.org/index.php/MAF/FullNewsItem/i_love_gitmo_campaign_launched/.

79. Joe Wierzbicki, "The Tea Party Express," Project Proposal—draft memo, April 17, 2009.

80. Williams, *Taking Back America One Tea Party at a Time*, 156.

81. Alex Brant-Zawadzki, "Mark Williams Posts Offensive Image of Muhammad," Huffington Post website, May 17, 2010, www.huffingtonpost.com/alex-brantzawadzki/mark-williams-posts-offen_b_576798.html.

82. Williams, *Taking Back America One Tea Party at a Time*, 19.

83. "Order Granting Plaintiff's Motion for Interlocutory Injunction," Tea Party Patriots, Inc. vs. Amy Kremer, Cobb County, Georgia, Superior Court, Civil Action No. 09-1-10603-42, November 10, 2009.

84. A neurosurgeon practicing in Florida, McKalip's action was later condemned by the Florida Medical Association. After the offending email surfaced and a controversy ensued, however, Kremer wrote to a Tea Party email list, "David, we all support you fully and are here for you. I can assure you of one

thing and that is we will protect our own. We all have your back my friend!" McKalip was a featured speaker when a Tea Party Express bus tour stopped in Orlando, Florida, the following November. See, for instance, Kremer's response to the Mark Williams attack on the NAACP, "Tea Party Racism Rift Reveals Fissures," CBS News website, July 20, 2010, www.cbsnews.com/stories/2010/07/20/politics/main6694191.shtml.

85. Amy Kremer, "College Football Saturday—Lawsuit Dismissed," Southern Belle Politics website, October 25, 2008, www.southernbellepolitics.com/2008/10/college-football-saturday-lawsuit.html.

86. Lloyd Marcus, "Exclusive: Tea Parties—It's the Media, Stupid!" Family Security Matters website, June 30, 2010, www.familysecuritymatters.org/publications/id.6601/pub_detail.asp; "Exclusive: Black Tea Party Spokesman Rebukes NAACP," Family Security Matters website, July 15, 2010, www.familysecuritymatters.org/publications/id.6751/pub_detail.asp; and "Exclusive: Tea Party 'Race' Issue Manipulated by the Media?" Family Security Matters website, July 20, 2010, www.familysecuritymatters.org/publications/id.6784/pub_detail.asp.

87. Joe Wierzbicki, "The Tea Party Express," Project Proposal.

88. Our Country Deserves Better—TeaPartyExpress.com PAC, query of individual donors, from "Detailed Files about Candidates, Parties, and Other Committees" databases, Federal Election Commission, downloaded June 15, 2010, http://fec.gov/finance/disclosure/ftpdet.shtml.

89. Jonathan Karl, "Far-Right John Birch Society 2010," The Note (blog), ABC News, February 19, 2010, http://blogs.abcnews.com/thenote/2010/02/farright-john-birch-society-2010.html.

90. "Conservative Republican Takes on Harry Reid!" Tea Party Express (blog), April 25, 2010, http://teapartyexpressblog.blogspot.com/2010/04/conservative-republican-takes-on-harry.html.

91. "Enjoy! Newspaper Ad to 'Defeat Harry Reid' and Elect Conservative Republican Sharron Angle!" Tea Party Express (blog), May 11, 2010, http://teapartyexpressblog.blogspot.com/2010/05/enjoy-newspaper-ad-to-defeat-harry-reid.html.

92. "The $150,000 Tea Party Express MONEY BOMB for Sharron Angle's U.S. Senate Bid," Tea Party Express (blog), May 16, 2010, http://teapartyexpressblog.blogspot.com/2010/05/150000-tea-party-express-money-bomb-for.html.

93. "Progress Report on $150,000 Money Bomb for Sharron Angle for U.S. Senate," Tea Party Express (blog), May 20, 2010, http://teapartyexpressblog.blogspot.com/2010/05/progress-report-on-150000-money-bomb.html.

94. Our Country Deserves Better—TeaPartyExpress.com PAC query of individual donors, from "Detailed Files about Candidates, Parties, and Other Committees" databases, Federal Election Commission, downloaded June 15, 2010, http://fec.gov/finance/disclosure/ftpdet.shtml.

CHAPTER 4

Astroturf versus Grass Roots

Scenes from Early Tea Party Mobilization[1]

CLARENCE Y. H. LO

Debate still rages in the blogs. Some condemn the Tea Party as Astroturf, a movement directly funded and organized from its very beginning by conservative leaders. Others argue that the Tea Party epitomizes grassroots politics, an outpouring of aggrieved citizens who spontaneously protested against big government.[2] Both arguments contain at least a grain of truth. In this chapter, I argue that, in its initial stage, the Tea Party was Astroturf—grassroots contrivance; in a second stage, however, the grass roots developed an autonomy (both strategically and organizationally) that revitalized the Republican Party.

The Astroturf metaphor asserts that conservative leadership organizations provided resources, direction, and standardized messages that were crucial in instigating Tea Party protests. This chapter will show that conservative groups favoring reduced social spending and lower taxes test marketed the concept of the Tea Party and thereby created its first protest wave in February and March 2009. The resulting mobilization gave the Tea Party a legitimate appearance as grassroots politics, and strengthened right-wing factions in their rivalry within the Republican Party establishment, setting the stage for the battles over the federal budget in 2011 and during the 2012 election campaign.

In contrast, the grass roots metaphor is above all a claim that the Tea Party resembles iconic phenomena such as the New England town hall meeting, the Iowa caucuses, or the clandestine collective action of the American Revolution. This chapter will show that, as the Tea Party's numbers grew precipitously, conservative organizations aided the growth of a second wave of Tea Party protests through *facilitated mobilization*, where local activists utilized preexisting networks and resources, like the Young Republicans, local campaign committees, donor lists, Internet blogs, and social networking sites, to build a grass-roots movement.

This second wave of Tea Party protests began on April 15, 2009, Tax Day, when three hundred thousand citizens protested in 350 American cities; these protests were followed by massive national demonstrations on July 4 and September 12, 2009. The second wave used a decentralized and federated mode of organization that proved crucial for establishing the overall character of the movement, allowing individual Tea Party factions to achieve some *marginal autonomy*[3] from conservative organizations as they navigated their own political terrain.[4] The Tea Party's marginal autonomy opened up choices about movement goals. Would the Tea Party emphasize electing Republicans and defeating President Obama by any means? Or would the movement focus more on electing a new breed of politician to drastically slash government and restore free enterprise?

This chapter argues that the goals pursued by individual Tea Party groups were influenced by their existing *affiliations* with different types of leadership groups. Pursuing electoral victory meant moving closer to a Republican establishment that generally favored an inclusive, big-tent vision of the Republican Party, and in particular meant embracing a well-funded group, the Tea Party Express. Emphasizing staunch fiscal conservatism entailed affiliating with groups that had orchestrated the test marketing of the Tea Party, such as FreedomWorks and Top Conservatives on Twitter, or joining the Tea Party Patriots—a Tea Party coalition that quickly rose to national prominence.[5]

Political pressure from new Tea Party coalitions led to headaches for established Republican leaders and subsequent readjustments in the Republican Party. Ironically, although the Tea Party mobilization was born of test marketing, its very mobilization loosened the scripted control of test marketers and the party establishment. The Republican Party is not what it once was before the Tea Party movement, and neither is the American democratic system.

WAVE ONE: TEST MARKETING

"From a marketing point of view, you don't introduce new products in August."[6] (Andrew Card, White House chief of staff for President George W. Bush, speaking of the public relations campaign to justify war in Iraq)

It was a scant month after Barack Obama's inauguration that Rick Santelli called for a "Chicago Tea Party." This "Santelli rant"[7] was the occasion for a coalition of leadership groups, mainly fiscal and business conservatives, to plan demonstrations on February 27 to protest President Obama's policies.[8] These plans were part of the "test marketing" of the Tea Party: Conservative leaders sought to take the concept voiced by Santelli in his rant, a Tea Party to protest Obama's proposals, and launch a coordinated test marketing of the concept to see if it would take hold in a variety of localities.[9] The Nationwide Tea Party Coalition (aka Nationwide Chicago Tea Party and later the Leadership Tea Party) constituted a "steering committee" of conservative leaders: Top Conservatives on Twitter (a following led by Michael Patrick Leahy and commonly called #tcot[10]), the dontgo movement[11] (now the American Liberty Alliance, founded by Eric Odom), and Smart Girl Politics (founded by Stacy Mott), with American Solutions (founded by Newt Gingrich) joining a month later.[12] Closely linked to the leadership network was Matt Kibbe, CEO of FreedomWorks. FreedomWorks was formed in 2004, out of Citizens for a Sound Economy, a group heavily funded by donations from the Koch family.[13] Although Koch-related foundations in 2010 denied that their funding for FreedomWorks was earmarked to support Tea Party factions,[14] the Koch family did create an extensive network of economically conservative political institutions, many of which were actively involved in test marketing the concept of a Tea Party.[15]

Beginning on the day after the Santelli rant, daily conference calls (twice weekly between February 28 and April 15) involved fifty-one conservative activists in eighteen cities.[16] (These "Founding Mothers and Fathers of the Tea Party Movement," were honored at an event held on the first anniversary of the February 27, 2009 Tea Parties.[17]) In a YouTube video distributed by Young Americans for Liberty, Brendan Steinhauser of FreedomWorks confirmed the existence of the daily "one PM" conference call and detailed the assistance his organization gave to local Tea Party groups.[18] Conservative leaders in Washington closely directed the activities of the fifty-one local activists, guiding them to oppose Obama's stimulus and health care bills,[19] and providing ready-to-use websites and advice on how to reach a larger audience. The leadership groups fielded a staff "support team" of nine professionals, skilled in marketing and public relations.[20]

The marketing activities of the Nationwide Tea Party Coalition typify a long-standing trend in which social movements become professionalized mobilizers of resources for public relations campaigns. Social movement scholars John McCarthy and Mayer Zald theorize that social movements in the United States have become national interest groups, led by entrepreneurs who seek to expand their organizations by developing new agendas that appeal to a mass audience.[21] Social movement organizations have evolved into enterprises, using the latest advertising techniques to sell memberships and solicit donations.

The test marketing of the Tea Party was similar to the rollout of a new consumer product that uses the techniques of cross-promotion. Cross-promotion uses one medium, such as television advertising or distributing free children's toys at chain restaurants, to promote an offering in another medium such as a Hollywood film. The Tea Party used Fox News and NASCAR racing events to cross-promote the Tea Party. Patrick Leahy and Eric Odom applied their expertise in Internet marketing and website development to promote the Nationwide Tea Party Coalition.[22] Immediately after the Santelli rant, Odom, who had been working for the conservative group Sam Adams Alliance (funded by the Koch family), set up websites using the words *Tea Party* whose domain names had been purchased many months earlier. Other Tea Party websites had been registered back in August 2008, and were owned by Zack Christenson, producer for a Chicago conservative talk radio program, and by Anthony Astolfi, a designer of conservative political websites.[23]

WAVE TWO: FACILITATED MOBILIZATION

The peak of the first wave of the Tea Party movement was the February 27, 2009 events held in eighteen U.S. cities, attracting some thirty thousand people, according to the organizers.[24] The test marketing of the Tea Party had been successful, but the outcome did not go exactly according to plan. The Tea Party protest held in Chicago only attracted three hundred demonstrators.[25] Santelli's rant focused on Obama's proposed assistance to defaulting homeowners. Organizers had reserved Internet domains such as angryrenter.com to target resentment against lower-income homeowners who might be seen as personally irresponsible and burdensome to taxpayers.[26] But as it turned out, Tea Partiers had greater animosity for the big-ticket bailout and stimulus programs that Obama launched in the face of the financial crisis. Conservative leaders sought to focus on the legislative priorities of the Obama administration, which drifted away from bailing out defaulting homeowners. Rage against undeserving homeowners never caught on, typical of the mercurial and situational character of Tea Party mobilization.

Less than one month later, on Tax Day, April 15, came the beginning of the second Tea Party wave, with three hundred thousand people demonstrating across the country.[27] The sudden and sharp increase in the scale of protest meant that the five conservative leadership groups could no longer directly administer the Tea Party on a day-to-day basis. After two months, direct control of local Tea Party groups by FreedomWorks-#tcot-Smart Girl Politics-dontgo-American Majority had faded. What remained was the ability to *facilitate mobilization* in the second wave. Facilitation was now in the hands of a broad network of Republican Party and staunch conservative organizations.

As will be seen in the following case studies, Young Republicans and Libertarian Party organizations provided facilitating networks and experienced local leaders who could produce volunteers and local publicity. Think tanks (Cato Institute and the Heritage Foundation) provided speakers for rallies and events, and leadership training for local organizers. Business-originated political and interest groups (Americans for Prosperity, Citizens for a Sound Economy, and National Federation of Independent Businesses) furnished fact sheets with arguments. Publications (*American Spectator*) and media outlets (Fox News) also reinforced the Tea Party's talking points and gave recognition and legitimacy to new local activists in both the February 27 and the April 15 Tea Party gatherings.

Sociologist and historian Charles Tilly used the term *facilitation* to describe assistance given to social movements like the Tea Party, whose members were political newcomers but who nevertheless gained support from "polity members" regularly included in deliberations.[28] Sometimes, as Craig Jenkins and Charles Perrow pointed out in the case of the United Farm Workers, insurgency is facilitated by liberal and labor leadership.[29] But elite facilitation is more common for conservative "countermovements" that have arisen in opposition to leftist movements.[30]

In short, facilitation provided resources to local groups that led to further Tea Party mobilization, a process common to many social movements. In many localities in the second wave, in the spring of 2009, mobilization ran high, producing Tea Party groups with much citizen involvement and activism. Some of the cases of high involvement, as will be seen in the following material, were in localities that had been targeted for test marketing the Tea Party by the Nationwide Tea Party Coalition. But there were also examples of highly mobilized Tea Party groups in localities that had not been included in the test marketing, demonstrating their relatively independent vitality.

Through the varied origins of mobilization in the second wave, high levels of Tea Party involvement came not only from facilitation by Republican organizations, but also from the rapid communication of credible signs that gave the appearance of strong popular mobilization, a phenomenon known as "demonstration effects."[31] A successful mobilization, such as the February 27, 2009 Tea Parties, changes the expectations of all those involved: activists, potential joiners, the authorities, and bystanders. Involved groups shift their views about the effort required, the costs of protest, the likelihood of successful mobilization, and the possibilities that recognition, power, and concessions will be granted to the movement. The first wave of thirty thousand protestors demonstrated the advantages of mobilization to the second wave, which soon became three hundred thousand strong.

MARGINAL AUTONOMY AND AFFILIATION AMONG TEA PARTY ORGANIZATIONS

The hallmark of the first wave was sites such as dontgo.com and chicagoteaparty.com that conservative leadership organizations had reserved in advance. The larger, second-wave mobilization made increasing use of inclusive and open local networks—social networking sites such as Facebook and Twitter, and Internet organizing tools such as Meetup. High levels of mobilization meant that the conservative leadership circle of FreedomWorks-#tcot-Smart Girl Politics-dontgo-American Majority had created a self-sustaining movement that had avoided the trap of continuing dependency on patrons. Successful mobilization in some localities created power bases,[32] at times headed by charismatic movement activists enjoying marginal autonomy from the direct authority of conservative leaders.[33] Local activists could chart their own political strategy somewhat independently, negotiating their way among different coalitions of Tea Party groups.

After their second wave of growth, Tea Party groups organized in loosely coupled networks. These networks formed several umbrella groups: the Patriotic Resistance (ResistNet), the Tea Party Express, and the Tea Party Patriots. The Patriots became the preeminent coordinating group. Of the twelve members on the national coordinating team of the Tea Party Patriots, three were first-wave founding mothers and fathers of the Tea Party movement. The Patriots included 2,200 affiliated groups and 115,000 registered members, the most among any coalition.[34]

From its earliest days, the Tea Party had spread the idea that it included not only Republicans, but also Independents, Libertarians, and even Democrats opposed to government and politicians as usual in the two-party system. The idea caught on like a Midwest grass fire among some activists and leaders affiliated with the Patriotic Resistance. Consequently, the Tea Party Express, which on the surface was a standard bus tour providing GOP campaign speakers and entertainment, became a flash point of controversy among Tea Party activists who wished to maintain autonomy from the Republican establishment. Many saw the Express as a vehicle for raising money for the political campaigns of Republicans who would be chosen by GOP elites, and not by the Tea Party itself. In the heyday of Tea Party growth, groups and entire Tea Party coalitions rejected the Tea Party Express, oblivious to the Freedom Works Republican leaders who had helped create the Tea Party in the first place.[35]

For the most part, the autonomy of Tea Party groups was limited because, even in the absence of direct hierarchical control, social forces such as resource dependency and conformity[36] influenced the affiliations of local Tea Party groups. Even in some Tea Party groups that were not coordinated by national organizations, zealous local leaders were eventually attracted to fiscal conservative organizations that promised the drastic change that mobilized Tea Party followings demanded.

The process of affiliation, negotiated by each Tea Party group in its own way, would determine the outcome of the debate over the Tea Party's place in the two-party system. At the end of 2009, many Tea Party groups, even those that were not initiated by the Nationwide Tea Party Coalition in February 2009, had affiliated with FreedomWorks, the economic conservative organization that had stood behind the founders. An economic conservative movement had opened the way for newly organized constituencies to rejuvenate the GOP.

THE GRASS ROOTS AND POLITICAL ORGANIZATION, RIGHT AND LEFT

Although the pattern of mobilization and goal adjustment in the Tea Party is unique in some ways, other social movements have followed a similar trajectory. A social movement of the left in the 1960s, Students for a Democratic Society (SDS), foreshadowed how the leadership of national organizations could be disrupted by the rapid mobilization of an intransigent movement.

The Tea Party began with a small circle of leadership groups, with a well-articulated ideology,[37] and a vision of a widespread movement that would transform American politics. SDS also started small, with a leadership circle based in universities in the Northeast and upper Midwest, and in the cities of Chicago and New York.[38]

Movement organization in both the first wave of the Tea Party and in SDS was based on principles and carefully designed strategy, all directed by central offices and punctuated with manifestos and national leadership conferences. But a larger wave of grassroots protest, both in the case of the Tea Party and SDS, changed the organizational form of the movement. A rapid expansion of antiwar protests brought into SDS new groups of "Prairie Fire" activists from the universities and cities of the Great Plains, overwhelming the established leadership of the movement.[39] Both SDS and the Tea Party held demonstrations and picketed against opposing politicians. The Prairie Fire of SDS was the analog of the Grassfire of the Tea Party, as the Astroturf of conservative leadership became the kindling for a movement. The sheer increase in the size of a movement made possible an increase in local autonomy and the formation of rival coordinating networks, as will be shown in the following case studies.

In the rapidly growing Tea Party of the second wave, where it seemed that any angry rant could bring cheers and determined action, images of militancy were king, as they were in the latter days of SDS. A media audience determined what was militant and effective: network television and the *New York Times* for SDS; and Fox News, video streaming, and social networking for the Tea Party.

But despite the spotlight on intransigents, these factions in the Tea Party, who condemned "Republicans in Name Only," competed with other factions who supported the Republican who could beat the Democrat regardless of stands on the issues. Although the moderates in the antiwar movement did prevail, how the Republican establishment, exemplified by the 2012 presidential candidacy of Mitt Romney, will change to accommodate the Tea Party has yet to be determined.

The remainder of this chapter develops case studies of local Tea Party groups. The cases illustrate the interconnection between test marketing, facilitation, mobilization, marginal autonomy, and affiliation in the Tea Party's progression through its first and second waves in 2009.[40] Considered first are four Tea Party groups from among the eighteen that participated in the first-wave test marketing. All of the four highly mobilized groups continued into the second wave. Even among these test-marketing groups, mobilization led to marginal autonomy sufficient for two local Tea Party activists to become national leaders of a new organization, the Tea Party Patriots. Later groups that emerged in the second wave demonstrated differences in the affiliations that decentralized Tea Parties had developed. Following, we consider the types of facilitation conservative groups provided, and the patterns of affiliation between second-wave groups and umbrella organizations and leadership groups that led to activities with different purposes.

BOSTON TEA PARTY: BRAD MARSTON AND CHRISTEN VARLEY

Brad Marston, organizer of the Boston Tea Party, participated in national conference calls with Tea Party organizers beginning in February 2009,[41] but the group's organizing efforts were mainly facilitated by Marston's position in established state and local GOP organizations. Marston describes himself on his Meetup page as a "life long Republican," and on his Facebook wall, his "likes" are the Massachusetts Republican Party and the Red Mass Group. The Boston Tea Party's assistant organizer, Christen Varley, ran a blog GOPmom.com, worked for the Coalition for Marriage and Family, and had worked for seventeen years in the state and local-level GOP, beginning with campaigns in Ohio.[42]

Facilitation from local GOP networks and the media helped push Boston Tea Party mobilization to high levels—a 2009 Tax Day attendance of two thousand, as reported in media accounts.[43] After Tax Day, the group maintained high mobilization through regular monthly meetings to organize events and hear speakers—twelve gatherings on Meetup in 2009, with a total attendance of 265.[44] Throughout Greater Boston, Tea Party meetings reenacted American traditions of town hall democracy, giving credence to their claim of grassroots virtue.[45]

Facilitation helped determine not only the level of mobilization, but also its focus. The strategy of the Republican establishment was to defeat President Obama's legislative agenda. After the stimulus bill was passed, health care reform became the overriding issue. For fiscally conservative leaders, taxes, regulation, spending on social welfare, burdens on small business, and the individual mandate to purchase heath insurance made health care reform anathema as well as a good target for GOP campaigning. The health care issue maintained the unity between the Republican establishment and staunch fiscal conservatives. In keeping with the fiscal-conservative priorities communicated through the conference calls, the Boston Tea Party held four meetings in 2009 to discuss and plan opposition to Obama's health care reform,[46] including a rally at Boston Common (October 17, 2009). When the Boston Common event was held, however, there was a relatively small turnout of 150,[47] suggesting that the local rank and file were less enthusiastic on this issue than national leaders.

High levels of mobilization in the Boston group around other issues opened the door to marginal autonomy. It meant that the Boston Tea Party would not have to rely on national leadership groups for an inflow of resources. In the second wave, the Boston Tea Party had no obvious affiliations with national organizations such as Tea Party Patriots, Patriotic Resistance, or FreedomWorks. By February 2010, Christen Varley had become president of the Greater Boston Tea Party, a coalition of suburban groups, but that coalition also lacked direct affiliation with conservative groups.[48] The group's limited autonomy from the GOP establishment allowed it to stick to its guns on certain issues rather than merely work for a GOP electoral victory.

In Boston, marginal autonomy fostered rhetoric that expressed a yearning for new policy departures beyond the compromises of the GOP. To move beyond big government spending was to think beyond the two-party system, to herald the rhetoric of nonpartisanship and appeal to independents, Libertarians, and even Democrats as well as Republicans. The speakers at the 2009 Tax Day rally included the standard Republican speakers from the Heritage Foundation and Smart Girl Politics, but also Carla Howell, the Libertarian candidate for Massachusetts's governor.[49] Members of the Boston Tea Party periodically expressed distaste for GOP politicians campaigning at Tea Party gatherings. After the July 4, 2009 Tea Party, an activist on the Meetup site wrote, "HAVING POLITICIANS CAMPAIGNING THERE WAS AWFUL. One of the good things about the Tea Parties we have attended was the lack of politicians. The next meeting we will be more careful to read the speakers list and not attend if there are too many" [caps in the original].[50] One member blurred party lines further to transcend the left–right distinction altogether. This member enthusiastically reported that he had spoken with a woman sympathetic to the peace movement who was concerned with government power, particularly the power of the Federal Reserve Board: "She was 100% on board with the reasoning behind End the Fed!!!"[51]

Despite the criticisms of GOP politicians, as the election of 2010 approached, GOP electoral victory began to seem more important to Tea Party members. True to Marston's and Varley's GOP roots, the Boston group hosted a stop on the Tea Party Express's bus tour, the heretofore-mentioned Republican campaign project. As 2009 turned into 2010, the Boston Tea Party began to organize events to support the election of Republican Scott Brown for U.S. Senate, which would bring the Tea Party into closer cooperation with the Republican Party. Beginning on December 29, 2009, Varley made individual postings to the Brown campaign's website (BrownBrigade).[52]

Varley's reasons for supporting Brown had to do with the tenacity of Brown's conservative positions, not how Brown would strengthen the GOP establishment, which was reluctant to support him at first: "I think Scott Brown has made clear his position on the Obama/Left agenda re: HC Reform, Cap and Trade, Amnesty and Card Check. To block these four agenda items is to save us all decades of economic disaster. . . . Scott will 'Kill the Bill!' [on health care reform]." In effect, the Scott campaign at the end of 2009 seemed the perfect fusion between the intransigence and activism of Tea Party volunteers and successful Republican National Committee (RNC) electoral strategy.[53] This fusion would eventually come apart due to Brown's votes in favor of the Dodd-Frank financial reform bill and other Democratic legislation.[54] The tension between fiscal intransigence and compromising Republicanism would continue in Boston and in the Tea Party generally.

PUNTA GORDA, FLORIDA: TEA PARTY PATRIOTS, ROBIN STUBLEN

Like Boston, Punta Gorda was targeted by the initial test-marketing effort. The Punta Gorda Tea Party received high levels of facilitation by fiscal conservative organizations, produced much mobilization, and consequently developed marginal autonomy. Facilitation of the Punta Gorda group became particularly significant in the first wave of the Tea Party movement, when American Majority offered a four-hour seminar to train activists in coalition building and the use of new media. As one group organizer wrote, "The cost to the Punta Gorda Tea Party, Inc. is zero," with American Majority paying for the trainers' travel and rental of the town's convention center.[55] The American Majority is an economic conservative group, led by Ned Ryun, formerly a writer for George W. Bush, and son of former Congressional Representative Jim Ryun. Seventy-five percent of American Majority's budget comes from the Sam Adams Alliance (an organization with a $4 million budget).[56] The training session was typical of the national, top-down approach of the first-wave Tea Party.

With this facilitation, Punta Gorda, a town of 17,000 on the less populated west coast of Florida, was able to achieve a relatively high mobilization, organizing a number of local meetings with good turnouts. That mobilization translated into marginal autonomy, and throughout 2009, the Punta Gorda group did little to strengthen its affiliation with any GOP organizations. On the contrary, Punta Gorda's leader Robin Stublen criticized some of those organizations for failing to reflect the true grassroots character of the Tea Party. Stublen criticized events such as a 2009 Tea Party Nation convention in Nashville for charging high attendance fees.[57]

On December 27, 2009, a Stublen post appeared on ResistNet (the Patriotic Resistance) sharply critical of how the Tea Party Express/Our Country Deserves Better PAC used the $1.2 million that it raised in 2009 for purchases of campaign advertising. Stublen concluded that the Tea Party Express was "GOP Astroturf."[58] Here, the idea that a part of the Tea Party was Astroturf was coming not from left-wing blogs, but from a faction of the Tea Party itself.

Stublen had misgivings about working for the GOP and eventually reaffiliated with economic conservative leadership groups, which began focusing on the November 2010 election. On September 12, 2010, Stublen was a featured speaker at the Taxpayer March on Washington, sponsored by FreedomWorks,[59] which had test-marketed the Tea Party concept in February 2009. FreedomWorks also had been a sponsor of the Tea Party Express bus tour that Stublen had roundly criticized, putting him in an awkward position. But by the end of 2010, all had been forgiven, or at least forgotten. On September 15, Stublen had an active page on the FreedomWorks website;[60] by March 2011, the Punta Gorda Tea Party website had the FreedomWorks logo at the top of its homepage.[61] It had taken sixteen months for Punta Gorda to reaffiliate with fiscal conservative leadership, much longer compared to other Tea Party groups.

SEATTLE: SONS AND DAUGHTERS OF LIBERTY, KELI CARENDER

Keli Carender's Seattle group is an example of a test-marketed local-ity and a facilitated group that developed some organizational and strategic autonomy before reentering the fiscal-conservative leadership fold, thereby reinvigorating the leadership from below. Carender's first protest action, directed against Obama's stimulus plan, is noteworthy because of its timing; it took place on February 16, 2009, three days before Rick Santelli's rant. Carender's first protest amounted to an ini-tial feasibility trial, a preview before the test marketing. Carender's pro-test against the "porkulus"[62] attracted about one hundred participants, some of whom wore pig noses. Describing the event, Michelle Malkin writes: "Others waved Old Glory and 'Don't Tread on Me' flags. Their handmade signs read: . . . 'Obama'$ Porkulu$ Wear$ Lip$tick' and 'I don't want to pay for the SwindleUs! I'm only 10 years old!' The event was peaceful, save for an unhinged city-dweller who barged onto the speakers' stage and gave a Nazi salute."[63]

Carender's work earned her a seat of honor at the daily FreedomWorks-#tcot-Smart Girl Politics-dontgo-American Majority conference calls. Carender, like Marston in Boston, was also cultivated by established Republican organizations, having joined the local Young Republicans late in 2008. In the liberal environs of Seattle, she rose to be chair of the state of Washington Young Republican Federation. Carender's February 2009 protest was aided by a plug from Seattle talk radio host Kirby Wilbur, and an announcement on the blog of Michelle Malkin, well known for her ties to leading conservatives. On February 17, 2009, a second Seattle protest turned out six hundred participants; the Tax Day protest drew 1,200. A one-year commemoration of the first porkulus protest attracted six hundred.[64]

Mobilization of the Seattle group was facilitated not only by Republicans and economic conservatives and their media, but also by inclusive networks and tools, such as locally administered Internet sites. Since January 2009, Carender had been writing as "Liberty Belle" on her own independent blog, *Redistributing Knowledge*. To organize her February 2009 protest, Carender developed her own email list of one thousand people in Seattle.

Carender continually strengthened her affiliations with well-known economic conservative leaders. In May 2009, she began to post a few of her libertarian blog entries on the website Red County.[65] Carender's fiscal conservative affiliations led her to work against Obama's legislative agenda, producing the memorable moment in 2009, when Carender challenged a Democratic House member at a town hall on health care reform. "If you believe that it is absolutely moral to take my money and give it to someone else based on their supposed needs," she said, waving a twenty dollar bill to boos and cheers, "then you come and take this $20 and use it as a down payment on this health care plan."[66] Libertarians and Republicans together could easily work against "Obamacare," but cutting Social Security and Medicare would be another matter.

Although facilitation by conservatives produced a group in Seattle that did its part to build the GOP opposition to Obama, Carender's role in that opposition was one of her own crafting, derived from libertarian principles. Carender did not quarrel with the GOP leadership over electoral tactics, as did members of the Boston group, and Stublen in Punta Gorda. Nevertheless, like Boston and Punta Gorda, Seattle showed signs of autonomy from Republican leadership despite Carender's history with the GOP and most likely due to her status as an early leader, a successful mobilizer, and a thoughtful strategist.

Throughout 2009, Seattle Sons and Daughters of Liberty remained unaffiliated with national Tea Party umbrella groups. It was not until February 24, 2010, that Carender's group was listed on the Tea Party Patriots website.[67] The Facebook page of Seattle Sons and Daughters lists the group as a Tea Party Patriots Affiliate, although only three entries on the Facebook page directly refer to activities of the Tea Party Patriots.[68] In January 2010, about a year after her first protest, FreedomWorks flew Carender to Washington for training by that conservative leadership organization.[69] Carender was profiled on March 15, 2010, on the blog of Stacy Mott, founder of Smart Girl Politics, linking her back to where she began—networking on the February 2009 conference calls.[70] In the Seattle case, as in Punta Gorda, organizational autonomy had turned out to be but a one-year detour to working with economic conservative elites. The detour, moreover, had strengthened the Tea Party in Seattle and elsewhere.

HOUSTON: TEA PARTY SOCIETY, FELICIA CRAVENS AND RYAN HECKER

Like Marston, Stublen, and Carender, Felicia Cravens in Houston took part in the post–Santelli conference calls that planned the February 27 Tea Party. The Houston case is noteworthy because national fiscal conservative groups facilitated the Tea Party Society at every turn. In Washington on February 23, Brendan Steinhauser listed the upcoming Houston event on the FreedomWorks website.[71] In addition, the incipient Houston Tea Party received facilitation from 9/12 Houston, an active chapter (with 220 past meetups) of the 9/12 organization, founded by former Fox News TV host Glenn Beck. Beginning on February 24, 2009, 9/12 Houston promoted the first Houston Tea Party gathering.[72] Later, Beck himself publicized an April 15 Houston event on his show, and interviewed Cravens.[73]

Houston's participation in the February test marketing provided ongoing access to conservative elite facilitation and guidance. Just two weeks after the February 27 protests, the Leadership Institute (whose president, Morton Blackwell, was a long-standing conservative leader) held a daylong training seminar in Houston for Tea Party members.[74] Soon afterward, confusion over the group's affiliations was resolved in favor of the original test-marketing leaders. A local organizer criticized the Houston group's Meetup site because it was created by an out-of-stater and because it was not controlled by the Houston group. Organizer Cravens then reminded the members that the Houston Tea Party Society continued to be affiliated with #tcot, Smart Girl Politics, and dontgo, the sponsors of the test marketing. Cravens created a new site, the Official Houston Tea Party Meetup.[75] Conservative leaders at the national level were instrumental in providing publicity, Internet marketing help, the time and expertise of staffers in DC, and speakers at events. Houston organizers communicated with Americans for Prosperity, funded by the Koch family, to recruit speakers.[76] Before the very first Houston rally, a local activist announced, "Americans for Prosperity will be attending the rally, and we encourage everyone to wear RED to show Congress how angry we are. . . ."[77]

Four hundred people attended that first rally on February 27. That day Ryan Hecker left his law firm of Vinson and Elkins for lunch and saw the crowd. "I went up and said, 'What is this?'" Hecker recalls. "And they said, 'It's pretty much an economic conservative protest,' which is just unheard of . . . before. And so I was very interested right away."[78]

Beginning in March 2009, the Houston Tea Party Society mobilized rapidly, reaching a very high level of mobilization—twenty-two meetings that were extensively documented through messaging on the Houston Tea Party Society website. Meetings included open microphones, where participants could do their own version of the Santelli rant that was "heard around the world." On Tax Day 2009, the Houston Tea Party organized demonstrations throughout the metro area, attracting 8,500 protesters at Jones Plaza in downtown Houston, 7,000 in Woodlands, 1,000 at Sugarland Town Hall, 900 at Clear Lake, and 800 in Tomball,[79] an overwhelming display of grassroots action.

The conference calls provided Houston with direction on conservative priorities such as opposing health care reform. As in Boston, a confluence developed in Houston between Republican and fiscal conservative strategies. After the 2009 Tax Day event, the Houston Tea Party organized eight actions to oppose the Obama health care bill, including two protests against House Speaker Nancy Pelosi (one drawing six hundred protestors, by a press account), picketing against an infomercial on ABC about the Democratic bill, a short-notice "flash mob,"[80] and vociferous protests at town hall meetings of congressional representatives, the signature event of Tea Parties in mid-2009.

After its rapid mobilization, the Houston Tea Party Society's principal affiliation was firmly with the Tea Party Patriots. As Joshua Parker, one of the original organizers, put it, "[T]he real one, the one that was formally Tax Day Tea Party is now TEA PARTY PATRIOTS!!! Clearing up the confusion . . . It's THE National Organizer and the one to plug into. We're in it, Sugarland is in it, The Woodlands is in it, heck, everyone! If your Tea Party is not in it, well you better get on board! If someone else is claiming to be national organizer, RUN!!! Non-Partisan, not Lobbyists, don't even have an office in DC."[81] Attorney Ryan Hecker was the Houstonian asked to join the National Coordinator Team of the Tea Party Patriots. Later in an interview, Hecker made clear his differences with the Republican establishment. "Hecker rejected any commonality with the GOP, declaring the Republican Party has lost its legitimacy. He called the vote for TARP (the Troubled Asset Relief Program), 'Republican cronyism at its worse,' and predicted [Representative John] Boehner would eventually come crawling to the Tea Party Patriots to endorse the Contract FROM America [a Tea Party platform Hecker developed]."[82]

In Houston, given the Tea Party's firm affiliation with the Patriots, there was little organizational autonomy from Tea Party coalitions or from fiscal conservative leadership. As in Punta Gorda, there was also limited strategic autonomy from the GOP establishment. The Houston Tea Party criticized the Tea Party Express bus tour as campaign activity controlled by GOP elites rather than highlighting conservative positions. Organizer Joshua Parker went so far as to tell the Express bus tour *not* to stop in Houston and Austin. Houston organizers, supported by many members on the Houston Tea Party site, engaged in a remarkable online, ninety-seven-response debate with Joe W (probably Joe Wierzbicki of the Express). The Express's fund raising for Republican candidates could not win the support of the Houston Tea Party, because it violated their 501(c) (4) tax exemption, and because mainstream Republicans were complicit with big government spending.[83] Houston's mobilized base and its affiliation with the Patriots, the largest and most grassroots of the umbrella organizations, enabled it to unexpectedly challenge GOP campaigning that had been controlled from above.

The idea of challenging the two-party establishment with resurgent economic conservatism, which would ultimately benefit Republicans, was planted by some national leaders from the beginning of the Tea Party. From February 2009, conservative grassroots organizer Eric Odom saw his approach as markedly different from that of the Republican National Committee and its chair, Michael Steele.[84] In Felicia Cravens's interview on the Glenn Beck show, a defining event for the Houston Tea Party, Beck established her grassroots credentials and helped her refine her public identity as independent from the Republican Party.[85]

ATLANTA, GEORGIA: THE PEACH STATE TEA PARTY, JENNY BETH MARTIN

Jenny Beth Martin heard the February 19, 2009 Santelli rant on CNBC, and the next day began organizing first-wave Tea Party protests. On February 20, she began participating in the daily conference calls.[86] Going back to June 2007, Martin had been blogging at *Jen's Genuine Life: Tips, Tales, and Thoughts from a Peach State Mom of Twins*. Martin did local campaign work for presidential candidate Mike Huckabee in 2008, although she was not as involved in the GOP as Marston in Boston or Carender in Seattle. At the end of 2008, she was learning from the Top Conservatives on Twitter site and Smart Girl Politics, funded and led by the stalwart economic conservative leaders who organized the conference calls.[87]

After the February 27 demonstration at the Georgia capitol mobilized a crowd of five hundred, Martin continued working with conservative elites organizing the April 15, 2009 Tax Day Tea Party protest. She spent twenty hours a week arranging speakers, holding local meetings, and publicizing the event. In an interview with the *Washington Post*, Martin reconciled the grassroots character of the Tea Party movement with the participation of economic conservative leaders, saying that they facilitated local activists and gave them credibility. Martin admitted that Americans for Tax Reform, the Heritage Foundation, and the National Taxpayers Union had compiled and distributed talking points for protests against the Obama health care legislation,[88] and seemed more helpful than the established Republican Party.

Martin was a leader in forming the Tea Party Patriots with the aim of providing an umbrella organization that could coordinate and offer national visibility for local groups. Less than a month after the Tax Day 2009 protests, Martin established a page and a blog on the Tea Party Patriots websites, containing posts from "Your Tea Party Patriots National Coordinator Team, Debbie Dooley, Jenny Beth Martin, Mark Meckler, Sally Oljar, Diana Reimer, and Dawn Wildman."[89]

In October 2009, Martin and the Patriots' national coordinator team signed a statement criticizing the Tea Party Express bus tour and its sponsor, Our Country Deserves Better PAC (OCDB) and thereby expressed strategic autonomy from the GOP establishment. The Patriots' coordinators argued, following the reasoning of Houston's stance earlier that month, that OCDB was a political action committee, most of whose expenditures went to the GOP consulting firm Russo Marsh and Rogers, which in turn passed on money to Republican candidates, listed on "page after page" of Federal Election Commission filings. While the Patriot coordinators admitted there was nothing wrong with PACs, they definitively emphasized, "This is not what the Tea Parties are about." A fundamental issue of identity was at stake here; the Patriots insisted that fiscal conservative issues came first, above any political party. Furthermore, the tax-exempt status of the Patriots prohibited direct partisan activity. The Patriot leaders categorically urged all local Tea Parties not to participate in the Tea Party Express's bus tour.[90] Many strongly mobilized groups had themselves evolved to the point where they eagerly agreed.

THE SECOND WAVE: ROCHESTER, NEW HAMPSHIRE; LAS CRUCES, NEW MEXICO; SPOKANE, WASHINGTON; PHILADELPHIA, PENNSYLVANIA; WACO, TEXAS

Neither part of the conference calls nor part of the first-wave mobilization, these Tea Party groups were facilitated in part by economic conservative leadership, but even more so by Republican institutions. They represented the wide germination of the grass roots, and their emergence would reshape the relation between conservative leaders and their political base—with lasting implications for American two-party politics.

The sources of facilitation varied. For the Rochester, New Hampshire, Tea Party (founded by Susan and Jerry DeLemus), facilitation (as in Houston) came through the 9/12 project, which was initiated through an on-air announcement by Glenn Beck on March 13, 2009, after the first wave but before the Tax Day rallies. New Hampshire leaders sought to imitate the demonstrated success of the February protests. The Rochester group experienced a surge in attendance, which was reflected on their Meetup site; 762 people attended twenty meetings between May 11, 2009 and the end of the year, a remarkable grassroots outpouring for a town of just 30,000.

Contrasting with the Rochester group, the Tea Party in Spokane (led by Dann Selle) relied on a mix of mainstream and conservative media, rather than just Fox News and its political groups:

> News Releases were sent out to all newspapers, TVs, and radio stations within a 100-mile area. Local talk show hosts Mike Fitzsimmons on KXLY radio [ABC affiliate], Spokane, WA. [and] Dr. Laurie Roth, a nationally syndicated host on KSBN [business] radio, Spokane, hosted [event organizer] Gary Edgington two times each. . . . Dann Selle dug into his own pocket and cut a public service announcement airing on KQNT [Clear Channel, featuring Fox News and Beck] news radio in Spokane that aired 15 times in a three-day period. . . . KHQ [NBC affiliate] television interviewed [m]edia rep., Dann Selle on the eve of the event, near the chosen location.[91]

Mainstream news was free publicity, but Fox News was charging for ads, a reversal of the usual media access for the Tea Party: free on Fox, but elsewhere, pay or be ignored.[92] In Spokane (population 200,000), Selle's group succeeded in organizing several events in 2009; the largest was a rally of five thousand on Tax Day 2009, followed by a July 4, 2009 demonstration, and a protest against health care reform directed against a congressional representative.[93]

The amount of time between the first event and an affiliation with a national group was unusually long in Spokane, indicating that mobilization had produced organizational autonomy as it did in Seattle and Punta Gorda. Selle's group affiliated with Patriotic Resistance eight months after its founding, and took seventeen months before affiliating with the Tea Party Patriots with a single posting on its national site. The Spokane Tea Party (because of its organizational autonomy and perhaps peripheral location) and the Rochester Tea Party (because of facilitated organizational strength) displayed some strategic autonomy from national GOP electoral politics, opening the door to varied political alternatives. The Spokane group was wary of supporting candidates for elected office due to its tax-exempt status, and focused on nonpartisan educational issues and state legislation instead,[94] using its marginal autonomy to distance itself from the DC leadership groups that wanted a focus on health care and greenhouse gas cap and trade. The Rochester group's marginal autonomy led it to local politics, resulting in (Meetup-registered) attendances of about 115 for local election campaigns, compared to 64 for national issues. Jerry and Susan DeLemus's runs for elected office also reflected Rochester's turn away from national to local partisanship. Jerry DeLemus ran for town mayor, as a pro-business fiscal conservative who nevertheless supported protective public services and improvements in education.[95] The Tea Party's sponsorship of numerous, well-attended events to discuss local elections gave the impression that the Tea Party was American grassroots politics at its finest.

For many Tea Party groups, the most common form of strategic autonomy was the pursuit of intransigent fiscal conservatism, borne not of organizational autonomy but rather affiliation with the Tea Party Patriots. Such marginal autonomy was exemplified by the history of the second-wave Philadelphia Tea Party Patriots. The Philadelphia group, led by Diane Reimer, affiliated with the Tea Party Patriots on March 17, 2009, as she was organizing her first events. Reimer rose to be a national coordinator of the Patriots, issuing memoranda in this role through at least January 2010. Most Tea Parties followed the lead of this main umbrella group and its more mobilized local groups like Houston and Philadelphia.[96] Members of Tea Party Patriots distanced themselves from the Tea Party Express and periodically asserted their independence from GOP big-tent politics.[97] After a group of local activists who were associated with the coalition DC Works for Us (founded by Karin Hoffman) announced their plans to meet with Republican National Committee chair Michael Steele, several Patriot leaders, including Jenny Beth Martin, asserted that the Patriots would not work closely with Republican leaders, and instead would prioritize fiscal conservative issues over party building.[98]

In contrast, the Las Cruces, New Mexico, Tea Party did become involved in national GOP campaigns. Lower levels of mobilization increased dependence on elite facilitation, reducing local organizational autonomy and discretionary judgments. The Las Cruces group played local host to a visit of the controversial Tea Party Express bus tour on September 1, 2009, attracting an audience of 1,300, according to press reports, including 53 from Las Cruces TEA who registered on Facebook. The group had three meetings in anticipation of the bus visit, indicating that national GOP linkages helped facilitate the activity of the local group. National media also facilitated; as Johnson exclaimed on the Facebook wall of the group, "FOX News will be doing 2 live shoots from the event!!! This is big! Be a part!!"[99]

The Tea Party Express bus tours were a divisive issue for the Tea Party movement. Another Tea Party group in Waco, Texas, like the one in Las Cruces, supported the Tea Party Express. The Waco group's support for the Express was noteworthy because Waco also had an early (by May 13, 2009) affiliation to the Tea Party Patriots, the group that five months later opposed the Express. In November 2009, both the Waco group and Toby Marie Walker, Texas state coordinator for the Patriots, quit the Patriots because of its criticism of the Express and because the Patriots sued its own board member that had gone over to work for the Express. The Waco group organized a rally of 4,000 when the Express bus stopped in Waco.[100] Striking the most effective balance between expediency in electoral campaigns and intransigence in fiscal conservatism would be an issue in 2010 and 2012. The mixture was cast not by reasoned decision, but by the actions of contending political organizations.

CONCLUSION

The Tea Party's use of its marginal autonomy revitalized the Republican Party. In response to the rise of the Tea Party, the GOP establishment could have dug in its heels, as the Democrats did in 1968, by nominating Hubert Humphrey for the presidency, a move that repudiated leftist grassroots pressures. For the Democrats, it would not be until 1972 that state and local rules changed to allow for more grassroots influence in the Democratic Party. Although grassroots revitalization led to the 1972 nomination of unsuccessful presidential candidate George McGovern, the Democratic grass roots triumphed in the election of the congressional Watergate Class of 1974, profoundly shaping not only foreign and domestic policy but the institution of Congress as well.

Republicans in 2010 were open to the Tea Party, allowing it to nominate some losing candidates like Christine O'Donnell, whose popular vote was only 2.5 percent better than George McGovern's. But the opening in the GOP for Tea Party candidates stimulated the turnout of conservative voters and led to the successful election of U.S. Senate candidates Rand Paul (KY) and Ron Johnson (WI), who will influence policy in the years to come, making at least one of the two major parties less of a catchall party and more of a European-style party with a consistent platform and message.

The debate over whether the Tea Party is Astroturf or grassroots is best understood in the context of whether political parties allow marginal autonomy in their ranks. Autonomy opens the possibility of energizing the base and revitalizing the party. The image of the Tea Party as grassroots, despite the fact that it belies how social movement mobilizations rely on facilitation and entrepreneurial leadership, has a crucial moral function in public discourse: to grant recognition to new groups not included in the formal party structure. The Tea Party members convinced themselves and convinced Republicans, even the big-tent variety, that the Tea Party was grassroots and deserved to nominate its candidates, win or lose, to energize the fight in elections.

Conversely, the metaphor that the Tea Party is Astroturf, despite highlighting the facilitation and the test marketing provided by leaders, has an important consequence for a political party: to delegitimize and therefore de-emphasize activity at the grassroots level. Democratic blogs say the Tea Party is Astroturf. Social movement analysis supports them. But being empirically correct has blindsided Democrats to the emerging strengths of GOP precinct organization at a time when the Democrats' own local organizations are under attack, be they trade unions, ACORN, the Green for All organization of Anthony K. "Van" Jones, the educational activism of William C. "Bill" Ayres, reproductive rights organizations, or the welfare rights movement and its intellectual leader, Frances Fox Piven.

Beginning in the 1970s, the new right assiduously studied the new left of the 1960s, with the specific aim of destroying left-wing movements that could reenergize the Democratic Party. The right also had an eye to adapting and applying leftist strategies, Alinsky included, to organize the conservative alternative. Today, liberals might learn from the experience of the Tea Party. Liberals ignore the Tea Party's grassroots record at their own peril.

NOTES

1. The author wishes to thank those who commented on earlier drafts, including J. Kenneth Benson, Victoria Johnson, and especially Nigel Lo, Darlaine Gardetto, Christine Trost, and Larry Rosenthal.

2. Scott Rasmussen and Doug Schoen, *Mad as Hell: How the Tea Party Movement Is Fundamentally Remaking Our Two-Party System* (New York: Harper Collins, 2010).

3. The autonomy was marginal in the sense that the increase was relatively small, at the margin in the terminology of economics, but nevertheless important in operational decision making.

4. A decentralized and autonomous structure is typical of large, rapidly growing social movements, which have the potential of regrouping political parties around issues of the right or the left.

5. Devin Burghart's chapter in this volume (Chapter 3) provides a detailed overview of the movement's national organizations.

6. Quoted in Elisabeth Bumiller, "Bush Aides Set Strategy to Sell Policy on Iraq," *New York Times,* September 7, 2002.

7. "Santelli's Tea Party," CNBC video, February 19, 2009, accessed May 23, 2011, http://video.cnbc.com/gallery/?video=1039849853; and "Rick Santelli's Chicago Tea Party in July," Facebook group, accessed on May 22, 2011, www.facebook.com/group.php?gid=51046649819&v=wall.

8. See Vanessa Williamson, Theda Skocpol, and John Coggin, "The Tea Party and the Remaking of Republican Conservatism," *Perspectives on Politics* 9, no. 1 (2011): 25–43. My application of the concept of test marketing to the first-wave Tea Party is consistent with the observations of Williamson, Skocpol, and Coggin, among others, that "National orchestrators draw their resources from a small number of very conservative business elites. . . ."

9. Nationwide Tea Party Coalition website, accessed March 30, 2011, www.nationwidechicagoteaparty.com/about.php; David A. Patten, "Party of the People," *Newsmax,* June 2010, 46–61, accessed October 31, 2011, http://w3.newsmax.com/a/jun10/party/; "The Local Organizers of 51 Tea Party Protests Held on February 27, 2009," Leadership Tea Party website, accessed on April 1, 2011, http://leadershipteaparty.com/pages/founders/. For connections between the Santelli rant, the Chicago Tea Party, the 9/12 Association, and February 27, 2009 events in Houston, see "Houston Tea Party—Feb. 27th 09 @ Discovery Green," 9/12 Members USA Meetup website, accessed September 18, 2011, www.meetup.com/912MembersUSA-Houston-Area-912ers/messages/boards/thread/6361623.

10. Milo Yiannopoulos, "A Message from Michael Patrick Leahy: Join the Chicago Tea Party!" *The Telegraph,* February 21, 2009, accessed October 4, 2011, http://blogs.telegraph.co.uk/technology/miloyiannopoulos/8662857/A_message_from_Michael_Patrick_Leahy_Join_The_Chicago_Tea_Party/.

11. So named as a slogan to stop House Speaker Nancy Pelosi from going on a tour in 2008 and delaying a House vote to extend offshore oil drilling. See the "Georgia Don't Go Movement" Facebook page, accessed May 25, 2011, www.facebook.com/group.php?gid=69575786803&v=info.

12. "Newt Joins the Party," Smart Girl Politics press release, March 19, 2009, accessed October 4, 2011, www.pr.com/press-release/139912.

13. Adam Brandon, "Citizens for a Sound Economy (CSE) and Empower America Merge to Form FreedomWorks," July 22, 2004, FreedomWorks.org website, accessed October 28, 2011, www.freedomworks.org/press-releases/citizens-for-a-sound-economy-cse-and-empower-ameri; "Citizens for a Sound Economy," Sourcewatch.org, accessed May 23, 2011, www.sourcewatch.org/index.php?title=Citizens_for_a_Sound_Economy; and "Attachment to CSE

President Paul Beckner's Response to Remarks Made by Oracle CEO Larry Ellison," FreedomWorks.org website, June 29, 2000, accessed May 23, 2011, www.freedomworks.org/press-releases/attachment-to-cse-president-paul -beckners-response. For earlier fiscal conservative leadership groups, see Jacob S. Hacker and Paul Pierson, "Tax Politics and the Struggle over Activist Government," in Paul Pierson and Theda Skocpol, ed., *The Transformation of American Politics: Activist Government and the Rise of Conservatism* (Princeton: Princeton University Press, 2007), 256–80.

14. Kenneth P. Vogel, "Tea Party's Growing Money Problem," Politico, August 9, 2010, accessed May 23, 2011, www.freedomworks.org/news/ tea-partys-growing-money-problem.

15. Jane Mayer, "Covert Operations: The Billionaire Brothers Who Are Waging a War against Obama," *The New Yorker*, August 30, 2010, 46–47.

16. "About Us," the Nationwide Tea Party Coalition website, accessed on March 30, 2011, www.nationwidechicagoteaparty.com/about.php.

17. "The Local Organizers of 51 Tea Party Protests Held on February 27, 2009," Leadership Tea Party website, accessed on May 22, 2011, http:// leadershipteaparty.com/pages/founders/.

18. "Jeff Frazee Interviews Brendan Steinhauser of FreedomWorks To Discuss the Tax Day Coalition," YouTube video, accessed May 23, 2011, www.youtube.com/watch?v=yHDFWViHL70.

19. Tim Dickinson, "The Lie Machine," *Rolling Stone* 1088 (October 1, 2009), 45–49.

20. Tim Dickinson, "The Lie Machine."

21. John D. McCarthy and Mayer N. Zald, "Resource Mobilization and Social Movements: A Partial Theory," *American Journal of Sociology* 82, no. 6 (1977): 1212–41.

22. Jane Hamsher, "A Teabagger Timeline: Koch, Coors, Newt, Dick Armey There from the Start," *HuffPost Politics* (blog), April 15, 2009, accessed May 22, 2011, www.huffingtonpost.com/jane-hamsher/a-teabagger-timeline -koch_b_187312.html; and Philip N. Howard, *New Media Campaigns and the Managed Citizen* (Cambridge: Cambridge University Press, 2005).

23. Information about the Santelli rant, Christenson domain registration, Odom, and Koch funding was the source of much controversy after it first appeared on the *Playboy* blog. See Mark Ames and Yasha Levine, "Backstabber: Is Rick Santelli High On Koch?" February 27, 2009, accessed May 25, 2011, www.freedomunderground.org/view.php?v=3&t=3&aid=25922; and "Whois Record for ChicagoTeaParty.com," DomainTools website, accessed May 22, 2011, http://whois.domaintools.com/chicagoteaparty.com; GinaMaria, "Set Up a Website in August for Future Outrage in February," February 21, 2009, DemocraticUnderground.com, last accessed October 29, 2011, www .democraticunderground.com/discuss/duboard.php?az=show_mesg&forum =389&topic_id=5102005&mesg_id=5102005; and Jonathan V. Last, "Gonna Have a Tea Party," *The Weekly Standard* 14, no. 24 (March 9, 2009), accessed May 22, 2011, www.weeklystandard.com/Content/Public/Articles/000/ 000/016/219pmhcs.asp.

24. "About Us," Nationwide Tea Party Coalition website, accessed March 30, 2011, www.nationwidechicagoteaparty.com/about.php; "Tea Party Update: Photos and Fox TV Video from Chicago," Instapundit.com, February 27, 2009, accessed May 22, 2011, http://pajamasmedia.com/instapundit/71537/; Brendan Steinhauser, "The Taxpayer Tea Party Movement is Growing," FreedomWorks .org website, February 23, 2009, accessed October 4, 2011, www.freedomworks .org/publications/the-taxpayer-tea-party-movement-is-growing; and Brendan Steinhauser, "2009 Taxpayer Tea Party," FreedomWorks.org website, accessed May 22, 2011, www.freedomworks.org/petition/iamwithrick/index.html.

25. "We had the pleasure of attending today's Chicago Tea Party rally in Daley Plaza. With the usual caveat that I am the worst estimator of crowd size I would call today's shindig in the 300 range." The Actual Chicago Chicago Tea Party!, posted by Jake in Uncategorized, January 27, 2009, accessed May 25, 2011, http://freedomfolks.com/?p=5748. Pictures and comment archived by author. Additional pictures and a smaller crowd estimate of the event are at www.foundingbloggers.com/wordpress/2009/02/breaking-chicago-tea-party-pictures/, last accessed November 4, 2011.

26. Michael M. Phillips, "Mortgage Bailout Infuriates Tenants (and Steve Forbes)—'Angry Renter' Web Site Has Grass-Roots Look, But This Turf Is Fake," *The Wall Street Journal,* May 16, 2008; and Alex Chadwick, "Big Money Backs Renters' Campaign," NPR's *Day to Day,* May 16, 2008, accessed May 25, 2011, www.npr.org/templates/transcript/transcript.php?storyId=90517606.

27. Patrik Jonsson, "Arguing the Size of the 'Tea Party' Protest," *The Christian Science Monitor,* April 18, 2009; and Nate Silver, "Tea Party Nonpartisan Attendance Estimates: Now 300,000+," *FiveThirtyEight* (blog), April 16, 2009, accessed May 25, 2011, www.fivethirtyeight.com/2009/04/tea-party-nonpartisan-attendance.html.

28. Charles Tilly, *From Mobilization to Revolution* (New York: Random House, 1978).

29. Craig J. Jenkins and Charles Perrow, "Insurgency of the Powerless: Farm Worker Movements (1946–1972)," *American Sociological Review* 42, no. 2 (1977): 249–68.

30. Clarence Y. H. Lo, "Countermovements and Conservative Movements in the Contemporary U.S." in *Annual Review of Sociology,* vol. 8, ed. R. H. Turner and J. F. Short Jr. (Palo Alto, CA: Annual Reviews, Inc., 1982), 107–34; Suzanne Staggenborg, *The Pro-Choice Movement: Organization and Activism in the Abortion Conflict* (New York: Oxford University Press, 1991); and Bert Useem, "Solidarity Model, Breakdown Model, and the Boston Anti-Busing Movement," *American Sociological Review* 45, no. 3 (1980): 357–69.

31. Theda Skocpol, *Social Revolutions in the Modern World* (New York: Cambridge University Press, 1979).

32. Clarence Y. H. Lo, "Communities of Challengers in Social Movement Theory," in *The Frontiers in Social Movement Theory,* ed. Aldon Morris and Carol Muller (New Haven, CT: Yale University Press, 1992), 224–27.

33. My analysis of marginal autonomy and its origins in the second-wave Tea Party is consistent with Williamson, Skocpol, and Coggin's assessment that "the Tea Parties are not operating under the guidance of official GOP

institutions. The Republican National Committee is not in charge, and neither are state party organs." See Williamson, Skocpol, and Coggin, "The Tea Party and the Remaking of Republican Conservatism."

34. Devin Burghart and Leonard Zeskind, *Tea Party Nationalism: A Critical Examination of the Tea Party Movement and the Size, Scope, and Focus of Its National Factions* (Kansas City, MO: Institute for Research and Education on Human Rights, 2010), 41.

35. Devin Burghart and Leonard Zeskind, *Tea Party Nationalism*, 54.

36. Clarence Y. H. Lo, *Small Property versus Big Government: Social Origins of the Property Tax Revolt*, 2nd ed. (revised and expanded paperback) (Berkeley: University of California Press, 1995).

37. Jerome L. Himmelstein, *To the Right: The Transformation of American Conservatism* (Berkeley: University of California Press, 1990).

38. Todd Gitlin, *The Whole World is Watching* (Berkeley: University of California Press, 2003), 82–85.

39. Gitlin, *The Whole World is Watching*, 129–39; and Wini Breines, *Community and Organization in the New Left, 1962–1968: The Great Refusal* (New Brunswick, NJ: Rutgers University Press, 1989).

40. The research methods used in this chapter are as follows:

Sampling: A sample was drawn from the universe of approximately one thousand local Tea Party groups that had existed through 2009. To sample the composition of a movement at an earlier time, one should rely on a printed documentary source whose content was frozen around that earlier date, that is, a printed source or a PDF of an Internet source taken at the earlier date.

An excellent printed source for a historical sample were the footnotes of Scott Rasmussen and Doug Schoen's book *Mad As Hell: How the Tea Party Movement Is Fundamentally Remaking Our Two-Party System* (New York: Harper Collins, 2010), which contained citations to printed and web articles in major daily newspapers (including the *New York Times*, the *Wall Street Journal*, and the *Washington Post*), magazines (again including web versions), and blogs from all parts of the political spectrum. From the footnotes to *Mad As Hell*, I compiled a comprehensive list of the names of nineteen activists and their associated groups that organized Tea Party protests going back through February 2009.

Mobilization: To find out about the 2009 actions of the nineteen local activists, the names of the activists and their groups were Googled, and at least the first twenty entries were examined. Sources included press accounts in national and community newspapers, Internet media and blogs from the left and the right (such as PJTV and NewsMax), and the activist's and the group's pages on the web, Facebook, and/or Twitter. On those sites, blogs and discussion boards were thoroughly examined, beginning with February 2009, if available. Pages on the site meetup.com were particularly useful, because they provided a comprehensive list of past announcements of business meetings and special events (collective actions such as demonstrations, picketing, and protests; speakers; and picnics and other celebrations), as well as members' reactions to the announcements, and evaluations of the events by attendees. The cases discussed in this chapter were the ones displaying the highest levels of mobilization.

Facilitation: One objective for the research was to discover for each of the nineteen groups the mix of resources that came from local donations, contrasted to support from conservative leadership organizations, and how various forms of support were instrumental in mobilizing Tea Party actions. The websites of local groups provided useful information, as did the discussion threads, the pages of individuals, and the staff directories on sites of national organizations like the Nationwide Tea Party Coalition, FreedomWorks, and Tea Party Patriots. Biographical information about individual activists provided clues to the networks (Young Republicans, Red County, previous campaign work) that may have contributed resources at the time of Tea Party mobilization. Publicity given to an activist by well-known blogs, organizations, or mass media outlets like Fox News was considered as an external resource and was noted, as were training sessions offered by conservative leadership groups.

41. My account of the Boston Tea Party adds to Williamson et al. who do not discuss Brad Marston in their case study of that group. See Williamson, Skocpol, and Coggin, "The Tea Party and the Remaking of Republican Conservatism."

42. David Riley, "Holliston Woman Leads Boston Tea Party," *Metrowest Daily News*, February 22, 2010.

43. Nate Silver, "Tea Party Nonpartisan Attendance Estimates: Now 300,000+," *FiveThirtyEight* (blog), April 16, 2009, accessed May 25, 2011, www.fivethirtyeight.com/2009/04/tea-party-nonpartisan-attendance.html.

44. Meetup attendance figures for large events are understated, and reflect only the number of followers on just the Meetup site who say they attended. Meetup attendance for the 2009 Tax Day rally was 105. Many members attend without notifying, and others use websites such as Facebook and Twitter to receive announcements and record their attendance. Assistant Organizer Christen Varley commented that 600 had signed up for the Tax Day rally on Facebook, and other political groups were bringing hundreds. Attendance at regular monthly planning meetings is more likely to be estimated accurately by Meetup. The number of meetings in a year is another good measure of group activity. The website Meetup provides the best account of the Boston Tea Party's meetings.

45. Robert N. Bellah, Richard Madsen, William M. Sullivan, Ann Swidler, and Steven M. Tipton, *Habits of the Heart: Individualism and Commitment in American Life* (Berkeley and Los Angeles: University of California Press, 1985); and Claude S. Fischer, *Made in America: A Social History of American Culture and Character* (Chicago: University of Chicago Press, 2010).

46. This number is equal to the median number of such meetings among Tea Party groups where documentation of meetings was available.

47. "Healthcare Reform Rally," October 17, 2009, Boston Tea Party Meetup page, accessed May 25, 2011, www.meetup.com/Boston-Tea-Party/events/11512555/.

48. David Riley, "Holliston Woman Leads Boston Tea Party."

49. "The Latest News—Boston Tax Day Tea Party," Boston Tea Party Meetup page, April 7, 2009, accessed May 25, 2011, www.meetup.com/Boston-Tea-Party/messages/boards/thread/6643748.

50. "Boston Independence Day Tea Party," Boston Tea Party Meetup page, July 4, 2009, accessed March 21, 2011, www.meetup.com/Boston-Tea-Party/events/10197681/.

51. "Boston Tax Day Tea Party Meetup," Boston Tea Party Meetup page, April 15, 2009, accessed March 27, 2011, www.meetup.com/Boston-TeaParty/events/9927674/.

52. "Reply by Christen Varley," Brown Brigade website, December 29, 2009, accessed April 17, 2011, http://brownbrigade.ning.com/forum/topics/will-the-conservative-tide?commentId=3990693%3AComment%3A10219.

53. "Reply by Phil," Brown Brigade website, December 29, 2009, accessed April 17, 2011, http://brownbrigade.ning.com/forum/topics/will-the-conservative-tide?commentId=3990693%3AComment%3A10219. David Catanese, on Politico, quoted Brendan Steinhauser that FreedomWorks thought Brown was a long shot until late December 2009, but then helped in the campaign, as did Tea Party Express: "The only way for somebody to raise the amount of money he [Brown] raised was through the tea party movement getting excited around the country. They were basically online bundlers. . . ." See David Catanese, "Did Tea Party Stir Brown's Victory?" Politico, January 22, 2010, accessed May 26, 2011, www.politico.com/news/stories/0110/31832.html.

54. Doug Powers, "Scott Brown Will Vote for Dodd-Frank Bill," MichelleMalkin.com, July 12, 2010, accessed May 25, 2011, michellemalkin.com/2010/07/12/scott-brown/.

55. "Training Seminar in Punta Gorda," Forum, June 5, 2009 entry, accessed May 23, 2011, http://pgteaparty.ning.com/forum/topics/training-seminar-in-punta.

56. Quin Hillyer, "After the Tea Parties," *The Grassroots Spectator*, June 2009.

57. Chris Good, "Is Palin's Tea Party Speech a Mistake?" *The Atlantic* website, February 4, 2010, accessed October 9, 2010, www.theatlantic.com/politics/archive/2010/02/is-palins-tea-party-speech-a-mistake-tea-partiers-have-mixed-opinions/35360/.

58. Stublen continued, "[W]hat would the true grassroots people think if they knew their money is being spent in this manner?" See "Robin Stublen Reports on Tea Party Express Expenses: Since ResistNet Backed Them Let's Take a Look," posted by Terrence Boggs, December 27, 2009, in Texas Patriotic Resistance website, copied to Patriot Action Network website, www.patriotactionnetwork.com/group/lonestarpatriots/forum/topics/robin-stublen-reports-on-tea-1; reposting archived by author. See also Chris Good, "Is Palin's Tea Party Speech a Mistake?"

59. Jacqueline Bodnar, "FreedomWorks and Allies Prepare for Historic 9/12 Taxpayer March on Washington," FreedomWorks.org website, September 2, 2010, accessed May 23, 2011, www.freedomworks.org/press-releases/freedomworks-and-allies-prepare-for-historic-912-t.

60. See http://teaparty.freedomworks.org/profile/RobinStublen256?xg_source=profiles_memberList, last accessed May 23, 2011, but no longer available.

61. See http://www.pgteaparty.org/1.html, accessed on May 23, 2011. Homepage and logo are visible at the bottom of the page; accessed November 4, 2011 at http://www.pgteaparty.org.

62. *Porkulus* = *pork* barrel spending + stim*ulus* spending. The Tea Party opposed both.

63. Michelle Malkin, "Rebel Yell: Taxpayers Revolt against Gimme-Mania," MichelleMalkin.com, February 20, 2009, accessed March 21, 2011, http://michellemalkin.com/2009/02/20/rebel-yell-taxpayers-revolt-against-gimme-mania/. See also Don Ward, "Protesting the Porkulus Package Postmortem," February 16, 2009, *Seattle Weekly.com* (blog), accessed May 25, 2011, http://blogs.seattleweekly.com/dailyweekly/2009/02/protesporkulus_package.php?print=true.

64. Parallel to the Seattle group, another early rally against the stimulus was facilitated by conservative leadership institutions. In Denver on February 17, 2009, "a crowd of nearly 300 gathered on the steps of the [state] Capitol on their lunch hour to flame-broil the spending bill and feast on roasted pig (also donated by yours truly [Malkin]). Jim Pfaff of Colorado's fiscal conservative citizens' group Americans for Prosperity condemned the 'Ponzi scheme, Madoff style' stimulus and led the crowd in chants of 'No more pork!'" Michelle Malkin, "Rebel Yell: Taxpayers Revolt against Gimme-Mania." For information on Americans for Prosperity being funded by the Koch family, see Jane Mayer, "Covert Operations: The Billionaire Brothers Who Are Waging a War against Obama," *The New Yorker*, August 30, 2010, 44–66.

65. Keli Carender, "Who Invited the Nanny to the BBQ?," May 27, 2009, Red County website, accessed May 25, 2011, www.redcounty.com/node/28103.

66. Kate Zernike, "A Young and Unlikely Activist Who Got to the Tea Party Early," *New York Times*, February 28, 2010, A1. A YouTube video of Carender making her statement, which has been seen by more than 76,000 viewers, can be found at www.youtube.com/watch?v=_IYLqtYEYeI. Last accessed October 4, 2011.

67. Tea Party Patriots website, accessed May 25, 2011, www.teapartypatriots.org/GroupNew/bc02b9bc-ac2c-45cc-9b83-d48cdbf27703/Seattle_Sons_and_Daughters_of_Liberty.

68. Seattle Sons and Daughters Facebook page, accessed May 25, 2011, www.facebook.com/group.php?gid=51707899093&v=wall.

69. Kate Zernike, "A Young and Unlikely Activist Who Got to the Tea Party Early."

70. Stacy Mott, "The Next Generation: Keli Carender," filed under Features, Profiles in Conservatism, March 15, 2010, last accessed October 1, 2010, www.sgpaction.com/sgn (archived by the author).

71. Brendan Steinhauser, "The Taxpayer Tea Party Movement is Growing: First Wave of Tea Parties a Huge Success," FreedomWorks.org website, February 23, 2009, accessed May 24, 2011, www.freedomworks.org/publications/the-taxpayer-tea-party-movement-is-growing; and Jube Dankworth, "Happy Birthday Tea Party," last accessed May 24, 2011, http://houstontps.org/?p=1542.

72. "Houston Tea Party—Feb. 27th 09 @ Discovery Green," posted on the Houston, Texas 9/12 Meetup website, February 24, 2009, accessed May 24, 2011, www.meetup.com/912MembersUSA-Houston-Area-912ers/messages/boards/thread/6361623; and "Beck Was Talking about the Houston Tea Party!" posted on the Houston, Texas 9/12 Meetup website, March 30, 2009, accessed

May 24, 2011, www.meetup.com/912MembersUSA-Houston-Area-912ers/messages/boards/thread/6590705.

73. "Houston's Head Organizer Felicia Speaks to Glenn Beck," Houston Tea Party Society website, April 1, 2009, last accessed May 24, 2011; view video at http://houstontps.org/?p=125.

74. Announcement for "Leadership Training in Houston," Houston Tea Party Society website, posted by Felicia Cravens on March 10, 2009, last accessed May 26, 2011, http://houstontps.org/?p=62.

75. Houston Tea Party Society Official Meetup website, accessed October 31, 2011, www.meetup.com/Houston-Tea-Party-Society/. Despite the positive labeling by leaders, the new site went largely unused.

76. Jube Dankworth, "Happy Birthday Tea Party," February 27, 2011, http://houstontps.org/?p=1542. Dankworth admits in the last line of his post that Americans for Prosperity "spearheaded" the Houston Tea Party, and Houston Tea Party organizer "Josh" admits that the Houston Tea Party spoke with Americans for Prosperity about getting speakers for their events. See "Stupid Tea Party Truther Tricks," April 13, 2009, accessed March 31, 2011, http://houstontps.org/?p=243.

77. Houston Tea Party Society Facebook group, accessed September 17, 2011, www.facebook.com/topic.php?uid=68423955662&topic=7279 (113 people responded positively online); and Houston Tea Party Society Facebook group, accessed September 17, 2011, www.facebook.com/event.php?eid=62664977287. A YouTube video of the event, beginning at 1 minute, 18 seconds, shows many at the event wearing red shirts, www.youtube.com/user/bryanxt#p/u/37/DgdWL8pjo6I (last accessed November 4, 2011). The video opens with a segment from an Obama speech, with no commentary offered. The mere replay of the speech itself is intended to fuel anger.

78. David A. Patten, "Party of the People," Newsmax, June 2010, 46–61, http://w3.newsmax.com/a/jun10/party/ (last accessed October 31, 2011).

79. Felicia Cravens, "Where Did You Have Your Tea Party?" Houston Tea Party Society website, April 16, 2009, accessed March 31, 2011, http://houstontps.org/?p=294. The New York Times estimated that 2,000 people attended the Jones Plaza event in downtown Houston. See Liz Robbins, "Tax Day is Met with Tea Parties," New York Times, April 15, 2009.

80. Cravens leads off a sixteen-post thread, recruiting for flash mobs and discussing a Democratic congressional representative and the ACORN office as targets. Houston Tea Party Society Facebook group, accessed September 17, 2011, www.facebook.com/topic.php?uid=68423955662&topic=7673.

81. "Displaying it Loud and Proud!" posted by "Josh" on the Houston Tea Party Society website, April 29, 2009, accessed March 31, 2011, http://houstontps.org/?p=495.

82. Eleanor Clift, "Weak Tea (Party)," TheDailyBeast.com, January 28, 2010, accessed September 18, 2011, www.thedailybeast.com/newsweek/2010/01/28/weak-tea-party.html.

83. "A Statement on the Tea Party Express," posted by "Josh" on the Houston Tea Party Society website, October 6, 2009, accessed March 31, 2011, http://houstontps.org/?p=957.

84. "Are the Tea Parties Tied to the GOP?" BlueCollarMuse.com, posted by "Blue Collar Muse" on April 11, 2009, accessed May 25, 2011, http://bluecollarmuse.com/2009/04/11/are-the-tea-parties-tied-to-the-gop/.

85. A transcript of nearly the entire interview, with nothing moved or deleted from the selection, follows:

BECK: OK. Tell me, Felicia, you are just [note declarative mood, but then a contrived switch to interrogative]—are you an average everyday person or a political organizer? [expecting the first alternative] What is your history?

CRAVENS: Hey, you call me a schmo. I'm a schmo.

BECK: [big smile] OK.

CRAVENS: I'm a mom who's got two kids and I teach drama after school to some kids [Beck nods], a little part-time job. And I just joined the precinct's chair position at the Republican Party [Beck looks intently, narrows eyes for an instant] locally, but this is beyond party, Glenn.

BECK: OK. [Beck looks to the side] Why are you doing it? Wait a minute. [Goes back to zero in on the precinct chair comment] You just joined into the Republican Party? So do you believe—[Beck points and waves his index finger]

CRAVENS: A couple of years ago.

BECK: OK. Do you believe the Republican Party is not part [with a chortle for emphasis] of this problem? [big smile]

CRAVENS: [responds to the negative in the leading question easily with her own negative, perhaps indicating prior coaching] Oh, au contraire. No way. I have worked locally to try to get the Republican Party to really pay attention to the messages that the spending bills are out of control. Republicans are just as guilty. We've done both ends of the spectrum finding people who are guilty.

BECK: OK. Felicia, this is what—you know, I'm looking for a rally that I'm going to attend. And I'm looking for the rallies that—because, to me, if they become about partisan politics, they're a waste of time.

CRAVENS: Absolutely.

BECK: They have to be about principles that both parties [pointing and waving two fingers for emphasis] now have claimed that they're against big spending, out-of-control spending, out-of-control budgets. But both parties are for that, actually. So this needs to be, "Both of you sit down and shut up and listen to the people."

"Houston's Head Organizer Speaks to Glenn Beck," video posted on the Houston Tea Party Society's website by "Josh" on April 1, 2009, accessed May 23, 2011, http://houstontps.org/?p=125. See also "Houston Tea Party on Glenn Beck with Lead Organizer Felicia Cravens," YouTube video posted on April 1, 2009, accessed May 23, 2011, www.youtube.com/watch?v=chOBJwxidUY.

86. "Nationwide Tea Party Coalition" website, accessed March 30, 2011, www.nationwidechicagoteaparty.com/about.php; and David A. Patten, "Party of the People." Newsmax, June 2010, 46–61, http://w3.newsmax.com/a/jun10/party/ (last accessed on October 31, 2011).

87. Mark Davis, "Jenny Beth Martin: The Head Tea Party Patriot: Woodstock Woman's Political Work Earns Her a Spot on 'Influential' List," Atlanta Journal-Constitution, May 9, 2010; and "Menu Plan Monday,"

JenuineJen.com website, February 4, 2008, accessed October 5, 2010, http://jenuinejen.com/category/politics/page/4/.

88. "Revolution! Nationwide Chicago Tea Party in Atlanta," JenuineJen.com website, February 24, 2009, accessed October 5, 2010, http://jenuinejen.com/category/politics/; "Ashley Fuller Area Woman Co-Organizing Anti-Tax 'Tea Party,'" *Cherokee Tribune*, March 26, 2009; and Jerry Markson, "New Media Help Conservatives Get their Anti-Obama Message Out," *Washington Post*, February 1, 2010, 1.

89. See http://teapartypatriots.ning.com/main/search/search?q=Jenny+Beth+Martin&page=13, and http://teapartypatriots.ning.com/main/search/search?q=JenuineJen&page=3 (last accessed March 30, 2011, and archived by author).

90. "Tea Party Patriots Statement on Tea Party Express," Tea Party Patriots website, October 16, 2009, http://teapartypatriots.ning.com/main/search/search?q=Martin+Express&page=3 (last accessed April 16, 2010, and archived by author).

91. Andrew Malcolm, "One Protester's Handwritten Notes from Behind the Tea Party Lines," *Los Angeles Times*, April 19, 2009.

92. Williamson, Skocpol, and Coggin, "The Tea Party and the Remaking of Republican Conservatism."

93. "Another Serving of 'TEA...,'" *The Spokesman-Review*, June 30, 2009, accessed October 31, 2011, www.spokesman.com/blogs/olympia/2009/jun/30/another-serving-tea/; and Jonathan Brunt and Kevin Graman, "Murray Says Health Reform Will Advance: Public-Option Protesters Greet Her Downtown," *The Spokesman-Review*, August 21, 2009, accessed on October 31, 2011, www.spokesman.com/stories/2009/aug/21/murray-says-health-reform-will-advance/.

94. See www.theteapartyofspokane.org/images/stories/docs/education%20bills.pdf (last accessed April 16, 2011).

95. Kenneth P. Vogel, "Tea Partiers Turn on Each Other," Politico, November 19, 2009, accessed April 15, 2011, www.politico.com/news/stories/1109/29744.html.

96. Philadelphia Tea Party Patriots website, accessed May 26, 2011, www.philateapartypatriots.com/default.html.

97. Kenneth P. Vogel, "Tea Party's Growing Money Problem," Politico, August 9, 2010, accessed May 23, 2011, www.politico.com/news/stories/0810/40800.html.

98. Zachary Roth, "Tea Party Leader on Steele Meeting: 'We Will Not Allow Our Movement To Be Hijacked,'" TalkingPointsMemo.com, February 16, 2010, accessed April 16, 2011, http://tpmmuckraker.talkingpointsmemo.com/2010/02/tea_party_leader_on_steele_meeting_we_will_not_all.php.

99. Post by Mary Johnson on Facebook wall, August 31, 2009, www.facebook.com/group.php?gid=77789743660&v=wall (last accessed March 31, 2011, and archived by author).

100. Waco Tea Party Newsletter, May 10, 2009, Waco Tea Party website, accessed April 15, 2011, http://wacoteaparty.forumcity.com/viewtopic.php?t=41; and Kenneth P. Vogel, "Tea Partiers Turn on Each Other."

PART TWO

"The Real Americans"

Motivation and Identity

CHAPTER 5

The Tea Party

A "White Citizenship" Movement?[1]

LISA DISCH

The South Carolina man who came forward at a town hall meeting in July 2009 with his infamous demand—"Keep your government hands off my Medicare"—exemplified for many liberals everything that should discredit Tea Party supporters[2]: Tea Partiers[3] are uninformed about the simplest facts of the programs on which they most depend. They seem hopelessly tethered to systematic misinformation coming out of propaganda machines like Fox News. How could legislators possibly respond to demands that do not have their roots in reality? How could they even answer criticisms that have no relationship to actual policy proposals? Tea Party supporters, liberals are convinced, are dupes. Seduced by right-wing wordsmiths, they have taken to the streets to sell out the very programs on which they depend.

Or have they? This chapter advances a counterintuitive argument: The Tea Party movement is sparked, in part, by the threat its supporters perceive to their share in two key programs of the liberal welfare state. Tea Party politics is conservative, but its supporters' material commitments and even aspects of their rhetoric place them in a *liberal* genealogy. They defend interests and identifications that they have inherited from the New Deal. Moreover, insofar as social welfare programs in the United States are and always have been racialized—despite that they are not explicitly segregated in terms of race—this inheritance is one in which they have a stake as *white* people. This makes Tea Party mobilization a "white citizenship" movement: action in defense of material benefits that confer "racial standing" in a polity that purports to deny precisely that—special standing based on race.[4]

I propose this counterintuitive understanding of Tea Party fear, anger, and resentment to counter the tendency among some on the left to "other" Tea Party mobilization as irrational, immoderate, racist— simply antithetical to liberal America.[5] This essay argues that Tea Party supporters are neither simply racist nor strictly libertarian nor straight-up fiscal conservatives. They are a constituency formed by the powerful framework for in-group/out-group politics that is an inheritance of liberal social welfare policy, and that has grouped individuals by race. The point of this argument is not to indict New Deal public policy. It is, rather, to hold liberals accountable for their share in the Tea Party phenomenon. I maintain that liberal social policy has a share in constituting the Tea Party, not just by provoking its backlash, but also by helping to define the terms in which Tea Party supporters recognize themselves. I aim to demonstrate that the Tea Party movement *belongs* to liberal America even as Tea Party rhetoric denounces liberalism and liberals denounce Tea Partiers.

WHOSE TEA PARTY?

The question from the beginning, which Clarence Lo explores in detail in Chapter 4 in this volume, was: Grass Roots? Or Astroturf? Former White House adviser David Axelrod gave one answer, when he denigrated Tea Party mobilization as "a grassroots citizens' movement brought to you by a bunch of oil billionaires."[6] Although Axelrod's framing is undeniably partisan, it does capture a grain of truth. Local Tea Parties and national Tea Party umbrella groups are entangled with and significantly funded by the United States' conservative establishment and by parts of the Republican Party. As Jane Mayer reported for the *New Yorker*, local Tea Parties (and, likely, Tea Party candidates) have quietly received significant financial resources and organizational support from oil magnate, climate change–denying libertarians Charles and David Koch through the Americans for Prosperity Foundation, the political advocacy group that David Koch founded in 2004.[7] Former Congressman Dick Armey's (R-TX) conservative nonprofit advocacy group FreedomWorks, which also received Koch family funding at its inception, has been much more visibly involved in building Tea Party organizational infrastructure and political capacity.[8] FreedomWorks trained Tea Party activists for the town hall meetings opposing health insurance reform in August 2009, and for the second round of Tax Day protests in 2010.

The Tea Party is not, then, a purely grassroots phenomenon or spontaneous force. As Clarence Lo argues, this does not make it an "Astroturf" phenomenon. Lo documents in detail the intensive involvement of conservative leadership groups in what he terms the initial "test-marketing" phase of Tea Party mobilization, when the "Tea Party" idea was an experiment and activists and organizers were waiting to see if it would take off. The results quickly became too popular and too unpredictable for any single force to coordinate or any single umbrella group to encompass.

Whereas partisan observers like Axelrod have emphasized what Tea Party groups take from the conservative establishment, it is important not to overlook what that establishment gets in return. The Tea Party has given conservative elites a face of popular protest, brought newly energized voters to the Republican Party, and has proven to be a revenue source for conservative advocacy groups. Most egregious on this last point is the Tea Party Express, the bus tours that were the brainchild of the California political consulting firm that ran the "Swiftboat" ad campaign against John Kerry in 2004, and founded the Our Country Deserves Better PAC in 2008 in opposition to Obama. The tours were launched to capitalize on the excitement of the Tea Party Tax Day protests, and capitalize they did: Donations to that PAC quadrupled, and the firm's earnings skyrocketed from $600,000 to $2.7 million.[9] Although Our Country Deserves Better contributed to the Massachusetts Senate campaign of Scott Brown in 2010, and the bus made stops at Tea Party rallies, the Express was not a Tea Party organization. It was, rather, parasitic on the Tea Party brand. As one of its executives acknowledged in an internal memo, "quite frankly, we are not only not part of the political establishment or conservative establishment, but we are also sadly not currently a part of the 'tea party' establishment."[10] As Lo reports, some Tea Party groups have rebuffed the Express for precisely that reason.

Reporters who covered the Tea Party mass rallies that took place in late 2009 and early 2010 had begun to put forward a romantic narrative of a movement composed of political neophytes "jolted into action by economic distress."[11] In those initial months, as Lo documents, Tea Party groups themselves claimed to be composed of Republicans, independents, Libertarians, even Democrats—all united by concerns about growing government and out-of-control spending. A series of polls published from late March to mid-April 2010 challenged both of these story lines.

The first demographic portrait of Tea Party support was surprising in many respects. Nearly one in five Americans were willing to express support for the Tea Party. Those supporters are, on average, more male, more white, and more educated than most Americans. Most always or usually vote Republican (66 percent); some have even volunteered for the Republican Party, although only 54 percent would identify as Republicans. Although financially secure, they are not wealthy, and they tend to be at or not far from retirement. What makes them stand out is not just that they are overwhelmingly white (90 percent compared to 77 percent of adults generally) but, as Alan Abramowitz points out (Chapter 8 in this volume), they are ideologically highly consistent. Tea Party supporters are uniformly conservative in their views on issues such as immigration, offshore oil drilling, deregulation, and, above all, limited government. Opinion surveys show that 92 percent of Tea Party identifiers support smaller government.[12]

It is important to underscore—contrary to those initial impressionistic reports from the field—that this is not a movement of outsiders. Although conservative to an extreme, Tea Party supporters are neither marginal nor fringe. They are married, largely male, well educated, solidly middle-class, and almost entirely white. To render the contradiction between their rebellious posture and their conventional lifestyles, commentators have termed them variously "the Radical Center," "Middle American Radicals," or "Wal-Mart Hippies."[13]

Polling revealed one feature that is significantly inconsistent with this profile: A substantial majority of the Tea Party base opposes cuts to Social Security and Medicare. In April 2010, 62 percent of Tea Party supporters affirmed that these programs are "worth" the expense to taxpayers.[14] In March 2011, Tea Party supporters "by a nearly two-to-one margin declared significant cuts to Social Security 'unacceptable.'"[15] The typical pattern in survey research is for "opposition to expansive government [to be] strongly and consistently associated with opposition" to government spending, and "to Social Security spending *in particular*."[16] The fact that Tea Party supporters who are otherwise so consistent in their conservative ideology affirm the value of these programs is a truly startling departure. This apparent ideological inconsistency may explain more about Tea Party supporters than do their demographic characteristics.

How to account for the contradiction? Is this simply a case where "self-interest trumps ideology when it comes to entitlements," as both liberal and conservative critics of the Tea Party have charged?[17] This is certainly possible, although Tea Party supporters do not present themselves as indulging in a highly public display of naked self-interest; they assert a claim to justice. They regard Social Security and Medicare (however erroneously) as benefits to which they are entitled because they have paid for them. Other government expenditures, specifically health care reform and the financial stimulus, strike them as irresponsible and unfair because (again erroneously) they believe they will both increase the scope of the United States government and inflate the deficit.

This is evident in the signs that they carry: "This democracy will cease to exist when you take it away from those who are willing to work and give it to those who would not,"[18] "You are not *entitled* to what I have earned," or "Redistribute my work ethic." It comes through in their responses to survey questions, where pollsters find that three-quarters of Tea Party supporters believe that spending on the poor "encourages them to remain poor," and that they are almost twice as likely to perceive that Obama administration policies "favor the poor" as Americans on average (56 percent versus 27 percent).[19] Simply put, Tea Party supporters are resentful.

Their particular resentment scenario presumes an antagonistic relationship between, on the one hand, the poor and an elite class of intellectual do-good social engineers who craft and defend the policies that serve the poor and, on the other hand, the hardworking independent Americans who will be made to foot the bill. The scenario dates to 1893, when social Darwinist William Graham Sumner introduced it in *What Social Classes Owe to Each Other*, his conservative libertarian manifesto. Attacking activist government at a time when the United States lacked even a federal income tax, let alone federally organized poverty relief, Sumner directed his argument against what he somewhat perversely portrayed as a class privilege being accorded to the poor, enjoining "democracy . . . [to] oppose the same cold resistance to any claims for favor on the ground of poverty as on the ground of birth and rank."[20] Sumner personified this argument through the figure of the Forgotten Man who appears throughout the text as the protagonist in various scenarios of injustice. Approximating the consciousness-raising genre long before its time, Sumner invited his readers to identify with this figure:

There are sanitary precautions which need to be taken in factories and houses. There are precautions against fire which are necessary. There is care needed that children not be employed too young, and that they have an education. . . . The system of providing for these things by boards and inspectors throws the cost of it, not on the interested parties, but on the tax-payers. . . . The real victim is the Forgotten Man again—the man who has watched his own investments, made his own machinery safe, attended to his own plumbing, and educated his own children, and who, just when he wants to enjoy the fruits of his care, is told that it is his duty to go and take care of some of his negligent neighbors.[21]

In this passage and many others like it, Sumner solicited the allegiance of those men who recognize themselves as independent, who take care of themselves, and who feel put upon by an elite that would have them compensate for the failings of others. Sumner cultivated a discourse of independence, coupled with an in-group/out-group dynamic that pits wage workers against the indolent poor and the educated elite—the Progressive-era state builders—who were their allies. He set a template for conflict that would carry over into the first comprehensive social welfare bill in the United States, and beyond.

SOCIAL SECURITY AND THE CONSTRUCTION OF WHITE CITIZENSHIP

The Social Security Act of 1935 played into this scenario. It established a two-tier system composed, on the one hand, of benefits deemed universal because they provided security to workers in old age (a common human condition), and, on the other hand, of need-based benefits that provided relief for the non-elderly poor (a special condition). Although the term *Social Security* was an umbrella for the entire aid package, policy makers created consequential symbolic differences among its components. They strategically branded old age and unemployment benefits as "insurance" and aligned them with independence and work, emphasizing that they are contributory and voluntary and, so, do not compromise the self-sufficiency of the recipient.[22] Much has been made of this explicit separation of the deserving from the dependent. There was a second distinction, however, *within* the so-called universal tier that may have been more consequential because it wrote race and sex difference into the construction of "worker." Congress made this universal subject into a particular one by voting "to exclude agricultural workers and domestic servants from participation in the program, which narrowed coverage to barely more than half of the civilian labor force and excluded most blacks" and childless women.[23] By excluding agricultural workers and domestics from the definition of what counted as work for the purposes of the act, Congress did not so much belie the rhetoric of universality as tap into the ideology of whiteness, whereby programs that selectively benefit middle-class whites pass as general, race neutral, and universal.[24] This selectivity did not make the Social Security Act racist, in the sense of either promoting racial segregation directly or explicitly affirming black biological difference and inferiority.[25] It did, however, give material, institutional expression to discourses that worked to gloss over class difference and mark race difference.

Specifically, the architecture of Social Security tapped the discourse of *dependency,* a term political theorist Nancy Fraser and historian Linda Gordon have analyzed regarding its significance to political subject formation in industrial capitalism.[26] Following the enfranchisement of white males in the 1820s in the United States and the acceleration of industrialization over the course of that century, the term *dependency* began to be juxtaposed against wage labor so as to elevate it from "wage slavery" to independence.[27] Contributing to the various forces that solicited workers to identify politically as white, dependency worked to combat group constitution and political mobilization along class lines. Fraser and Gordon emphasize that as a condition, dependency was not literally and materially the opposite of independence. It was, on the contrary, a symbolic opposite that, "through linguistic sleight of hand," secured a precarious independence for "white working men" who were, in fact, dependent in two crucial senses of the term: subordinated to an employer and reliant on the uncompensated domestic labor of wives and children.[28] This symbolic opposition was so powerful that "the honorific term 'independent' remain[ed] firmly centered on wage labor, no matter how impoverished the worker."[29] With wage labor thus effectively "exempted" from dependency (despite its economic and social insufficiency) and held up as paradigmatic of independence, independence could become an attribute of whiteness, not just a privilege of the propertied class.[30]

By contrast, dependency was increasingly stigmatized as "a defect of individual character."[31] In promoting his two-track Social Security framework in the State of the Union Address in 1935, Roosevelt tapped this stigma even as he attempted to legitimate the new federal antipoverty programs as assistance to those who were unable to "maintain themselves independently—for the most part, through no fault of their own."[32] By presenting poverty assistance as doing away with "dependence on relief," which he likened to a "narcotic" that induced a "spiritual and moral disintegration fundamentally destructive to the national fibre," Roosevelt affirmed that dependency is pathological. He thereby reproduced and further entrenched the ideology of independence that would come to stigmatize these new programs even more than their predecessors.[33] In the second half of the twentieth century, the "negative connotations" of dependency and its "individualization" only intensified.[34] As the civil rights movement did away with the explicit forms of political and legal subordination that had remained in the wake of emancipation, and as the decline of the family wage precipitated more white working-class women and even numbers of middle-class women into the workforce, "postindustrial society appear[ed] . . . to have eliminated every social-structural basis of dependency."[35] Whatever remained could "be interpreted as the fault of individuals," a social pathology not the grounds for a legitimate claim to social insurance.[36]

As a package, the New Deal helped to construct "white citizenship."[37] This is not because it was racist but, rather, precisely because it differentiated citizens into racialized groups while appearing to be race-blind. In addition to the facially neutral definition of worker that excluded agricultural workers and domestics, Federal Housing Administration (FHA) mortgages were disproportionately approved for white borrowers and structured to encourage purchase in redlined suburbs. These suburbs, in turn, developed with federal and state funding of infrastructure that served the white commuter, routing highways through city centers in ways that instituted racial segregation as geography.[38] These acts, among many others, invested whiteness with standing but made it invisible as race privilege.

This invisibility, characteristic of white citizenship, serves to differentiate it from white supremacy, an essentialist ideology that makes individual whites feel naturally superior, and materializes that sense of superiority in whites-only schools, buses, restaurants, and other public accommodations. By contrast, white citizenship is constituted by benefits and freedoms that white citizens take for granted as being theirs by "natural right, [as] a normal condition, or a deserved advantage"—not as race privileges.[39] As Lawrie Balfour has noted, the "role of white entitlement in structuring virtually every dimension of American life is imperceptible to many Americans."[40] It is constituted by an independence that seems to have been personally earned when it is, in fact, publicly subsidized.

Within two decades of its enactment, the Social Security program was extended to cover most occupations predominantly held by Black Americans. With that extension, the material basis for white citizenship and its invisibility was no longer explicit, as in the New Deal era. It shifted, rather, to the broader apparatus in which many significant U.S. social programs participate: the "submerged state."[41] This is Suzanne Mettler's term for the various government-sponsored social benefits that do not appear as such because they are delivered in the form of "tax breaks for individuals and families" or tax exemptions that foster employer provision of such elements of social security as health care and retirement savings accounts.[42] Mettler found that over 60 percent of individuals who have benefited from such provisions are oblivious to their dependence on government subsidy; they deny having "used a government program."[43] The most lucrative of submerged state benefits (the home mortgage deduction and tax exemption for employer-sponsored health insurance) accrue disproportionately to households with incomes of $75,000 or more—the income bracket in which 31 percent of Tea Party supporters placed themselves in March 2010.[44] One-third of all households who identified as "white only" in the U.S. census are above that threshold, as compared to 17 percent of blacks and 21 percent of Hispanics, with white households accounting for 76 percent of all households at that level.[45] In other words, whites, in far greater numbers than blacks and Hispanics, and in a substantial proportion of the white population overall, receive government benefits in forms that render them invisible as such.

The "submerged state" indirectly perpetuates the sense of independence that New Deal programs rendered an explicit material prerogative of whiteness. Although the initial patently discriminatory aspects of the welfare state are gone, the association of whiteness with independence persists through indirect government programs that disproportionately benefit high-income households. In fact, this association intensified as poverty began to be represented (contrary to fact) as predominantly a condition of Black Americans. That linkage came about in the mid-1960s, in part due to social protests, which called attention to the living conditions of African Americans in U.S. cities. More significantly, it was engineered by means of a sharp sudden shift by the news media, which began putting a black face on poverty by "overrepresenting the proportion of blacks among the poor," and inaugurating a decades-long "pattern of associating African Americans with the least sympathetic aspects of poverty."[46] In this context, where a stigmatized dependence is juxtaposed against benefits for which government responsibility is either "submerged," or, as in the case of Social Security, where individual contribution looms larger than government sponsorship, social policy continues to support white citizenship. Because it is seen to epitomize the ideal of self-sufficiency, Social Security remains racialized: It is associated "with *whiteness* in a mirror image of the association of welfare with blackness."[47]

This account casts the dynamics of Tea Party mobilization in a new light by situating them in the context not of race antagonism but of white racial identification facilitated by liberal social welfare policy. It also suggests a hypothesis that could account for the apparent contradiction between the extreme conservatism of Tea Party supporters and their affirmation of both Social Security and Medicare. This is no contradiction but an expression of resentment that is proof of Tea Party supporters' identification with whiteness. To borrow the provocative phrase of sociologist George Lipsitz, Tea Party supporters are defending their share in "racialized social democracy."[48] It is in this respect that their mobilization can be seen as a "white citizenship" movement: It is collective political action in defense of material benefits that (while seeming neutral) have perpetuated racial inequality.

TEA PARTY RESENTMENT

Could such a hypothesis be tested? In fact, survey researchers have a way of measuring resentment. It is operationalized by a four-question series that registers attitudes about whether members of different racial and ethnic groups are hardworking, and solicits judgments as to the validity of claims about structural discrimination. Subjects are asked for their responses to statements that focus on black achievement relative to special favors, slavery and discrimination, deservingness, and effort, without any specific reference to government assistance or to public policy like affirmative action. The scale aims to separate a respondent's ideological commitment to limited government from the respondent's sense that blacks enjoy unfair or unearned advantages. Researchers disagree as to whether these questions measure specifically "racial resentment,"[49] or whether they tap a conservatism that values independence, opposes government spending, and can just as well be ideologically as racially motivated.[50] Researchers have been so focused on the relationship between white resentment and antiblack prejudice that they have given little thought to the role resentment may play in soliciting an attachment to whiteness. Some researchers go so far as to explicitly disavow such an attachment.[51]

Without presuming to settle this dispute, a task properly suited to empirical scholars, it is important to point out the parallels between these questions and the Forgotten Man scenario. At stake in both is an in-group/out-group dynamic that breaks along the fault line of dependency. The Forgotten Man scenario worked both to denigrate a nondeserving out-group for failing to live up to ideals of individualism and hard work, and to invite the "forgotten" men to identify with one another as the responsible ones on whom the lazy and the social reformers who are their advocates rely to take up the slack. Quite apart from whether it measures underlying antiblack prejudice, I suggest that the resentment index captures identification with hard work and possessiveness regarding its just rewards—signal features of whiteness and the defining characteristics of the Forgotten Man.

The University of Washington Multi-State Survey of Race and Politics, a poll that was administered in six battleground states plus California in early Spring 2010, tested the resentment measure specifically on Tea Party supporters. Researchers found that relative to other white Americans, Tea Party "true believers" score highly on this index. Similarly, a 2010 New York Times/CBS Poll found that Tea Party supporters were almost twice as likely (73 percent) as nonsupporters (38 percent) to agree with the statement that "providing government benefits to poor people encourages them to remain poor."[52] That poll also found that they were significantly more likely to affirm that whites and blacks have an equal chance of getting ahead (73 percent) than were respondents on average (60 percent). Put simply, Tea Party supporters are resentful.[53] Could there be any better illustration of this than Tea Party activist Keli Carender? As related by Clarence Lo (Chapter 4 in this volume), Carender incarnated the Forgotten Man at a 2009 town hall meeting on health care. Brandishing a $20 bill, she challenged a Democratic legislator: "If you believe that it is absolutely moral to take my money and give it to someone else based on their supposed needs, then you come and take this $20 and use it as a down payment on this health care plan."[54]

Christopher Parker, who oversaw the University of Washington study, reads the resentment score, together with thermometer measures of attitudes toward blacks, as evidence of racism.[55] Without disputing his argument, I draw on an article by political scientist Nicholas J. G. Winter to develop an additional interpretation.[56] Winter's work analyzes how the resentment measure affects approval of Social Security among respondents who otherwise favor limited government. Winter's analysis makes it possible to test the hypothesis that the central contradiction of Tea Party ideology—their consistent conservatism combined with their support for Social Security and Medicare—is a consequence of their identification with whiteness.

Winter's study, though conducted several years prior to the emergence of the Tea Party phenomenon, examined the constellation of factors that have proven to give rise to Tea Party activism. Using National Election Studies data, Winter looked at correlations among the resentment measure, positive feelings about/positive conceptions of whites as a group, and support for Social Security spending. Factoring in thermometer readings of respondents' warmth toward whites, measures of their propensity to stereotype whites as hardworking, and the resentment index, Winter found that "resentful whites are substantially more supportive of spending on Social Security" than are the less resentful.[57] He explained this support by the fact that characteristics associated with Social Security, "hard work and self reliance, are stereotypically associated with whiteness."[58] Winter concluded that the resentful favor Social Security spending because of their positive feelings toward "whites as a group."[59] In other words, people who are otherwise individualists, and would be typically inclined to oppose government spending, make an exception for Social Security (which they racialize as white) insofar as they hold positive feelings toward whites. His work points, then, to the affective identification with whiteness as a way of making sense of how a group that is otherwise both consistently conservative and adamantly in favor of limited government could affirm the value of this liberal legacy.

The contemporary Republican Party is infamous for its "Southern Strategy," which it used to fracture the New Deal coalition by capturing the so-called Reagan Democrats.[60] These were the southern whites alienated from the Democratic Party that were mobilized as a constituency by George Wallace's third-party runs for the presidency. Wallace tapped their antipathy to civil rights and to the affirmative action policies that they blamed for taking their jobs and destroying their schools. The Southern Strategy gave the Republican Party a makeover from its public face as the party of corporate elites and old money to that of a party with an energetic popular base.[61] Tea Party support serves a similar function for the Republican Party today, although it is composed of very different popular elements. As Alan Abramowitz demonstrates (Chapter 8 in this volume), Tea Party supporters were already Republican, those at the extreme right wing of the party. Thus, they have not been captured from the Democrats but, rather, given new visibility and leverage by their mobilization as Tea Partiers. In addition, Tea Party supporters are not segregationists. Whereas race difference and identification do play an undeniable role in Tea Party politics, it is as important to consider their identification with whiteness as it is to note their prejudice against blacks. In other words, whereas Tea Party politics is unquestionably a racialized politics, it is not necessarily a racist one, in the usual sense of that term.

It is puzzling that the racial dynamics of Social Security would favor the Republican Party, rather than the Democratic Party. Interestingly, Winter thought the partisan advantage would go the other way. He predicted that because "Social Security has traditionally been associated with the Democratic Party, . . . the mirror-image racialization of Social Security should increase somewhat the appeal of the Democratic Party among some of those same voters."[62] Winter suggests that Democrats might tap white citizenship and turn it to a broader force for liberal social policy (much as Reagan tapped southern Democrats). This essay has aimed to shed some light on why this has not been so. To begin with, Tea Party supporters are staunch Republicans. It is not likely that anything would make them shift their allegiance to the Democrats. The question in their case is not "Why do they not switch parties?" but, as I stated at the outset of this chapter, "What can reconcile their consistent and deep-seated conservatism with their attachment to Social Security?" I have suggested that aspects of the discourse of Social Security resonate with conservative ideology, especially its emphasis on the virtues of work and vices of dependency.

CONCLUSION

I have pursued this line of argument not to indict liberal social welfare. Social insurance for the aged is a valuable achievement of liberalism, one whose continued survival cannot be taken for granted. I have aimed to cast the Tea Party phenomenon in a new light so as to prompt liberals and progressives to offer a different response to their claims and demands. Rather than distancing and ridicule, the Tea Party movement calls for a positive counterforce, one that would counter the historic distinction between social "insurance" and social "welfare" and displace the glorification of markets for an ethic of mutual responsibility. In other words, rather than scold and correct the Tea Party base, liberals and progressives ought to mount a positive counterforce by exemplifying— in speech and action—alternatives to the politics of resentment.

"Social citizenship" is a powerful vocabulary for such a counterforce. The concept is credited to British sociologist T. H. Marshall. Marshall conceived social citizenship as the "right to defend and assert all one's rights on terms of equality with others and by due process of law."[63] This is in contrast to the more familiar dimensions of citizenship, those constituted by civil rights that guarantee individual freedoms and political rights that afford participation in government. Practically speaking, social citizenship entails publicly secured welfare, broadly understood not as transfer payments but as economic and health security. It is also intangible, involving having a share in the "social heritage" and "life of a civilized being according to the standards prevailing in the society."[64] Social citizenship, then, is both material and cultural; it ensures inclusion, equal respect, and equal recognition not of one's humanity in the abstract but of one's equal title to membership and status in a specific linguistic and cultural community.

Social citizenship is distinct from social welfare as U.S. citizens know it because it aims not simply to relieve the worst excesses of poverty but to alter the "pattern of social inequality," particularly inequalities of status.[65] It begins from the radical notion that these various forms of security, and these matters of cultural access that an American might think of as lifestyle choices, are not contingent on earning a good wage at a job with benefits. They are, rather, "an integral part of the rights of the citizen."[66] A two-track welfare system that makes fundamental distinctions between its clientele—the worker valued as independent and the poor stigmatized as dependent—violates these notions of equal membership and status at a most basic level, as do the vast disparities between urban and suburban public schools, the inadequacy of the health and legal services available to the poor, their lack of access to legitimate banks and properly stocked grocery stores, and so on. It is not simply, and perhaps not even primarily, the distributional inequity that is troubling, but the status inequity, the existence of a second-class system that imbues its clients with a sense of shame.

Imagined as a system-wide principle, social citizenship is a daunting project that would seem unlikely to take hold in the United States context because it runs counter to so much of what its citizens take for granted as common sense. As Fraser and Gordon note, in the American context, "'social citizenship'. . . sounds almost oxymoronic."[67] They attribute this to the primacy of contractual relations and the attendant ideology of independence in the United States, which is a side effect of its strong tradition of constitutionally protected individual rights—Marshall's "civil citizenship."[68] Fraser and Gordon argue that the predominance of civil citizenship, which takes contract as its model of reciprocity, had two consequences that worked against the development of social citizenship. First, "noncontractual forms of reciprocity were increasingly assimilated to contractual exchange" (except for those within the family which became a domain of altruism). Second, "interactions that seemed neither contractual nor familial now appeared to be unilateral and entirely voluntary, entailing neither entitlements [on the part of the recipient] nor responsibilities" on the part of the doer.[69] Although "kinship, neighborly, and community obligations continued strong," and people participated in a range of practices of "informal mutual aid," it became difficult to regard these as relations governed by legitimate claims and enforceable debts, as participants were not bound to one another contractually.[70]

Opposition to the 2010 health insurance reform exemplifies United States citizens' resistance to social citizenship. A program that makes a minimal step in Marshall's direction by virtue of its (unfulfilled) aspiration toward universality, but which is utterly at odds with his vision in its reliance on market mechanisms, still strikes a substantial portion of the public as an unacceptable extension of government control over economic systems and individual choice. If social citizenship is difficult to imagine at a system level, it is not so implausible on a smaller scale. There is the example of the monthlong occupation of the state capitol in Madison, Wisconsin, in the winter of 2011. Although participants did not use the language of social citizenship, these protests manifested its spirit. A range of citizens, union and nonunion alike, took up a defense of collective bargaining rights not simply (or perhaps not at all) out of support for unions but because they regarded the freedom to negotiate the terms of a labor contract as a fundamental freedom, not as a private matter between employer and employee. The Wisconsin protests cast collective bargaining rights as Marshall regarded them, as an "institution of citizenship."[71]

The South Carolina man who came forward with his seemingly absurd demand may appear extreme; however, the belief that individuals have an inviolable claim to certain benefit programs because they get back from them just what they put in is a misperception held by many Americans, not just Tea Party supporters.[72] Put in Marshall's terms, United States citizens have a tendency to read social citizenship as civil citizenship; transposing their dependencies into individual rights, they regard Social Security as theirs because they contributed to it not because of a broad social commitment to solidarity. Given how they see such benefits, it should not be surprising that Tea Party supporters respond with resentment when they perceive them to be threatened. I have suggested that the resentment frame is something they have inherited not only from conservative individualism but also from the structure of liberal social policy in the United States. Social Security has taught them about the benefits that derive from whiteness. Rather than denounce Tea Party supporters' investment in that identity as illiberal and intolerant, the left needs to put forward a counterforce to white citizenship through new languages and practices of solidarity.

NOTES

1. This essay was produced with the support of a fellowship at the Institute for the Humanities at the University of Michigan, Ann Arbor. I am grateful to Larry Rosenthal, Christine Trost, Lawrence Jacobs, Joe Lowndes, Joel Olson, and Sam Chambers for comments on various drafts.

2. Paul Krugman, "Health Care Realities," *New York Times*, July 30, 2009.

3. Throughout this essay, when I speak of the Tea Party and its supporters, I am referring to the people who make up the base of the Tea Party movement, not to elites in the legislature or Republican Party. As Williamson et al. have argued, there are some significant differences between the Tea Party base and its representatives and sympathizers in the Republican Party, specifically with respect to reform of Social Security and Medicare. See Vanessa Williamson, Theda Skocpol, and John Coggin, "The Tea Party and the Remaking of Republican Conservatism," *Perspectives on Politics* 9, no. 1 (2011): 25–43. See also Theda Skocpol and Vanessa Williamson, *The Tea Party and the Remaking of Republican Conservatism* (Oxford University Press, 2011).

4. Joel Olson, *The Abolition of White Democracy* (Minneapolis: University of Minnesota Press, 2004), xix, xviii.

5. See, for example, Ben McGrath, "The Movement: The Rise of Tea Party Activism," *The New Yorker*, February 1, 2010; Eugene Robinson, "Racism and the Tea Party Movement," RealClearPolitics.com, November 2, 2010, accessed March 24, 2011, www.realclearpolitics.com/articles/2010/11/02/race_and_the _tea_partys_ire_107805.html; HuffPost Citizen Journalists, "10 Most Offensive Tea Party Signs and Extensive Photo Coverage from Tax Day Protests," April 16, 2009, accessed March 24, 2011, www.huffingtonpost.com/2009/04/16/ 10-most-offensive-tea-par_n_187554.html; Frank Rich, "The Rage is Not about Health Care," *New York Times*, March 27, 2010; and Brian Stelter, "NPR Executive Caught Calling Tea Partiers 'Racist,'" Media Decoder (blog), *New York Times*, March 8, 2011, accessed March 24, 2011, http://mediadecoder.blogs .nytimes.com/2011/03/08/npr-executive-caught-calling-tea-partiers-racist/.

6. Quoted in Jane Mayer, "Covert Operations," *The New Yorker*, August 30, 2010.

7. Jane Mayer, "Covert Operations."

8. Kate Zernike, *Boiling Mad: Inside Tea Party America* (New York: Times Books, Henry Holt and Co., 2010), 35.

9. Kenneth Vogel, "GOP Operatives Crash the Tea Party," Politico, April 14, 2010.

10. Quoted in Vogel, "GOP Operatives Crash the Tea Party."

11. Zernike, *Boiling Mad: Inside Tea Party America*.

12. New York Times/CBS Poll, "National Survey of Tea Party Supporters," April 5–12, 2010.

13. Sam Tanenhaus, "The Radical Center: The History of an Idea," *New York Times*, April 14, 2010; and David Brooks, "The Wal-Mart Hippies," *New York Times*, March 4, 2010.

14. New York Times/CBS Poll, 2010.

15. Neil King and Scott Greenberg, "Poll Shows Budget-Cuts Dilemma," *Wall Street Journal*, March 3, 2011.

16. Nicolas J. G. Winter, "Beyond Welfare: Framing and the Racialization of White Opinion on Social Security," *American Journal of Political Science* 50, no. 2 (2006): 409, emphasis added.

17. Steve Pendlebury, "Poll of Tea Party Supporters Reveals Surprises," AolNews.com, April 15, 2010.

18. This is a quote they wrongly attribute to Thomas Jefferson.

19. New York Times/CBS Poll, 2010.

20. William Graham Sumner, *What Social Classes Owe to Each Other* (Caldwell: Caxton Press, [1883] 2003), 32.

21. Sumner, *What Social Classes Owe to Each Other*, 118–19.

22. Martha Derthick, *Policymaking for Social Security* (Washington: Brookings Institution, 1979).

23. Jacob S. Hacker, *The Divided Welfare State: The Battle over Public and Private Social Benefits in the United States* (Cambridge: Cambridge University Press, 2002), 107; compare to Jill Quadagno, *The Color of Welfare: How Racism Undermined the War on Poverty* (New York: Oxford University Press, 1994).

24. Ruth Frankenberg, *White Women, Race Matters: The Social Construction of Whiteness* (Minneapolis: University of Minnesota Press, 1993).

25. Racism was enacted through its federal structure, which allowed southern states to administer veterans' benefits, community health services, school lunch, and other federally funded programs in ways that explicitly discriminated against blacks.

26. Nancy Fraser and Linda Gordon, "A Genealogy of 'Dependency': Tracing a Keyword of the U.S. Welfare State," in *Justice Interruptus: Critical Reflections on the 'Postsocialist' Condition*, ed. Nancy Fraser (New York: Routledge, [1994] 1997), 121–50.

27. Nancy Fraser and Linda Gordon, "A Genealogy of 'Dependency,'" 127.

28. Nancy Fraser and Linda Gordon, "A Genealogy of 'Dependency,'" 130.

29. Nancy Fraser and Linda Gordon, "A Genealogy of 'Dependency,'" 139.

30. Fraser and Gordon's argument is not that only whites identified with discourses linking wage labor to independence. As Amy Dru Stanley has argued, following emancipation, contract principles—the emblem of independence—emerged as a new common sense and constituted an ideal to which both black

and white citizens subscribed. See Amy Dru Stanley, *From Bondage to Contract: Wage Labor, Marriage, and the Market in the Age of Slave Emancipation* (New York: Cambridge University Press, 1998). Their point is that wage labor could not guarantee independence without the further protections accorded to workers by the state, protections that were not extended to job categories that were populated predominantly by African Americans.

31. Fraser and Gordon, "A Genealogy of 'Dependency,'" 131.

32. Franklin D. Roosevelt, "Annual Message to Congress," in *The Era of Franklin D. Roosevelt, 1933–1945,* ed. Richard Polenberg (Boston: Bedford/ St. Martin's, [1935] 2000), 51.

33. Franklin D. Roosevelt, "Annual Message to Congress," 51.

34. Fraser and Gordon, "A Genealogy of 'Dependency,'" 136.

35. Fraser and Gordon, "A Genealogy of 'Dependency,'" 136.

36. Fraser and Gordon, "A Genealogy of 'Dependency,'" 136.

37. Olson, *The Abolition of White Democracy*, xix.

38. Douglas S. Massey and Nancy Denton, *American Apartheid: Segregation and the Making of the Underclass* (Cambridge, MA: Harvard University Press, 1993).

39. Olson, *The Abolition of White Democracy*, xxi.

40. Lawrie Balfour, "Reparations after Identity Politics," *Political Theory* 33, no. 6 (2005): 793–94.

41. Suzanne Mettler, "Reconstituting the Submerged State: The Challenges of Social Policy Reform in the Obama Era," *Perspectives on Politics* 8, no. 3 (2010): 803–24.

42. Suzanne Mettler, "Reconstituting the Submerged State," 804.

43. Suzanne Mettler, "Reconstituting the Submerged State," 809.

44. New York Times/CBS Poll, 2010.

45. Carmen DeNavas-Walt, Bernadette D. Proctor, and Jessica C. Smith, U.S. Census Bureau, Current Population Reports, P60-239, *Income, Poverty, and Health Insurance Coverage in the United States: 2010* (Washington, DC: U.S. Government Printing Office, 2011), 34–38.

46. Martin Gilens, "How the Poor Became Black: The Racialization of American Poverty in the Mass Media," in *Race and the Politics of Welfare Reform*, ed. Sanford F. Schram, Joe Soss, and Richard C. Fording (Ann Arbor: University of Michigan Press, 2003), 119, 123.

47. Winter, "Beyond Welfare," 400, 401.

48. George Lipsitz, "The Possessive Investment in Whiteness: Racialized Social Democracy and the 'White' Problem in American Studies," *American Quarterly* 47, no. 3 (1995): 369–87. It could be objected that Social Security is not racialized "social democracy" but a racialized program of the "'liberal' social welfare state," which social scientist Gøsta Esping-Andersen differentiates from social democracy by virtue of its eschewing full employment, and providing only "an equality of minimal needs" by means-testing aid to the poor and allocating limited funding for social insurance. See Gøsta Esping-Andersen, *The Three Worlds of Welfare Capitalism* (Princeton: Princeton University Press, 1990), 27, 26. Although this typology differentiates between liberal and social democratic approaches to welfare, Esping-Andersen emphasizes that all welfare

regimes are mixed and, in fact, singles out Social Security as an exception within the "social assistance system" of the United States for incorporating the principles of the "social-insurance tradition" of the European social democracies (p. 49). Thus, Lipsitz might well be entitled to his polemical phrase.

49. Donald R. Kinder and Lynn M. Sanders, *Divided by Color: Racial Politics and Democratic Ideals* (Chicago: University of Chicago Press, 1996).

50. Stanley Feldman and Leonie Huddy, "Racial Resentment and White Opposition to Race-Conscious Programs: Principles or Prejudice?" *American Journal of Political Science* 49 (2005): 168–83; Paul M. Sniderman, Gretchen C. Crosby, and William G. Howell, "The Politics of Race," in *Racialized Politics: The Debate about Racism in America*, ed. D. O. Sears, J. Sidanius, and L. Bobo (Chicago: University of Chicago Press, 2000), 236–79; and Paul M. Sniderman and Edward G. Carmines, *Reaching beyond Race* (Cambridge: Harvard University Press, 1997).

51. David O. Sears, Colette Van Laar, Mary Carrillo, and Rick Kosterman, "Is It Really Racism? The Origins of White Americans' Opposition to Race-Targeted Policies," *Public Opinion Quarterly* 61 (1997): 33.

52. New York Times/CBS Poll, 2010.

53. See http://depts.washington.edu/uwiser/racepolitics.html.

54. See http://www.youtube.com/watch?v=_IYLqtYEYeI.

55. Christopher Parker, "Race and the Tea Party: Who's Right?" Salon.com, May 3, 2010, accessed March 24, 2011, www.salon.com/news/feature/2010/05/03/race_and_the_tea_party.

56. Winter, "Beyond Welfare," 400–20.

57. Winter, "Beyond Welfare," 415.

58. Winter, "Beyond Welfare," 406.

59. Winter, "Beyond Welfare," 413.

60. Kevin Phillips, *The Emerging Republican Majority* (New York: Arlington House, 1969).

61. Joseph E. Lowndes, *From the New Deal to the New Right: Race and the Southern Origins of Modern Conservatism* (New Haven: Yale University Press, 2008).

62. Winter, "Beyond Welfare," 417.

63. Thomas H. Marshall, "Citizenship and Social Class," in *Class, Citizenship and Social Development*, ed. Seymour Martin Lipset (Westport: Greenwood Press, 1973 [1949]), 71.

64. Marshall, "Citizenship and Social Class," 72.

65. Marshall, "Citizenship and Social Class," 103, 115.

66. Marshall, "Citizenship and Social Class," 80.

67. Nancy Fraser and Linda Gordon, "Contract versus Charity: Why Is There No Social Citizenship in the United States?" *Socialist Review* 22, no. 3 (1992): 46.

68. Fraser and Gordon, "Contract versus Charity," 64.

69. Fraser and Gordon, "Contract versus Charity," 59.

70. Fraser and Gordon, "Contract versus Charity," 60.

71. Marshall, "Citizenship and Social Class," 111.

72. For a powerful defense of this position, see Suzanne Mettler, "Our Hidden Government Benefits," *New York Times*, September 19, 2011.

CHAPTER 6

The Past and Future of Race in the Tea Party Movement

JOSEPH LOWNDES

Conflicting interpretations of the Tea Party movement abound. Chief among these debates for scholars, pollsters, and partisans is the role of race and racism.[1] Those for whom race is central to the Tea Party movement see a continuation of the racial coding that marked the rise of modern conservatism, or they see widespread racial anxiety triggered by the election of the nation's first African American president. They point to demonized portrayals of Obama on placards and racial epithets hurled at rallies, to the prevalence of Tea Partiers who do not believe Obama was born in the United States, and to the antigovernment sentiments steeped in traditions of racial coding.[2] Those who deny the role of race see the Tea Party as driven by broadly held populist resentment against a government that spends with abandon. Asserting that Tea Party goals are racially neutral, they point to high-profile Tea Party politicians of color, note that civil rights leaders are figures of inspiration for movement activists, and argue that actual racists in the movement are a small minority whose presence is continually overblown by the media.[3]

Race is indeed central to the Tea Party movement, but in ways not fully appreciated by its supporters or its critics. First, while the movement inherits the racial framings of the modern conservative movement, the contemporary context alters its field of racial meaning. In the populist imagination of the modern right forged in the 1960s and 1970s, hardworking white Americans were threatened by blacks below and their liberal elite allies above. The current absence of a black freedom movement, along with the election of a black president, has shifted white populist anger almost entirely upward toward the state itself. Second, while it is tempting to see the Tea Party disavowal of racism as merely color-blind window dressing, conservatives over the last decade have attempted to forge new interpretations of the civil rights movement. Third, the successful dismantling of welfare and the full realization of a prison industrial complex largely removed welfare and crime as animating policy issues for Tea Partiers. Thus, its targets have increasingly been nonracial, such as public-sector unions and universal entitlement programs. What does it mean then for a movement, forged in racial populism, to forgo explicit racial commitments as it seeks to dismantle the welfare state and protect wealthy interests from tax burdens? Ultimately, the Tea Party's racial ambivalence defines both its possibilities and limitations, and will reveal the historic importance of race to the modern conservative project.

THE TEA PARTY AND THE RACIAL LEGACY OF ANTISTATIST POPULISM

In sympathetic portraits, the Tea Party is a spontaneous people's movement that has come together to wrest power from corrupt elites. For legal scholar Glenn Harlan Reynolds, it is "the next Great Awakening," a movement that is neither right nor left, but "a symptom of a much broader phenomenon, exemplified by earlier explosions of support for Howard Dean via Meetup and Barack Obama and Sarah Palin via Facebook. They were triggered by the growing sense that politics has become a cozy game for insiders, and that the interests of most Americans are ignored."[4] Similarly, in their book *Mad as Hell: How the Tea Party Movement is Fundamentally Remaking Our Two-Party System*, pollsters Scott Rasmussen and Douglas Schoen write, "*For the first time in history, the majority of Americans qualify as populists. And make no mistake: their anger is real. We have seen it*" (italics theirs). Having asserted the hegemonic character of this new movement, they go on to specify this feeling upon the land: "There is a deep distrust of the elite in government and business, and a pervasive sense, which is wholly justified by outrageous current events, that the powerful are conspiring against ordinary Americans."[5] Such portrayals participate in the populist romance they claim to describe, overstate the popular influence of the Tea Party movement, and deny its ideological and affective link to contemporary conservatism.

As Skocpol and Williamson have recently argued, the movement's rhetoric has been fiscally conservative in ways consistent with the rest of the right. Tea Partiers are antiregulation, antitax, and antispending—particularly on programs for the poor. The latter, the authors point out, is in sync with racially framed opposition to welfare spending that marked the rise of the right.[6] Indeed, the fusing of race, populism, and antistatist fiscal conservatism is in many ways the story of the rise of modern conservatism itself.[7]

Goldwater's 1964 GOP presidential campaign marked the first national attempt to wed racism to fiscal conservatism, when the Arizona senator's opposition to civil rights gave him enough southern delegate votes for a conservative capture of the Republican nomination that year, but nationally he won only his home state and five more in the Deep South. Conservatives had thus extended their base by embracing racial politics, but were still associated with wealthy interests. Soon after, however, Alabama Governor George Wallace forged a politics that framed both racism and antistatist conservatism as populist, attacking "pointy-headed bureaucrats" and social meddlers in rants against busing, welfare, crime, and civil rights protest. Such themes proved popular not just in the white South, but also among white working- and middle-class voters in the Northeast, Midwest, and West.[8]

Kevin Phillips, then a young elections analyst working for John Mitchell on Nixon's 1968 presidential campaign, saw the political potential of Wallace's populist rhetoric. Nixon began using the terms *silent majority, forgotten Americans,* and *Middle America* to describe an aggrieved white majority squeezed by both the unruly poor and government elites. Meanwhile, Phillips sought ways to link up various groups—white southerners, urban ethnics, western populists, and middle-class dwellers of the emergent Sunbelt—into a new majoritarian voting bloc. After the 1968 election, Phillips wrote that what he called the emerging Republican majority "spoke clearly . . . for a shift away from the sociological jurisprudence, moral permissiveness, experimental residential, welfare, and educational programming and massive federal spending by which the Liberal establishment sought to propagate liberal institutions and ideology." This political identity was revived and made hegemonic in Reagan's 1980 presidential campaign through his simultaneous demonization of government and "welfare queens."[9]

Race was central in shifting populism from left to right, and thus was key to the success of modern conservatism more generally. As the state itself became more tightly linked to people of color in this political logic, it became less identified with hegemonic views of national identity. State was thus increasingly split from nation in this politics, allowing Reagan himself to be iconographic of (white) America, even while he continually disparaged the state.

TEA PARTY ANTISTATISM

The Tea Party movement was called into being by antigovernment rage, through Seattle blogger Keli Carender's "porkulus package" demonstration, NBC business news editor Rick Santelli's rant on the floor of the Chicago Mercantile Exchange against a government plan to refinance mortgages, and other protests against anti–recessionary spending, most of which were organized by FreedomWorks and given ample coverage on Fox News. The nascent movement solidified over the summer of 2009, through the public spectacle of protests at town hall meetings across the country where elected officials at public fora discussed federal health care reform legislation. The movement soon took on the Gadsden "Don't Tread on Me" flag as its unifying symbol, an icon that at once evokes patriotism and antigovernment dissent.[10]

The contemporary Tea Party movement evinces the thundering antistatist fury of its forebears in its attacks on the stimulus package, Troubled Asset Relief Program (TARP), the auto industry bailout, health care reform, and in attacks on public-sector workers. Tea Party leaders describe the movement as driven first and foremost by a concern to stave off encroaching state power over the lives of individuals. The mission statement of the Tea Party Patriots (the largest network of the Tea Party organizations) reads: "The impetus for the Tea Party movement is excessive government spending and taxation. Our mission is to attract, educate, organize, and mobilize our fellow citizens to secure public policy consistent with our three core values of Fiscal Responsibility, Constitutionally Limited Government, and Free Markets." FreedomWorks says in its mission statement that it "fights for lower taxes, less government and more economic freedom for all Americans." Similarly, Tea Party Express advertises on its website that its aim is to "speak out against the out-of-control spending, higher taxes, bailouts, and growth in the size and power of government!"[11] The movement has pushed Republicans in Congress past their comfort zone to radically reduce spending on programs for the poor as well as on middle-class entitlements such as Medicare and Social Security.

Part of the antistatism of the Tea Party reflects a libertarian movement that has had an important impact on it. The libertarian movement has grown since 2008, and has thus been well placed to have an influence. Ron Paul, who had surprising visibility in the 2008 GOP primaries, has garnered much more support in the 2012 primaries. Libertarian antistatism has roots in the 1960s counterculture as well as on the right, and Libertarians part company with mainstream conservatives over such issues as prisons and sentencing, drug legalization, foreign intervention, and civil liberties. Libertarians who have joined the Tea Party movement tend to emphasize commonalities with other conservatives, although as I discuss later, differences occasionally emerge.[12]

RACE AND THE TEA PARTY MOVEMENT

While Tea Party spokespeople tend to claim that the movement is purely fiscal, it is hard to imagine that such antistatist rage is unconnected to the racism that fueled it in prior decades. Prior to publicized charges of racism in the movement, Obama was portrayed as both a figure of racial abjection and a symbol of totalitarian control on Tea Party placards and in supporters' rhetoric, suggesting a powerful link between race and the state in Tea Party rage. For an antistatist populism that contrasts a virtuous white middle against black dependents below and controlling elites above, Obama represents both poles.

Obama's taking office coincided not just with the rise of the Tea Party movement but also with what became known as the "birther" movement. Birthers argue that Obama holds the office of the presidency illegally because of the constitutional requirement that presidents be born on U.S. soil. Beyond the geographic fact of his birth in the state of Hawaii, Obama has successfully claimed political and cultural birthright through maternal forebears in the American heartland, through the strivings of an immigrant father, and through his national creedal commitments to equality and pluralism redeemed by his blackness in a post–civil rights era. Thus his birther opponents seek to nullify his claims by locating him outside the boundaries of the nation not ideologically, but rather bodily. This movement has had strong resonance for Americans unable to accept a black president. However, such open attacks are tricky in an increasingly multicultural nation. Racial claims about Obama's American authenticity cannot stand on their own because they obviously violate the self-understanding of most Americans as egalitarian and color-blind. On the other hand, a constitutional challenge to legitimacy could not get anywhere without underlying racial appeals. Try to imagine, for instance, an American president of Irish or Australian parentage being challenged on birthright grounds. While distinct phenomena, there was clear overlap between birthers and Tea Partiers. Indeed, five of the six national Tea Party organizations have birthers in their leadership.

The link between racism and Tea Party politics publicly came to a head on March 19, 2009: While walking to the Capitol, Representatives André Carson of Indiana, Emanuel Cleaver II of Missouri, and John Lewis of Georgia, all black, were subject to racial epithets and spitting by Tea Partiers who were there to protest the passage of federal health care reform.[13] Increasing links to racism between groups and individuals associated with the Tea Party movement led the National Association for the Advancement of Colored People (NAACP) to pass a resolution calling on the Tea Party movement to denounce racist elements in its midst.[14] The NAACP also partnered with the Institute for Research and Education on Human Rights to analyze the presence of racism in the Tea Party movement. The resulting report, *Tea Party Nationalism*, evaluates the presence of racism through the language of Tea Party leaders and participants, of racial symbolism at Tea Party rallies, and of Tea Partiers who are also associated with white supremacist organizations.[15] The report is a thorough investigation of the major Tea Party organizations at both the national and local level. It provides evidence that there are racists in the movement, and that in certain locales, particularly in the South, there is overlap between racist organizations like the Council of Conservative Citizens and Tea Party groups. Professional Islamophobes such as Pamela Geller have close ties to some Tea Party organizations, and Burghart and Zeskind document hundreds of Tea Party blog posts expressing anti-Muslim sentiment. Nativist activity, particularly in Arizona around Senate Bill 1070, and the campaign to repeal birthright citizenship, has had Tea Party groups in the vanguard. Klan, neo-Nazi, militia, and border vigilante groups have all tried to make inroads to the Tea Party movement at the local level as well.

This open racist influence on the Tea Party is in the context of a major upsurge in racial nationalism in the United States since 2008. On one end of the spectrum are the birthers and the campaign to repeal the Fourteenth Amendment's birthright citizenship clause, and on the other end, open hate groups. The Southern Poverty Law Center issued a report in February 2011, stating that there are over a thousand Klan and neo-Nazi groups in the United States right now, more than it has ever reported, and over 850 patriot and militia groups in a separate category.[16]

Yet evidence of occasional racist signs at Tea Party rallies, of shared membership with racial conservatives in regionally specific locations, or of a few individuals on boards of national Tea Party organizations who are also associated with racist or nativist movements only goes so far in illuminating the role of race in the Tea Party movement. The Tea Party is a decentralized phenomenon without any organizational structure of accountability, so it is unclear how representative such displays are. Indeed, given the racial history of the modern right, the current spike in white supremacist organizations, and the broad-based nature of any populist movement, the absence of racism would be far more surprising than its presence.

AMBIGUITIES OF RACE IN THE POST-CIVIL RIGHTS ERA

A clear understanding of the role of race in the Tea Party is elusive for a number of reasons. Although much suggests that the movement has powerful racial motivations, race does not signify for modern conservatism as it did during its ascent in the 1960s and '70s. Indeed, conservatives today claim not only color-blindness but also often an emphatic embrace or appropriation of the civil rights movement. More complicated still is the fact that conservatives today must disavow any racial intent. This is a defining paradox of the political moment: Even as the conservative movement has lurched rightward, racial appeal—indeed even racial coding—has become discredited as a form of political address. While Tea Party leaders loudly denounced the NAACP after the call to expunge racists from Tea Party ranks, openly bigoted figures such as Tea Party Express leader Mark Williams were promptly ousted from the movement, and racially charged signs quickly disappeared from Tea Party rallies.[17]

Indeed Tea Party organizations and spokespeople have adamantly refuted claims of racism in a manner distinct from the era of the rise of the right, when conservatives would code language but the issues themselves had transparent racial referents, such as crime, busing, welfare, and affirmative action. In response to Christopher Parker and Matt Barreto's survey[18] that revealed racial animus among Tea Party supporters, Tea Party leader Michael Patrick Leahy wrote: "The Tea Party movement has rejected the discussion of social issues as an unwanted distraction that will hurt the movement's ability to accomplish its constitutional and fiscal objectives. I know this because I helped start the movement, and I have participated in hundreds of conference calls where this position has been deliberated and confirmed—both publicly and privately—innumerable times." The quote is revealing for the emphasis Tea Party leaders have placed on avoiding racial issues, but also for the essential admission that racial identification runs so deep that the effort required deliberation over "hundreds of conference calls."[19]

In his 2010 U.S. Senate campaign memoir, Tea Party-backed Kentucky senator Rand Paul spends pages defending himself from charges of racism. He writes, "It is worth pointing out that my political philosophy, which values the importance of the individual over the collective, is the antithesis of the mind-set of not only bona fide racists but race-obsessed liberals, both of whom always see people as belonging to a group."[20] Referring to the Tea Party's focus on issues of spending and debt, he writes, "The Tea Party doesn't see politics in black and white, but black and red." Such refutations of racial intent are common staples of "color-blind" rhetoric of contemporary conservatives, requiring a denial of the myriad forms of race-based inequality built into U.S. political, economic, and social institutions. And yet the repeated, vehement repudiation of racism speaks to the changed landscape of U.S. politics, where race baiting cannot be openly achieved. Indeed, Paul was in part responding to the moment in his campaign when he appeared on the Rachel Maddow Show and, echoing Goldwater's position in 1964, stated his belief that government should not force private businesses to abide by civil rights law. Compelled to reverse his position because of controversy it caused, he issued a statement the next day that read, "Let me be clear: I support the Civil Rights Act because I overwhelmingly agree with the intent of the legislation, which was to stop discrimination in the public sphere and halt the abhorrent practice of segregation and Jim Crow laws."[21] Tea Partiers are perhaps particularly sensitive to the charge of racism. FreedomWorks campaign director Brendan Steinhauser, who counts civil rights leader Bayard Rustin as one of his inspirations, starkly stated, "Being a racist is one of the worst things you can be in this society. No one wants to be labeled this."[22]

RACIAL INNOCENCE AND APPROPRIATION

To dismiss Tea Party disavowals of racism as merely color-blind window dressing would be to underestimate complex changes afoot. How does one account for the high-profile Tea Party–associated black, Latino, and Asian American politicians, such as Representative Allen West and Senator Marco Rubio from Florida; and Governor Nikki Haley and Representative Tim Scott from South Carolina—the latter who defeated one of Strom Thurmond's (white) children for the Republican nomination? They are not evidence of an embrace of Tea Party politics by significant numbers of voters of color, as the Republican base of each of these candidates is largely white. But their successful candidacies do perhaps speak to a strong desire for racial innocence, a notion that Lawrie Balfour, following James Baldwin, explains as an expressed affirmation of racial equality that nevertheless disavows the very historical conditions and contemporary practices that continue to reproduce racial stratification.[23] More than just disavowal, Tea Partiers often affirm innocence through appropriation. "We want to put a young, edgier face on this movement," said FreedomWorks's Steinhauser about a decision to feature a rapper named Hi-Caliber at 9/12 events. "This isn't a bunch of boring people who just listen to one kind of music. Don't get me wrong. I love country music, but we have an edge, too." Steinhauser's affection for country music is meant to affirm the Tea Party's conservative cultural basis even as he explains his desire to breathe new life into this identity in a black idiom—which, as Toni Morrison has argued, has been used to signal what is modern, hip, and urbane in the white American imagination.[24]

Perhaps the most powerful example of racial appropriation associated with the Tea Party movement was Glenn Beck's emphatic identification with the very struggle against which modern conservatism was built. On his radio show on May 24, 2010, Beck described himself and his allies as "the inheritors and the protectors of the civil rights movement." He said he "wouldn't be surprised if in our lifetime dogs and fire hoses are released or opened on us. I wouldn't be surprised," he went on, "if a few of us get a billy club to the head. I wouldn't be surprised if some of us go to jail—just like Martin Luther King did—on trumped-up charges. Tough times are coming."[25] Where color-blind conservatives deracialize King to make him into one of them, here Beck almost racializes conservatives to make them more like King. Beck's followers become the scorned, the beaten, the jailed—those who will be the first sacrificed to "tough times." In the spring and summer of 2010, Beck, who at the time was the icon of the Tea Party movement, organized an event called "Restoring Honor" on the anniversary of the 1963 March on Washington. The well-attended event featured speeches by both Sarah Palin and Martin Luther King Jr.'s niece, Alveda King. Beck has a long history of making racist comments and jokes, and famously accused Obama of having a "deep-seated hatred of white people." Beyond racism directly, he trades in a demonological style that places him squarely within what Michael Rogin called countersubversion, an American political tradition rooted in the nation's origins in black slavery and Indian land theft.[26] And yet Beck's ability to draw hundreds of thousands of revelers for an event to memorialize King and the March on Washington, and his own dramatic identification with the violence suffered by civil rights marchers, takes us beyond the territory of color-blind conservatism. But to where? Significantly, Beck decided that this rally, unlike his television and radio shows, would not be a political event but a spiritual one. Beck's own fantasies of racial identification notwithstanding, the historical contradictions between populist conservatism and civil rights struggle could not easily be contained in such a symbolically charged rally. Or perhaps it is simply that without Beck's countersubversion on display, there are no politics.

POLITICAL CHANGES IN THE RACIAL TERRAIN OF U.S. POLITICS

How should we understand a movement that expresses the antistatist discourse borne of the racial logic of the modern right, and which demonizes a black president, but which emphatically disavows racial motivations, appropriates icons and narratives of the civil rights movement, and successfully backs prominent political candidates of color? There are no clear answers yet to be had, but there are a number of dynamics at work worth considering.

First, the current U.S. right is not being built directly in opposition to a developing black freedom movement as it was in the era from the late 1950s through the 1970s. Racial discourse, both open and coded, across a spectrum of issues including crime, welfare, housing, education, and employment stoked fears and resentments and greatly expanded the popular base of the Republican Party. In the post-civil rights era, however, such appeals have far less affective power, and people of color have become celebrated national figures not just in sports and entertainment, but also in politics. Yet the same period has seen the further isolation and targeting of the black poor through the simultaneous processes of neoliberal deindustrialization, dismantling of the welfare state, and the massive expansion of the prison system. The combination of symbolic victories and political defeats of the civil rights movement has produced a context that constrains the right from deploying racial affect, robs it of the political resistance against which it was constructed, and yet offers new possibilities for racial appropriation.

Related to this, certain forms of multiculturalism and even antiracism have made inroads among conservatives in the last two decades. Steven Teles has shown that more than mere rhetoric, "compassionate conservatism" has a policy legacy advanced by conservatives seeking to embrace a conservative version of black civil rights.[27] Critics argued that Bush's "compassionate conservatism" rhetoric was cynical at best.[28] Yet scholars have begun to show that a number of conservatives, particularly within the Bush administration, sought to reclaim and recast the civil rights legacy as something more meaningful than color-blindness.[29] Historian Gary Gerstle has argued that George W. Bush held and expressed a strong personal commitment to racial equality, influenced strongly by Latino friends and associates in Texas, and by his evangelical religious faith.[30] Bush's appointment of Colin Powell as secretary of state and Condoleezza Rice as both national security advisor and secretary of state placed African Americans in prominent and very visible positions in the executive branch for the first time. Further, Republican National Committee Chair Ken Mehlman and later Bush himself apologized to the NAACP for the very Southern Strategy that brought their immediate conservative forebears to national power. And as Victoria Hattam and I have argued, Mehlman, Rice, Bush, Michael Gerson, and others sought to re-narrate the civil rights movement to advance Bush initiatives ranging from education policy to the Iraq War.[31] While such repurposing was greeted with skepticism on the left and within the civil rights community, it represented a micropolitical opening among conservatives in their own relationship to race politics—one that challenges the presumption that black politics naturally resides in progressive identifications. Unlike color-blindness, phenotype is neither ignored nor disavowed by these conservatives. Rather it is meaningfully resignified—along with the civil rights movement itself—as potentially conservative.

Finally, many fiscal conservatives and libertarians strongly oppose involvement in social and cultural issues, splitting antistatists from cultural nationalists. The issue of crime for instance, long a fundamental component of conservative racial strategy, is largely absent in Tea Party rhetoric. And the issues of race and culture that have emerged as conservative concerns have seen Tea Partiers take different sides. In the spring of 2010, when the Arizona State Senate introduced S.B. 1070, the subsequent fight found people associated with the Tea Party split over the issue, even while conservatives generally took up the cause.[32] Nationally, both Tea Party Patriots and FreedomWorks opposed any discussion of the issue, compelling anti-immigrant former Colorado U.S. Representative Tom Tancredo to complain, "The national Tea Party Patriots, which is affiliated with the FreedomWorks organization, has been vocal and systematic in excluding immigration-related concerns from its 'Contract from America.'"[33] Nevertheless, in Arizona, Tea Party groups were at the forefront of the battle on behalf of S.B. 1070 throughout the state, providing the organizing network capacity to turn people out at community meetings and public hearings.[34]

Another example was the debate over the plan for Park51, a proposed thirteen-story Muslim community center two blocks from Ground Zero in lower Manhattan. As with their support for S.B. 1070, conservatives nationally were energized in their fierce opposition to the construction of the center. The Rand Paul campaign, for instance, sought to distance itself from the issue, putting out a statement that simply said, "We don't want New York intervening in our local Kentucky issues, and we don't look to interfere with New York's local issues."[35] Andrew Ian Dodge, Maine state coordinator for Tea Party Patriots told Politico .com, "Most Tea Party–minded people I talk to say it's in bad taste, but it doesn't fall under our remit. And if it did, we would look at the states' rights and property rights and say, 'OK, they can do whatever they want.' We're very wary about taking up any of these emotional issues, because it dilutes our main focus—which is fiscal, fiscal, fiscal— and we have got the gig down so most Tea Party people don't want to be dragged off on tangents."[36] Some remain ambivalent. "I am torn," conceded Mark Lloyd, chairman of the Lynchburg, Virginia, Tea Party and an advisory board member of the National Tea Party Federation. "I personally want to see the Tea Party stay focused on constitution-ally limited government, fiscal responsibility, and personal liberties, but not everything we are concerned with as individuals can be put into a category."[37] Mark Williams, former head of Tea Party Express who was removed from that post for making racist statements about both blacks and Muslims, began his own non-Tea Party group for people who wanted to be vocal in criticism of the center.

More dedicated racial nationalist groups, even ones that have promoted the Tea Party movement like the Council of Conservative Citizens (CCC) in Mississippi, also have reservations. A leader of the CCC assessed the Tea Party's racial prospects stating, "The fact that hundreds of thousands of white people got up the nerve to oppose the government [was] astonishing. Yet the negative tendency that plagues Tea Party activism is to deny the racial dynamic empowering the movement. The future of this revolution, if that is what it is, depends on white zealots."[38]

SOCIALIST OBAMA AND THE DEMONIZED STATE

It remains to be seen whether the Tea Party movement will endure, but for now racial affect has made the movement successful even in the absence of a black freedom movement to stoke it. This returns us to Obama, whose office taking coincided with the emergence of the Tea Party movement. Obama was inaugurated in the midst of the mortgage crisis and subsequent Great Recession, sharply increased nativist anxieties about immigration from Mexico, and within the long shadow of 9/11. For Obama's racial opponents, he represents a notion of blackness linked to irresponsible welfare spending, foreignness linked to nativist anxieties, and Islam, depicted as a violent, anti-American religion.

But Obama signifies for fiscal conservatives in specific ways as well. As animus toward Obama built in the battle over health care reform, Tea Partiers increasingly labeled Obama not as a taxing, spending, liberal, but as a socialist. This extraordinary claim, which would in no way have been credible even for conservatives prior to Obama's election, has far greater purchase now. TARP, the stimulus package, and health care reform, all of which were moderate pro-market state responses to a historic economic crisis, and TARP actually the product of the Bush administration, were rendered dangerous, threatening expressions of socialism when associated with a black president.

It is instructive to look closely at how Obama was made a socialist in the Tea Party imagination. The most widely circulated symbol associating Obama with socialism among Tea Partiers was the Obama/Joker socialism poster (see Figure 6.1). During the first few months of 2009, an image began circulating of Obama as the Joker from *The Dark Knight*. By summer, tens of thousands of reproductions of the image with the caption *Socialism* were wheat-pasted across the Los Angeles area. As the Tea Party opposition to health care reform developed over the summer of 2009, the Obama/Joker socialism poster was omnipresent. Defenders of the image claimed that there was nothing identifiably racial in the otherwise demonic image, and that the message, *socialism*, is a clear political statement unconnected to race.

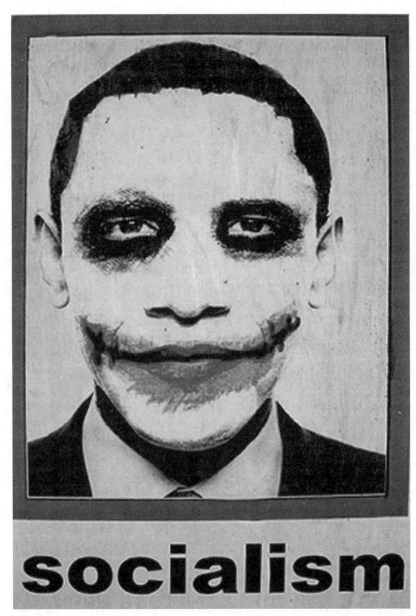

FIGURE 6.1. Obama/Joker socialism poster.

Those who assert that the image is racist, however, have rightly pointed to the minstrelsy connotations of Obama's painted face and the symbolism of the Joker as a figure of uncontrolled urban violence and nihilism. But it is not merely that a racially demonized image of Obama got juxtaposed to the political charge of socialism in the text below it. Indeed, the "Socialism" caption points not away from race, as its defenders would have it, but toward it. The modern conservative movement in the United States, from the late 1940s onward, linked the advance of black civil rights with the threat of a totalitarian state, and of socialism specifically. The modern right, as argued earlier, continually depicted an unholy alliance of invasive state elites above and criminal, parasitic blacks below against a virtuous middle of hardworking white Americans. As a form of political address, there is nothing muddled about the poster's message. Image and text refer to each other along an already well-developed chain of associations.

But again, the changed political landscape means the symbolic relationship between race and state has also changed. The last significant instance of the right's deployment of a menacing black face for political purposes was Lee Atwater's use of convicted rapist William Horton ("Willie" was Atwater's invented nickname) in the 1988 Bush campaign.[39] There, as here, blackness was linked to criminality to discredit a Democratic opponent. The difference is that in the 1988 Bush campaign, "liberalism" was meant to evoke fears of a white president, unleashing black criminals on a vulnerable nation. For contemporary Tea Partiers, "socialism" is meant to evoke fears of a black president unleashing a criminal state on a vulnerable nation. In the former, the state enabled unchecked black aggression, whereas in the latter, blackness enables unchecked state aggression. Without black social unrest as a political issue (or even recent memory), assaults on the modern right's virtuous middle come from above, not below.

RACE AND THE FUTURE OF THE TEA PARTY

What does it mean politically that the Tea Party movement is an articulation of conservative politics directed less at people of color than at the state more generally? The successes of the modern right were achieved through the refashioning of political identities of working- and middle-class whites away from the Democratic liberalism and toward conservative Republicanism. This meant splitting off and racializing the poor as welfare dependents and criminals. But welfare has been largely dismantled, and the prison industrial complex fully realized. Indeed, as noted previously, the issue of crime is mostly absent for Tea Partiers.

Racial affect for the Tea Party circulates most powerfully in attacks on Obama, but as such, these lack substantive policy targets. The birther issue, for instance, has fired the countersubversive imagination, but does not translate directly into more punitive crime legislation or further attacks on affirmative action. Thus, attacks on Obama become assaults on taxation, social spending, and more recently public-sector unions. To be sure, this is precisely the direction FreedomWorks, Americans for Prosperity, and other corporate-funded entities associated with the Tea Party movement want to go. But such a strategy of putting forth fiscal conservatism, antistatism, and libertarian individualism without a clearly identifiable racial frontier against which to shore up popular sentiment may deplete the Tea Party movement of its populist affect.

Fiscal conservatives in the Tea Party movement may want to avoid cultural questions in their quest to dismantle the welfare state in its entirety, but these individualists still require a language of nation or community to advance their politics popularly. Absent specified racial targets against whom to produce an identity on the order of "the silent majority" or "Middle America," attempts to eradicate middle-class entitlements, weaken wage and benefit security for large sectors of the workforce, and preserve tax breaks for the very rich may falter or, as Occupy Wall Street has demonstrated, can become the target of new popular social movements. If we are all Black Americans now, as Melissa Harris-Perry recently suggested, then racial populist exhortations begin to lose their meaning.[40]

NOTES

1. I would like to thank Kevin Bruyneel, Daniel HoSang, Joel Olson, George Shulman, and Priscilla Yamin for helping me think through the peculiarities of the Tea Party movement. I would also like to thank the Columbia University Center for Urban Research and Policy and participants in the City University of New York American Politics Colloquium.

2. See for instance, Devin Burghart and Leonard Zeskind, *Tea Party Nationalism: A Critical Examination of the Tea Party Movement* (Kansas City, MO; Institute for Research and Education on Human Rights, 2010); Christopher Parker, Principal Investigator, "2010 Multi-State Survey of Race and Politics," University of Washington Institute for the Study of Ethnicity, Race, and Sexuality, http://depts.washington.edu/uwiser/racepolitics.html; and Theda Skocpol and Vanessa Williamson, *The Tea Party and the Re-making of Republican Conservatism* (New York: Oxford University Press, 2011).

3. See Scott Rasmussen and Douglas Schoen, *Mad as Hell: How the Tea Party Movement is Fundamentally Remaking Our Two-Party System* (New York: Harper Collins, 2010).

4. Glenn Harlan Reynolds, "At Issue: Is the Tea Party the Next Great Awakening?" *CQ Researcher* 20, no. 11 (2010): 257.

5. Rasmussen and Schoen, 20.

6. Skocpol and Williamson, 2011.

7. Joseph Lowndes, *From the New Deal to the New Right: Race and the Southern Origins of Modern Conservatism* (New Haven: Yale University Press, 2008).

8. Mary C. Brennan, *Turning Right in the Sixties: The Conservative Capture of the GOP* (Chapel Hill: University of North Carolina Press, 1995), 12; Robert Alan Goldberg, *Barry Goldwater* (New Haven: Yale University Press, 1995); Lowndes, *From the New Deal to the New Right*, 45–76; and Rick Perlstein, *Before the Storm: Goldwater and the Unmaking of the American Consensus* (New York: Hill and Wang, 2001).

9. Lowndes, *From the New Deal to the New Right*, 106–139; and Kevin Phillips, *The Emerging Republican Majority* (New Rochelle, NY: Arlington House, 1968).

10. Kate Zernike, *Boiling Mad: Inside Tea Party America* (New York: Times Books, 2010).

11. "Tea Party Patriots Mission Statement and Core Values," Tea Party Patriots website, accessed May 24, 2011, www.teapartypatriots.org/mission .aspx; "About FreedomWorks: Our Mission," FreedomWorks website, accessed May 24, 2011, www.freedomworks.org/about/our-mission; and "Contribute," TeaPartyExpress.org, accessed May 24, 2011, www.teapartyexpress.org/ contribute/.

12. Personal interview with Jack Hunter, libertarian radio host and coauthor with Rand Paul, *The Tea Party Goes to Washington* (Nashville: Center Street, 2010).

13. Robert Pear, "Spitting and Slurs Directed at Lawmakers," *Prescriptions* (blog), *New York Times,* March 20, 2011, accessed May 24, 2011, http:// prescriptions.blogs.nytimes.com/2010/03/20/spitting-and-slurs-directed-at -lawmakers/.

14. Ashley Southall, "NAACP Challenges Tea Party on Racism," *The Caucus* (blog), *New York Times,* July 13, 2010, accessed May 24, 2011, http://thecaucus .blogs.nytimes.com/2010/07/13/n-a-a-c-p-challenges-tea-party-on-racism/ ?scp=1&sq=%20jealous%20naacp%20resolution%20on%20tea%20party% 20%20&st=cse.

15. Burghart and Zeskind, *Tea Party Nationalism.*

16. "SPLC Hate Group Count Tops 1,000 as Radical Right Expansion Continues," *Hatewatch* (blog), Southern Poverty Law Center, accessed May 24, 2011, www.splcenter.org/blog/2011/02/23/new-report-splc-hate-group -count-tops-1000-as-radical-right-expansion-continues/.

17. Matt DeLong, "Tea Party Leader Expelled over Slavery Letter," *Washington Post*, July 18, 2010, accessed May 24, 2011, http://voices .washingtonpost.com/44/2010/07/mcconnell-on-tea-party-racism.html.

18. "Research: 2010 Multi-State Survey of Race and Politics, Christopher S. Parker, Principal Investigator," http://depts.washington.edu/uwiser/racepolitics .html.

19. Michael Patrick Leahy, "Bruce Bartlett's Intellectually Dishonest Smear of the Tea Party Movement," *American Thinker*, June 10, 2010, accessed May 24, 2011, www.americanthinker.com/2010/06/bruce_bartletts_intellectually.html.

20. Rand Paul, *The Tea Party Goes to Washington*, 92–99.

21. Krissah Thompson and Dan Balz, "Rand Paul Comments about Civil Rights Stir Controversy," *Washington Post*, May 21, 2011, accessed May 24, 2011, www .washingtonpost.com/wp-dyn/content/article/2010/05/20/AR2010052003500 .html.

22. Amy Gardner and Krissah Thompson, "Tea Party Groups Battling Perceptions of Racism," *Washington Post*, May 5, 2010, accessed May 24, 2011, www.washingtonpost.com/wp-dyn/content/article/2010/05/04/ AR2010050405168.html.

23. Lawrie Balfour, *The Evidence of Things Not Said: James Baldwin and the Promise of American Democracy* (Ithaca, NY: Cornell University Press, 2001).

24. Toni Morrison, *Playing in the Dark: Whiteness and the Literary Imagination* (New York: Vintage, 1993).

25. Bob Herbert, "America Is Better Than This," *New York Times*, August 27, 2010, accessed May 24, 2011, www.nytimes.com/2010/08/28/ opinion/28herbert.html.

26. Michael Rogin uses "countersubversive tradition" to describe "the creation of monsters as a continuing feature of American politics by the inflation, stigmatization, and dehumanization of political foes. . . . These monsters—the Indian cannibal, the black rapist, the papal whore of Babylon, the monster-hydra United States Bank, the demon rum, the bomb-throwing anarchist, the many-tentacled Communist conspiracy, the agents of international terrorism—are familiar figures in the dream-life that so often dominates American politics." See Michael Rogin, *Ronald Reagan, the Movie and Other Episodes in Political Demonology* (Berkeley: University of California Press, 1987), xiii.

27. Steven Teles, "Compassionate Conservatism, Domestic Policy, and the Politics of Ideational Change," in *Crisis of Conservatism? The Republican Party, the Conservative Movement, and American Politics after Bush*, ed. Joel D. Aberbach and Gillian Peele (New York: Oxford University Press, 2011).

28. Bob Herbert, "In America, a Slick Mix," *New York Times*, August 3, 2000; and Brent Staples, "The Editorial Observer: The Republican Party's Exercise in Minstrelsy," *New York Times*, August 2, 2000.

29. Teles, "Compassionate Conservatism, Domestic Policy, and the Politics of Ideational Change."

30. Gary Gerstle, "Minorities, Multiculturalism, and the Presidency of George W. Bush," in *The Presidency of George W. Bush: A First Historical Assessment*, ed. Julian E. Zelizer (Princeton, NJ: Princeton University Press, 2010), 252–81.

31. Victoria Hattam and Joseph Lowndes, "From Birmingham to Baghdad: The Micropolitics of Political Change," in *Unstructuring Politics: New*

Perspectives on Institutional Diversity and Change, ed. Gerald Berk, Dennis Galvan, and Victoria Hattam (University of Pennsylvania Press, forthcoming).

32. Arizona libertarian and Tea Party radio personality Ernest Hancock was a prominent opponent of the bill, and there was much debate on Arizona Tea Party websites. See David Safier, "SB1070 Update: Tea Party Split on Immigration," *Baja and Alto* (blog), Arizona.com, June 19, 2010, accessed May 24, 2011, www.blogforarizona.com/blog/2010/06/sb1070-update-tea-party-split-on-immigration.html.

33. Tom Tancredo, "The Tea Party *Does* Care about Immigration Issue," WorldNetDaily, June 19, 2010, accessed May 24, 2011, www.wnd.com/index.php?pageId=168369.

34. See Bennett Grubbs, *The Tea Party and the Virtuous Middle: An Analysis of Racialized Language and Political Identity*, MA thesis, Northern Arizona University, 2011.

35. Marion County Line blog, "Rand Paul, Sane Person," August 16, 2010, accessed May 24, 2011, www.marioncountyline.com/2010/08/rand-paul-sane-person.html.

36. Kenneth Vogel, "Mosque Debate Strains Obama, Tea Party and GOP," NBC New York, August 18, 2010, accessed May 24, 2011, www.nbcnewyork.com/news/local/Mosque_debate_strains_tea_party__GOP-100964969.html.

37. Kenneth Vogel, "Mosque Debate Strains Obama, Tea Party and GOP."

38. Burghart and Zeskind, *Tea Party Nationalism*, 61.

39. Tali Mendelberg, *The Race Card: Campaign Strategy, Implicit Messages, and the Norm of Equality* (Princeton: Princeton University Press, 2001).

40. Melissa Harris-Perry, "Are We All Black Americans Now?" *The Nation*, April 18, 2011.

CHAPTER 7

Of Mama Grizzlies and Politics

Women and the Tea Party

MELISSA DECKMAN

. . . All across this country, women are standing up and speaking out for common-sense solutions. These policies coming out of DC right now—this fundamental transformation of America—well, a lot of women, who are very concerned about their kids' futures, say, "We don't like this fundamental transformation, and we're gonna do something about it." It seems like it's kind of a mom awakening in the last year-and-a-half, where women are rising up and saying, "No, we've had enough already." Because moms kinda just know when something's wrong. Here in Alaska, I always think of the mama grizzly bears that rise up on their hind legs when somebody's comin' to attack their cubs, to do something adverse toward their cubs. Ya thought pit bulls were tough! Well, ya don't wanna mess with the mama grizzlies. And that's what we're seeing with all these women who are banding together, rising up, saying, "No—this isn't right for our kids and for our grand-kids. And we're gonna do something about this. . . ." [. . .] Look out, Washington!—'cause there's a whole stampede of pink elephants crossing the line and the ETA stampeding through is November Second, 2010. (Sarah Palin, Web ad, SarahPAC[1])

In 2010, women established themselves as leaders in the Tea Party movement when a record number of GOP women rode the Tea Party wave to win their first seats in Congress—notwithstanding the failures of the Tea Party's most visible and controversial candidates, Christine O'Donnell in Delaware and Sharron Angle in Nevada.[2] The success and visibility of Tea Party women in 2010 stands in contrast to the limited role of women leaders in the GOP's 1994 takeover of Congress and in earlier politically conservative movements in American politics, such as the Christian right.

But how much support for the Tea Party is drawn from women nationally? Is there a "stampede of pink elephants" in our midst as Sarah Palin suggests? Approaching the Tea Party as a relatively new political phenomenon, one in which conservative women seem to be playing a large role in its development, I offer a preliminary assessment of women who support the Tea Party. Using data from a cross-sectional, national survey jointly conducted by the Pew Research Center for the People and the Press and the Pew Forum on Religion and Public Life in July and August 2010,[3] I analyze how much support the Tea Party is drawing from women nationally. I also consider how Tea Party women differ from Republican women, specifically, and American women, more generally, in terms of their personal backgrounds, religious behavior, and political and policy leanings. Lastly, I compare Tea Party women with Tea Party men to uncover how or if the roots of their support for the movement differ. The chapter concludes with a discussion of the challenges that the Tea Party faces in reaching beyond a narrow slice of female supporters to recruit a broader segment of women to the movement.

MAMA GRIZZLIES AND PINK ELEPHANTS:
WOMEN ACTIVISTS IN THE TEA PARTY

Women have assumed pronounced roles as leaders and activists within the Tea Party. Case studies of grassroots Tea Party organizations[4] indicate that there may be more women than men in leadership positions at the local level. Arguably the two most well-known Tea Party politicians nationally are women: former Alaska Governor and 2008 GOP nominee for Vice President Sarah Palin, and Michele Bachmann, the Minnesota congresswoman who started the Tea Party Caucus in the U.S. House and who gained national recognition as a serious contender for the 2012 GOP presidential nomination.

Women are making their mark in the Tea Party as organizational leaders and activists. Amy Kremer, who has gained prominence as the chair and spokesperson of the Tea Party Express, routinely appears on news outlets to promote the views of the Tea Party. Women dominate the board of the Tea Party Patriots, another leading Tea Party organization. Hanna Rosin of *Slate* reported in May 2010 that of its eight board members who serve as national coordinators, six were women, including Jenny Beth Martin, the Tea Party Patriots' founder.[5] Martin, who took a prominent, public role in the "9/12" Washington, DC tax protest organized by former Fox News personality Glenn Beck, was named by *Time* magazine as one of the 100 most influential people in 2010.[6] She claims that women are a natural fit for the Tea Party because as mothers, they have experience in balancing family finances: "Many women are the primary decision makers when it comes to the household budget. . . . [F]rom firsthand experience, they know you cannot spend your way out of debt at home and they know that philosophy translates to businesses and to the government."[7]

Several prominent women's Tea Party organizations have emerged as well, including Smart Girl Politics, which was launched when Stacy Mott, a stay-at-home mom, began blogging about her conservative political views during the 2008 presidential campaign.[8] What started with one woman's blog has grown into an organization with more than 50,000 members that trains and mobilizes women as future activists and political candidates. Their motto is "Engage. Educate. Empower," which they do through a web-savvy blend of social media, active blogs, and their digital Smart Girl Magazine. Since 2009, they have held an annual political summit, featuring key Tea Party movement leaders and conservative female icons such as Michelle Malkin, Liz Cheney, Michele Bachmann, and Phyllis Schlafly. In 2011, the organization held its first presidential straw poll; not surprisingly, Bachmann won. Smart Girl Politics spokeswoman Rebecca Wales described the group to *Slate* as made up of "a lot of mama bears worried about their families."[9]

Wales added that the Tea Party is a compelling place for conservative women activists because "for a long time people have seen the parties as good-ole'-boy, male-run institutions. In the Tea Party, women have finally found their voice."[10] The Republican Party, historian Melanie Gustafson points out, has never been particularly welcoming of women activists or candidates, and the Tea Party effectively allows conservative women who want a voice in politics to bypass the national party structure. Adds Gustafson, "[I] think women are comfortable with [this] type of organizing, because it's community organizing" that revolves around family rituals.[11] Indeed, it is in the grassroots trenches or local and state political arenas that conservative women have proven adept at organizing politically throughout American history, whether fighting against the evils of alcohol in the temperance movement,[12] the "red menace" of communism in the 1950s,[13] or the "second-wave" women's liberation movement in the 1970s and early 1980s and its perceived threats to traditional gender roles.[14]

Mothers may have found a particular niche within the Tea Party as well, drawn in by movement leaders who are adept at framing their messages to appeal to them, none more so than Sarah Palin. Palin likens conservative women activists in the Tea Party to "mama grizzlies" who want to protect their "cubs" from an overreaching federal government—one that places too great a debt burden on future generations.[15] But Palin is not alone among Tea Party leaders in calling "mama grizzlies" to action. The 2010 film produced by the conservative nonprofit organization Citizens United, *Fire from the Heartland: The Awakening of the Conservative Woman*, features prominent women Tea Party leaders and conservative activists. Nearly all of them link their activism to their roles as mothers. Take Dana Loesch, the conservative talk radio host and editor in chief of the political blog Big Journalism, who says the following to explain the Tea Party's appeal to mothers: "Motherhood is a political act. Women realize that their involvement with politics is part of motherhood. Their involvement in the national discourse about where our country is heading is about motherhood because we are raising the next generation." Or, as Janine Turner, an actress turned conservative radio show host and cofounder of the nonprofit educational group Constituting America, explains in the film: "American women are seeing the writing on the wall and mothers are seeing the writing on the wall. Wait a minute—our children may end up living in tyranny."

"Defending the family" is certainly not a new theme employed by political leaders to galvanize parents—particularly mothers—into conservative political activism. This theme was taken up by the Christian right in recent years to justify opposition to policies that challenged their views on social issues such as the legalization of abortion or same-sex marriage. Christian right activists—both mothers and fathers—involved in the local grassroots arena of school boards have opposed comprehensive sex education and evolution because such policies are both an affront to their religious beliefs and because their instruction in public schools directly challenges the ability of Christian parents to guide the moral upbringing of their children.[16]

What is new among Tea Party activists, especially Tea Party women when compared with previous conservative political activists, is the direct linkage between their stances on fiscal issues and their perceived need to protect their families. Tea Party activists frame reducing both the size and scope of government as a moral obligation to reduce the debt burden passed down to the next generation. When couched in such a way, this rhetoric could potentially appeal to a larger swatch of American women than, say, just those who identify with the Christian right.

At the same time, however, the Tea Party faces a challenge in building support among American women. Women's strong support nationally of policies such as welfare and other assistance to the poor has driven the long-standing gender gap which finds that American women are significantly more likely to support the welfare state, identify as Democrats, and vote for Democratic candidates than American men.[17]

Whether we can expect a "stampede of pink elephants" in future elections, as Sarah Palin predicted in her 2010 SarahPAC advertisement, depends in large part on how successful the movement is in convincing American women that smaller government is good for families. But before we can speculate about how appealing the Tea Party message may be to American women in 2012 and beyond, we must first understand the views and backgrounds of women who currently support the movement. What do women who support the Tea Party believe? How do Tea Party women compare with American women nationally in terms of public policy attitudes and likely voting behavior? Are Tea Party women just a more conservative faction within the GOP? Are Tea Party women merely Christian right activists using a different name and taking up the cause of fiscal conservatism along with social conservatism? And does the gender gap in American politics carry over to Tea Party activists? Do Tea Party women differ in their politics from Tea Party men?

TEA PARTY WOMEN: DRAWN FROM THE CHRISTIAN RIGHT?

Tables 7.1 through 7.4 offer an exploration of the background and political views of Tea Party women. Here, I use the 2010 Pew Survey data to examine three separate groups of women: women who self-identify as Tea Party supporters (17.9 percent of the sample); women

TABLE 7.1   TEA PARTY WOMEN, GOP WOMEN, AND WOMEN AT LARGE:
DEMOGRAPHICS

	Tea Party Women	GOP Women	Women Nationally
Race			
White	82.3%	86.4%	68.9%
African American	5.3%	2.3%	11.4%
Latino	6.2%	5.5%	12.5%
Other	3.9%	4.1%	6.1%
Age			
18–24	7.6%	12.2%	12.0%
25–34	6.4%	12.2%	15.8%
35–44	12.4%	15.3%	16.4%
45–54	24.2%	22.3%	19.6%
55–65	17.9%	15.6%	15.4%
65+	27.8%	19.9%	18.4%
Region			
Northeast	17.8%	18.4%	19.8%
Midwest	25.1%	24.6%	23.6%
South	35.3%	40.1%	36.7%
West	21.8%	16.9%	19.9%
Income			
Less than $30,000	16.4%	21.2%	28.0%
$30,000 to under $50,000	17.5%	17.3%	16.4%
$50,000 to under $75,000	17.2%	15.4%	13.3%
$75,000 to under $100,000	10.1%	9.7%	9.6%
$100,000 and over	15.4%	16.5%	5.6%
DK/Refused	23.4%	19.8%	19.3%
Education			
Less than high school	6.7%	8.7%	11.9%
High school graduate	29.8%	30.8%	33.8%
Some college	27.1%	30.4%	25.1%
College degree	35.6%	29.5%	28.6%
Marital Status			
Married or partnered	64.4%	66.6%	58.5%
Not married or partnered	34.2%	32.5%	41.5%

SOURCE: Summer 2010 PEW Survey.[18]

who self-identify as Republicans, which includes Tea Party supporters (26.3 percent); and all women in the sample, inclusive of Tea Party supporters and Republicans.

As Table 7.1 demonstrates, Tea Party women are overwhelmingly white and older when compared to either Republican women or women nationally. Their geographical composition is similar to women nationally, although it is interesting that they are less likely to come from the South than are Republican women. Their incomes are similar to Republican women but are higher than women nationally. And Tea Party women are well educated, being more likely than both Republican women and American women to have a college degree. Along with Republican women, they are slightly more likely to be married than women nationally.

Table 7.2 shows that Tea Party women look a lot like other Republican women when it comes to religious tradition and born-again status: They are drawn disproportionately from the ranks of Protestants and born-again Christians. However, on other measures of religious behavior and religious belief, Tea Party women are more devout and theologically more conservative than even their Republican sisters. Tea Party women report attending church more often than GOP women or American women nationally, are more likely than the other two groups of women to say that religion is very important to their lives, and have the most conservative view of scripture of all groups. In other words, Tea Party women are the most likely of the three groups of women to share similarities with Christian right activists, which suggests at the very least that the Tea Party has done a good job of recruiting devout, religiously conservative women to their ranks.

Turning to their political and policy views, we find in Table 7.3 that Tea Party women are overwhelmingly Republican in their party identification and are much more likely than even Republican women to identify themselves as very conservative. They are the group least likely to approve of Barack Obama's performance as president. They are also the group who appear most inclined to vote (the pro-voting bias of all survey respondents notwithstanding), and they are more than twice as likely as women nationally to intend to vote for a Republican. However, Tea Party women are somewhat less likely than Republican women to vote for a Republican candidate, which may be indicative of Tea Party activists' efforts to distance themselves officially from any one party.

TABLE 7.2   TEA PARTY WOMEN, GOP WOMEN, AND WOMEN AT LARGE:
RELIGIOSITY

	Tea Party Women	GOP Women	Women Nationally
Religious Tradition			
Protestant	56.0%	55.0%	44.1%
Roman Catholic	24.0%	20.2%	23.8%
Mormon	2.0%	2.1%	1.4%
Jews	1.0%	.6%	1.7%
Other Christian	14.3%	17.9%	18.1%
Other religious tradition	.0%	.0%	1.3%
Secular/unsure	2.8%	4.2%	9.4%
Born-Again Christian			
Yes	55.8%	54.3%	46.1%
No	41.0%	42.7%	49.0%
Church Attendance			
Once a week or more	61.8%	50.9%	43.1%
Once/twice a month	14.5%	14.7%	14.0%
A few times a year	9.0%	16.9%	19.0%
Seldom	9.3%	12.4%	14.1%
Never	4.4%	4.4%	8.4%
Importance of Religion in your life			
Very important	83.8%	72.9%	65.7%
Somewhat important	10.4%	19.9%	21.6%
Not too important	2.5%	3.8%	6.4%
Not at all important	2.7%	2.8%	5.7%
Views on Holy Book			
Word of God, literally true	52.0%	44.4%	37.7%
Word of God, not everything is literally true	31.3%	34.4%	30.9%
Word of man	10.4%	11.7%	19.3%
Don't know/unsure	6.3%	9.5%	12.1%

SOURCE: Summer 2010 PEW Survey.[19]

On a number of issues, Tea Party women place the same importance as GOP and American women generally when considering their
intended congressional vote. Not surprisingly, all women respondents
say that the economy is paramount on their minds, as is energy (recall
that this survey was taken at a time of record gas prices and during
the middle of the BP oil spill crisis in the Gulf of Mexico in the summer of 2010). All women express fairly similar levels of concern about

TABLE 7.3 TEA PARTY WOMEN, GOP WOMEN, AND WOMEN AT LARGE:
POLITICAL PROFILE

	Tea Party Women	GOP Women	Women Nationally
Party Identification			
Republican	80.0%	N/A	26.3%
Democratic	14.0%		36.8%
Independent	5.3%		29.7%
DK/unsure	.7%		7.2%
Ideology			
Very conservative	17.8%	11.2%	5.5%
Conservative	53.6%	50.5%	31.7%
Moderate	20.7%	30.5%	35.2%
Liberal	3.0%	3.4%	15.7%
Very liberal	2.1%	1.7%	5.3%
Obama Approval			
Approve of job	13.2%	16.6%	50.0%
Disapprove of job	84.2%	72.9%	38.6%
DK	2.7%	10.5%	11.4%
Intention to Vote			
Yes	97.2%	86.0%	80.1%
No	2.8%	11.1%	16.2%
Intended Congressional Vote			
Republican candidate	82.4%	88.1%	39.5%
Democratic candidate	12.6%	6.6%	49.5%
Unsure	5.0%	5.3%	11.1%
The Following Issues are "Very Important" to Intended Congressional Vote:			
Economy	90.3%	88.9%	89.8%
Gay marriage	40.6%	37.5%	31.5%
Abortion	59.2%	57.0%	48.1%
Environment	38.6%	47.4%	64.4%
Afghanistan	78.7%	64.0%	56.4%
Jobs	63.5%	59.4%	59.7%
Energy	89.6%	90.5%	91.0%
Financial system	53.5%	51.9%	64.7%
Immigration	74.1%	63.7%	67.1%
Terrorism	78.4%	79.3%	73.4%
Health care	83.0%	81.0%	83.9%
Taxes	75.6%	74.5%	65.7%
Federal budget	85.4%	76.2%	67.2%

SOURCE: Summer 2010 PEW Survey.[20]

jobs, terrorism, and immigration, whereas Tea Party women and GOP women are similar in terms of their emphasis on the importance of taxes and two social issues: gay marriage and abortion. With respect to the latter, however, Tea Party women are the most likely of all groups of women respondents to say that gay marriage and abortion are very important to their intended congressional vote, which suggests again that the Tea Party may be successful in recruiting conservative Christian women to their cause. Where do Tea Party women differ from GOP women? Tea Party women are more likely than GOP women (and women nationally) to say that Afghanistan and immigration are important factors in their intended vote choice; moreover, they are far less likely than GOP women (and women nationally) to say that the environment is a very important consideration in their intended vote.

Table 7.4 compares issue attitudes—not just the salience of certain issues in the voting calculus of respondents—among Tea Party women, GOP women, and American women nationally. On all seven public policy issues, Tea Party women, by far, hold the most conservative viewpoints. While it is not surprising to find that Tea Party women are far more conservative than women at large in the United States, some of the differences are striking, especially regarding social issues. More than two-thirds of Tea Party women believe that abortion should be illegal in most or all cases compared with 46.7 percent of women nationally. Just 26.8 percent of Tea Party women support gay marriage compared with 51.8 percent of women nationally. But it is not just social issues where differences are stark: Tea Party women are far less likely than American women or Republican women to favor government assistance to the poor—58.1 percent oppose or strongly oppose such programs compared with just 28.9 percent of American women and 48.5 percent of GOP women. Tea Party women are the group least likely to favor stronger environmental laws and most likely to favor better border security as a way to deal with immigration problems in the United States.

What do these data tell us about Tea Party women in America? As expected, women who support the Tea Party have consistently conservative views on financial and governmental regulatory policy (such as environmental concerns), even more so than their GOP counterparts. More surprising is that Tea Party women are more religiously devout and theologically orthodox than Republican women and they hold more conservative positions on gay rights and abortion than other Republican

	Tea Party Women	GOP Women	Women Nationally
Immigration			
Better border security	52.9%	41.5%	28.7%
Path to citizenship	10.9%	16.6%	25.9%
Both	36.1%	41.1%	44.6%
None of these	.1%	.8%	.8%
Death Penalty			
Strongly favor	37.2%	35.8%	29.4%
Favor	38.8%	41.8%	33.5%
Oppose	17.6%	16.9%	25.4%
Strongly oppose	6.4%	5.5%	11.7%
Same-Sex Marriage			
Strongly favor	7.5%	10.2%	22.8%
Favor	19.3%	24.6%	29.0%
Oppose	32.6%	27.8%	22.9%
Strongly oppose	40.6%	37.4%	25.4%
Government Assistance to Poor			
Strongly favor	13.9%	21.1%	31.2%
Favor	28.0%	30.4%	39.9%
Oppose	44.0%	35.9%	20.6%
Strongly oppose	14.1%	12.6%	8.3%
Stronger Environmental Laws			
Strongly favor	22.7%	27.5%	40.3%
Favor	50.3%	53.8%	48.0%
Oppose	20.9%	13.1%	7.4%
Strongly oppose	6.1%	5.6%	4.4%
Gays in Military			
Strongly favor	12.6%	15.5%	28.2%
Favor	43.2%	44.7%	44.0%
Oppose	25.9%	21.9%	16.1%
Strongly oppose	18.3%	17.9%	11.6%
Abortion			
Legal in all cases	9.5%	12.0%	19.2%
Legal in most cases	23.2%	26.9%	34.1%
Illegal in most cases	40.1%	36.5%	26.9%
Illegal in all cases	27.3%	24.5%	19.8%

SOURCE: Summer 2010 PEW Survey.[21]

women. While the public face of the Tea Party is one that touts its economic concerns, social issues still resonate with Tea Party women. But are their views at all different compared with Tea Party men?

TEA PARTY WOMEN AND TEA PARTY MEN: A GENDER GAP?

An analysis of the demographics of Tea Party women and Tea Party men show few substantial differences. Women and men in the Tea Party are remarkably similar in terms of their education background, their incomes, their race, their geographic location, and their marital status. One difference between Tea Party women and Tea Party men concerns age. Support for the Tea Party among men appears more uniform across age categories, whereas for women it increases in older age groups. For example, 14.9 percent of male Tea Party supporters reported being between the ages of 25 and 34 compared with just 6.4 percent of female Tea Party supporters; likewise, 27.8 percent of Tea Party women can be found in the 65 years and older age group compared with just 18.9 percent of Tea Party men.

There are notable differences between Tea Party men and Tea Party women when it comes to religion (see Table 7.5). Tea Party women are more likely than Tea Party men to be Protestants—and less likely to be secular.[22] They are also more likely to report being born-again Christians than are Tea Party men. Perhaps most striking are the findings concerning church attendance, salience of religion, and views of the Bible. On all three measures, Tea Party women profess more religiously orthodox beliefs and practices than do Tea Party men. Part of this tendency may be attributable to the larger gender gap in religiosity that exists nationally and that has been well documented for years, one that finds that American women of all stripes are more religiously observant than men[23]—but the gap between Tea Party women and Tea Party men on these measures is approximately 10 percentage points larger than the religious gender gap nationally.[24] In fact, Tea Party men look much more like Americans generally when it comes to their religious background on matters concerning church attendance, religious salience, and views on the Bible. Tea Party women, however, are notably more religious than all Americans, American women, *and* Republican women.

Does religion continue to be an important differentiator between women and men in terms of support for the Tea Party while

TABLE 7.5   TEA PARTY WOMEN AND TEA PARTY MEN: A RELIGIOUS COMPARISON

	Tea Party Women	Tea Party Men
Religious Tradition		
Protestant	56.0%	44.7%
Roman Catholic	24.0%	21.0%
Mormon	2.0%	3.5%
Jews	1.0%	2.3%
Other Christian	14.3%	17.6%
Other religious tradition	.0%	.5%
Secular	2.8%	10.4%
Born-Again Christian (If Christian)		
Yes	55.8%	48.1%
No	41.0%	49.0%
Church Attendance		
Once a week or more	61.8%	41.2%
Once/twice a month	14.5%	14.9%
A few times a year	9.0%	18.5%
Seldom	9.3%	11.7%
Never	4.4%	12.4%
Importance of Religion in Your Life		
Very important	83.8%	55.4%
Somewhat important	10.4%	27.9%
Not too important	2.5%	6.4%
Not at all important	2.7%	9.8%
Views on Holy Book		
Word of God, literally true	52.4%	36.8%
Word of God, not everything is literally true	31.3%	32.5%
Word of man	10.4%	23.1%
Don't know/unsure	6.3%	6.6%

SOURCE: Summer 2010 PEW Survey.[25]

considering other factors? Table 7.6 presents the results of two separate logistic regression analyses that predict support for the Tea Party, first for women and then for men.[26] I use similar control variables as Abramowitz (Chapter 8 in this volume) to predict support for the movement including age, education, income, Republican party status, conservative ideology, and support for Obama. Regrettably, there are no questions in the Pew Survey that tackle racial resentment (included in the Abramowitz model); however, my models include three religious variables instead of just one like Abramowitz's model: frequency of

TABLE 7.6 PREDICTING SUPPORT FOR THE TEA PARTY: WOMEN VERSUS MEN

Independent Variables	Support for Tea Party: Women	Support for Tea Party: Men
Age	−.010(.005)*	−.005(.005)
Education	−.198(.058)***	.063(.053)
Income	.137(.033)***	−.042(.032)
Republican	1.995(.227)***	1.365(.191)***
Conservative ideology	.350(.103)***	1.001(.100)***
Support for Obama	−2.421(.213)***	−2.442(.185)***
Church attendance	.142(.066)*	−.064(.062)
Scripture interpretation	.449(.066)*	.024(.208)
Born-again Christian	.300(.220)	.209(.188)
Constant	−3.065	−4.134

SOURCE: Summer 2010 PEW Survey.

NOTE: Significance levels based on one-tailed tests; standard errors in parentheses:

*p < .05

**p < .01

***p < .001

church attendance, views on the Bible (the higher the score, the more literally respondents view the Bible or scripture), and self-identified born-again status.[27]

The models show that Republican status, conservative ideology, and opposition to Obama all help to predict support among both women and men for the Tea Party. However, there are some important distinctions between the sexes. Support for the Tea Party among women (but not men) comes independently from their age, education levels, and income—all of which have a positive impact on support for the Tea Party. Religion appears to have an independent effect on support for the Tea Party only among women. According to the models, two religious independent variables (church attendance and views of scripture) are significant predictors for women in terms of Tea Party support; men's support for the movement does not hinge on religion. What does this mean? The data demonstrate that men support the Tea Party movement for largely political reasons whereas women's support is also conditioned by their socioeconomic status and their religious behavior and beliefs.

While we see that Tea Party women and Tea Party men are different religiously, what about politically? Do any gender gaps appear in terms of their support for public policy issues or other political measures?

TABLE 7.7   TEA PARTY WOMEN VERSUS TEA PARTY MEN: ISSUE POSITIONS
AND CONGRESSIONAL VOTE

	Tea Party Women	Tea Party Men
Intended Congressional Vote		
Republican candidate	82.4%	70.8%
Democratic candidate	12.6%	11.0%
Unsure/other	5.0%	8.1%
The Following Issues are "Very Important" to Intended Congressional Vote:		
Economy	90.3%	93.3%
Gay marriage	40.6%	31.0%
Abortion	59.2%	45.6%
Environment	38.6%	35.8%
Afghanistan	78.7%	79.2%
Jobs	63.5%	54.8%
Energy	89.6%	82.6%
Financial system	53.5%	60.2%
Immigration	74.1%	63.7%
Terrorism	78.4%	79.2%
Health care	83.0%	67.8%
Taxes	75.6%	82.0%
Federal budget	85.4%	81.0%
Immigration		
Better border security	52.9%	60.6%
Path to citizenship	10.9%	7.7%
Both	36.1%	31.0%
None of these	.1%	.7%
Death Penalty: Favor	76.0%	85.4%
Same-Sex Marriage: Favor	26.8%	22.2%
Gov't Assistance to Poor: Favor	41.9%	31.8%
Stronger Environmental Laws: Favor	73.0%	62.7%
Gays in Military: Favor	55.8%	45.1%
Abortion: Legal in all or most cases	31.7%	40.0%

SOURCE: Summer 2010 PEW Survey.

When it comes to party identification, ideology, approval of Obama as president, and intention to vote, Tea Party women and Tea Party men are similar. And they place similar amounts of emphasis on most issues when it comes to considering their intended congressional vote choice (see Table 7.7). Yet, while well over 90 percent of Tea Party support- ers of both genders indicate an intention to vote for a congressional candidate, Tea Party women seem more committed to GOP candidates than Tea Party men: There is an 11 percentage-point difference between men and women in terms of their intention to vote for the Republican candidate for Congress. When it comes to the issues that are very important to their intended congressional vote, Tea Party women are much more likely than Tea Party men to say that gay marriage and abortion are very important. Health care, immigration, and jobs are also more likely to factor into the voting calculus of Tea Party women than Tea Party men, while Tea Party men are more concerned about taxes and the financial system.

Table 7.7 also includes a brief summary of support for the seven policy issues considered in earlier tables.[28] Make no mistake—both Tea Party women and Tea Party men are much more conservative than most Americans on all seven issues. But there are some interesting gender "fissures" (if not large gaps) that emerge between the two groups. Tea Party men are more likely than Tea Party women to stake out more conservative positions on six out of seven public policies, which corresponds to other research that finds that men have more conservative attitudes about the death penalty[29] and social welfare policies,[30] for example. On the issue of gay rights, women have more liberal views than Tea Party men, which follows national trends that show the same.[31] On one important social issue, however, the trend is reversed: Tea Party men are more likely to say that abortion should be legal in all or most cases than are Tea Party women.

BROADENING THE BASE: CHALLENGES TO RECRUITING MORE WOMEN TO THE TEA PARTY

This chapter offers a first look at women who support the Tea Party and considers both how they compare with other women politically and with Tea Party men. The previous analysis shows that Tea Party women are more religious and more socially and fiscally conservative than Republican women or women in general. Moreover, women and men are likely drawn to the Tea Party for different reasons. While men's support is rooted in their ideological conservatism, women's support is strongly linked to their religiosity. These findings suggest that there are at least two challenges to efforts by the Tea Party to bring more women into the fold.

The Tea Party is successfully capturing support among women for whom mixing their conservative religious values and conservative politics is a good thing—women who would likely feel right at home in the Christian right. But to broaden its base among women, Tea Party leaders will need to appeal to women who are less religious and less socially conservative. Yet doing so may alienate the women who currently make up the Tea Party membership. In fact, representatives of the Tea Party, including its women leaders, have largely avoided an emphasis on social issues and religious appeals in their public rhetoric—likely in an attempt to gain broader support among an American public that, while increasingly more economically conservative, has grown suspect of those who mix religion and politics.[32] For example, in an appearance on the ABC syndicated show *The View* in May 2010, Amy Kremer, director of the Tea Party Express, maintained that the movement was "all about the fiscal issues . . . no social issues. We don't go there." When pressed by Joy Behar, one of the show's hosts and an outspoken political liberal about whether the Tea Party was pro-choice on abortion, Kremer was resolute: "It doesn't matter. We don't talk about it."[33]

Whether Tea Party women activists successfully maintain this barrier between their public rhetoric regarding economic concerns and their conservative positions on social issues remains to be seen, however. Take the case of Smart Girl Politics' online monthly magazine *Smart Girl Nation*, which began publication in March 2011.[34] Each magazine has about a dozen or so short articles and most stories touch on economic issues, such as wasteful government spending or taxes. But there is space in most editions for other concerns, such as support for Israel (a favorite cause of the Christian right), support for gun rights, and opposition to unions. In several editions, there are also articles about abortion, which take a decidedly pro-life bent.

For instance, in its August 2011 profile of conservative Republican congresswoman Cathy McMorris Rodgers, who founded the Down Syndrome Caucus in Congress and is the mother of a child with Down's, the article notes that Rodgers "believes every life begins at conception and is a gift from God."[35] This approach to the abortion issue certainly employs the softer rhetoric adopted by leaders of the second wave of the Christian right, as discussed in Cohen's chapter (Chapter 9 in this volume). And perhaps it is not too surprising that such stories about social issues are cropping up given that the national data show that Tea Party women are very religious (and very pro-life)—much more so than Tea Party men or American women more generally. Yet any emphasis on these social issues may work against efforts by the Tea Party to recruit more women to its cause in the longer term.

Another sticking point that the Tea Party faces in recruiting more women is the national gender gap with respect to social welfare programs, in which women nationally are more supportive of government safety net programs than men, likely because of their roles as primary caregivers and because they are more dependent on such social welfare programs.[36] While the previous analysis shows that there is also a gender gap in the Tea Party, with Tea Party women holding less conservative views on social welfare concerns than Tea Party men, at the end of the day Tea Party women are still much more conservative than women at large on this issue. Given that the overarching goal of the Tea Party is to reduce the size and role of government in larger society, Tea Party leaders in search of expanding their base have to find a compelling narrative that speaks to women, who are more inclined to support the government safety net than are men. Attempts to rally more women to the Tea Party cause will need to convince women, particularly mothers, that the Tea Party's philosophy about the role of government in society comports with women's roles as caregivers and mothers. As discussed previously, these themes appear in the rhetoric of Tea Party leaders, for example, in references to "mama grizzlies" that Sarah Palin includes in her stump speeches. More empirical research needs to be conducted to determine whether Tea Party activists and candidates who identify with the Tea Party—especially Tea Party women—routinely employ such rhetoric in their campaign appeals, and if so, whether such appeals are effective in gaining electoral support from a broader group of women.

The findings presented in this chapter are preliminary, and it remains to be seen if a stampede of "pink elephants" will develop in time for the 2012 election. As of this writing,[37] support for the Tea Party among women is still limited; only 17 percent of American women identify themselves as supporters of the movement. One thing is clear: The extent to which the Tea Party succeeds in making a lasting impact on American politics will be determined by whether it continues to hold appeal for a relatively small slice of conservative women or whether, by framing its message around the role of women as caregivers and mothers called to put the state's fiscal house in order, it is able to appeal to and mobilize a broader segment of American women.

NOTES

1. Transcript from an advertisement for Sarah Palin's political action committee, SarahPAC. The transcript was accessed at www.youtube.com/watch?v=fsUVL6ciK-c.

2. Noreen Malone and Hanna Rosin, "The Mama Grizzlies You Don't Know: Meet the New Crop of GOP Women Elected to Congress in 2010," *Slate,* November 12, 2010, www.slate.com/id/2274446/.

3. The Religion and Public Life Survey, 2010, is free and available to researchers at the Association of Religion Data Archives website, www.thearda.com/Archive/Files/Descriptions/RELPUB10.asp. The survey is based on telephone interviews conducted between July 21 and August 5, 2010, with a nationally representative sample of 3,003 adults living in the continental United States. I have weighted the data according to criteria established by the study's authors. Please see the previous weblink for more information about how the study was conducted.

4. For example, see Lo, Chapter 4 in this volume.

5. See Lo, in this volume.

6. Alex Altman, "The 2010 Time 100: Jenny Beth Martin," April 29, 2010, www.time.com/time/specials/packages/article/0,28804,1984685_1984864_1985462,00.html.

7. Quoted in Kenneth P. Vogel, "Face of the Tea Party is Female," Politico, March 26, 2010, www.politico.com/news/stories/0310/35094.html.

8. Eleanor Clift, "Smart Girls Back Bachmann," *The Daily Beast,* July 30, 2011, www.thedailybeast.com/articles/2011/07/30/smart-girls-summit-michele-bachmann-wins-straw-poll.html.

9. Quoted in Hanna Rosin, "Is the Tea Party a Feminist Movement?" *Slate,* May 12, 2010, www.slate.com/id/2253645/.

10. Quoted in Hanna Rosin, "Is the Tea Party a Feminist Movement?"

11. Quoted in Vogel, "Face of the Tea Party is Female."

12. Holly Berkley Fletcher, *Gender and the American Temperance Movement of the Nineteenth Century* (New York: Routledge, 2008).

13. Mary C. Brennan, *Wives, Mothers, and the Red Menace: Conservative Women and the Crusade against Communism* (Boulder, CO: University Press of Colorado, 2008).

14. Jane Mansbridge, *Why We Lost the ERA* (Chicago: University of Chicago Press, 1986); Donald T. Critchlow, "Mobilizing Women: The 'Social' Issues," in *The Reagan Presidency: Pragmatic Conservatism and Its Legacies*, ed. W. Elliot Brownlee and Hugh Davis Graham (Lawrence, KS: University Press of Kansas, 2003), 293–326; and Catherine E. Rymph, *Republican Women: Feminism and Conservatism from Suffrage through the Rise of the New Right* (Chapel Hill: The University of North Carolina Press, 2006).

15. Sarah Palin calls this "generational theft" in her book *America by Heart: Reflections on Family, Faith, and Flag* (New York: Harper, 2010).

16. Melissa M. Deckman, *School Board Battles: The Christian Right in Local Politics* (Washington, DC: Georgetown University Press, 2004).

17. Karen Kaufmann and John R. Petrocik, "The Changing Politics of American Men: Understanding the Sources of the Gender Gap," *American Journal of Political Science* 43, no. 3 (1999): 864–997; Karen Kaufmann, "Culture Wars, Secular Realignment, and the Gender Gap in Party Identification," *Political Behavior* 24, no. 3 (2002): 283–307; Karen Kaufman, "The Partisan Paradox: Religious Commitment and the Gender Gap in Party Identification," *Public*

Opinion Quarterly 68, no. 4 (2004): 491–511; and Susan J. Carroll, "Voting Choices: Meet You at the Gender Gap," in *Gender and Elections: Shaping the Future of American Politics,* ed. Susan J. Carroll and Richard L. Fox (Cambridge: Cambridge University Press, 2006), 74–96.

18. Numbers do not always add up to 100 percent because I omitted those respondents who neglected to provide information about these characteristics.

19. Numbers do not always add up to 100 percent because I omitted those respondents who neglected to provide information about these characteristics.

20. Numbers do not always add up to 100 percent because I omitted those respondents who neglected to provide information about these characteristics.

21. On these seven policy questions, respondents who answered "don't know" or "refused" are coded as missing.

22. Whether such differences can be considered statistically significant can be determined by a chi-square test. However, chi-square tests are heavily influenced by sample size. When using large amounts of data, even the smallest numerical differences yield a statistically significant result. I have opted not to report chi-square statistics here because I have employed weights developed by Pew researchers to account for demographic discrepancies in the survey data, but which have the effect of inflating the sample size to more than 9,000 cases. When running chi-square tests, then, virtually all differences between men and women Tea Party respondents are "statistically" significant, although many such differences may not be substantially meaningful.

23. Pew Forum on Religion and Public Life, "The Stronger Sex—Spiritually Speaking," February 26, 2009, http://pewforum.org/The-Stronger-Sex—Spiritually -Speaking.aspx; Wade Clark Roof, *Spiritual Marketplace: Baby Boomers and the Remaking of American Religion* (Princeton: Princeton University Press, 1999).

24. For example, in the 2010 Pew Survey, 43.7 percent of American women report attending church weekly compared with 33.5 percent of American men, whereas 61.8 percent of Tea Party women and 41.2 percent of Tea Party men report attending church weekly. Likewise, 66.2 percent of American women and 51.0 percent of American men indicate that religion is "very important" in their lives, compared with 83.8 percent of Tea Party women and 55.4 percent of Tea Party men.

25. Numbers do not always add up to 100 percent because I omitted those respondents who neglected to provide information about these characteristics.

26. I include only respondents who either support or oppose the movement; those survey respondents who do not have or are unsure about a position on the Tea Party are excluded from the analyses. The dependent variable, support for the Tea Party, is coded 1 for support and 0 for opposition.

27. Another version of the model also included a control for importance of religion, a variable that was reported in Table 7.5; however, importance of religion was highly correlated with church attendance, so I opted to exclude it from the final version of the models.

28. Where possible, I combine strongly favor and favor into one category.

29. Richard Seltzer, Jody Newman, and Melissa Voorhees Leighton, *Sex as a Political Variable: Women as Candidates and Voters in U.S. Elections* (Boulder, CO: Lynne Rienner Publishers, 1997).

30. Carole Kennedy Chaney, R. Michael Alvarez, and Jonathan Nagler, "Explaining the Gender Gap in U.S. Presidential Elections, 1980–1992," *Political Research Quarterly* 51, no. 2 (1998): 311–39; Kaufmann, "Culture Wars, Secular Realignment, and the Gender Gap in Party Identification"; and Kaufman, "The Partisan Paradox: Religious Commitment and the Gender Gap in Party Identification."

31. Gregory M. Herek, "Gender Gaps in Public Opinion about Lesbians and Gay Men," *Public Opinion Quarterly* 66, no. 1 (2002): 40–66; and Melissa Deckman, Sue E. S. Crawford, and Laura Olson, "The Politics of Gay Rights: A Perspective on the Clergy," *Religion and Politics* 1, no. 3 (2008): 384–410.

32. Robert D. Putnam and David E. Campbell, *American Grace: How Religion Divides and Unites Us* (New York: Simon and Schuster, 2010); and David E. Campbell and Robert D. Putnam, "Crashing the Tea Party," *New York Times*, August 16, 2011, www.nytimes.com/2011/08/17/opinion/crashing-the -tea-party.html.

33. ABC's *The View*, first broadcast, May 6, 2010, www.youtube.com/ watch?v=ngzyXKakHug.

34. Copies of *Smart Girl Nation* can be accessed on Smart Girl Nation's website: http://sgpaction.com/sgn.

35. Quoted in Tami Nantz, "Game Changers: Cathy McMorris Rodgers on the Congressional Down Syndrome Caucus," *Smart Girl Nation*, August 7, 2011, accessed on September 17, 2011, http://sgpaction.com/august-2011.

36. Virginia Sapiro, *The Political Integration of Women: Roles, Socialization and Politics* (Champaign: University of Illinois Press, 1983); Kaufmann and Petrocik, "The Changing Politics of American Men: Understanding the Sources of the Gender Gap"; Kaufmann, "Culture Wars, Secular Realignment, and the Gender Gap in Party Identification"; and Laurel Elder and Steven Greene, "Parenthood and the Gender Gap," in *Voting the Gender Gap*, ed. Lois Duke Whitaker, (Champaign: University of Illinois Press, 2008), 119–40.

37. Fall of 2011.

PART THREE

New on the Bloc

Political Impact

CHAPTER 8

Grand Old Tea Party

*Partisan Polarization and the Rise of
the Tea Party Movement*

ALAN I. ABRAMOWITZ

The Tea Party movement has attracted enormous attention from journalists, candidates, and elected officials since it first appeared on the U.S. political scene in early 2009. However, there has been considerable disagreement among political observers about the numbers and motivations of those participating in Tea Party protests; the prevalence of racist sentiments among Tea Party activists; the role played by wealthy individuals, conservative groups, and media figures in fomenting these protests; and the potential long-term impact of the movement.[1] A key question raised by the spread of Tea Party protests and the emergence of Tea Party candidates in numerous House, Senate, and gubernatorial elections is whether this movement represents a new force in American politics or whether it is simply the latest, and perhaps the noisiest, manifestation of the long-term rightward shift of the Republican Party—a shift that can be seen as part of a larger trend toward increasing partisan polarization in American politics.[2]

Political analysts aligned with the liberal wing of the Democratic Party have tended to criticize the Tea Party protests as a largely top-down phenomenon driven by well-funded conservative interest groups and media figures.[3] It is clear that right-wing organizations such as Americans for Prosperity and FreedomWorks have provided important logistical support for the movement and that conservative media figures, mainly associated with Fox News, have played crucial roles in publicizing and encouraging attendance at Tea Party rallies.[4] However, these efforts could not have succeeded without the existence of a large, receptive audience among the public. Any successful social movement requires both leadership and organization and a grassroots army of sympathizers to respond to those leaders and organizations, and the Tea Party movement is no exception.[5]

In this chapter, I analyze the sources of support for the Tea Party movement within the American public. I also explain why the Tea Party movement emerged when it did, immediately following the election of a Democratic president and Congress in 2008, and whether the movement is likely to last beyond the 2010 midterm elections. Using data from the American National Election Studies (NES) cumulative file, I argue that grassroots support for the Tea Party movement can best be understood as a product of the increasing conservatism of the Republican Party's activist base over the past several decades. While only a small fraction of this base has actually participated in Tea Party protests, the expansion of the activist conservative base of the Republican Party has produced a large cadre of politically engaged sympathizers from which such participants can be recruited.

Along with a growing number of conservative Republican activists, the other factor crucial to the emergence of the Tea Party movement at the grass roots was the Democratic victory in the 2008 election and especially the election of Barack Obama as president. Obama is not only the first African American president, but he's also the first non-southern Democratic president since John F. Kennedy and arguably the most progressive Democratic president since Franklin D. Roosevelt.

Obama's mixed racial heritage, his ambitious policy agenda, and the extraordinarily diverse coalition of liberals, young people, and racial minorities that supported him in 2008 all contributed to a powerful negative reaction on the part of many economic and social conservatives aligned with the Republican Party and perhaps among whites who were simply upset about having a black man in the White House. While any Democratic president pursuing a progressive policy agenda would probably have provoked a strong reaction from conservatives, Obama's presence in the White House may have intensified that reaction by activating racial fears and resentments among some whites. These fears and resentments were of course stoked by right-wing politicians, media commentators, and websites.

A recurring theme on the right since even before the 2008 election has been that, because of his mixed racial heritage, Barack Obama's values were different from those of the large majority of white Americans. The widespread promotion by right-wing talk show hosts and websites of claims that Obama was really a Muslim and may not have been born in the United States sought to exploit this sentiment.[6] Acceptance of these beliefs, along with intense opposition to specific policies such as the economic stimulus and health care reform, helped to create a large pool of individuals who were receptive to calls for action by conservative organizations and media figures during 2009 and 2010.

BREWING THE TEA: THE GROWTH OF THE CONSERVATIVE REPUBLICAN BASE, 1972–2008

To understand the origins of the Tea Party movement, one needs to go back many years before the appearance of Barack Obama on the national political scene. The Tea Party movement can best be understood in the context of the long-term growth of partisan-ideological polarization within the American electorate and especially the growing conservatism of the activist base of the Republican Party.

Over the past several decades, the U.S. party system has undergone an ideological realignment at both the elite and mass levels. At the elite level, conservative Democrats and liberal Republicans who once held key leadership positions in the congressional parties have almost disappeared, and the number of moderates in both parties has gradually diminished, leaving a predominantly liberal Democratic Party battling a predominantly conservative Republican Party.[7] At the mass level, change has not been quite as dramatic but citizens have gradually brought their party loyalties into line with their ideological orientations with the result that Democratic identifiers have been moving to the left while Republican identifiers have been moving to the right.[8]

While the alignment of partisanship with ideology is not as close at the mass level as it is at the elite level, the sharpest ideological divide within the American public is found among the most politically engaged citizens. In general, partisan-ideological polarization is greatest among the most interested, informed, and active members of the public: Active Democrats are far more liberal than inactive Democrats and active Republicans are far more conservative than less active Republicans. Moreover, as the parties have become more polarized, the size of each party's activist base has been increasing.[9]

Rather than turning off the public, the growing polarization of the parties appears to have led to increased interest and participation in the electoral process since the 1980s, because citizens perceive that more is at

TABLE 8.1   CAMPAIGN ACTIVISM BY DECADE AMONG REPUBLICAN IDENTIFIERS

Campaign Activities	1952–60	1962–70	1972–80	1982–90	1992–2000	2002–08
0	13%	16%	21%	28%	22%	13%
1	41%	42%	39%	40%	39%	37%
2	24%	22%	23%	21%	26%	31%
3+	22%	20%	17%	11%	13%	19%

SOURCE: American National Election Studies Cumulative File.

stake in elections. Table 8.1 displays the trend in electoral participation among Republican identifiers (people who self-identify as Republicans) over the past six decades according to data from the American National Election Studies. The electoral participation scale is based on responses to six questions about election-related activities—(1) voting; (2) trying to influence someone else's vote; (3) displaying a campaign button, yard sign, or bumper sticker; (4) giving money to a candidate or party; (5) attending a campaign rally; and (6) working for a campaign. Therefore, scores range from 0 for individuals who engaged in no activities to 6 for those who engaged in all six activities.

The data in Table 8.1 show that the percentage of Republican identifiers participating in two or more activities—generally individuals who did more than just vote—reached a low point during the 1980s, but then rebounded in the 1990s and reached an all-time high in the most recent decade. As partisan polarization has increased in recent years, so has the level of activism of Republican identifiers. While only about a third of Republican identifiers reported engaging in at least two activities in the 1980s, fully half reported engaging in at least two activities in the 2000s. At the same time, the percentage of Republican identifiers engaging in at least three activities almost doubled, going from 11 percent in the 1980s to 19 percent in the most recent period.

These results indicate that over the past three decades there has been a marked increase in the size of the activist base of the Republican Party—an increase that preceded the rise of the Tea Party movement. Moreover, as the GOP's activist base was growing, it was also becoming increasingly conservative. Figure 8.1 displays the trend in the average score of Republican identifiers on a 7-point liberal–conservative scale between the 1970s and the 2000s.[10]

Over this time period there has been a fairly steady increase in the average conservatism score of Republican identifiers. Rank-and-file

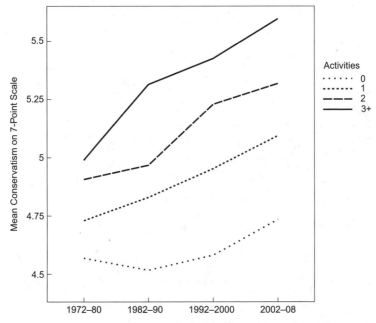

FIGURE 8.1. Average conservatism by decade of Republican identifiers.

Republicans have been following their party's leaders to the right. Moreover, this increase has been greatest among the most active party identifiers—those who presumably pay the most attention to what their party's leaders are doing. While the increase in conservatism was fairly modest among inactive Republicans, it was very substantial among the most active group—those engaging in at least three activities. This group was the most conservative to begin with and it became much more conservative during this time period, going from an average score of 5.0 to an average score of 5.6 on the 7-point scale.

Thus far we have seen that the most active segment of the Republican base almost doubled in size between the 1980s and 2000s, and that it also became considerably more conservative during this time period. But that was not the only important shift in outlook that occurred. Figure 8.2 displays the trend in the average rating of Democratic presidential candidates on the NES feeling thermometer scale over the past five decades. Since 1968, the NES has asked respondents to rate a variety of individuals and groups on this feeling thermometer scale, which ranges from 0 (very cold) to 100 (very warm). A score of 50 is considered neutral.

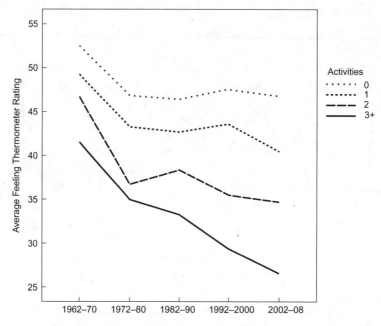

FIGURE 8.2. Average feeling thermometer rating of Democratic presidential candidate by decade among Republican identifiers.

The data in Figure 8.2 show that as Republican identifiers have become increasingly conservative, they have also become increasingly negative in their evaluations of Democratic presidential candidates. A very similar trend is evident in evaluations of the Democratic Party itself. And once again, the most dramatic change occurred among the most active Republican identifiers—those engaging in at least three election activities. Among this group, the average feeling thermometer rating of Democratic presidential candidates fell from a lukewarm 42 degrees in the late 1960s to a very chilly 26 degrees in the 2000s.

Over the past several decades, the active Republican base has become increasingly conservative and increasingly hostile to the Democratic Party and its presidential candidates. By 2008, as the data in Table 8.2 demonstrate, the active Republican base was primed to respond positively to calls from conservative organizations and media figures to engage in protest activity against a newly elected Democratic president and Congress with an ambitious progressive policy agenda. This table compares the social characteristics and political attitudes of active Republican identifiers (those who engaged in two or more

TABLE 8.2   SOCIAL CHARACTERISTICS AND POLITICAL ATTITUDES OF ACTIVE
REPUBLICANS VERSUS OVERALL ELECTORATE IN 2008

	Active Republicans	Overall Electorate
Social Characteristics		
White	92%	75%
Male	50%	45%
College graduates	44%	29%
18–29 years old	16%	21%
50 and older	50%	43%
Income $75K or more	55%	37%
Weekly churchgoer	50%	33%
Political Attitudes		
Conservative	83%	42%
Very conservative	59%	26%
Oppose health care reform	74%	37%
Pro-life on abortion	58%	42%
Oppose gay marriage	83%	61%
Favor reduced government role	75%	41%
Negative rating of Obama	69%	29%
Positive rating of Palin	84%	46%

SOURCE: 2008 American National Election Studies.

election-related activities in 2008) with the social characteristics and
political attitudes of the overall electorate.

In 2008, active Republicans were overwhelmingly white, older, better educated, wealthier, and more religious than the overall electorate.
They were also much more conservative than the overall electorate.
Compared with the electorate as a whole, active Republicans were
much more likely to place themselves on the right side of the 7-point
liberal–conservative scale, to oppose the creation of a single-payer
health care system, to oppose gay marriage, to take a pro-life position
on the issue of abortion, and to favor a reduced role for government in
dealing with social problems. They were also much more likely to give
Barack Obama a negative rating and Sarah Palin a positive rating on the
feeling thermometer scale. Given the decidedly conservative and anti-
Obama attitudes of the active Republican base, the size of this group,
and its relatively high level of previous political engagement, the success
of the Tea Party movement in mobilizing large numbers of anti-Obama
protesters is not surprising.

DRINKING THE TEA: ANALYZING PUBLIC SUPPORT FOR THE TEA PARTY MOVEMENT IN 2010

While several million individuals may have taken part in Tea Party protests or contributed money to Tea Party organizations or candidates since the movement first appeared on the political scene in early 2009, these active participants clearly constitute only a small fraction of a much larger group of Tea Party sympathizers. I will concentrate here on analyzing the sources of support for the Tea Party movement among the American public, using data from the October 2010 wave of the American National Election Study Evaluations of Government and Society Survey (EGSS).[11]

It is important to understand the characteristics and attitudes of Tea Party supporters within the public because protest participants and contributors are recruited from this group. It is also important to understand this larger group because it constitutes a bloc of voters that Tea Party candidates can look to for electoral support—a constituency that has proven large enough to carry a number of Tea Party candidates to victory over more mainstream or moderate candidates in Republican primaries. Tea Party supporters undoubtedly played major roles in the upset victories of Sharron Angle in Nevada, Christine O'Donnell in Delaware, and Ken Buck in Colorado in 2010, over candidates the Republican establishment backed. However, the fact that all three of these candidates went on to lose in the general election, possibly costing the Republican Party three U.S. Senate seats, suggests that the Tea Party movement poses serious risks for the GOP in areas that are not solidly Republican by supporting candidates whose views are far to the right of the overall electorate.

The 2010 EGSS included questions about the Tea Party and a series of questions about current domestic policy issues in addition to questions about racial attitudes, political activities, and demographic characteristics. This made it possible to analyze the sources of support for the Tea Party movement and to compare the political activities, social characteristics, and the racial and political attitudes of Tea Party supporters with the attitudes of members of the general public and Republicans who did not support the Tea Party movement.

Respondents were asked if they considered themselves supporters of the Tea Party movement. Those who described themselves as supporters were then asked a follow-up question about whether they supported the Tea Party strongly or not too strongly. Overall, 23 percent of the

TABLE 8.3 SOCIAL CHARACTERISTICS AND POLITICAL ATTITUDES OF TEA PARTY
SUPPORTERS VERSUS NONSUPPORTERS

	Tea Party Supporters	Non Supporters
Social Characteristics and Attitudes		
Age (45 and older)	70%	59%
White	85%	75%
Male	63%	45%
Married	62%	49%
Income $75,000+	31%	24%
College grad	27%	30%
Born-again/evangelical	52%	33%
Weekly churchgoer	50%	36%
Believe Bible actual word of God	49%	28%
Gun owner	43%	29%
Political and Racial Attitudes		
Republican ID or Lean	86%	32%
Conservative ID	85%	29%
Dislike Obama	84%	27%
Like Palin	77%	19%
Birther	44%	22%
Oppose ending DADT	67%	31%
Oppose clean energy	74%	21%
Oppose health care reform	81%	33%
Oppose stem cell research	66%	29%
Oppose economic stimulus	87%	41%
Disagree blacks are victims	74%	39%
Disagree blacks have gotten less	77%	42%
Agree blacks need to try harder	66%	36%
Agree no favors for blacks	80%	48%

SOURCE: American National Election Study Evaluations of Government and Society Survey,
October 2010.

survey respondents described themselves as supporters of the Tea Party
movement, including 13 percent who described themselves as strong
supporters.

Table 8.3 compares the social characteristics and political attitudes
of Tea Party supporters with those of nonsupporters. The findings
regarding the social characteristics of Tea Party supporters indicate that
the widely held stereotype of this group as made up predominantly of
older white males is largely correct. Tea Party supporters were overwhelmingly white, they were somewhat older than nonsupporters, and

they were disproportionately male. In addition, Tea Party supporters were somewhat more affluent than nonsupporters, they were considerably more religious than nonsupporters, and they were more likely to be gun owners. In terms of education, Tea Party supporters were slightly less likely to have graduated from college than nonsupporters.

When we turn our attention from social characteristics to political attitudes, the differences between Tea Party supporters and the overall electorate become striking. Although some Tea Party leaders have tried to stress the movement's independence from the Republican Party, it is clear from these data and from other surveys that supporters of the Tea Party movement overwhelmingly identify with the Republican Party. In this case, 86 percent of Tea Party supporters were Republican identifiers or independents leaning toward the Republican Party compared with only 32 percent of nonsupporters. Tea Party supporters make up a very large proportion of the Republican electoral base. Forty-five percent of all Republican identifiers and leaners and 63 percent of strong Republican identifiers described themselves as supporters of the Tea Party movement.

Going along with the strongly Republican Party loyalties of Tea Party supporters, the data from the EGSS show that, compared with nonsupporters, Tea Party supporters held much more negative views of President Obama and much more positive views of the Republican politician who has been perhaps most frequently associated with the Tea Party movement—Sarah Palin. Fully 84 percent of Tea Party supporters had an unfavorable opinion of Barack Obama, and 77 percent had a favorable opinion of Sarah Palin. In contrast, only 27 percent of nonsupporters had an unfavorable opinion of Obama, and only 19 percent had a favorable opinion of Palin. And Tea Party supporters were also much more likely than nonsupporters to have doubts about whether Barack Obama was born in the United States—44 percent of supporters believed that Obama either probably or definitely was not born in the United States compared with only 22 percent of nonsupporters.

When it comes to ideology and issue positions, the data in Table 8.3 show that Tea Party supporters were far to the right of the rest of the public. Eighty-five percent of Tea Party supporters described themselves as conservative compared with only 29 percent of nonsupporters. Similarly, compared with the overall public, Tea Party supporters were much more likely to take the conservative side on a wide variety of policy issues, opposing key Obama administration initiatives, including repeal of the "don't ask, don't tell" (DADT) policy toward gays in the military, government support for clean energy development, health care reform, stem cell research, and the economic stimulus program.

The fact that Tea Party supporters were much more likely than non-supporters to identify themselves as born-again or evangelical Christians and to accept a literal interpretation of the Bible, as well as the fact that they were substantially more opposed to repealing the "don't ask, don't tell" policy toward gays in the military suggest that support for the Tea Party was based on social as well as economic conservatism. Moreover, the fact that Tea Party supporters scored substantially higher than nonsupporters on four questions measuring resentment toward African Americans suggests that racial attitudes were also a contributing factor.

An important question here is: To what extent are differences between the social characteristics and political attitudes of Tea Party supporters and nonsupporters explained simply by the fact that Tea Party supporters were overwhelmingly Republicans? To answer this question, we need to know whether Republicans who supported the Tea Party differed from those who did not. Table 8.4 compares the social characteristics and political attitudes of these two types of Republicans.

The results displayed in Table 8.4 indicate that Republican supporters of the Tea Party movement differed in a number of important respects from other Republicans, sometimes fairly dramatically. In terms of social characteristics, the most striking differences involved gender, age, and religiosity. Tea Party Republicans were disproportionately male, somewhat older, and much more religious than other Republicans. More importantly, there were substantial differences between the political attitudes of supporters and nonsupporters. Compared with other Republicans, Tea Party supporters were much more likely to identify strongly with the GOP, to describe their political views as conservative, to dislike Barack Obama, to like Sarah Palin, to question whether Obama was born in the United States, and to oppose a variety of Obama administration policy initiatives.

The results in Table 8.4 show that the characteristics and attitudes of Tea Party supporters cannot be explained simply by their Republican loyalties. Tea Party supporters clearly stood out from other Republicans in terms of their characteristics and especially in terms of their political outlook. In addition, Tea Party supporters scored substantially higher on the racial resentment items than other Republicans. These findings raise the question of how much each of these factors contributed to support for the Tea Party movement.

TABLE 8.4 SOCIAL CHARACTERISTICS AND POLITICAL ATTITUDES OF
REPUBLICAN TEA PARTY SUPPORTERS VERSUS OTHER REPUBLICANS

	Tea Party Supporters	Other Republicans
Social Characteristics and Attitudes		
Age (45 and older)	70%	59%
White	86%	89%
Male	66%	48%
Married	62%	63%
Income $75,000+	32%	27%
College grad	28%	32%
Born-again/evangelical	52%	38%
Weekly churchgoer	52%	42%
Believe Bible actual word of God	47%	34%
Gun owner	44%	42%
Political and Racial Attitudes		
Strong Republican ID	45%	21%
Conservative ID	90%	62%
Dislike Obama	90%	55%
Like Palin	82%	38%
Birther	46%	37%
Oppose ending DADT	71%	44%
Oppose clean energy	81%	32%
Oppose health care reform	88%	58%
Oppose stem cell research	71%	41%
Oppose economic stimulus	91%	62%
Disagree blacks are victims	74%	54%
Disagree blacks have gotten less	77%	58%
Agree blacks need to try harder	65%	42%
Agree no favors for blacks	82%	65%

SOURCE: American National Election Study Evaluations of Government and Society Survey, October 2010.

EXPLAINING TEA PARTY SUPPORT: A MULTIVARIATE ANALYSIS

To determine the relative contributions of party identification, ideological conservatism, racial resentment, and demographic characteristics to support for the Tea Party movement among the public, I conducted a logistic regression analysis of Tea Party support among white respondents. I excluded nonwhites from the analysis because there were very few nonwhite supporters of the Tea Party movement in the sample. However, including nonwhites has almost no impact on the results. The

TABLE 8.5   PREDICTING TEA PARTY SUPPORT AMONG WHITES

Independent Variable	Beta	Standard Error	Significance	Change in Probability
Age	.141	.060	.01	+.027
Female	−.511	.191	.01	−.024
Education	.073	.055	.10	+.016
Income	−.033	.025	.10	−.013
Church attendance	−.011	.057	(not significant)	−.000
GOP ID	−.188	.064	.01	−.034
Conservative ideology	.354	.041	.001	+.187
Obama dislike	.227	.071	.001	+.063
Racial resentment	.155	.034	.001	+.118
Constant	−6.137			

SOURCE: American National Election Study Evaluations of Government and Society Survey, October 2010.

NOTE: Significance levels based on one-tailed test.

independent variables in this analysis are a nine-item ideology scale[12] combining ideological identification with opinions on eight policy issues (repeal of DADT, health care reform, expansion of government-funded health insurance for children [SCHIP], the economic stimulus program, federal funding of stem cell research, federal funding of clean energy research and development, financial reform, and raising taxes on upper income households), the seven-point party identification scale, the four-item racial resentment scale, the Obama like–dislike scale, and five social characteristics—age, gender, education, family income, and frequency of church attendance. The results are displayed in Table 8.5.

The independent variables included in the analysis do a very good job of predicting support for the Tea Party movement with an overall accuracy rate of 85 percent. To compare the effects of the independent variables, I calculated the change in the probability of supporting the Tea Party associated with an increase of one standard deviation above the mean on each independent variable with all other independent variables set at their means. For example, an increase of one standard deviation above the mean on the ideology scale is estimated to produce an increase of almost 19 percentage points in Tea Party support.

The results in Table 8.5 show that ideological conservatism was by far the strongest predictor of Tea Party support. In addition to conservatism, however, both racial resentment and dislike for Barack Obama had significant effects on support for the Tea Party. These two variables had much stronger effects than party identification. Racial resentment had a somewhat stronger effect than dislike for Obama. Moreover, dislike for Obama was itself very strongly related to racial resentment with a correlation of .46. Finally, two social background characteristics, age and gender, had significant effects on Tea Party support with older respondents and men more likely to support the Tea Party. However, these effects were much smaller than those for ideology, racial resentment, and dislike of Obama. After controlling for political attitudes and other demographic characteristics, education, income, and frequency of church attendance had little impact on Tea Party support.

TEA PARTY SUPPORT AND POLITICAL ACTIVISM

We have seen thus far that Tea Party supporters differed from other Republicans in their demographic characteristics and especially in their political attitudes. However, the significance of these differences depends on the relative levels of political activism of these two types of Republicans. Table 8.6 displays data comparing Republicans who supported the Tea Party movement with those who did not support the movement on several measures of political activism. In every case, Tea Party supporters were substantially more active than nonsupporters. Tea Party supporters were much more likely than nonsupporters to be registered to vote and to report that within the past year they had contacted a public official to express an opinion on an issue, given money to a candidate or party, attended a political meeting or rally, and displayed a yard sign or bumper sticker.

The relatively high levels of activism of Republicans supporting the Tea Party movement mean that the composition of various groups of GOP activists is skewed toward supporters of the movement. Tea Party supporters made up 45 percent of all Republican respondents but they made up 63 percent of Republicans who reported contacting an elected official to express an opinion, 65 percent of Republicans who reported giving money to a party or candidate, and 73 percent of Republicans who reported attending a political rally or meeting. Thus, the impact of the Tea Party movement on the Republican Party is magnified by the greater political activism of its supporters compared with other rank-and-file Republicans. This finding suggests that Tea Party supporters are very likely to comprise a disproportionate share, and an outright majority of voters in 2012 Republican presidential and congressional primaries in many states and congressional districts.

TABLE 8.6 POLITICAL ACTIVITIES OF REPUBLICAN TEA PARTY SUPPORTERS
VERSUS OTHER REPUBLICANS

Activity	Tea Party Supporters	Other Republicans
Registered to vote	92%	75%
Contacted public official	44%	20%
Given money to campaign	22%	9%
Attended rally/meeting	24%	7%
Displayed sign/bumper sticker	25%	11%

SOURCE: American National Election Study Evaluations of Government and Society Survey, October 2010.

CONCLUSION

The evidence presented in this study indicates that the Tea Party movement did not suddenly emerge on the American political scene in 2009 in response to the progressive policy agenda set forth by President Obama and the Democratic Congress. Rather it was the natural outgrowth of the growing size and conservatism of the activist base of the Republican Party during the preceding decades. By 2009, a large cadre of very conservative Republican activists was available for mobilization by conservative organizations and media outlets.

Although it is unlikely that more than 5 percent of voting-age Americans have ever participated in a Tea Party rally or contributed money to a Tea Party organization, more than one-fifth of the American public considered themselves to be supporters of the Tea Party movement according to the October 2010 wave of the American National Election Study Evaluations of Government and Society Survey. These Tea Party supporters were overwhelmingly white, disproportionately male, somewhat older, and a good deal more religious than the overall electorate—all characteristics also present among active Republican identifiers. But by far the most striking differences between Tea Party supporters and the overall public involved their political beliefs. Tea Party supporters overwhelmingly identified with the Republican Party and they were much more conservative than the overall public and even other Republicans on a wide range of issues including social issues and economic issues. Moreover, Tea Party supporters displayed high levels of racial resentment and held very negative opinions about President Obama compared with the rest of the public and even other Republicans. In a multivariate analysis, racial resentment and dislike of Barack Obama, along with conservatism, emerged as the most important factors contributing to support for the Tea Party movement.

These findings suggest that the Tea Party movement is not likely to fade away any time in the near future. While a Republican majority in the House of Representatives might reduce some of the concern among conservative Republicans about liberal policies emanating from Washington, as long as Barack Obama remains in the White House, Tea Party supporters are likely to remain highly motivated to oppose his policy agenda and remove him from the White House. And given the fact that Tea Party supporters make up almost half of Republican identifiers and a much larger proportion of active Republicans, the Tea Party movement appears to have the potential to strongly influence Republican congressional and presidential primaries in 2012. Any serious Republican presidential contender will have to find a way to appeal to Tea Party supporters. The risk, of course, is that this may make it very difficult for the eventual Republican nominee to appeal to more moderate swing voters in the general election.

NOTES

1. John B. Judis, "Tea Minus Zero," *The New Republic*, May 27, 2010, 19; James Crabtree, "Reading the Tea Leaves," *Prospect*, October 21, 2010; and Christopher Parker, "Race and the Tea Party: Who's Right?" Salon.com, May 21, 2010, www.salon.com/news/feature/2010/05/03/race_and_the_tea_party 2010; Joe Scarborough, "Is the Tea Party Over?" *Newsweek*, February 1, 2010, 26; and Jacob Weisberg, "A Tea Party Taxonomy," *Newsweek*, September 27, 2010, 32.

2. Alan I. Abramowitz, *The Disappearing Center: Engaged Citizens, Polarization, and American Democracy* (New Haven: Yale University Press, 2010); Joseph Bafumi and Robert Y. Shapiro, "A New Partisan Voter," *Journal of Politics* 71 (2009): 1–24; and Nolan McCarty, Keith T. Poole, and Howard Rosenthal, *Polarized America: The Dance of Ideology and Unequal Riches* (Cambridge, MA: MIT Press, 2006).

3. Paul Waldman, "Tea Party Standard," *The American Prospect*, web ed., September 21, 2010, www.prospect.org/cs/articles?article=tea_party_standard.

4. Paul Bedard, "Poll: Tea Party Amped Up by Fox, Glenn Beck," *USNews .com*, July 19, 2010, http://politics.usnews.com/news/washington-whispers/articles/2010/07/19/poll-tea-party-amped-up-by-fox-glenn-beck.html.

5. See Lo, Chapter 4 in this volume; Roberta A. Garner, *Social Movements in America*, 2nd ed. (Chicago: Rand McNally, 1977); James L. Wood and Maurice Jackson, *Social Movements: Development, Participation, and Dynamics* (Belmont, CA: Wadsworth Publishing, 1982); and Doug McAdam and David S. Snow, eds., *Social Movements: Readings on their Emergence, Mobilization, and Dynamics* (Los Angeles: Roxbury Publishing, 1997).

6. Sheryl G. Stolberg, "In Defining Obama, Misperceptions Stick," *New York Times*, August 18, 2010, A19.

7. Keith T. Poole and Howard Rosenthal, *Congress: A Political-Economic History of Roll Call Voting* (New York: Oxford University Press, 2000); Barbara Sinclair, "The New World of U.S. Senators," in *Congress Reconsidered*, 8th ed., ed. Lawrence C. Dodd and Bruce I. Oppenheimer (Washington, DC: CQ Press, 2005); and Lawrence C. Dodd and Bruce L. Oppenheimer, "A Decade of Republican Control: The House of Representatives, 1995–2005," in *Congress Reconsidered*, 8th ed., ed. Lawrence C. Dodd and Bruce I. Oppenheimer (Washington, DC: CQ Press, 2005).

8. Abramowitz, *The Disappearing Center: Engaged Citizens, Polarization, and American Democracy*; and Bafumi and Shapiro, "A New Partisan Voter."

9. Abramowitz, *The Disappearing Center: Engaged Citizens, Polarization, and American Democracy*.

10. This is as far back in time as we can go since the ANES did not begin asking this question until 1972.

11. The October 2010 survey is the first of several cross-sectional studies being conducted by ANES in 2010, 2011, and 2012, to test new instrumentation and measure public opinion between the 2008 and 2012 presidential elections. The surveys are being conducted entirely on the Internet using nationally representative probability samples. Respondents are members of the Knowledge Networks KnowledgePanel, an omnibus panel of respondents recruited using telephone and address-based sampling methods who are provided free Internet access and equipment when necessary.

12. Cronbach's alpha = .92, indicating a high degree of internal consistency among the items that make up this scale.

CHAPTER 9

The Future of the Tea Party

Scoring an Invitation to the
Republican Party

MARTIN COHEN

At this stage in the political life of the Tea Party movement, there are almost as many angles to explore as there are signs at a typical rally. Part of the popular allure of the fledgling movement is the notion that these are political outsiders tired of the way the two parties are conducting the people's business. The movement has tapped into the anxiety and frustration prevalent in our nation today, but we know from our political history that if outsiders want to accomplish anything substantive, they must come in from the outside and inject themselves into our two-party system. In the case of the Tea Party, this necessarily means working within the Republican Party to impact public policy. One way to analyze this compelling new movement is to study its relationship with the Republican Party.

Everyone wants to know whether the Tea Party will ultimately be a flash in the pan, a footnote in our political history, or whether it will significantly influence American politics for decades to come. History shows that this will depend almost entirely on whether the Tea Party is first able to significantly influence the Republican Party. The ability to get the party to stress its issues, to move the party toward its views on the issues, and to take control over at least some of the official party apparatus will all be necessary for the Tea Party to achieve anything of value in upcoming years. Previous movements have also been faced with this test. Abolitionists, populists, progressives, and suffragettes all found their greatest successes not when they ran third-party candidates but when they worked within the two-party system.

The recent rise of the Tea Party can be understood best by comparing it to the last great influx of political outsiders seeking to reconfigure the Republican Party—the Christian right. The best analogue to current Tea Party efforts to remake the Republican Party in its image is the influx of social conservatives, with the first wave of organizing beginning in the late 1970s and the second wave commencing in the early 1990s. While the first wave of Christian right organizing saw limited gains in both policy and stature, the second wave corrected many of the faults of the earlier approach and the Christian right built itself into *the* major faction in GOP politics. A comparison of the Christian right with the Tea Party will show that the Tea Party movement, as it is constructed now, is ill-suited to successfully influence the Republican Party. The Tea Party must make significant changes as a movement to gain a permanent, meaningful foothold within the Republican Party.

PARTIES AS COALITIONS

"Modern democracy is unthinkable save in terms of parties."[1] These were the words of the eminent political scientist E. E. Schattschneider, and to this day, very few scholars would deny how important parties are to how our system of government works. The centrality of parties in our political system was proved early on when Thomas Jefferson won election to the presidency as the head of an organized party. If Jefferson, who famously wrote in 1789 that he would not go to heaven if he needed a party to get there, acknowledged the need for political parties by starting one only a few years later, then clearly parties are vital to achieving political success.[2]

From the beginning of partisan conflict in this country, political parties have attempted to cobble together majorities to win elective office and pursue certain public policies. For Schattschneider, a party is "an organized attempt to control government."[3] Cohen et al. argue that parties are the creation of interest groups, ideological activists, and others they call intense policy demanders. The direction a party takes is determined by the tug-of-war between groups of activists within the party.[4] The New Deal Coalition was an example where the main coalition members—blacks, Jews, Southerners, Catholics, labor—all placed themselves firmly behind governmental policies designed to stimulate the economy and provide a safety net for its citizens. As long as the goals of the group members complemented each other, intra-party conflict would be relatively minor. Of course there were intra-party conflicts, but impressively, southern segregationists and northern liberals both continued to vote "D" for roughly two decades after the Dixiecrats walked out of the 1948 Democratic National Convention. The New Deal Coalition eventually broke apart when different sets of issues, namely civil rights, the Vietnam War, and the 1960s counter-culture, created intractable disagreements among the party's coalition members.

Not every party coalition is as long-lasting or electorally potent as the New Deal Coalition was between 1933 and 1968, and not every party coalition collapses as dramatically as that same coalition did in the years that followed. The post-war Republican Party has had to overcome par-tisan infighting that first revolved around ideology. In the 1950s and '60s, so-called liberal and moderate Republicans accepted general New Deal economic principles and only differed from the Democrats in terms of degree—how much the government should be involved. Conservative Republicans fundamentally disagreed with activist government and sought to dismantle the New Deal. This fight played out during the 1952 Republican National Convention when Eisenhower and Robert Taft battled for the nomination. Of course, Eisenhower and his side's outlook prevailed.[5] But twelve years later, moderate Republicanism was booed off the stage in San Francisco when Barry Goldwater led the ultraconservative wing of the party to prominence.[6]

When new groups enter a partisan coalition, if they really want to have a say in the direction the party takes, they must seek to influence the nomination process. They must play an active role in determining who will be the nominee. Ideally, a group would be able to shepherd its own handpicked candidate to victory. At the very least, a new group should be able to have some influence on the nomination process in exchange for gaining assurances that their particular interests will be addressed if the party's candidate gets elected. It is not a surprise that GOP intraparty conflict reached a head at the nomination conventions in 1952 and 1964. Nominations are the most important activities a party undertakes. Selecting a candidate, at any level, to represent the party on the November ballot obviously goes a long way to determin-ing how successful a party will be. It also shows which groups within the party are preeminent. When Goldwater won the nomination, it was clear that the Republican Party had been taken over by its conservative wing. Indeed, Goldwater supporters traversed the country in the years prior to the convention, looking to gain the support of party leaders. This effort was handsomely rewarded when their candidate became the party's standard bearer. Winning nominations is how a group gains control of a party, regardless of whether it is the presidential nomination or a nomination for state senator. The nominee is the party's representative and signals what the party will stand for if he or she is elected.

Minority factions like religious conservatives and the Tea Partiers have to go through one of the two major parties, but it is rarely easy. They figure to encounter some resistance even if it is just from establishment leaders protecting their turf. Resistance may also come from those in the establishment who do not want to see the party move in the direction of the newcomers. This is usually an ideological struggle but it can also be about socioeconomic status or other intraparty divisions. Parties are coalitions. When a party adds groups, current coalition members either accept the newcomers and everything they bring with them, or they desert the party. Adding new groups is helpful only when the concurrent losses are not greater. Some political outsiders are less attractive than others and may meet more resistance.

For this analysis, I have identified three criteria that will impact how welcome a new group, in this case the Tea Party, will be to the party establishment. The first one deals with issue popularity. Are the new issues pushed by the insurgents broadly popular? Are they popular among those groups that already make up the party? And what are the prospects for appealing to other voters if these issues are brought to the forefront of the party agenda? The second criterion has to do with electoral gain. The new group must bring in enough new voters to justify the losses that might be incurred—the loss of leadership positions, the loss of other voters. Plus, the new voters must truly be "new" or else *any* losses are unacceptable. The third criterion relates to political rhetoric and tactics. Moderation and sophistication are most helpful to political insurgents attempting to gain prominence within a major political party.

After providing some brief background, I will compare the first two waves of Christian right organizing with the Tea Party on these three criteria to draw conclusions about the latter's potential for bringing the Republican Party more in line with its ideals and goals and ultimately influencing public policy. The first "wave" of Christian right activism ended around the time the 1980s drew to a close. In 1986, Jerry Falwell disbanded the Moral Majority and Pat Robertson's presidential campaign in 1988 was judged a failure when he failed to win a single primary. So when the 1990s dawned, the movement was thought to be dead. However, Robertson and Ralph Reed soon founded the Christian Coalition and the second wave was said to have begun.[7]

BACKGROUND ON THE TWO WAVES OF THE CHRISTIAN RIGHT MOVEMENT

First Wave

The Christian right's roots are not so much ideological as they are doctrinal. Religion, of course, plays a large role in how evangelical Christians see the world and therefore how they behave politically.[8] The latter half of the nineteenth century was the heyday of American evangelicalism. Evangelicals not only focused on winning souls to Christ, but they also sought during this time to reform society. Abolition, prohibition, and alleviating poverty were a few of the causes evangelicals actively pursued. As society modernized and secularized—with increases in industrialization, urbanization, and immigration, as well as advances in transportation—evangelicals found themselves ostracized from society. They became cultural outsiders. Evangelicals withdrew from, compromised with, or resisted society. Those who resisted simply refused to accept the new thinking. They continued to insist the Bible was the word of God, miracles really happened, that unless one had experienced religious conversion they were destined to hell, and that the book of Genesis provided an accurate account of the origin of life and species. They also believed in pre-millennialism. This meant that instead of Jesus coming back after the millennium, he would return and usher in the new millennium and save the world from Armageddon. Thus, good Christians should concentrate only on spreading the gospel rather than bettering society. Evangelicals made their withdrawal from public and political life complete after the embarrassment of the Scopes Monkey Trial. They basically gave up on public life and retreated into their separate religious entities not to reemerge until the mid-1970s.[9]

For the most part, these religious conservatives, residing mostly but not exclusively in the South, were consciously brought back into politics by conservative activists focused on remaking the Republican Party in their image. Activists such as Paul Weyrich, Richard Viguerie, and Howard Phillips realized these individuals might be more easily mobilized through their churches. So they set out to recruit fundamentalist preachers to the politically conservative cause. Through the preachers, they had a built-in entrée into their politically conservative congregations. These congregations were in effect pre-mobilized and could be reached easily through the structure of the church.

At this time, several evangelists had made inroads into television. They were televangelists and they were very popular. They were already raising money for the churches. They already had donor lists. The possibilities for a mutually beneficial relationship between conservative Republican operatives and leaders were endless. Both sides agreed that the country was becoming too permissive. Morality needed to be tightened up in the wake of the 1960s. Issues like abortion, gay rights, and feminism were bothering both groups.

The biggest fish in the televangelist pool was a Fundamentalist preacher named Jerry Falwell. Falwell's congregation numbered 17,000 in the late 1970s. His *Old-Time Gospel Hour* was seen weekly on 373 television stations and more importantly raised $35 million from the 2.5 million people on its mailing lists. In May 1979, Bob Billings of the National Christian Action Conference invited Falwell to a meeting with new right secular operatives Howard Phillips, Richard Viguerie, and Paul Weyrich. Ed McAteer of the Religious Roundtable was also in attendance. The four men told Falwell of their shared opposition to abortion and pornography and how they wanted to influence the 1980 GOP platform. Weyrich felt if they could persuade the Republican Party to take a strong stance against abortion, this would split the strong Catholic voting bloc within the Democratic Party. The new right leaders wanted Falwell to spearhead an organization to put pressure on the GOP. Weyrich proposed the name "Moral Majority," and the first wave of Christian right organizing had begun in earnest.[10]

Second Wave

The seeds of the so-called second wave were planted when the Reverend Pat Robertson revealed that God had called him to run for president in 1988. Robertson put to use his considerable fund-raising prowess and tapped millions of people who already supported him through his ministry and his popular television show, *The 700 Club*. After a surprising second-place finish in Iowa, Robertson failed to win a single primary. And after being beaten handily by Vice President Bush in South Carolina, his campaign was finished.[11] However, the long-term impact of this effort was much more consequential for two reasons. First, those activists who supported Robertson in his bid for convention delegates remained active in Republican Party affairs. They fought to gain prominent positions within the party hierarchy. On the one hand, this was a threat to the establishment since their turf was being encroached upon, and in many states leadership of the party was hanging in the balance. But many Republicans realized that here was a large group of newly active, highly motivated voters who were now beginning to identify with the Republican Party.[12] Second, Robertson's campaign lists were put to good use in the early 1990s when Robertson and Ralph Reed started a national organization designed to channel the political energy of conservative Christians. It was called the Christian Coalition. The basic purpose of the Christian Coalition was to make government more responsive to the concerns of evangelical Christians and pro-family Catholics.[13] It was to be primarily a grassroots organization and its leaders hoped to improve on some of the faults of earlier New Christian Right groups.

COMPARING THE CHRISTIAN RIGHT AND THE TEA PARTY: ISSUE POPULARITY AND ELECTORAL GAIN

In this section, I utilize various survey data to compare, with their contemporaries, religious conservatives during the first and second waves of Christian right activism and Tea Partiers using the first two criteria of an effective insurgent movement previously set forth: issue popularity and electoral gain. I use National Election Studies from 1980 and 1992 to analyze religious conservatives at the beginning of the first and second waves of Christian right activism.[14] For the Tea Party, I use the *New York Times*'s April 2010 survey of Tea Party supporters as well as several Gallup polls reported in July 2010.[15]

Criterion #1: Issue Extremism?

First Wave

Abortion was clearly the most important issue for evangelicals who reemerged onto the American political scene beginning in the 1970s. In fact, for many religious conservatives, abortion was the primary reason they decided to become politically active. Jerry Falwell had always believed that politics and the pulpit should remain completely separate. However, he claims he changed his mind the day the Supreme Court

TABLE 9.1   CHRISTIAN RIGHT: FIRST-WAVE ISSUES

	Religious Conservatives	All Respondents	Republicans	Independents	Democrats
Abortion illegal in all cases	21%	12%	9%	12%	13%
Abortion illegal except in cases of rape, incest, and to save mother's life	41%	33%	34%	30%	33%
Disapprove of ERA	47%	39%	56%	33%	29%

SOURCE: 1980 American National Election Studies.[18]

handed down its decision in *Roe v. Wade*. In *The Fundamentalist Phenomenon*, Falwell argues that life begins at fertilization and that abortion is the murder of human life. For these reasons, he and his followers led the charge in the early 1980s for a constitutional amendment to ban abortion. There would be no exceptions and no compromises.[16]

In general, so-called women's issues were extremely important to evangelicals at this time. They wholeheartedly resisted threats to traditional gender roles. Phyllis Schlafly, a well-known moral traditionalist, led the fight against the Equal Rights Amendment (ERA) and many credit Schlafly and her organization, Eagle Forum, with keeping the ERA from passing in the requisite number of states. In late 1978, even before the Moral Majority was formed, Jerry Falwell helped defeat a state version of the ERA in Florida.

Religious conservatives had strong views on abortion, the Equal Rights Amendment, and a woman's role in society more generally. Table 9.1 compares religious conservatives with other Americans on these two issues. By comparing our target group with all Americans, we can get a sense for how far out of the mainstream religious conservatives were on these issues. Just over one-fifth of religious conservatives believed abortion should be illegal in all cases.[17] When we add in those who believed abortion should be illegal except in cases of rape, incest, and when the mother's life is in danger, 62 percent of religious conservatives took this view compared to 45 percent of all respondents. A strong pro-life stand at this time was a minority position.

By comparing religious conservatives with Republicans, we can get a sense for how receptive the GOP would be to this new group coming in and pushing a strong pro-life position. Only 43 percent of Republicans agreed that abortion should be either banned completely or banned except for the most difficult cases. And finally, what can we say about independents? Any party looking to increase its chances of winning elections has to pay attention to the unaffiliated, those who might be "up for grabs." The advantages of bringing in a new group have to be weighed against the chances that independents will be turned off to a more extreme party, and, as Table 9.1 shows, independents were significantly less pro-life than the insurgents.

To summarize, religious conservatives were much more pro-life than the rest of the country's citizens. In 1980, Republicans and independents were also significantly less likely to take strong pro-life stands. This suggests that unless religious conservatives would be willing to compromise on abortion, their views probably would not be welcome on this issue. And sure enough, many first-wave activists were quite assertive and quite unwilling to accept anything less than a total ban on abortion. New right stalwarts such as Paul Weyrich and Richard Viguerie sharply criticized President Reagan for his unwillingness to put his full weight behind the cause.[19] Looking at the survey data, it is not much of a surprise that the president chose not to take on this relatively unpopular cause.

On the Equal Rights Amendment, 47 percent of religious conservatives disapproved compared with 39 percent of all respondents. This is not a huge difference in magnitude but is still statistically significant. Interestingly, on the ERA, Republicans would seem to be willing to welcome additional activists who were against the ERA since they were actually more conservative on this issue. In 1980, 56 percent of Republicans were against the ERA, and indeed, the 1980 GOP platform reversed its long-standing support for the Equal Rights Amendment. Independents were a different story, as only one-third disapproved of the ERA.

Second Wave

Abortion continued to be a hot-button issue for Christian conservatives during the early 1990s. The Supreme Court had come extremely close to overturning *Roe* but stopped short in *Planned Parenthood of Southeastern Pennsylvania v. Casey*. High-profile protests led by Operation Rescue kept the issue in the national spotlight, and pro-choice

TABLE 9.2 CHRISTIAN RIGHT: SECOND-WAVE ISSUES

	Religious Conservatives	All Respondents	Republicans	Independents	Democrats
Abortion illegal in all cases	20%	11%	12%	9%	10%
Abortion illegal except to save mother's life	41%	28%	34%	25%	24%
Approve of parental consent	86%	76%	82%	77%	70%
Disapprove of using state funds	63%	50%	61%	49%	41%
Approve of spousal notification	80%	65%	70%	69%	61%
Disapprove of gays in the military	56%	41%	55%	39%	32%
Disapprove of gay adoption	85%	72%	82%	74%	65%
Prayer should be allowed in public schools	94%	88%	92%	90%	85%

SOURCE: 1992 American National Election Studies.[20]

groups responded to the pressure with an intense mobilization effort of their own. Taking a look at Table 9.2, we see that religious conservatives still were much more likely to support banning abortion except in cases of rape, incest, and life of the mother.

Despite abortion being such a controversial issue, or maybe because of it, we see very little movement in public opinion between 1980 and 1992. The key difference in the relationship between the Christian right and the Republican Party, however, lies in the approach taken by second-wave activists. One of the lessons Ralph Reed took from the failures of groups like the Moral Majority was their unwillingness to compromise—rather than accepting a half loaf, they often got nothing. The Christian Coalition realized the futility of screaming for a constitutional amendment to ban abortion. Instead, members focused their energy and rhetoric on restrictions to abortion that were more widely popular. By focusing on parental consent, disallowing state funds to be used for abortion, and spousal notification, conservatives were able to turn the tables and paint as extremist liberals who opposed these restrictions. On these three items, religious conservatives were predictably much stronger supporters than the rest of the country. However, unlike with making abortion illegal for most women, majorities of Republicans, independents, and even Democrats in some cases also supported these restrictions. This change in strategy and expectations on the important issue of abortion made the religious right much more attractive to Republicans hoping to rebuild a majority coalition in the wake of Bill Clinton's election and the return of unified Democratic government.

On other issues important to religiously conservative activists, the Christian right also found common ground with Republicans and even some independents. Just over half of religious conservatives *and* Republicans came out against gays serving in the military. Independents were much more tolerant on this issue, but religious conservatives found themselves with the median voter on gay adoption. Eight-five percent of religious conservatives disapproved of gay adoption in 1992, and while that number was much higher than the rest of the country, it was not much different than Republicans. In addition, 74 percent of independents were also against gay adoption. And on allowing prayer in schools, large majorities of all subgroups agreed. Of course, religious conservatives led the way but they were not significantly more in favor of it than Republicans and independents.

By showing a willingness to compromise on abortion and coming out against gays in the military and gay adoption, second-wave insurgents did not ruffle the feathers of many Republicans, nor did it appear they would repel too many independents. Coupled with a change in tactics and rhetoric (discussed later in this chapter), the 1990s version of the Christian right became a much more palatable coalition member than it was in the 1980s.

Tea Party

The Tea Party first emerged on the national scene in the spring of 2009. Obama's plan to bail out struggling homeowners had become particularly controversial in the wake of the Troubled Asset Relief Program that many saw as a bailout of the banks. To many, the word *bailout* meant government giving something to people who did not deserve it. These

TABLE 9.3 TEA PARTY: ISSUES THOUGHT TO BE "EXTREMELY SERIOUS THREATS"
TO FUTURE U.S. WELL-BEING

	Tea Party Supporter	Neutral	Tea Party Opponent
Federal government debt	61%	44%	29%
Terrorism	51%	43%	29%
Size and power of federal government	49%	30%	12%
Health care costs	41%	37%	33%

SOURCE: May 2010 and June 2010 Gallup Poll.[21]

bailouts, along with the $787 billion stimulus package, convinced many on the right that government spending was raging out of control. Many Tea Partiers worried about the debt that was piling up and wanted to restrain their government from spending more than it could afford. And with the rolling out of Obama's complex plan to reform our health care system, the perceived big-spending, meddling government trifecta was complete. Bailouts, stimulus, and "Obamacare" combined to create a compelling narrative for those who were afraid of an overbearing, over-spending, federal government. This narrative fit nicely with the ideology of libertarian-leaning groups like FreedomWorks that played a large role in financing and organizing the Tea Party.

In a Gallup poll report published in July 2010, citizens were asked what issues they thought to be "extremely serious threats" to the future well-being of the United States. Among Tea Party supporters, 61 per-cent cited "federal government debt," making it easily the most salient issue for this group of Americans. After terrorism at 51 percent, the next two issues were "the size and power of the federal government" (at 49 percent) and "health care costs" (at 41 percent). As Table 9.3 shows, Tea Party supporters were much more concerned about these four issues than Tea Party opponents or even those who considered themselves neutral toward the Tea Party.

Besides differing from other Americans in terms of how important these issues were for the well-being of the United States, Tea Partiers also distinguished themselves in terms of their views on what should be done to solve these problems. Touching on the size and power of government as well as government debt, 92 percent of Tea Party sup-porters would prefer smaller government and fewer services to bigger government and more services. Among all Americans, only half would choose that option. On health care, 85 percent of Tea Party supporters

TABLE 9.4 TEA PARTY ISSUES: SUPPORTERS VERSUS ALL AMERICANS

	Tea Party Supporters	All Americans
Smaller government, fewer services	92%	50%
Don't require all to have health insurance	85%	45%
Don't raise taxes on rich to pay for health insurance	80%	39%

SOURCE: April 2010 New York Times Poll.[22]

believe the government should not require that everybody purchase health insurance. Only 45 percent of all Americans are in agreement with that position. And finally, 80 percent of Tea Partiers as opposed to 39 percent of all Americans think that the government should not raise taxes on the rich to pay for health insurance.

It is clear from Tables 9.3 and 9.4 that on the issues that matter most to the Tea Party, Tea Party supporters are considerably further to the right of the median voter. In fact, the only group equally conservative on the federal government's role in the economy is Republicans. When asked whether the government is doing too much that should be left to individuals and businesses, 80 percent of Tea Party supporters say yes while 81 percent of Republicans agree. In Chapter 8 of this book, Alan Abramowitz echoes and expands upon these findings. He looks at several additional issues and finds that the Tea Party is far more conservative than the overall electorate. And while he shows that the plurality of Americans is slightly left of center, over half of Tea Partiers are strong conservatives.[23]

Using the standards I laid out earlier in the chapter, it would appear that the Tea Party is rather extreme when it comes to the issues they most care about. However, they should not expect much resistance ideologically from the GOP. This makes sense considering several groups indirectly affiliated with the Republican establishment, like FreedomWorks, have shown their support for the Tea Party movement. But this could ultimately prove problematic for both the Tea Party movement and the Republicans that display agreement with it. Many in the media have argued that the Tea Party's ideology consists only of broad ideas— lowering taxes, cutting spending—that have not yet been tied to any specific policies. In other words, if Tea Party supporters actually got their way, what exactly would they do? How would their ideology play out when they have to govern? Specific cuts to popular programs like Social Security, Medicare, or the defense budget would undoubtedly alienate even more voters and presumably many Republicans, too. And promises to abolish the Departments of Education and Energy, among others, have been widely panned by voters and pundits alike. It would appear that the policy manifestations of their main principles can only lead to political actions that would be quite unpopular with many Americans, including some of those with whom they have been in agreement so far.

Comparing the Movements

One of the main reasons the first wave of Christian right organizing failed to live up to early expectations of its political prowess is that those involved aggressively pushed issue positions that were unpopular with sizable majorities of the public. The second wave took one of the same issues—abortion—and realized that extreme policies would never be enacted, and that trying to do so would only alienate the Republican establishment, let alone independents and conservative Democrats. So Ralph Reed led an effort to seek compromises on the issue of abortion and led the fight for state-level restrictions with which most of the country agreed. This strategy allowed religious conservatives to gain power and influence within the Republican Party, not to mention actually restrict abortion. In addition, Reed focused a good deal of his movement's energies on other types of issues that were more broadly popular within the Republican Party. This bought him some respect from establishment Republicans who realized the party was more important than one group's pet issues.[24]

Given this history, it would appear that the Tea Party movement can be successful and make progress on its main issues even though supporters' beliefs might not be shared by anyone but conservative Republicans. The key would be to stop short of advocating extreme positions and seek compromises that are more palatable to the American people. If it can be done on such a controversial, life-or-death issue as abortion, it can certainly be done on something like taxes and spending that would seem to evoke a less emotional and visceral reaction.

Criterion #2: Electoral Gain?

First Wave

The second criterion that should have an impact on how easily a group of political outsiders can make its presence felt in one of the major parties has to do with how much of an electoral gain it figures to provide.

As discussed previously, parties are coalitions of groups and acceding to one group's demands usually means that other groups in the coalition are getting less of what they want. Almost always, it is a case of issue emphasis, as most of the time parties do not contain groups directly opposed to one another. But when a new group appears, all bets are off. When Lyndon Johnson signed the Civil Rights Act of 1964, he famously remarked that he was signing away the South to the Republicans. White southerners were significant members of the New Deal coalition prior to this point. It was not long before they were gone. Besides the desire to right historical wrongs, President Johnson, and Truman before him, calculated that the electoral gain of moving more quickly toward civil rights would be worth the loss that would surely be incurred. This calculation helped Truman win the election of 1948. Johnson's Democratic Party was not so fortunate. The bottom line is that the more electoral gain that can be achieved by cozying up to a new group, the more likely it will occur. The members of the establishment will be that much less resistant to potential attacks on their positions of power *inside* the party if they sense that their positions of power *outside* the party will get stronger. It may not always be as easy to gauge as it was in 1964, but to the extent it can be, electoral gain provides an objective measure of what the electoral consequences will be of a new group entering the party coalition.

To estimate the potential for electoral gain, it is necessary to consider who these new people are who are coming into the party. What is their partisan and ideological breakdown? At what rate do they vote? Those are the major questions that will help determine relative electoral gain. Looking at Table 9.5, in 1980, religious conservatives virtually mirrored the partisanship breakdown found among all Americans. They were a bit more conservative and a bit less likely to be liberal. They were registered to vote at almost exactly the same rate as the nation at large. And most importantly, when they voted in the past, they were more likely to have voted Democratic. This looks exactly like the group Paul Weyrich and others had in mind when they set out to fashion a realignment out of moral and cultural issues. The potential for major political gain was great. And indeed, the early returns after the 1980 presidential election suggested that some of these gains were realized.

The strategy of the Moral Majority and other similar organizations in the first wave was to connect moral and religious conservatism to the Republican Party. But for this to pay off, these groups would have to also get their congregations to vote at higher levels than they were accustomed. Table 9.6 shows that this effort was largely a fruitful one.

TABLE 9.5   PARTISANSHIP, IDEOLOGY, AND PAST VOTING BEHAVIOR OF
RELIGIOUS CONSERVATIVES, 1980

	Religious Conservatives	All Respondents
Republican	33%	33%
Independent	11%	13%
Democratic	56%	53%
Conservative	53%	44%
Moderate	29%	31%
Liberal	18%	25%
Registered to vote	72%	74%
Always voted Republican	10%	13%
Have voted for both parties	53%	57%
Always voted Democratic	37%	30%

SOURCE: 1980 American National Election Studies.

TABLE 9.6   VOTER TURNOUT BY RELIGIOUS GROUPS AND REGION, 1980

	South		Non-South	
	Evangelicals	Others	Evangelicals	Others
Turned out for all/most of prior presidential elections	61.1%	70.5%	60.8%	73.2%
Voted in 1980	77.0%	65.9%	74.6%	73.3%
Change in mobilization	+15.9%	−4.6%	+13.8%	+0.1%

SOURCE: Statistics taken from Table 5.5 in Clyde Wilcox, God's Warriors: The Christian Right in Twentieth-Century America (Johns Hopkins University Press, 1991), 116.

In 1980, evangelicals across the country became a much larger proportion of the electorate than they had been in the previous election. And
this newly enlarged group moved toward Reagan and the Republicans.
Among self-identified born-again white Protestants, Reagan received
65 percent of their votes compared to Ford's 50 percent in 1976. Clyde
Wilcox, an eminent Christian right scholar concluded the following:

> There is mixed evidence concerning the possible mobilization of previously
> apolitical evangelicals and fundamentalists by the Moral Majority. Although
> supporters did not turn out at a significantly higher rate than nonsupport-
> ers, there are hints in the data that they voted more often than others with a
> similar demographic and participatory background. *Moreover, although the
> vote choice of the Moral Majority is fully consistent with their partisanship,
> there is some evidence that they have changed their partisanship at some
> point in their life.*[25] (italics mine)

TABLE 9.7   PARTISANSHIP, IDEOLOGY, AND PAST VOTING BEHAVIOR OF
RELIGIOUS CONSERVATIVES, 1992

	Religious Conservatives	All Respondents
Republican	37%	38%
Independent	12%	12%
Democratic	51%	50%
Conservative	53%	41%
Moderate	30%	31%
Liberal	17%	28%
Registered to vote	64%	75%
Always voted Republican	N/A	N/A
Have voted for both parties	N/A	N/A
Always voted Democratic	N/A	N/A

SOURCE: 1992 American National Election Studies.

Second Wave

Table 9.7 shows that, in 1992, religious conservatives were still divided between the parties in a similar proportion as the rest of the country. They were significantly more conservative, however, and it is well known that they had moved sharply toward the Republican Party in presidential elections. Party identification is always slowest to transition and that is probably what was happening here. The troubling number for Republicans looking to become the majority party backed by its newest coalition member is the 64 percent of religious conservatives that were registered to vote in 1992, compared to 75 percent of the entire country. That means the full potential of the moral/cultural realignment was not being realized. Religious conservatives were still rightly seen as the target group, but in the 1990s and 2000s, it became more about mobilization than conversion. These Americans, when they did vote during this time, went strongly for Republicans—generally at a 3:1 clip.

Ralph Reed and the Christian Coalition invested a great deal of resources and effort into ensuring that Christian conservative turnout increased. The organization worked extremely hard to build structures that would identify sympathetic voters in certain states and localities, and turn them out on Election Day. They did this for candidates overtly affiliated with them and also for candidates who they either endorsed or just agreed with on important issues. In addition, they also utilized the

TABLE 9.8   PARTISANSHIP, IDEOLOGY, AND PAST VOTING BEHAVIOR OF TEA
PARTY SUPPORTERS, 2010

	Tea Party Supporters	All Respondents
Partisanship		
Republican	57%	30%
Independent	38%	36%
Democratic	5%	34%
Ideology		
Conservative	75%	37%
Moderate	21%	41%
Liberal	4%	22%
Past voting behavior		
Registered to vote	97%	84%
Always or usually voted Republican	69%	32%
Voted equally for both parties	26%	36%
Always or usually voted Democratic	5%	32%

SOURCE: April 2010 New York Times Poll.[26]

built-in organizational structure of the churches and oversaw "in-pew" voter registration drives. These efforts paid off immediately when, in 1994, the Republican Party finally took control of Congress after four decades of being in the minority.

Even after the millennium, it was essential to the electoral success of the GOP to continue to seek out evangelical Christians and get them to the polls in large numbers. After the 2000 election, Karl Rove believed there were at least three million Christian conservatives across the nation (that is, slam-dunk Bush voters) that did not come to the polls. This calculation led directly to the Bush campaign's unprecedented strategy in 2004 of virtually ignoring swing voters and simply looking to enlarge their base. With the help of the gay marriage issue, religious conservatives kept Ohio in the Republican column and Bush in the White House.

Tea Party

In terms of partisanship, ideology, and past voting behavior, the current Tea Party movement differs dramatically from both the first and second wave of Christian right organizing. According to data from an April 2010 *New York Times* survey (presented in Table 9.8), Tea Party supporters are much more likely to be Republican and conservative than the rest of the country. Whereas the *Times* survey found that the country was essentially split between Republicans, Democrats, and independents, the numbers were considerably skewed toward the GOP among Tea Party supporters. Of Tea Party supporters, 57 percent called themselves Republicans. Along with 38 percent claiming independent status, that only leaves 5 percent of Tea Partiers in the Democratic column. In addition, the Tea Party contains twice as many conservatives as are found in the population at large. As far as voting behavior goes, 97 percent of Tea Party supporters are registered to vote, compared to 84 percent of the total population. And when they have voted in the past, it has been mostly for Republican candidates. Once again, among all respondents, we see almost an exact split in thirds between those who always vote Republican, those who have voted for both parties, and those who always vote Democrat. Among Tea Partiers, those numbers are 69 percent, 26 percent, and 5 percent, respectively. Clearly the Tea Party is not representative of our nation when it comes to partisanship, ideology, and voting behavior.

The results of several Gallup polls published in July 2010 provide corroborating evidence for the previous findings. Gallup found that there is significant overlap between the Tea Party movement and those who identify as conservative Republicans. Gallup found that eight out of ten Tea Party supporters are Republican compared with 44 percent of the general population. In addition, Tea Partiers are no more enthusiastic than conservative Republicans—the GOP's base. And finally, about 80 percent of Tea Party supporters say they will vote for the Republican candidate in their district, slightly lower than the projected 95 percent Republican vote among conservative Republicans but almost double that of the entire electorate. Gallup concludes, "Their similar ideological makeup and views suggest that the Tea Party is more a rebranding of core Republicanism than a new or distinct political movement."[27]

Now to anybody who has been even remotely following this fledgling movement, these numbers and conclusions are not very surprising. However, looking at them from the perspective of the relationship between the Tea Party and the Republican establishment, they are potentially very important. Equally well known to the general public is that the Tea Party brought incredible passion and intensity to the 2010 midterm elections. But looking beyond 2010, one has to wonder how much the Republican establishment will feel they need to cater to the Tea Party. They already vote at incredibly high rates for Republican candidates. The odds that these voters will turn to the Democratic

Party if left unfulfilled by the GOP are highly unlikely. Of course, there is another possibility. The Tea Party and its followers may become disillusioned with the political process and simply stay home: Some might, but the chances that enough will to damage Republican electoral prospects is improbable considering many Tea Party supporters have been consistently voting Republican since before there was a Tea Party.

Comparing the Movements

The electoral gain from acceding to Tea Party demands seems much less than it was when religious conservatives were attempting to reshape the Republican Party in their image. The potential was much greater for the Republicans in the early 1980s and early '90s since there were so many more Democrats, independents, and nonvoters among religious conservatives. Plus, those religious conservatives who began voting Republican were not traditionally Republican. If anything, they were historically Democrats. Therefore, the threat was greater that they would fade from the GOP and even go back to the Democrats if their issues were not being addressed adequately.

This does not seem like a problem the Tea Party can consciously address. They could display their independence in the near future by defecting from the Republicans to support Democrats or they could look to form their own party or run independent candidates in 2012 and beyond. But both of these options seem remote when one considers that the Tea Party is widely believed to be either entirely a Republican creation or a completely organic, decentralized, leaderless movement. If the former is true, one cannot expect any considerable movement toward the Democrats, and if the latter is the case, then one can hardly imagine the various grassroots groups across the country coordinating on any sort of a third-party strategy. From the perspective of electoral gain, things do not look good for the Tea Party in their efforts to impact the Republican Party in the long term.

COMPARING THE CHRISTIAN RIGHT AND THE TEA PARTY: RHETORIC AND NOMINATION POLITICS

The way our politics plays out these days is far from genteel. Thin skin, an unwillingness to get dirty, and expectations of fair treatment from the other side will not get anybody very far. However, there is something to be said for at least some modicum of restraint, that is, an ability to play nicely with others. This can prove problematic for some, especially those involved in a grassroots uprising hoping to fan the flames of indignity for political gain. The squeaky wheel still gets the grease, and increasingly in our politics, the squeaky wheel that speeds through a mud puddle splattering everyone in sight gets even more grease. The third criterion for success measures the ability of political insurgents to smooth out some of their sharp edges and make themselves more palatable to the party they hope to influence. In this section, I compare the first and second waves of Christian right organizing to the Tea Party movement on two aspects of playing nicely: rhetoric and nomination politics. In each case, I argue that a bit of gentility and grace can go a long way in helping political outsiders gain power and influence in the two-party system. The two parties by definition seek to build majorities. Majorities cannot be built if the party is constantly repelling voters with harsh rhetoric, in-your-face tactics, and the nomination of extremist candidates.

Criterion #3: Playing Nicely?

First-Wave Rhetoric

To gain attention and legitimacy, first-wave Christian right leaders came out with both rhetorical guns blazing. During the 1980 presidential campaign, the Religious Roundtable sponsored a National Affairs Briefing that boasted Ronald Reagan as its keynote speaker. The salvos from the stage during the speeches leading up to Reagan's were inflammatory and immediately branded the movement as intolerant and exclusive. First it was the Reverend James Robison, who complained, "I am sick and tired of hearing about all of the radicals and the perverts and the liberals and the leftists and the communists coming out of the closet. It is time for God's people to come out of the closet and the churches and change America."[28] Then Reverend Bailey Smith asserted, "It is interesting at great political rallies how you have a Protestant to pray, and a Catholic to pray, and then you have a Jew to pray. With all due respect to these dear people, my friends, God Almighty does not hear the prayer of a Jew."[29] Jerry Falwell said Jimmy Carter "wasn't a good Christian," and Pat Robertson told *U.S. News and World Report* that "we have enough votes to run the country. And when the people say, 'We've had enough,' we are going to take over."[30] Robertson also threatened the Republican Party during his presidential campaign by telling the Republican Party to let his supporters in or they will kick down the door. This overheated rhetoric spawned liberal and moderate criticism. Norman Lear formed the liberal group People for the American Way in direct response to the mobilization of Christian conservatives and the perceived threat they posed. The entire movement was accused of being racist, anti-Semitic, and against the separation of church and state. In many cases, the exact words of Christian right leaders lent credence to these charges. This portrayal damaged the movement's credibility among the nation at large, and understandably made the GOP resistant to their efforts to influence the party.

Second-Wave Rhetoric

The second wave of political organizing, epitomized by Ralph Reed and his Christian Coalition, made toning down the rhetoric one of their chief goals. They did not get off to a great start as Pat Buchanan and Pat Robertson gave notoriously inflammatory speeches at the 1992 Republican National Convention in Houston, Texas. Buchanan declared famously that there was a "cultural war" going on in America. He condemned the Democratic convention as "that giant masquerade ball up at Madison Square Garden, where 20,000 radicals and liberals came dressed up as moderates and centrists in the greatest single exhibition of cross-dressing in American political history."[31] Buchanan went on, charging that Clinton was hostile to "the Judeo-Christian values and beliefs upon which this America was founded. . . . The agenda that Clinton and the Democrats would impose on America—abortion on demand, a litmus test for the Supreme Court, homosexual rights, discrimination against religious schools, women in combat units . . . not the kind of change we can abide in a nation that we can still call God's country."[32] Robertson warned, "When Bill Clinton talks about family values, he is not talking about either families or values. He is talking about a radical plan to destroy the traditional family and transfer its functions to the federal government."[33] Because of where this rhetoric was being broadcast, the scent of extremism and bigotry stained the Republican Party as well. Reed realized if his movement had any hope of working with the GOP in the future, they would have to tone it down. In January 1993, Reed advised his followers to avoid hostile and intemperate rhetoric: "When stating our own convictions we must acknowledge the opinions of others and the sincerity of their beliefs. We must emphasize inclusion, not exclusion. We must adopt strategies of persuasion, not domination. We must be tolerant of diverse views and respectful of those who present them." Reed made a point of criticizing the notion that religious conservatives speak for God in matters of public policy: "There may be only one way to get to heaven according to one's theology, but there is probably more than one way to balance the budget or reform health care."[34] While this change in style may not have won over many liberal Democratic converts, it made Republicans much less fearful of associating themselves with this insurgent movement. In sharp contrast to 1992, at the 1996 convention, the Christian right was content to stay out of the spotlight and happy to concentrate on controlling the platform.

Tea Party Rhetoric

The Tea Party has been plagued by intemperate rhetoric that has attracted charges of intolerance and even racism. Much of this occurred during the 2009 town hall protests over the Democratic health care plan. Tea Partiers showed up with guns on their hips and provocative signs in their hands, not to mention armed with harsh insults meant for hurling at politicians attempting to explain their reasons behind supporting the bill. Calling Obama a Muslim, accusing him of not being a U.S. citizen, and suggesting armed rebellion against a "tyrannical Democratic regime" rivals anything ever said by Christian conservatives in terms of combative rhetoric. The anger is fine for firing up the base but it does not bode well for expanding movement support. In fact, this rhetoric has an excellent chance of turning off voters who might otherwise agree with the political sentiments behind the rhetoric. This type of rhetoric is hardly the kind with which a major political party would want to associate.

First-Wave Nomination Campaigns

The importance of nominations has been discussed earlier in this chapter. During the 1980s, religious conservatives consistently backed extremist candidates who ran in-your-face campaigns that alienated their fellow Republicans as well as the rest of the electorate. Several Republican congressional primary campaigns pitted evangelical Christians against establishment candidates. These candidates backed by the Christian right took harsh and uncompromising stands on social issues. They flaunted their orthodox religiosity and portrayed anyone who failed to agree with them on either the issues or the scripture as unfit for office. When the religious conservative candidates won the primary, they often lost the support of moderate Republicans in the general election. When they lost the primary, many times their supporters held a grudge and refused to back the nominee in November. Either way, this proved extremely problematic for the GOP. These internecine battles were one of the main reasons why the Republicans could not gain more ground on the Democrats in Congress even while they were consistently winning presidential elections.

Second-Wave Nomination Campaigns

During the second wave of organizing, there were still nomination fights going on within the Republican Party. However, Christian right leaders made conscious changes in how they were going to approach these battles. For the most part, when Christian right candidates lost primaries in the 1990s, elites backed the nominee and urged their followers to do so as well. This curried favor with local, state, and national party leaders. Furthermore, religious conservatives ceased to reflexively get behind the most socially conservative candidate. They wanted a social conservative but one who could win. When Christian right–backed candidates did gain the nomination, they often downplayed their religiosity and moral conservatism in the general election. Ralph Reed and other leaders utilized what they called stealth campaigns. The idea was to essentially run two campaigns. One campaign would be directed at the base and would reassure them that the candidate was sufficiently pro-life, anti–gay rights, and so on. This message would be disseminated through the churches and by local Christian right groups only to those who were friendly to the cause. A separate campaign was waged for the media and the general electorate. Here, candidates would focus on more broadly popular issues like cutting taxes and spending. They did not have to wear their morality on their sleeve because the base did not have to see it to know it was there.

Tea Party Nomination Campaigns

Throughout the tumultuous primary season of 2010, we saw many examples of Tea Party–backed candidates taking on establishment

Republicans with an uncompromising ideology and a brash style. Rand Paul shocked the nation with his easy victory over Mitch McConnell's protégé Trey Grayson in Kentucky. Like his father, Paul appears to be a staunch libertarian fighting to drastically limit the role of the federal government. He was one of the first Senate candidates to ride the wave of Tea Party enthusiasm to victory, yet soon after his triumph he was in the middle of a controversy about his position on the Civil Rights Act of 1964. In Alaska, armed with a high-profile endorsement from Sarah Palin, Joe Miller upset an incumbent senator and member of one of Alaska's political royal families, Lisa Murkowski. Despite the primary victory, his prospects in the general election were hurt by his strong belief in eschewing federal money for a state that has lived off of it since its admittance to the union. Rand Paul was able to overcome his relatively extreme views to win the general election; however, Joe Miller was not so fortunate falling to Murkowski's surprising write-in campaign.

In addition to issue positions that appear to be far from the median voter, other candidates displayed a stunning lack of experience that led to repeated gaffes and may have ultimately kept the Republicans from regaining control of the Senate. With help from Tea Partiers across the country, Christine O'Donnell came from out of nowhere in Delaware to defeat a man who had been winning statewide elections for decades. But her past pronouncements on celibacy, masturbation, evolution, and witchcraft essentially handed this seat to the Democrats. In Nevada, Sharron Angle proved to be one of the few people who could single-handedly resurrect Senate Majority Leader Harry Reid's hopes of getting reelected. Angle once pushed for a prison rehabilitation program modeled on the teachings of Scientology founder L. Ron Hubbard. She also suggested it might be a good idea to go back to the days when patients bartered with their doctors for health care. Both O'Donnell and Angle were defeated on Election Day in races that Republicans were favored to win prior to their nominations.

These are just a few examples of U.S. Senate candidates who look a lot like early Christian right candidates. Their extremist views have been broadcast loud and clear to a bemused and sometimes dumbfounded electorate. As of this writing, there is no study that systematically looks at how many independents and moderate Republicans pulled the Democratic lever because they were turned off by these candidates. But in such a closely divided electorate *and* U.S. Senate, losing even relatively small numbers of voters can be the difference between taking over the Senate and staying in the minority.

CONCLUSION

The story of the Tea Party and how it ultimately will fit into the Republican Party is far from over. The passionate belief in fiscal responsibility unleashed by this movement and manifested in the 2010 midterm elections will not soon fade. However, I would argue the Tea Party got off to a rocky start in 2011. Many pundits focused more on the high-profile races lost by Tea Party candidates than those they won. The new RNC chairman seems to be friendly to the movement but the Republican congressional leadership remains firmly in the hands of establishment leaders who figure to be at least somewhat resistant to the rabidly conservative cries of the Tea Party–supported freshmen.

If the Tea Party has any designs on significantly influencing American politics through the Republican Party, they will have to make changes—changes similar to those the Christian right made in the 1990s. Finding a way to make their specific policy proposals palatable to a larger segment of the population is the first adjustment that should be made. Abolishing the Department of Education and repealing the Fourteenth Amendment figure to be nonstarters and only serve to crystallize the extremist nature of the movement to the general public. Compromises similar to those religious conservatives sought on abortion will keep their supporters motivated while tagging those who oppose the compromises as out of the mainstream.

In the Tea Party's favor, I believe that compromising over fiscal issues that are not always clearly understood by the electorate, and therefore able to be spun as less of a compromise than they actually might be, is not as difficult as compromising on abortion, which for many is seen as a life-or-death, "good versus evil" type of an issue. Another difference between the Tea Party and the Christian right that bodes well for the former is that while religious conservatives had to change the entire issue focus of the GOP in the 1980s and 1990s, the current Republican Party already is focused on fiscal conservatism. The Tea Party's goal should simply be to shift them further to the right on these issues.

Finally, the Tea Party will have to make a decision regarding the kinds of Republican candidates they will support in the future. In 2012, the Tea Party once again mounted several challenges to incumbent Republican senators who they view as insufficiently conservative. The question is whether the 2012 election cycle will be a repeat of 2010 when Tea Party–backed insurgents knocked off GOP incumbents only to be deemed unfit for office and defeated by Democrats in the general election. With control of the Senate hanging in the balance, there exists the real possibility that the Tea Party and its uncompromising nature will stand in the way of a Republican senatorial majority. That kind of an outcome surely does not bode well for the long-term prospects of the Tea Party, either within the Republican Party, or within American politics as a whole.

NOTES

1. E. E. Schattschneider, *Party Government* (Westport, CT: Greenwood Press, 1942), 1.

2. Cited in Robert Allen Rutland, *The Democrats: From Jefferson to Clinton* (Columbia: University of Missouri Press, 1995), 3.

3. Schattschneider, *Party Government*, 35.

4. Marty Cohen, David Karol, Hans Noel, and John Zaller, *The Party Decides* (Chicago: University of Chicago Press, 2008), 30.

5. On the 1952 Republican presidential nominating campaign, see Richard Norton Smith, *Thomas E. Dewey and His Times* (New York: Simon and Schuster, 1982); and Stephen E. Ambrose, *Eisenhower: Soldier, General of the Army, President-Elect 1890–1952* (New York: Simon and Schuster, 1983).

6. On the 1964 Republican presidential nominating campaign, see Theodore H. White, *The Making of the President, 1964* (New York: Atheneum, 1965); and Nicol C. Rae, *The Decline and Fall of the Liberal Republicans: From 1952 to the Present* (Oxford: Oxford University Press, 1989).

7. A change in groups was not the only standard for delineating the two waves. As I explain later in the chapter, the tactics and strategies of the second wave differed dramatically from those of the first wave.

8. The word *evangelical* comes from the Greek *euangelion*, which means "good news." Evangelicalism came to symbolize the revival movements sweeping the nation through the various Great Awakenings in the eighteenth and nineteenth centuries. These revival meetings consisted of emotionally charged preaching and singing that sought to arouse an immediate experience of conversion or rededication to the Christian faith. Preachers actively worked to evangelize, to give the "good news" to others—the "good news" being the existence of the savior Jesus Christ. People were encouraged to accept Jesus Christ as their Lord and personal savior. This was seen as the only way to save one's soul. The idea was that Jesus Christ would return to earth and those who accepted Him would be saved and those who hadn't would be damned. This new acceptance, conversion, or rededication to the Christian faith was known as a born-again experience. See Duane Oldfield, *The Right and the Righteous: The Christian Right Confronts the Republican Party* (Lanham, MD: Rowman and Littlefield, 1996); and Steve Bruce, *The Rise and Fall of the New Christian Right* (Oxford: Oxford University Press, 1988).

9. Oldfield, *The Right and the Righteous*; Bruce, *The Rise and Fall of the New Christian Right*; and David Bromley and Anson Shupe, *New Christian Politics* (Macon, GA: Mercer University Press, 1984).

10. On the new right's involvement with the first wave of Christian right organizing and the Moral Majority in particular, see Bromley and Shupe, *New Christian Politics;* Sara Diamond, *Spiritual Warfare: The Politics of the Christian Right* (Cambridge, MA: South End Press, 1999); Matthew Moen, *The Transformation of the Christian Right* (Tuscaloosa: University of Alabama Press, 1992); and Jeffrey Hadden and Charles Swann, *Prime Time Preachers: The Rising Power of Televangelism* (Reading, MA: Addison-Wesley Publishers, 1981).

11. See Oldfield, *The Right and the Righteous;* and Sara Diamond, *Roads to Dominion: Right-Wing Movements and Political Power in the United States* (New York: The Guilford Press, 1995).

12. Allen Hertzke, *Echoes of Discontent: Jesse Jackson, Pat Robertson, and the Resurgence of Populism* (Washington, DC: CQ Press, 1993); and James Penning, "Pat Robertson and the GOP: 1988 and Beyond," *Sociology of Religion* 55 (1994): 327–44.

13. Justin Watson, *The Christian Coalition: Dreams of Restoration, Demands of Recognition* (New York: St. Martin's Press, 1997).

14. The American National Election Studies (www.electionstudies.org). *The ANES Guide to Public Opinion and Electoral Behavior* (Ann Arbor, MI: University of Michigan, Center for Political Studies [producer and distributor]). In this analysis, I am denoting religious conservatives as those survey respondents who chose the most orthodox response to a question about their attitudes toward the Bible. In 1980, that was "The Bible is God's work and all it says is true." In 1992, the NES asked a slightly different question with the orthodox response reading "The Bible is the actual word of God and is to be taken literally." On biblical inerrancy (1980, NES): Here are four statements about the Bible, and I'd like you to tell me which is closest to your own view: (1) The Bible is God's work and all it says is true; (2) the Bible was written by men who were inspired by God but it contains some human errors; (3) the Bible is a good book because it was written by wise men, but God had nothing to do with it; or (4) the Bible was written by men who lived so long ago that it is worth very little today. On biblical literalism (1992, NES): Which of these statements comes closest to describing your feelings about the Bible? (1) The Bible is the actual word of God and is to be taken literally, word for word; (2) the Bible is the word of God but not everything in it should be taken literally, word for word; or (3) the Bible is a book written by men and is not the word of God.

Using the Bible question as opposed to religious denomination makes sense because, in the era of the "culture wars," moral appeals are widely believed to cross traditional religious barriers. (The "culture war" idea was proposed by James Davison Hunter, *Culture Wars* [New York: Basic Books, 1991].) In addition, one is not really considered an evangelical or fundamentalist Christian if he or she has not had a born-again experience and does not believe the Bible is the literal word of God. Several notable studies of religion and politics rely heavily on attitudes toward the Bible. Geoffrey Layman, *The Great Divide* (New York: Columbia University Press, 2001); and Lyman Kellstedt and Corwin Smidt, "Doctrinal Beliefs and Political Behavior: Views of the Bible," in *Rediscovering the Religious Factor in Politics,* ed. David Leege and Lyman Kellstedt (Armonk, NY: M. E. Sharpe, 1993), 177–98, are two among many studies that utilize the NES questions on the Bible. For discussions of the wording change of the Bible question, see Ted Jelen, "Biblical Literalism and Inerrancy: Does the Difference Make a Difference?" *Sociological Analysis* 50 (1989): 421–29; and Ted Jelen, Clyde Wilcox, and Corwin Smidt, "Biblical Literalism and Inerrancy: A Methodological Analysis," in *Sociological Analysis* 51 (1990): 307–13. I conducted a similar analysis using self-reported evangelicals and supporters of the Moral Majority as the target group. The results were extremely similar.

15. In these cases, the survey's classification of "Tea Party supporter" was self-evident.

16. Ed Dobson, Edward Hindson, and Jerry Falwell, *The Fundamentalist Phenomenon: The Resurgence of Conservative Christianity* (Grand Rapids, MI: Baker Publishing, 1986).

17. This number is important on its own. Out of the most pro-life groups in the country, only one in five supported a complete ban on abortion. It is no wonder then that a constitutional amendment banning abortion got nowhere.

18. On abortion: There has been some discussion about abortion during recent years. Which one of the opinions on this page best agrees with your view? (1) By law, abortion should never be permitted; (2) the law should permit abortion only in cases of rape, incest, or when the woman's life is in danger; (3) The law should permit abortion for reasons other than rape, incest, or danger to the woman's life, but only after the need for the abortion has been clearly established; or (4) by law, a woman should always be able to obtain an abortion as a matter of personal choice. On the ERA: Do you approve or disapprove of the proposed Equal Rights Amendment to the Constitution, sometimes called the ERA amendment? (1) Approve; or (5) disapprove.

19. Weyrich said, "As conservatives we kid ourselves if we think the president's reelection in 1984 is going to deliver major gains to our movement" (reprinted in Diamond, *Spiritual Warfare*, 64–65). Viguerie said, "Alas, like Jimmy Carter, the man he defeated and replaced, Ronald Reagan has turned his back on the populist cause" (reprinted in Oldfield, *The Right and the Righteous*, 120).

20. On abortion: Same as in 1980. On parental consent, on state funds, and on spousal notification: Would you favor or oppose (strongly or not strongly) a law in your state that would require parental consent before a teenager under eighteen can have an abortion/allow the use of government funds to help pay for the costs of abortion for women who cannot afford them/require a married woman to notify her husband before she can have an abortion? (1) Favor strongly; (2) favor not strongly; (3) oppose not strongly; or (4) oppose strongly. Gays in the military and gay adoption: Do you feel strongly or not strongly that homosexuals should be allowed to serve in the United States Armed Forces/legally permitted to adopt children? (1) Feel strongly should be allowed; (2) feel not strongly should be allowed; (3) feel not strongly should not be allowed; or (4) feel strongly should not be allowed. Prayer in public schools: Which of the following views comes closest to your opinion on the issue of school prayer? (1) By law, prayers should not be allowed in public schools; (2) the law should

allow public schools to schedule time when children can pray silently if they want to; (3) the law should allow public schools to schedule time when children, as a group, can say a general prayer not tied to a particular religious faith; or (4) by law, public schools should schedule a time when all children would say a chosen Christian prayer.

21. Jeffrey M. Jones, "Debt, Government Power among Tea Party Supporters' Top Concerns," July 5, 2010, accessed at www.gallup.com.

22. "Polling the Tea Party," April 14, 2010, accessed at www.nytimes .com.

23. See Table 8.3 in Abramowitz, Chapter 8 in this volume.

24. In a forthcoming publication, I focus on the process by which Christian conservative activists infiltrated, and in some cases took over state and local Republican Party structures. As a result, when George W. Bush entered the White House, social conservatives were considered a full-fledged party faction with significant influence over GOP candidates, platforms, and strategies. Their place alongside economic conservatives and neoconservatives was secured.

25. Clyde Wilcox, *God's Warriors: The Christian Right in Twentieth-Century America* (Baltimore: Johns Hopkins University Press, 1991), 121.

26. "Polling the Tea Party," April 14, 2010, accessed at www.nytimes .com.

27. Frank Newport, "Tea Party Supporters Overlap Republican Base," July 2, 2010, www.gallup.com. Data from polls conducted in March, May, and June 2010.

28. Howell Raines, "Reagan Backs Evangelicals in Their Political Activities," *New York Times*, August 23, 1980, 8.

29. "Baptist Leader Criticized for Statement about Jews," *New York Times*, September 18, 1980, A18.

30. "Preachers in Politics," *U.S. News and World Report*, September 24, 1979, 37.

31. Diamond, *Roads to Dominion*, 292.

32. Richard Wolf, "Reagan, Buchanan Ignite Party," *USA Today*, August 18, 1992, 3A.

33. Oldfield, *The Right and the Righteous*, 204.

34. Quotes come from *Christian American*, which was an internal publication of the Christian Coalition.

CHAPTER 10

The Tea Party and the Religious Right Movements

Frenemies with Benefits

PETER MONTGOMERY

The religious right movement is comprised of grassroots political organizations, legal advocacy groups, traditional and new media outlets,
and educational institutions that work to engage conservative evangelical Christians and their allies in efforts to elect like-minded officials and
shape culture, law, and public policy in accordance with their religious
and political views. Since Republican operatives met with evangelical
leaders in the late 1970s to create the political movement we call the
religious right, the movement's top priorities have consistently been
opposition to legal abortion, opposition to the advancement of social
and legal equality for gay and lesbian Americans, and opposition to the
separation of church and state—or using their terms, the right to life,
traditional family values, and religious liberty.

The religious right's success at using church-based organizing to
deliver voters made the movement and its followers a crucial and
influential part of the Republican Party's base, particularly once the
Christian Coalition in the early 1990s made it an explicit goal of
the movement to take over working control of the Republican Party
from the ground level up. Martin Cohen (Chapter 9 in this volume)
describes how, as part of that process, religious right leaders like
Ralph Reed worked assiduously to expand the movement's definition
of "family values" to embrace Republicans' antitax and antigovernment agendas.

Nevertheless, there have frequently been tensions between the "social issue" priorities of religious right groups and the pro-business economic priorities and election-winning concerns of "establishment" Republicans. For years, religious right leaders and activists have complained that Republican politicians embraced their issues to gain electoral support but rarely made passage of their policy goals, such as eliminating legal abortion and restricting marriage to a man and a woman in the U.S. Constitution, a sufficiently high priority. Religious right leaders, for example, worked hard to help elect Ronald Reagan but were bitterly disappointed when he nominated Sandra Day O'Connor to the Supreme Court. Two decades later, to boost religious right enthusiasm for his reelection, a visibly uncomfortable George W. Bush publicly embraced a federal constitutional amendment on marriage but made little effort to advance such an amendment through Congress.[1]

The 2008 election of President Barack Obama and Democratic majorities in both houses of Congress sent shockwaves through the entire conservative political establishment. Religious right leaders, who had been largely unenthusiastic backers of GOP nominee John McCain until the selection of Sarah Palin as his running mate, announced well before Obama's inauguration that they now viewed themselves, in the words of Concerned Women for America's Wendy Wright, as part of a "resistance movement."[2]

Some conservative strategists began calling immediately for a grassroots movement that would challenge insufficiently conservative Republicans. Just weeks after the 2008 election, Richard Viguerie told the secretive Council for National Policy that "there needs to be a flowering of grassroots conservative activism and local groups, local PACs." An attendee recounted Viguerie's strategy: "He's basically saying you've got a Republican county commissioner in Buzzard's Breath, Texas, and he's not a conservative? Run a conservative against him."[3]

At the same time, some conservative commentators challenged the prominent public role played by the religious right in the Republican Party. Shortly after the election, pundit Kathleen Parker declared that "[a]rmband religion is killing the Republican Party." Parker bemoaned the fact that "[t]he choir has become absurdly off-key, and many Republicans know it," even as she acknowledged the GOP's dilemma: "*But they need those votes!*"[4]

The rightward shift of the GOP's activist base and the 2008 electoral failures of the party establishment and religious right political groups set the stage for a conservative backlash to the Obama administration and Democratic congressional leadership that was distinct from the traditional religious right groups that had not proven themselves capable of delivering a sufficient electoral impact in 2008. Some consider CNBC commentator Rick Santelli's February 19, 2009 rant against the Obama administration's planned intervention in the mortgage market to be a pivotal spark for the Tea Party movement. A week later, at the annual Conservative Political Action Conference, Senator Jim DeMint, the religious right's point man in the U.S. Senate, declared that Americans were ready to "take to the streets to stop America's slide into socialism."[5]

Public anger at the extraordinary bailout of Wall Street and other interventions in the financial markets was quickly exploited by corporate-funded conservative groups such as FreedomWorks and Americans for Prosperity, which helped mobilize antitax protests around the country on April 15, 2009.[6] Even at this nascent moment of the Tea Party movement, the religious right was present. The American Family Association, one of the oldest and largest religious right organizations, used its extensive online networks to encourage activists to participate in the Taxed Enough Already (TEA) protests.[7]

By the summer of 2009, religious right leaders had enthusiastically joined GOP-led and Tea Party–fueled opposition to health care reform efforts, moving well beyond their claims that reform would lead to taxpayer funding of abortions to fully embrace the Tea Party's antigovernment talking points.[8] This rhetoric reflected conservative leaders' belief that the fight against health care reform was a way to reinvigorate the off-again, on-again coalition between social and economic conservatives that is essential to advancing right-wing political objectives. Toward that end, the Heritage Foundation published *Indivisible*, a book of essays in which people known primarily for "social issue" activism were asked to contribute essays on an economic topic and vice versa. "In the long run," writes editor Jay Richards, "economic prosperity and limited government depends on moral principles like respect for the property of others and social institutions such as marriage."[9]

The same strategy is apparent in the creation of the Freedom Federation, a confederation of religious right groups launched in the summer of 2009. The Federation published a Declaration of American Values that declared groups' allegiance not only to the social agenda of the religious right but also to a system of taxes that "are not progressive in nature, and within a limited government framework, to encourage economic opportunity, free enterprise, and free market competition."[10]

The overriding shared goals of economic and social conservatives in the wake of President Obama's election have been to diminish his administration's ability to advance its policy goals and to build toward the defeat of Democratic lawmakers in 2010 and Obama himself in 2012. The importance of those electoral goals to both groups ultimately overwhelms the significance of the sometimes public squabbles over priorities or the question of the visibility or lack thereof of the religious right's social agenda at Tea Party events and in Tea Party documents. As Richard Land, president of the Southern Baptist Convention's Ethics and Religious Liberty Commission, said in March 2010, "I don't see the Tea Party movement as a threat at all—I see it as additional allies and fellow travelers."[11] Or, as Mississippi Governor and former GOP Chair Haley Barbour bluntly wrote in September in the *Wall Street Journal*, "Republican and tea party voters united means Mr. Obama defeated."[12]

IDEOLOGY: GOD, LIMITED GOVERNMENT, AND AMERICAN EXCEPTIONALISM

In 2010 and 2011, conservative leaders worked hard to maintain close working relationships among the three (overlapping) groups of activists that make up what many refer to as the three-legged stool of conservatism: social conservatives, economic conservatives, and national security conservatives. That coordination goes well beyond electoral tactics to encompass long-term strategic planning. At an early October 2010 meeting between Tea Party Patriot leaders and the Council for National Policy, "TPP leaders handed out a 'secret' strategy memo . . . that lays out an ambitious goal: to 'renew the commitment to limited government and free markets in the hearts and minds of at least 60 percent of the American people over the next 40 years.'"[13] That memo also implicitly points to a role for religion, quoting John Adams:

> The Revolution was effected before the War commenced. The Revolution was in the minds and hearts of the people; a change in their religious sentiments of their duties and obligations. This radical change in the principles, opinions, sentiments, and affections of the people, was the real American Revolution.[14]

This convergence of libertarianism and fundamentalist religion has coalesced into the Tea Party's concept of American exceptionalism: The American Constitution, which restricts the powers of government, was divinely inspired. Other interpretations that allow for a more expanded role for government are therefore not only un-American but are also ungodly and unchristian. Glenn Beck not only portrays President Obama, congressional Democrats, and liberals in general as pro–big government and antireligion, but he also characterizes their antireligion as a *means* to achieve big government. Beck describes the "progressive dream" as requiring first the destruction of the religious and moral roots of the people: "That was the number one thing they had to destroy. They had to get God out of our schools." And secondly, "they had to take apart our understanding of the Constitution."[15]

In February 2010, Damon Linker, writing for *The New Republic*, noted that claims by right-wing pundits that President Obama is an enemy of "American exceptionalism" is a belief "so widely held and so frequently asserted on the right, in fact, that it can almost be described as conservative conventional wisdom."[16] Newt Gingrich offers another example of this view of American exceptionalism. In his book *To Save America: Stopping Obama's Secular Socialist Machine*, he writes:

> Most of us know who we are. We know that America is an exceptional country with unique genius for combining freedom and order, strength and compassion, religious faith and religious tolerance. But today we have given power in Washington and in state capitols nationwide to a radical left-wing elite that does not believe in American exceptionalism.[17]

American exceptionalism became a familiar phrase on the 2010 campaign trail, where Tea Party–backed candidates waved it as a banner and wielded it as a weapon against President Obama and Democrats. Senator Marco Rubio of Florida, one of the Tea Party's biggest success stories to date and one of their brightest hopes for the future, made American exceptionalism a theme of his campaign, which pushed the notion that disagreements about spending and the role of government are not just about policy disagreements but about the very identity and character of America.[18] In March 2011, a reporter for the Christian Broadcasting Network reported that "political analysts" are predicting that "American exceptionalism" is "likely to become one of the buzzwords" of the 2012 presidential race:

> The expression has already been a major talking point at CPAC—the Conservative Political Action Conference. It's the focus for a chapter in former Alaska Governor Sarah Palin's latest book *America by Heart*. It was also the theme at this year's Ronald Reagan Symposium at Regent University.[19]

At the September 2010 Values Voter Summit, Senator Jim DeMint pointedly argued for a necessary connection between fiscal and social conservatism: "You can't be a true fiscal conservative if you do not understand the value of a culture that is based on values."[20] As Sarah Posner put it in *The Nation,* "Many tea partiers, like religious right activists, find the roots of their thinking on government in the Bible."[21]

Adele Stan locates the origins of this ideological campaign in the Constitution Party. "If the Tea Party could be said to have a founding father," she writes, "I'd name him as Constitution Party founder Howard Phillips." According to the preamble to the Party's platform:

> The Constitution Party gratefully acknowledges the blessing of our Lord and Savior Jesus Christ as Creator, Preserver and Ruler of the Universe and of these United States. [. . .] The goal of the Constitution Party is to restore American jurisprudence to its Biblical foundations and to limit the federal government to its Constitutional boundaries.[22]

At the Freedom Federation's April 2011 "Awakening" conference at the Jerry Falwell–founded Liberty University, religious right leaders and activists embraced the Tea Party's focus on diminishing the size and restricting the actions of the federal government. Participants were told that their "common enemy" was a growing and intrusive federal government. The federal health care reform "monstrosity" that conservatives failed to prevent from being signed into law was portrayed as a dangerous step toward European-style socialism.

Baylor University sociologist Paul Froese has argued that a shared hatred for atheistic socialism has functioned as a unifying factor between conservative Christians and libertarians in the Tea Party movement:

> The historical roots of the Tea Party are not really found in the deism of the Founding Fathers nor the racism of the segregated South. Rather this growing movement is a direct descendent of the Red Scare. And, like the Red Scare, the Tea Party appeals to a wide range of Americans, many of whom are at direct odds over very central issues of freedom and religion. By reducing libertarian and conservative Christian concerns to a common enemy, the Tea Party has become a very potent political force.[23]

Supporting Froese's analysis is the reemergence of the John Birch Society as a welcome member of the conservative coalition. William F. Buckley and *National Review* had drummed the John Birth Society out of respectable conservative circles in 1962.[24] But the group had a visible presence at the 2011 Conservative Political Action Conference. Among the founders of the John Birch Society was Fred Koch, whose son David is now a major funder of the Americans for Prosperity Foundation, one of the "Astroturf" groups that has worked to organize Tea Partiers into an effective political force.[25]

Another shared characteristic of the two movements is resentment, bordering on contempt, for the "establishment" of the Republican Party. Tea Party leaders reviled national Republicans for having abandoned small-government principles by endorsing earmarks and supporting federal spending on programs many Tea Partiers believe are unconstitutional. In June 2010, Richard Viguerie put out a press release expressing "delight" that Tea Party–backed candidates had beaten establishment GOP picks in runoff primaries. "This is alarming news for GOP establishment politicians such as John Boehner, Mitch McConnell, and all closely associated with them. The Tea Party steamroller is rolling big government Republicans right out of town."[26]

Over the years, James Dobson and other religious right leaders have also frequently criticized GOP elected officials for not doing enough to push the agenda of religious right voters. Dobson has repeatedly threatened to punish the party by keeping his voters home, but has always backed down in the face of the alternative. The Tea Party's aggressive and remarkably successful backing for insurgent challengers to the establishment accomplished in short order more than Dobson was ever able to do in terms of threatening the party establishment.

So Dobson was happy to join the Tea Party. When he endorsed Tea Party candidate Rand Paul's successful Senate primary bid, Dobson reversed his earlier endorsement of Mitch McConnell's candidate Trey Grayson. Dobson blasted "senior members of the GOP" who he said had given him flawed information about Paul's antiabortion credentials.[27] Mark Silk commented on Paul's primary win:

> Not only is Rand Paul's victory a wake-up call for the national GOP establishment but it should also be one for those who imagine that the Tea Party movement is somehow unfriendly territory for the religious right. Other than Paul himself, the big winner was Dr. James Dobson, who weighed in with a video endorsement that seems to have driven the last nail into the coffin of Paul's Mitch McConnell–anointed opponent. Therein, Dobson slams "senior members of the GOP" for lying to him about Paul's positions and chalks it up to Paul's credit that he "identifies with the Tea Party movement."[28]

In the words of Democratic political strategist Ed Kilgore:

> [I]t's hard to identify Christian Right pols who haven't strongly identified themselves with the Tea Party Movement . . . and hard to find Tea Party spokesmen who favor any policies that would in any way discomfit the

Religious Right. Where they aren't the same people, they are certainly strong allies, and essentially two sides of the same radicalized conservative coin with the same apocalyptic vision of a righteous nation led hellwards by evil progressives.[29]

TENSIONS AND RIVALRIES

The convergence of the movement's ideologies and political goals has not prevented public disputes and rivalries. During the 2010 campaign season, religious right leaders complained about Tea Party groups' inattention to abortion and gay rights issues and warned the GOP not to abandon social conservatives in the rush to embrace the Tea Party.

Some of these sparks are probably a result of the role that Dick Armey's FreedomWorks has played in fostering the Tea Party movement. Armey is a rare Republican critic of the religious right movement, and he has suggested that the religious right's social agenda runs counter to the Tea Party's small-government, pro-individual liberty message:

> When the social conservatives and the economic conservatives work well together is when they work with a common resistance to the growth of the power of the state. And what happened was there was a small cadre of very strongly assertive people on the social issues side that were saying "let's expand the power of the state" in order to impose our values on the community. . . . [M]y point is very simple: you live a righteous life, you're an encouragement to other people; use the state to impose it and you're a tyrant.[30]

The victory of libertarian-leaning Ron Paul in the presidential straw poll at the 2010 Conservative Political Action Conference also dismayed some religious right leaders.[31] "There's a libertarian streak in the tea party movement that concerns me as a cultural conservative," Bryan Fischer, director of Issue Analysis for Government and Public Policy at the American Family Association, has complained. "The tea party movement needs to insist that candidates believe in the sanctity of life and the sanctity of marriage."[32]

A number of Tea Party leaders and Republican Party officials—including those with strong religious right credentials—angered religious right leaders during the 2010 election cycle by making a case grounded in pure electoral politics that groups should stay focused on voters' economic concerns and shy away from social issues. Among them were Mississippi Governor Haley Barbour, Indiana Governor Mitch Daniels, and Wisconsin Representative Paul Ryan. The anti-abortion LifeNews.com noted unhappily that Representative Ryan told

CNBC in September 2010, "We will agree to disagree on those issues. But let's rally around the tallest pole in our tent: fiscal conservatism, economic liberty."[33]

In response, the Family Research Council's Tony Perkins acknowledged that "economic issues are currently at the forefront of the minds of most voters," but he said many socially conservative voters make abortion the top issue in deciding how to vote. Perkins says the libertarian leanings of Armey's FreedomWorks don't represent "true" Tea Partiers.[34]

In these disputes, the Tea Party generally had the upper hand through 2010, one that grew even stronger as Tea Party–backed candidates—running mostly under the antitax, small-government banner—defeated incumbent senators and other candidates backed by the Republican establishment. That political reality is reflected in the blunt comments by FreedomWorks's director of federal and state campaigns in response to religious right complaints that abortion and gay marriage were not in the Contract From America: "People didn't come out into the streets to protest gay marriage or abortion."[35]

NATIONAL LEADERSHIP CONNECTIONS

The decentralized nature of the Tea Party movement and its relative lack of a formal leadership structure contrast with the highly structured religious right. Still, some leadership-level connections are clear, reflected in collective Tea Party–religious right events. In October 2010, leaders of the Tea Party Patriots, a group that has maintained a focus on fiscal issues and eschewed public discussion of religion or social issues, met with the members of the Council for National Policy (CNP) to try to raise money for its election plans.[36] The CNP's national director Bob Reccord also moderated a Tea Party panel at the September meeting of Ralph Reed's Faith and Freedom Coalition conference.[37]

A number of high-profile political figures who are seen as advocates of one of the movements are also strongly associated with the other. Among the examples of movement-bridging national leaders are Jim DeMint, Newt Gingrich, Sarah Palin, David Barton, Glenn Beck, Ralph Reed, Mike Pence, and Michele Bachmann.

Jim DeMint

Senator Jim DeMint (R-SC) is in many ways the embodiment of the intersection between the two movements. DeMint, who has argued that gays and single mothers should not be allowed to teach in public schools, has long been a folk hero to conservative religious activists and established himself as the religious right's go-to guy in Congress. At the same time, DeMint is also at the fringe of antigovernment sentiment in the Senate, and has abused rules to routinely obstruct Senate action on executive and judicial branch nominees as well as other legislation.[38] In 2010, DeMint and his Senate Conservatives Fund PAC were the most prominent backers of insurgent candidates, including some who dethroned incumbents and GOP-backed candidates in primary elections. His endorsement and financial backing in many ways defined the crop of Tea Party candidates for the U.S. Senate.[39]

In April 2010, the Christian Broadcasting Network's David Brody asked DeMint if he was worried about social issues taking a "backseat" to fiscal concerns. DeMint responded:

> No, actually just the opposite because I really think a lot of the motivation behind these Tea Party crowds is a spiritual component. . . . I think people are seeing this massive government growing and they're realizing that it's the government that's hurting us and I think they're turning back to God in effect is our salvation and government is not our salvation and in fact more and more people see government as the problem and so I think some have been drawn in over the years to a dependency relationship with government and as the Bible says you can't have two masters and I think as people pull back from that they look more to God. It's no coincidence that socialist Europe is post-Christian because the bigger the government gets the smaller God gets and vice versa. The bigger God gets the smaller people want their government because they're yearning for freedom.[40]

Before the 2010 election, some believed DeMint would challenge Senator Mitch McConnell for the Republican leadership. That possibility evaporated after DeMint-backed Senate candidates lost in Nevada, Delaware, and Colorado. Grumbling by some party regulars that DeMint cost the party the chance to achieve parity with Democrats in the Senate provoked a harsh backlash from religious right leaders and other conservatives who warned critics in an open letter that they would send their financial support to DeMint's Senate Conservative Fund rather than the National Republican Senatorial Committee.[41]

DeMint, who has been ranked the Senate's most conservative member on spending, gave the keynote address to a March 26, 2011 "Conservative Principles Conference" on American exceptionalism organized by Representative Steve King.[42] He was featured on the cover of the February 2011 issue of Focus on the Family's *Citizen* magazine, which said DeMint "remains convinced" that a majority of Tea Party participants are social conservatives. "I have been to a lot [of the rallies]," he said. "I have waded into the crowd. I know there is a strong faith component there because I always hear three things: 'Thanks for fighting, we are praying for you and what can I do?' I hear that everywhere. . . . Most of the values and principles that make this country work derive from biblical faith."[43]

Newt Gingrich

Newt Gingrich, whose 1994 "Contract with America" helped engineer a Republican takeover of Congress with an agenda focused on fiscal and accountability issues, has in recent years been working to build greater visibility among conservative evangelicals by promoting books and DVDs under the rubric of "Rediscovering God in America."

In March 2009, Gingrich launched an organization called "Renewing American Leadership" and hired Jim Garlow, a California pastor who mobilized church involvement in the Prop 8 campaign, to run it. Renewing American Leadership describes its mission statement this way: "to preserve America's Judeo-Christian heritage by defending and promoting the three pillars of American civilization: freedom, faith and free markets." Renewing American Leadership joined forces with the American Family Association to promote the Taxed Enough Already rallies on April 15, 2009. Dan Gilgoff observed, "The antitax rallies illustrate the new group's quest to unite religious and fiscal conservatives, two flanks of the Republican base that have squabbled with one another since Election Day [2008]."[44]

In preparation for launching a bid for the presidency, Gingrich aggressively courted religious right leaders and sought to defuse potential resistance to the candidacy of someone who cheated on and divorced two wives in unsavory circumstances. In this effort, Gingrich used religious right outlets like the Christian Broadcasting Network, where David Brody invited him to talk about "God's forgiving nature."[45] Gingrich also embraced evangelist John Hagee, whose support was controversial enough to be disavowed by John McCain in 2008. At Hagee's church in a March 2011 visit, Gingrich said "I have two grandchildren—Maggie is 11, Robert is 9. I am convinced that if we do not decisively win the struggle over the nature of America, by the time they're my age they will be in a secular atheist country, potentially one dominated by radical Islamists and with no understanding of what it once meant to be an American."[46] In April 2011, Gingrich was the featured speaker at an invitation-only "leadership luncheon" held as part of the Freedom Federation's Awakening 2011 conference at Liberty University; he shared the podium with Joseph Farah of WND (formerly World Net Daily), the leading online "birther" outlet.

Gingrich still works the Tea Party side of the GOP, of course. His think tank, American Solutions, organized a letter signed by 86 local and national Tea Party activists in support of the antiunion activities of Wisconsin Governor Scott Walker.[47] American Solutions has reportedly "been holding regular conversations with more than 300 tea party leaders throughout the country."

Sarah Palin

Former Alaska Governor Sarah Palin's choice as John McCain's running mate in 2008 energized religious right leaders and activists who until then had been generally reluctant supporters of McCain's candidacy. Palin's membership in a Pentecostal church and her routine references to the "prayer warriors" who support her made her popular among religious conservatives. In a May 2010 appearance on *The O'Reilly Factor*, Palin said, "I think we should kind of keep this clean, keep it simple, go back to what our founders and our founding documents meant. They're quite clear that we would create law based on the God of the Bible and the 10 Commandments. It's pretty simple."[48]

Politico noted in the fall of 2010 that Palin's political operation was further hitching its wagon to the Tea Party movement with a video that praises the Tea Party as the "future of politics." In a note promoting the video, she tells supporters to "support commonsense conservative candidates who will work with you, and for you, to provide solutions to America's challenges. Constitutionalists who are running for the right reasons will put our country back on course—for opportunity and freedom for all."[49]

In Palin's postgubernatorial role as part pop culture figure, part conservative political icon, she has achieved folk-hero status among her followers while earning relatively low approval ratings among the public at large. An October 2010 poll by the Public Religion Research Institute found that Palin was the most popular likely 2012 presidential candidate among voters who consider themselves part of the Tea Party. Her favorable rating among white evangelical voters was 61 percent; among voters who identify with the Tea Party, a remarkable 84 percent had a favorable view of Palin, more than double the figure for the public at large.[50] More recent polling has suggested that her popularity has declined among Republicans and Republican-leaning independents, including Iowa and New Hampshire Republicans.[51]

David Barton

David Barton is a longtime religious right activist and Republican political operative. Through his WallBuilders ministry and its for-profit affiliates, he has built a small empire as a self-declared historian who specializes in documenting the purported religious roots of the nation's founding. The fact that historians have widely and repeatedly criticized Barton's scholarship does not stop GOP officials from embracing him.[52] Mike Huckabee, former presidential candidate, has called Barton America's greatest historian.[53] Barton was invited by Representative Michele Bachmann to address sessions on the Constitution for members of her Tea Party Caucus.

Barton is a former chair of the Texas GOP who campaigned for George W. Bush in evangelical churches and has produced a "documentary" aimed at convincing black Christians that they should abandon the Democratic Party because it was responsible for slavery, lynching, and Jim Crow.[54] Barton's "history" stops with passage of landmark civil rights legislation in the 1960s, conveniently ignoring the Republican Party's subsequent "Southern Strategy" of building power by fanning racial resentment among southern whites. Barton has also been a key player in the religious right's effort to influence the content of textbooks in Texas and throughout the nation.

Barton, well known in religious right circles for years, was given a vastly expanded audience by Glenn Beck, who made Barton a sidekick of sorts in his efforts to "teach" Americans about the nation's history and Constitution. Barton shared the stage with Beck at the "America's Divine Destiny" event on the eve of the "Restoring Honor" rally at the Lincoln Memorial in August 2010, and was a frequent guest on Beck's "Founders' Fridays."

Barton is actively promoting messages designed to unite the religious right and Tea Party movements by claiming a biblical grounding for the Tea Party's views of the Constitution and radically right-wing economics. Barton has also enlisted Jesus in the attack on unions, asserting that Jesus is opposed to progressive taxation, the minimum wage, the capital gains tax, the estate tax, and collective bargaining (or "socialist-union kind of stuff").[55] Beck is a major promoter of Barton's notion of a divinely inspired American exceptionalism: Barton teaches that America's founders were inspired by God through colonial preachers whose theology of individual salvation is responsible for constitutional protections of individuals.[56]

Glenn Beck

Glenn Beck, the former Fox News Channel personality and political pop culture phenomenon, has played an extraordinarily powerful supporting role for the Tea Party movement. Along with his Fox colleagues, Beck promoted Tea Party events and validated the movement's most extreme antigovernment, anti-Obama elements. Beck has made a specialty of denouncing President Obama and members of his administration as socialists, communists, racists, fascists, and simply evil.

In 2010, Beck embraced an increasingly messianic view of his role in bringing America back to God—and a particular vision of God. At "America's Divine Destiny," an event held on the eve of his "Restoring Honor" event at the Lincoln Memorial in August, Beck proclaimed his gathering to be "the beginning of the end of darkness. We have been in darkness a long time." He said Saturday's rally would be a "defibrillator to the spiritual heart of America" and said participants would be "fundamentally transforming the United States of America."[57] He repeatedly insisted that his "Restoring Honor" event at the Lincoln Memorial in August was not political, but he filled it with predictably conservative political speakers and messages.[58]

Beck has also urged Americans to abandon churches that are committed to "social justice" and told his viewers that "[y]our church is either for socialist government, or the living of the gospel."[59] Beck has partnered with David Barton to promote the idea that America's founding documents were cribbed from colonial preachers' sermons, and that a dramatically limited role for government is inseparable from America's divinely inspired founding.

While Beck lost a powerful pulpit when he left Fox News in 2011, he continues to reach an audience via his website, radio show, online video channel, books, and speaking appearances.

Ralph Reed

Ralph Reed built the Christian Coalition into a political force in the 1990s, but had a spectacular flameout when his unsavory dealings with disgraced lobbyist Jack Abramoff were exposed and he lost his bid for the lieutenant governorship in Georgia. Reed is making his political comeback with an organization he created in 2009 called the Faith and Freedom Coalition, which journalist Adele Stan calls "the Tea Party movement's get-out-the-vote operation."[60]

At its Washington, DC conference in September 2010, Reed said he would never again allow conservatives to be out-mobilized the way they were in 2008, and bragged about the Coalition's growing network of state-level affiliates and its huge database of faith-based conservative voters. Reed predicted that below-the-radar voter identification and turnout work by conservative activists tapping into his database would turn November's elections into a historic victory for conservatives, including races not considered at play.

After the election, Reed bragged that due to his coalition's efforts, evangelical turnout was at a record high in 2010, contributing to the GOP–Tea Party electoral victories. Reed is intensely focused on preparing for an even bigger turnout operation in 2012. In January 2012, presidential hopefuls Mitt Romney, Rick Santorum, Newt Gingrich, Ron Paul, and Rick Perry all appeared before a pre-debate rally hosted by Reed's Faith and Freedom Coalition in South Carolina.[61]

Mike Pence

In 2006, Representative Mike Pence, former chair of the conservative Republican Study Committee, ran against John Boehner in a bid to lead the House Republicans. Pence framed his unsuccessful campaign as a challenge to Republicans' own betrayal of the values of the 1994 Contract with America. He held the title of Republican Conference Chairman, the third highest-ranking position in Republican leadership; he resigned his leadership post in 2010 and announced in 2011 that he would pass up a run for the presidency in order to run for governor of Indiana.[62]

Pence has appeared at events sponsored by FreedomWorks and Americans for Prosperity. In addition, he was the dark-horse winner of the presidential straw poll at the September 2010 Values Voter Summit, which is sponsored by the Family Research Council and a number of other religious right organizations:

> At the Values Voter Summit, Pence offered the following rationale for the melding of the two movements. "We must not remain silent when great moral battles are being waged," he said. "Those who would have us ignore the battle being fought over life, marriage, religious liberty have forgotten

the lessons of history. As in the days of a house divided, America's darkest moments have come when economic arguments trumped moral principles. Men and women, we must demand, here and now, that the leaders of the Republican Party stand for life, traditional marriage and religious liberty without apology."[63]

In February 2011, Pence helped lead a push in the House of Representatives that led to a 240–185 vote to block all federal funding for Planned Parenthood, a longtime target of the religious right.[64] Pence celebrated the vote as "a victory for taxpayers and a victory for life."[65]

Michele Bachmann

Minnesota Republican Representative Michele Bachmann is another elected official with folk-hero status among both the religious right and Tea Party movements, even though some Missouri Tea Party activists were livid when she endorsed incumbent Roy Blunt in the 2008 GOP primary.[66]

In interviews and speeches, Bachmann moves effortlessly back and forth between discussions of policy and religious exhortation. For example, in one interview on the Christian Broadcasting Network, Bachmann complained about big government "oppressing the American people with too much spending, too much taxes, too much regulatory burden," and she repeated religious right charges that federal hate crimes legislation is about "restricting free speech and free expression of American citizens" before shifting into a conversation about how her faith guides her life and work, all while denouncing the Obama administration as radical.[67]

Bachmann has said that "God called me to run for the U.S. Congress."[68] After the 2010 elections, she made a brief and unsuccessful run for a leadership position as chair of the House Republican Conference, a bid that was backed by a number of religious right leaders.[69] She upstaged GOP leaders by giving an alternative Tea Party response to President Obama's 2011 State of the Union speech. And by spring of 2011, she had set her sights higher and was preparing her campaign for the 2012 Republican presidential nomination.[70] In April 2011, Bachmann hired the organizer of Mike Huckabee's successful 2008 Iowa campaign.[71] In August 2011, she won the Iowa Straw Poll, though her poor showing in the January 2012 Iowa caucuses led her to withdraw from the presidential campaign.

LOCAL ACTIVIST-LEVEL CONNECTIONS

Polling conducted in September 2010 by the Public Religion Research Institute confirmed extensive overlap between the two movements and their ideologies. The survey report found that 47 percent of those who considered themselves part of the Tea Party movement, and 57 percent of Tea Partiers who identified as Christians, said they are also part of the Christian conservative or religious right movement. The survey also found that those who call themselves part of the Tea Party movement are much more socially conservative than they are libertarian. Nearly two-thirds (63 percent) said abortion should be illegal in all or most cases, and only 18 percent supported allowing gay and lesbian couples to marry, which put them far to the right of American voters and nearly as far to the right as those who identify as Christian conservatives. On the question of whether America is a Christian nation, those who called themselves part of the Tea Party movement were actually more likely to say America is now a Christian nation (55 percent) than those who called themselves part of the Christian conservative movement (43 percent).[72]

The Pew Forum on Religion and Public Life released a similar analysis in February 2011, noting that:

> Tea Party supporters tend to have conservative opinions not just about economic matters, but also about social issues such as abortion and same-sex marriage. In addition, they are much more likely than registered voters as a whole to say that their religion is the most important factor in determining their opinions on these social issues. And they draw disproportionate support from the ranks of white evangelical Protestants.[73]

Pew found that "Overall, the Tea Party appears to be more widely known and to garner broader support than the religious right." It reported the following:

> While most people who agree with the conservative Christian movement support the Tea Party, many people who support the Tea Party are unfamiliar with or uncertain about the religious right. In the August [2010] poll, almost half of Tea Party supporters said they had not heard of or did not have an opinion on the conservative Christian movement (46%). Among those who did offer an opinion, however, Tea Party supporters agreed with the religious right by a roughly 4-1 margin (42% agreed with the religious right, 11% disagreed).[74]

Earlier polls identified affinities between the two movements. In June 2010, the *Seattle Times* reported that a poll by the University of Washington found that "52 percent of strong tea party supporters agreed with the statement that 'compared to the size of their group, lesbians and gays have too much political power,' compared to 25 percent of all voters surveyed." University of Washington political science professor Matt Barreto concluded that, "The tea party movement is not just about small government or frustration. It's [also] about a very specific frustration with government resources being used on minorities and gays and lesbians and people who are more diverse."[75]

Given that religious conservatives make up a significant portion of Tea Party membership, it is not surprising that in the lead-up to the 2010 elections, local Tea Party organizations were routinely engaging with local Christian conservatives. In May 2010, for example, the South Atlanta Tea Party sponsored a breakfast for pastors that featured speakers from two national religious right groups, Ken Fletcher of the Alliance Defense Fund and Gary DeMar of American Vision. According to a news report, topics included "the threats to religious freedom and the persecution of the church" and "restoring the church to its Biblical foundations and America's Christian heritage."[76]

People For the American Way's *Right Wing Watch* blog reported an array of national religious right leaders appearing at Tea Party events in the spring of 2010:

> For instance, WallBuilders' Rick Green is speaking at a rally in Texas, and the Eagle Forum's Phyllis Schlafly is addressing an event in Michigan, while Ralph Reed is joining Bob Barr and Virginia Thomas, wife of Supreme Court Justice Clarence Thomas, for a Tea Party rally in Atlanta.
>
> On top of that, the AFA's Bryan Fischer is speaking at an event in Mississippi and Alan Keyes was at one in Ohio, while Vision America's Rick Scarborough is speaking at an event in Oklahoma where he will share the microphone with Oklahoma state Senator Randy Brogdon, who is trying to create Tea Party militia to defend the state's sovereignty from federal encroachment.[77]

At the 2010 Values Voters Summit in September, a panel of three Tea Party activists discussed their efforts. While the representative of the Tea Party Patriots kept her focus on fiscal issues, the other two activists talked about feeling that they were being instructed by God, just like Glenn Beck. One of those organizers, Katy Abram, told journalist Sarah Posner that the 350 members of her Lebanon, Pennsylvania, group are getting training on the Constitution from the Institute on the Constitution, which offers a twelve-part course on the biblical basis of the Constitution.[78] Another, Billie Tucker, described a disagreement among organizers of her local Tea Party group: When one argued against adding moral issues to the mission, Tucker responded that "God did not wake me up for four months at four in the morning to say, 'Billie, we've got a tax issue.' He woke me up because he said 'my country doesn't love me like it used to love me.'"[79]

That kind of collaboration continued in 2011. For example, an April 16 "Community Awareness and Outreach" event sponsored by the Chino Tea Party in Chino, California, included on its list of speakers both the California state director for Americans for Prosperity and the president and founder of Radical Truth Ministry, which reportedly focuses on how Christians should address the threats posed by Islam.[80]

2010 CANDIDATES AND ELECTORAL STRATEGIES

FreedomWorks's Dick Armey told a group of reporters before the 2010 election that he believed Tea Party and religious right conservatives would end up working together in an embrace of economic and fiscal issues: "If we lose this nation, if it falls into insolvency, then all of these [social] issues pretty well fall by the wayside too, don't they. So I think there is a setting of priorities." Richard Land, president of the Southern Baptist Convention's Ethics and Religious Liberty Commission, also made a point about the benefits to both libertarians and religious conservatives from making common cause: "They can either hold their nose vis-à-vis social issues and get economic policies that they like, or they can vote for the social issues they like with the liberals, and have their pocketbooks raided by confiscatory liberal economic policies. I have no doubt which one they will choose, given the choice."[81]

One thing on which Tea Party and religious right leaders agreed in 2010 was that the midterm election would be the most important of our lifetimes, because it, along with the 2012 presidential election, would be the last chance to stop the Obama administration and its congressional allies from destroying American exceptionalism and replacing it with a form of European socialism. At the 2010 Values Voter Summit, Amy Kremer of the Tea Party Express urged activists to focus on the fall elections: "The time has come to put down the protest signs and pick up the campaign signs and engage," she said. "If we're going to truly effect change it's going to be at the ballot box."[82]

For all the election-season sniping about whether or not social conservative voters were being given enough respect and attention by Tea Party and Republican leaders, the fact is that religious right leaders and activists had nothing to complain about when it came to Tea Party–backed candidates.[83]

Tea Party candidates who beat establishment Republicans to win their primaries were not only committed to radical views of the role of government when it comes to spending, but they were also conservative on social issues. For example, at least six Republican Senate candidates wanted to criminalize all abortion, even in the case of rape or incest.[84] The success of antiabortion candidates, and the antiabortion commitments of many Tea Party–identified candidates, were reflected in a wave of state and federal legislative efforts to further restrict access to abortion in the first months of 2011.

For the Tea Party, the ability to defeat some high-level Republican incumbents and bigger-name candidates—and throw a scare into others—was a heady introduction to political power. Some of the movement's leaders clearly believe that to sustain that influence, the proudly decentralized movement needed to learn from the pros, like those who worked with Ralph Reed on 2010 turnout:

> . . . [T]he uprising energy of the tea party movement is beginning to coalesce with the organizing savvy of the religious right—and putting the force of religious zeal behind the tea party's anti-government fanaticism. Reed is focused on get-out-the-vote drives in key districts where, he told activists at his conference, just a few votes could make a difference. In a session on how to organize a state chapter, Colorado Faith and Freedom chair John Ramstead told activists that the "most receptive" people attending training sessions are coming from tea parties.[85]

Religious right leaders also worked hard to ensure that their own activists were as energetically engaged. For many conservative Christian activists, the prospect of victory over President Obama and congressional Democrats was a force far more powerful than the desire to have social issues front and center on the campaign trail. More than a half dozen programs promoted prayer and fasting as well as electoral activism by conservative religious voters.[86] David Barton asserted after the election that it was historically "irrefutable" that prayer and fasting for conservative election victories had an impact: "There's no way from a biblical or historical standpoint you can do that and not see God intervene or move."[87]

Religious right voters could look to Virginia Governor Bob McDonnell, elected in 2009, as what one Faith and Freedom Coalition leader called "a perfect example" of a "social conservative who talked about economic issues." After McDonnell's election, Mark Silk noted:

> The newly elected governor of Virginia has impeccable Christian Right credentials—a degree from Regent University Law School and a perfect record of pushing social conservatism while representing Virginia Beach in the House of Delegates from 1993 to 2006. But in 2009, he ran for governor as a fiscal, not a social, conservative.[88]

Since his election, McDonnell and his even more aggressively conservative Attorney General Ken Cuccinelli have pursued policies to warm the hearts of religious right activists (restricting state abortion funding[89]) as well as Tea Party activists (filing a legal challenge to federal health care reform legislation[90]). McDonnell spoke at the 2010 Faith and Freedom Federation–sponsored conference at Liberty University, and both he and Cuccinelli took part in a Tea Party gathering in Richmond the weekend of October 8–9, 2010, along with other Tea Party–religious right bridgers like Representative Steve King and former Senator Rick Santorum.[91]

Indeed, in a March 2011 interview with religious right leader and broadcaster James Dobson, Ralph Drollinger, the head of an organization that hosts Bible studies for members of Congress, celebrated the conservative religious orientation of most Tea Party–affiliated candidates:

> . . . [T]he Tea Party is this huge voter block that is bigger than, say, our old Religious Right voter blocks because it's all kinds of people that are trying to elect fiscal conservatives to save the country economically. And when you elect a fiscal conservative with this big engine called the Tea Party, you typically get a social conservative [and often a Christian]. . . . And so now we've got this flood of new believers that have snuck in under the radar. And before, the secular media would always shoot our horses in the corral before they got out on the track. And now they've all snuck in under the radar and through the guise of being fiscally conservative they've rallied huge voter bases. They get elected and they happen to be believers and they're saying, "let's fuel a movement for Christ in the nation's capital."[92]

2011: WIELDING POWER AND NEGOTIATING PRIORITIES

Having worked together to help the Republican Party achieve historic gains in the U.S. House of Representatives and state legislatures, tensions between libertarian-leaning Tea Partiers and religious conservatives broke into open hostility around the 2011 Conservative Political Action Conference (CPAC), an annual gathering sponsored by the American Conservative Union. When conference organizers announced that GOProud, a group for politically conservative gay Republicans, would be welcomed as a conference cosponsor, many religious right groups, joined by the Heritage Foundation, publicly complained and withdrew their sponsorship for the event. Some encouraged a boycott by religious conservatives.

GOProud had angered religious right leaders when, shortly after the 2010 election, its chairman Christopher Barron and sixteen Tea Party leaders and conservative bloggers sent a letter to Senator McConnell and Representative Boehner urging them to put forward a legislative agenda reflecting "the Tea Party's laser focus on issues of economic freedom and limited government" and to "resist the urge to run down any social issue rabbit holes.... We recognize the importance of values but believe strongly that those values should be taught by families and our houses of worship and not legislated from Washington, DC."[93] The letter was denounced by religious right leaders and socially conservative Tea Party activists.

Meanwhile, in early 2011, the leader of the Republican Study Committee, a caucus for conservative Republicans in the House of Representatives, made an effort to signal that House conservatives would not neglect social conservatives' agenda. Representative Jim Jordan began pushing House Speaker John Boehner to advance a proposal that would force the District of Columbia to subject its marriage equality law to a referendum, something that local officials and courts have ruled would violate the city's Human Rights Act.[94]

House Republicans delivered on a promise to both Tea Party and religious right activists by voting to repeal the health care reform legislation that President Obama had signed into law. Religious right leaders call the reform measure a "monstrosity." Passage of repeal in the House was widely seen as a symbolic gesture, given that Democratic Senate leaders had no intention of bringing the repeal legislation to the floor. Still, religious right and Tea Party activists planned to push forward a series of smaller steps to try to slow implementation in hope of enacting a full repeal in the wake of the 2012 elections. As part of the deal to keep the federal government operating through fiscal year 2011, Republicans were promised a Senate vote on their repeal measure, something conservative strategists hope will give them political ammunition that can be used to turn out conservative voters against Senate Democrats up for reelection in 2012.

Passage of a federal budget for fiscal year 2011 was the major legislative battleground of the first quarter of 2011. Daniel Burke of the Religion News Service wrote in February that the debt had become the "new hot issue for evangelicals," citing Concerned Women for America, the Family Research Council, and the Faith and Freedom Coalition. "America's growing debt is not just a financial issue, it's a spiritual one," said Jerry Newcombe, host of *The Coral Ridge Hour,* a television program broadcast by Coral Ridge Ministries. "The Bible is very clear about the moral dangers of debt."[95] At the Freedom Federation's Awakening 2011 conference in April, Hispanic evangelical leader Samuel Rodriguez equated "big government" with "the spirit of Pharaoh."[96]

Republican lawmakers at federal and state levels moved quickly in 2011 to push a wave of legislation designed to further restrict women's access to abortion and family planning services, including proposals to stop all federal funding for family planning services. GOP insistence that the 2011 budget include a rider to ban federal funding for Planned Parenthood nearly led to a federal government shutdown.

In March, after the House had voted on the Pence Amendment to block funding for Planned Parenthood, antitax activist Grover Norquist, president of Americans for Tax Reform, and antiabortion activist Marjorie Dannenfelser, president of the Susan B. Anthony List, issued a joint declaration demanding that congressional Republicans make the cuts stick:

> Mike Pence's battle is not just another social-issue skirmish. It's a test of economic and budgetary seriousness. . . . Planned Parenthood must be privatized. Economic and social conservatives agree—this one is non-negotiable.[97]

After recounting a litany of right-wing criticisms of Planned Parenthood, Norquist and Dannenfelser threw down the gauntlet: "If a sparkling new Tea Party Congress won't cut off this bunch, what will it cut?"

As the deadline to avoid a government shutdown approached, religious right leaders urged House Republicans to draw a line in the sand, and to shut down the government if the Democrats and Obama administration would not agree to defund Planned Parenthood. In the end, though, the Obama administration refused to accept a ban on Planned Parenthood funding, and a deal was reached with additional budget cuts and a ban on the District of Columbia using its own money to pay for poor women's abortions. Pollster and political analyst Robert P. Jones noted that Michele Bachmann was among the high-profile religious right and Tea Party leaders who backed down, or gave cover to House leadership for the decision not to shut down the government over Planned Parenthood's funding, even though just weeks earlier she had declared that "there is a point where you draw the line in the sand and you have a hill where you die on. I think this is our issue."[98]

Some religious right leaders were bitterly angry that the deal would continue funding for Planned Parenthood, suggesting that once again, economic issues had been given priority. A month earlier, journalist Steve Benen recounted the religious right's frequent disappointment with GOP leaders, characterizing religious right leaders as Charlie Brown, the Republican establishment as Lucy, and the culture-war agenda as the football: "Republicans don't want to lose, and the American mainstream isn't on board with the religious right wish list."[99]

But strongly antiabortion Senator Tom Coburn of Oklahoma demonstrated just how successfully government spending and debt had become transformed into a moral issue when he suggested that reducing the deficit might even be a bigger moral question than abortion. Coburn asked, "[W]hat's the greatest moral dilemma of our day? Abortion certainly is a big one, but if we don't address all these other financial issues that are going to cripple those that are with us, we'll be making a big mistake."[100]

The University of Akron's John C. Green, a well-known scholar of religion in America, summarized how the focus on the federal debt had something to offer everyone in the conservative coalition:

> First, the national debt is a good mobilizing issue for the Republican coalition, able to unite social conservatives and deficit hawks, whose alliance has sometimes been strained. Secondly, it allows religious leaders to ride the Tea Party wave of anger against government spending. And lastly, it broadens the conservative Christian agenda beyond such culture war battles as abortion and gay marriage.[101]

CONCLUSION

The history of religious right support for a conservative small-government ideology has led some political observers to question whether the Tea Party phenomenon should actually be considered a new movement or an organizing vehicle for the GOP's right-wing base, "nothing more than the Republican Party masquerading as a grass-roots phenomenon."[102] But Chip Berlet, a longtime scholar of right-wing movements in America, suggested before the 2010 election that even with the overlap in the movements, the Tea Party had energized a number of people who have not previously been involved in politics. He said, "If those newbies are even another five percent of the population, the Democrats aren't going to know what hit them."[103]

In Chapter 9 of this volume, Martin Cohen compares the Tea Party to two separate waves of religious right movement building. Cohen says the first wave, in the late 1970s and early 1980s, insisted on absolutist agenda items that the GOP was unwilling to push in the face of popular opinion, while a second wave in the 1990s was more successful because it was willing to accept more popular incremental moves toward an ultimate goal, offering Republican elected officials a legislative strategy that helped rather than hurt them. Cohen suggests that what will determine whether the Tea Party is a flash in the pan "will depend almost entirely on whether they are able to first significantly influence the Republican Party."[104]

In the short term, the Tea Party has already shown its ability to have an impact on the GOP, moving the party's congressional caucus to the right and having an impact on elected officials' own policies and legislative strategies. Whether the Tea Party movement and the candidates it elects will move the GOP so far to the right that the party loses the support of independent voters and moderates who swung its way in the 2010 elections is a major open question. One arena in which that question will be played out is the public relations, political, and legislative battle over the fiscal year 2012 budget. That struggle will pit the two parties' best strategic minds against each other, along with contrasting visions of the nation's history, the meaning of the Constitution, and the relative importance of fiscal and social issues. It is too early to tell whether Tea Party activists (and their religious right allies) are able to negotiate their own competing priorities and strategic differences to meet Cohen's test of long-term success, that is, whether they will be able to "stop short of advocating extreme positions and seek compromises that are more palatable to the American people."[105]

Richard Flory of the Center for Religion and Civic Culture at the University of Southern California has suggested that journalists pondering the future of the movement "should be asking questions about how values, economics and religion are related":

> Does economics really trump values, or are values really about "me" and my beliefs as opposed to "them" and their needs? Was the apparent economic vote of the 2010 midterm election really a proxy for underlying values

concerns, or even prejudices, whether racial, religious or class-oriented? Reporters should keep an eye out for how these shifting concerns and political alliances play out as the economy recovers and we head toward the 2012 presidential election.[106]

Religious right leaders have a powerful incentive to continue to strengthen connections with the Tea Party movement, which has helped to energize a broader constituency of conservative voters and elect candidates who back the religious right's social issues agenda as well as the Tea Party's economic agenda. Moreover, it seems certain that the concerted efforts by conservative strategists to meld the movements by building a religious and moral underpinning for right-wing economics and the Tea Party's view of constitutionally limited government will continue through 2012 and beyond.

The February 2011 issue of the *AFA Journal,* published by the American Family Association, included an article entitled "Rise of the Teavangelicals," which decried efforts by libertarian-leaning Tea Party elements to define the movement as part of a "leave-me-alone-coalition" uninterested in social issues: "Perhaps it is precisely because many social conservatives have come to see the economy in moral terms that so many of them have found a home in the Tea Party movement." The article also quotes Ralph Reed saying that the Tea Party and religious right movements are inextricably intertwined. Whether or not they like the idea, Tea Partiers are now married to the religious right. And as Reed insisted, "Those who ignore or disregard social conservative voters and their issues do so at their own peril."[107]

As for the perennial questions about the survival of the religious right as a movement, author and longtime movement analyst Rob Boston says, "The Religious Right's political strategy may involve some high-tech tools like social networking and tweets, but at the end of the day, it's anchored in something old school: identifying your voters, rallying around candidates and getting people to the polls on Election Day. As long as the movement remains focused on this, it will be a force to reckon with in American politics."[108]

Making predictions about a young political movement is a particularly dicey business. Back in February 2010, David Waters, then editor of the *Washington Post*'s *On Faith* blog, asked, "Will the Christian Right join the Tea Party? Will the Tea Partying fiscal conservatives make room for social conservatives? Should they? I doubt it."[109] The last two years, it seems, have proven Waters wrong. But he is not the only one who made faulty predictions. Religious broadcaster Pat Robertson reports annually on his year-end one-on-one conversations with God. In the wake of the 2008 election, Robertson reported that God had declared, "The people will welcome socialism in order to relieve their pain. Nothing will stand in the way of a plan by Obama to restructure the economy in the same fashion as the New Deal in the '30s."[110] In other words, even God didn't see the Tea Party coming.

NOTES

1. Z. Byron Wolf, "No Rose Garden for Bush's Anti-Gay Marriage Speech," *ABC News*, June 5, 2006.

2. Kyle Mantyla, "Viva La Resistance!" *Right Wing Watch* (blog), November 17, 2008.

3. Sarah Posner, "The Fundamentalist (No. 58)," Prospect.org, November 19, 2008.

4. Kyle Mantyla, "Kathleen Parker Invites More Hate Mail," *Right Wing Watch* (blog), November 19, 2008, www.rightwingwatch.org (emphasis in original).

5. Peter Hamby, "Senator Calls Obama 'World's Best Salesman of Socialism,'" *CNN Politics Political Ticker* (blog), February 27, 2009, http://politicalticker .blogs.cnn.com/2009/02/27/senator-calls-obama-world's-best-salesman-of -socialism/.

6. "Americans for Prosperity," Source Watch, www.sourcewatch.org/index .php?title=Americans_for_Prosperity.

7. Rob Boston, "Having a Party: Religious Right Gets an Invitation to Tea," *The Wall of Separation* (blog), Americans United for Separation of Church and State, http://blog.au.org/2010/02/18/having-a-party-religious-right-gets-an-invitation -to-tea/.

8. "To Hell with Health Care Reform: Religious Right Leaders Attack Obama, Spout GOP Dogma about 'Socialism' While Fanning Flames on Abortion," report published by People For the American Way (undated), www .pfaw.org/rww-in-focus/to-hell-with-health-care-reform-religious-right-leaders -attack-obama-spout-gop-dogma-about-so.

9. *Indivisible: Social and Economic Foundations of American Liberty*, Washington, DC: Heritage Foundation, 2010. The book includes an essay from antigay activist Bishop Harry Jackson on the moral evils of the minimum wage, while Club for Growth founder (and current *Wall Street Journal* editorialist) Stephen Moore opines on the importance of the family. Jay Richards, "Indivisible: Social and Economic Conservatism," *The Enterprise* (blog), February 5, 2010, http://blog.american.com/?p=10221.

10. Kyle Mantyla, "When the Going Gets Tough, the Right Starts a New Group," *Right Wing Watch* (blog), June 30, 2009, www.rightwingwatch .org/content/when-going-gets-tough-right-starts-new-group. The Freedom Federation describes itself as a collaboration among religious groups, but

among its founding members is Americans for Prosperity, a corporate-backed group that has become a leading Tea Party movement organizer. The How to Take Back America conference in September 2009, convened by Phyllis Schlafly and religious right radio host Janet Porter, also demonstrated a merging of messaging and organizing strategies among the religious right and Tea Party right. For example, a session about health care reform focused less on the threat of publicly funded abortion than on the "fascist" government "takeover" of the economy as a "power grab" by the president.

11. Ben Smith, "Tea Parties Stir Evangelicals' Fears," Politico, March 12, 2010, http://dyn.politico.com/printstory.cfm?uuid=4FB3D910-18FE-70B2-A855734169AC4037.

12. Haley Barbour, "GOP, Tea Party Unity Spells Defeat for Obama," Wall Street Journal, September 21, 2010, http://online.wsj.com/article/SB10001424052748703989304575503921088554324.html.

13. Stephanie Mencimer, "Tea Party Courts GOP's Evangelical Wing," Mother Jones, October 6, 2010, motherjones.com/mojo/2010/10/tea-party-patriots-tim-lahaye-evangelicals.

14. Stephanie Mencimer, "Tea Party Courts GOP's Evangelical Wing," Mother Jones, October 6, 2010, motherjones.com/mojo/2010/10/tea-party-patriots-tim-lahaye-evangelicals.

15. "The Black Robe Brigade," Glenn Beck transcript, Fox News Channel, April 28, 2010, www.foxnews.com/story/0,2933,591785,00.html.

16. Damon Linker, "Taking Exception," The New Republic, February 26, 2010, www.tnr.com/blog/damon-linker/taking-exception.

17. "Gingrich, Obama, and American Exceptionalism," DailyKos, June 14, 2010, www.dailykos.com/story/2010/6/14/185248/897.

18. George Bennett, "Rubio Casts Senate Race as Referendum on American Exceptionalism," Post on Politics (blog), Palm Beach Post, October 3, 2010, www.postonpolitics.com/2010/10/rubio-casts-senate-race-as-referendum-on-american-exceptionalism/.

19. Heather Sells, "'American Exceptionalism' Next Political Hot Button?" CBN News, March 30, 2011.

20. Peter Montgomery, "Value Voter Recap: We're All Tea Partiers Now (Including God)," Right Wing Watch (blog), September 21, 2010, www.rightwingwatch.org/content/value-voter-recap-were-all-tea-partiers-now-including-god.

21. Sarah Posner, "Tea Party Values," The Nation, September 21, 2010, www.thenation.com/article/154944/tea-party-values. See also Robert P. Jones and Daniel Cox, "Religion and the Tea Party in the 2010 Election: An Analysis of the Third Biennial American Values Survey," Public Religion Research Institute, October 2010, http://publicreligion.org/research/2010/10/religion-tea-party-2010/.

22. Adele Stan, "What Rand Paul and Sharron Angle Have in Common: A Far-Right 'Biblical Law' Political Party," AlterNet, June 15, 2010.

23. Paul Froese, "The Tea Party's Unifying Bogeyman: the Socialist," USA Today, September 16, 2010.

24. William F. Buckley, Jr. "Goldwater, the John Birch Society, and Me," *Commentary*, March 2008.

25. Adele Stan, "Tea Party's Rand Paul Squashes GOP Candidate in KY Primary," AlterNet, May 18, 2010.

26. "Richard Viguerie: South Carolina Tea Party Steamroller Sweeps Establishment Republicans Out of Office," ConservativeHQ.com press release, June 22, 2010, www.christiannewswire.com/news/2821514203.html.

27. David Weigel, "James Dobson Endorses Rand Paul, Apologizes for Having Previously Backed His Opponent," *Right Now* (blog), *The Washington Post*, May 3, 2010, http://voices.washingtonpost.com/right-now/2010/05/james_dobson_endorses_rand_pau.html.

28. Mark Silk, "Rand Paul's Victory," *Spiritual Politics* (blog), Leonard E. Greenberg Center for the Study of Religion in Public Life, May 19, 2010, http://b27.cc.trincoll.edu/mt/mt-search.cgi?search=rand+paul+dobson&IncludeBlogs=13&limit=20.

29. Ed Kilgore, "The Tea Party and the Christian Right Redux," *The Democratic Strategist*, February 3, 2011.

30. Kyle Mantyla, "Armey Accuses Religious Right of Trying to Impose Its Will through Tyranny," *Right Wing Watch* (blog), September 16, 2010.

31. Smith, "Tea Parties Stir Evangelicals' Fears."

32. Smith, "Tea Parties Stir Evangelicals' Fears."

33. Steven Ertelt, "Congressman Paul Ryan Latest to Call for Truce on Pro-Life, Social Issues," LifeNews.com, September 20, 2010, www.lifenews.com/nat6701.html.

34. Steven Ertelt, "Congressman Paul Ryan Latest to Call for Truce on Pro-Life, Social Issues."

35. Smith, "Tea Parties Stir Evangelicals' Fears."

36. Mencimer, "Tea Party Courts GOP's Evangelical Wing."

37. Mencimer, "Tea Party Courts GOP's Evangelical Wing."

38. Manu Raju, "Jim DeMint Vows Roadblock," Politico, September 27, 2010, www.politico.com/news/stories/0910/42807.html#ixzz1JEmM41T5.

39. "The Rogues' Gallery," People For the American Way, 2010, www.pfaw.org/rww-in-focus/the-rogues-gallery-right-wing-candidates-have-dangerous-agenda-for-america-and-could-tu.

40. David Brody, "Senator DeMint to Brody File: Tea Party Movement Will Bring on 'Spiritual Revival,'" interview with Senator Jim DeMint, *The Brody File* (blog), Christian Broadcasting Network, April 21, 2010, http://blogs.cbn.com/thebrodyfile/archive/2010/04/21/senator-demint-to-brody-file-tea-party-movement-will-bring.aspx.

41. Michael Falcone, "Conservative Leaders Threaten Critics of Sen. Jim DeMint," The Note, ABC News, November 12, 2010.

42. Craig Robinson, "King Drives Issues at Conservative Principles Conference," *The Iowa Republican*, March 28, 2011. See also "Steve King Announces Conservative Principles Conference," *The Iowa Republican*, January 28, 2011.

43. Catherine O. Snow, "The Cost of Discipleship," *Citizen Magazine*, February 2011.

44. Dan Gilgoff, "Newt Gingrich Steps Up Efforts to Mobilize Religious Conservatives," *US News and World Report*, March 20, 2009.

45. David Brody, "Newt Gingrich Tells The Brody File He 'Felt Compelled to Seek God's Forgiveness,'" interview with Newt Gingrich, *The Brody File*, Christian Broadcasting Network, March 8, 2011.

46. Kendra Marr, "Newt Gingrich Talks Faith—Not Affairs—at Cornerstone Church in Texas," Politico, March 27, 2011.

47. Jeanne Cummings, "Questions for Newt Gingrich in 2012," Politico, March 26, 2011.

48. *The O'Reilly Factor*, Fox News, May 6, 2010.

49. Andy Barr, "Sarah Palin PAC: Tea Party is the 'Future of Politics,'" Politico, September 21, 2010, www.politico.com/news/stories/0910/42488.html.

50. Jones and Cox, "Religion and the Tea Party in the 2010 Elections."

51. John Avlon, "The Palin Implosion," The Daily Beast, March 17, 2011.

52. "Barton's Bunk: Hack 'Historian' Hits the Big Time in Tea Party America," People For the American Way, April 2011.

53. Kyle Mantyla, "David Barton: America's Greatest Historian," *Right Wing Watch* (blog), October 20, 2008.

54. "David Barton: Propaganda Masquerading as History," People For the American Way, September 2006, www.pfaw.org/media-center/publications/david-barton-propaganda-masquerading-history.

55. Peter Montgomery, "Jesus Hates Taxes: Biblical Capitalism Created Fertile Anti-Union Soil," Religion Dispatches, March 14, 2011, www.religiondispatches.org/archive/politics/4366/jesus_hates_taxes%3A_biblical_capitalism_created_fertile_anti-union_soil/.

56. Peter Montgomery, "Glenn Beck's Salvation Army," Religion Dispatches, September 7, 2010.

57. Peter Montgomery, "Glenn Beck and God Are Ready to Rock," *Right Wing Watch* (blog), August 27, 2010, www.rightwingwatch.org/content/glenn-beck-and-god-are-ready-rock.

58. Michael B. Keegan, "Glenn Beck's Political, Hypocritical, Me-Party, Tea Party Weekend," *The Huffington Post*, August 30, 2010, www.huffingtonpost.com/michael-b-keegan/glenn-becks-political-hyp_b_699686.html.

59. "Beck: 'Your church is either for socialist government, or the living of the gospel,'" Media Matters, May 18, 2010, http://mediamatters.org/mmtv/201005180056.

60. Adele Stan, "Del. Tea Party Senate Candidate O'Donnell Opposes Women in Military," AlterNet, September 15, 2010, http://blogs.alternet.org/speakeasy/2010/09/15/del-tea-party-senate-candidate-odonnell-opposes-women-in-military-n-h-candidate-lamontagne-endorses-creationism/.

61. Peter Montgomery, "GOP Presidentials Line Up to Kiss Ralph Reed's . . . Ring," *Right Wing Watch* (blog), January 18, 2012, www.rightwingwatch.org/content/gop-presidentials-line-kiss-ralph-reedsring.

62. Michael Muskal, "Mike Pence to Run for Indiana Governor," *Los Angeles Times*, May 5, 2011.

63. Adele Stan, "Religious Right to Tea Party: Join Us or Die!" AlterNet, September 21, 2010, www.alternet.org/story/148246/.

64. Brian Tashman, "Right-Wing Leaders Hail House Vote to Strip Planned Parenthood of Funding," *Right Wing Watch* (blog), February 18, 2011.

65. "Pence Hails Passage of Amendment Eliminating Federal Funding for Planned Parenthood: 'Victory for Taxpayers and a Victory for Life,'" February 18, 2011 press release distributed via ChristianWire, http://christiannewswire .com/news/7745816271.html.

66. Elyse Siegel, "Michele Bachmann's Roy Blunt Endorsement Sparks Tea Party Fury," *The Huffington Post,* July 28, 2010.

67. David Brody, interview with Michele Bachmann, *The Brody File,* Christian Broadcasting Network, February 18, 2011, http://blogs.cbn.com/ thebrodyfile/archive/2011/02/18/michele-bachmann-to-brody-file-on-2012 -seeking-prayerful-innner.aspx.

68. Peter Fenn, "Michele Bachmann Is a Real Face of the GOP and Tea Party," USNews.com, January 28, 2011.

69. Kyle Mantyla, "Religious Right Lining Up behind Bachmann," *Right Wing Watch* (blog), November 9, 2010.

70. Paul West, "Michele Bachmann Moves Closer to Presidential Bid," LAtimes.com, March 24, 2011.

71. Peter Hamby, "Bachmann Nabs Top Huckabee Aide in Iowa," CNN, April 4, 2011.

72. Jones and Cox, "Religion and the Tea Party in the 2010 Elections: An Analysis of the Third Biennial American Values Survey."

73. "The Tea Party and Religion," The Pew Forum on Religion and Public Life, February 23, 2011.

74. "The Tea Party and Religion."

75. Andrew Garber, "New Poll Looks at Tea Party Views toward Minorities," *The Seattle Times,* June 1, 2010, http://seattletimes.nwsource.com/ html/politicsnorthwest/2012005031_new_poll_looks_at_tea_party_vi.html.

76. Ben Nelms, "Tea Party Group Holds Pastors Breakfast," TheCitizen.com, May 18, 2010, www.thecitizen.com/articles/05-18-2010/tea-party-group-holds -pastors-breakfast.

77. Kyle Mantyla, "Tea Party Activism and the Religious Right's Unrequited Love," *Right Wing Watch* (blog), April 15, 2010, www.rightwingwatch.org/ content/tea-party-activism-and-religious-rights-unrequited-love.

78. Posner, "Tea Party Values."

79. Peter Montgomery, "Values Voters' Angry Afternoon Tea," *Right Wing Watch* (blog), September 18, 2010, www.rightwingwatch.org/content/ values-voters-angry-afternoon-tea.

80. "Tea Party to Hold Awareness and Outreach Event," Chino Tea Party press release, April 4, 2011, www.chinohills.com/news-articles-details/Tea_Party _To_Hold_Awareness_Outreach_Event-1770.

81. Stan, "Religious Right to Tea Party: Join Us or Die!"

82. Montgomery, "Values Voters' Angry Afternoon Tea."

83. "The Rogues' Gallery," People For the American Way, 2010, www .pfaw.org/rww-in-focus/the-rogues-gallery-right-wing-candidates-have-dangerous -agenda-for-america-and-could-tu.

84. And on the House side, The Huffington Post's Amanda Terkel reported that antiabortion activists counted sixty-three candidates who share this "pro-life without discrimination" position.

85. Posner, "Tea Party Values."

86. Kyle Mantyla, "Lucky Number Seven: Liberty Counsel Launches Election Prayer Effort," *Right Wing Watch* (blog), October 7, 2010, www.rightwingwatch .org/content/lucky-number-seven-liberty-counsel-launches-election-prayer -effort.

87. Peter Montgomery, "Tealigious Right Gloats, Thanks God for GOP Victories," *Right Wing Watch* (blog), November 4, 2010.

88. Mark Silk, "The End of the Christian Right," Religion in the News, Winter 2010, http://caribou.cc.trincoll.edu/depts_csrpl/RIN1203/End%20of %20Christian%20Right%20Ed%20Colm.htm.

89. Julian Walker, "McDonnell Bid To Restrict Abortion Funding Upheld," *The Virginian Pilot*, April 22, 2010.

90. Jim Nolan, "McDonnell Backs Cuccinelli on Challenge to Health-Care Bill," *Richmond Times Dispatch*, March 23, 2010.

91. Rosalind S. Helderman, "Attorney General Cuccinelli's Star Keeps Rising at Va. Tea Party Gathering," *The Washington Post*, October 9, 2010, www .washingtonpost.com/wp-dyn/content/article/2010/10/09/AR2010100903894 .html?hpid=moreheadlines.

92. Kyle Mantyla, "Meet the Religious Right/Tea Party Ministry at the Heart of Capitol Hill," *Right Wing Watch* (blog), March 16, 2011.

93. Ben Smith and Byron Tau, "GOP Is Urged to Avoid Social Issues," Politico, November 14, 2010.

94. Alan Ota, "RSC Sees D.C. Marriage Law as Chance to Renew Social Agenda," Congressional Quarterly Today Online News, March 29, 1011.

95. Daniel Burke, "National Debt is New Hot Issue for Evangelicals," Religion News Service, February 16, 2011.

96. Peter Montgomery, "Tea Party Jesus: Koch's Americans For Prosperity Sidles Up to Religious Right for 2012 Campaign," Alternet, April 15, 2011.

97. Grover Norquist and Marjorie Dannenfelser, "Economic and Social Conservatives Agree: Cut Planned Parenthood," National Review Online, March 7, 2011.

98. Robert P. Jones, "What's the Role of the Tea Party and Religion in the Shutdown Showdown?" On Faith (blog), *The Washington Post*, April 8, 2011, www.washingtonpost.com/blogs/on-faith/post/the-tea-party-and-religions -hand-in-the-shutdown-showdown/2011/04/08/AFdnUF2C_blog.html.

99. Steve Benen, "Religious Right Leader Sticks Up for the Culture War," *Washington Monthly*, March 5, 2011.

100. David Weigel, "Bachmann, Huckabee, Coburn: Cut a Deal," Slate .com, April 8, 2011.

101. Daniel Burke, "National Debt is New Hot Issue for Evangelicals," Religion News Service, February 16, 2011.

102. Glenn Greenwald, "Palin and the Tea-Party 'Movement': Nothing New," Salon, February 7, 2010.

103. Posner, "Tea Party Values."

104. Cohen, Chapter 9 in this volume.

105. Cohen, Chapter 9 in this volume.

106. Richard Flory, "Was There a Values Vote?" USC Trans/Missions, November 5, 2010.

107. Peter Montgomery, "AFA: Tea Party Married to Religious Right, Like it or Not," *Right Wing Watch* (blog), January 31, 2011.

108. Rob Boston, "In Play in Iowa: Ralph Reed Confab Shows Religious Right is in the Game for 2012," Talk to Action, March 8, 2011.

109. David Waters, "Will Christian Right Join the Tea Party?" *On Faith* (blog), *The Washington Post*, February 10, 2010, http://newsweek.washingtonpost.com/onfaith/undergod/2010/02/will_christian_right_join_the_tea_party.html.

110. Kyle Mantyla, "It's That Time of the Year," *Right Wing Watch* (blog), January 5, 2009, www.rightwingwatch.org/content/it%E2%80%99s-time-year.

Epilogue

A Tale of Two Movements

While our primary goal in this book has been to analyze the origins and early takeoff of the Tea Party, we have ineluctably touched upon the movement's influence on American politics beyond its formative two years. It seems to us both appropriate and vital to take the story as far as the vicissitudes and deadlines of publishing permit. Hence these comments on where things Tea Party currently stand.

As of early March 2012, two months into the presidential primaries, the Republican campaign has had a singular rhythm. Former Massachusetts Governor Mitt Romney, while maintaining his position in the front of the pack, has been unable to close the deal due to his inability to convince primary voters of his conservative bona fides. Before the primaries began in January 2012, a series of contenders emerged, seemingly willed forward by the depth of conservative unhappiness with Romney. Some were merely names promoted by conservative media, like Sarah Palin, Haley Barbour, or Chris Christie, who never entered the race. Others, like Minnesota Congresswoman Michele Bachmann, Texas Governor Rick Perry, and businessman Herman Cain, threw their hats in the ring, but finally posed little threat to Romney—their popularity with primary voters resembling short-lived swells that challenged Romney and then receded.[1] With uncanny timing, former Pennsylvania Senator Rick Santorum was the last candidate to surge and, along with former House Speaker Newt Gingrich, found himself the final alternative to Romney. Both Santorum and Gingrich won early primary elections and diminished any hopes Romney had of a cakewalk to the nomination.

The palpable desire among Republicans for a candidate other than Romney illustrates a cleavage in the Republican Party and in American conservatism that emerged explicitly with the election of Barack Obama. The cleavage has been the dominant story of politics on the right ever since, with the Tea Party, like an inspired walk-on, assuming the central role in the drama.

In his first column after the 2008 election, the *New York Times* house conservative, David Brooks, announced the division between what he called the traditionalists and the reformers in the Republican Party. According to Brooks, the traditionalist view was that Republicans lose elections when, as with the presidential candidacy of John McCain, they fail to field "real conservatives."[2] In contrast, the reformers, with whom Brooks identified, believed traditionalists were stuck in a 1970s view of conservatism and were losing touch with an American electorate that was rapidly changing both ethnically and in terms of their economic life chances.

Inside the Republican Party, the deck was stacked against the reformers, Brooks lamented. The traditionalists had managed to build up their ranks in the party infrastructure and would continue to dominate the party's nominating process. The near future looked bleak:

> [T]he Republican Party will probably veer right in the years ahead, and suffer more defeats. Then, finally, some new Reformist donors and organizers will emerge. They will build new institutions, new structures and new ideas, and the cycle of conservative ascendance will begin again.[3]

Brooks was half right. The traditionalists maintained their hold on the party. But electoral defeat did not materialize. In the 2010 election year, the party won a stunning sixty-three seats in the House of Representatives to take over as majority party.

It was the Tea Party that upset Brooks's calculations. He had it right about the issues that would bring change in the party. When the reformers would have their day, Brooks wrote, they would "propose new policies to address inequality and middle-class anxiety." But he had the agent of change all wrong. As chapters in this volume illustrate, notably those of Berlet and Disch, inequality and middle-class anxiety indeed mobilized the Tea Party. But it was not a mobilization to solve these problems; rather, it was a movement to oppose any measures that attempted to solve them.

In *The Tea Party and the Remaking of Republican Conservatism*, political scientists Theda Skocpol and Vanessa Williamson identify "deservingness" as the Tea Partiers' key discriminator between themselves and those they oppose.[4] The Tea Partiers see themselves as the people who have worked hard, achieved comfort and security and, with respect to entitlements like Social Security and Medicare, are merely getting what they have earned. They feel besieged by the "undeserving" and the liberal politicians who are colluding with them. They see the long-term unemployed and the legions of homeowners with underwater mortgages as parasitical, refusing to work and yet demanding what they, the Tea Partiers, have earned—hence, for example, the extraordinary mobilization to defeat the Obama administration's program to expand health insurance coverage, and support for politicians who promise to repeal the law that finally passed through Congress.

But there has been another turn of the screw in American politics. Two years after the Tea Party's appearance, another new movement burst onto the political stage. Occupy Wall Street (OWS) emerged at the end of a convulsion over the national debt in the summer of 2011.[5] If "deservingness" is the Tea Party's central theme, a concern with "fairness" characterizes the Occupiers. Rising economic inequality, the concentration of wealth in the hands of a few, and corporate greed are central complaints of OWS supporters, whose slogan is "We are the 99%."[6]

At first glance, the Occupy movement seems like a countermovement to the Tea Party. Their respective activists come from opposite ends of the American cultural and political spectrum. Largely young and ethnically diverse, the ranks of the Occupiers are made up of students, vets, unemployed workers, former homeowners, teachers, and union organizers. Could there be a greater contrast to the late middle-aged, white, and buttoned-down Tea Party? Instead of large one-day rallies, such as those held by the Tea Party on Tax Day, movement organizers set up tent villages in city parks and in the shadow of financial institutions across the nation. Run by "general assemblies" and equipped with makeshift health clinics and media centers, these "occupations" represented a novel form of grassroots protest—encampments in which activists "put down roots and grow the movement" by exercising their First Amendment right to assemble peaceably.[7]

But on closer examination, the Tea Party and the Occupy movement have something fundamental in common. They are both expressions of pain from differing points of view of the same social process. This process has been the dismantling of American middle-class life. In effect, the Tea Party movement is reacting to the feeling that prosperity is being taken away from them. The Occupy movement is reacting to the feeling that they will never have it.

In fact, the "American Dream,"[8] the unprecedented middle-class economic security that characterized the quarter century after the Second World War, has been undergoing slow-motion erosion since the first oil shock of 1973.[9] One measure of this is how large the gap in wealth has become between young people, from whose numbers the successor middle class emerges, and their elders. According to a recent Pew Research report, "households headed by adults 35 and under have 68 percent less wealth than those their age a quarter century ago." At the same time, households headed by adults age 65 and older "have seen their wealth increase 42% compared to their counterparts 25 years ago." Consequently, older households are 47 times wealthier than younger households today, compared to only 10 times wealthier in 1984.[10] This transformation is of a piece with a gradual unfolding of large-scale changes in social habits driven by economic necessity. In the past three decades, to take one example, even conservatives most closely tied to a notion of the "traditional family" have come to accept the two-earner family. It has become an economic given, and stands in contrast to the image of the stay-at-home mom of the 1950s, '60s, and early '70s.

The United Autoworkers (UAW) were once the iconic beneficiaries of the American dream, realizing both stable blue-collar jobs and middle-class levels of affluence. The 2009 financial rescue of Chrysler and General Motors (anathema to the Tea Party and one of the notable successes of the Obama administration's response to the financial crisis) saved this dying industry, yet the new UAW contracts of 2011 firmly institutionalized a two-tier system where new workers will earn half of what veteran workers make, about $14 an hour. This comes to about $30,000 a year. The UAW bellwether has now gone from working at a middle-class level to working at the level of the working poor.[11]

The great financial meltdown of 2008 brought a shocking and explosive ending to what had been a gradual process of decay. In its final stage before the financial collapse, the erosion of middle-class life was masked by easy credit, in particular, the ability of homeowners to borrow against what seemed like the continuous upward valuations of their property. In September 2008, this all came apart. Millions would find themselves underwater on their homes—owing more than the home's current value; grinding recession and large-scale, long-term unemployment was on the horizon.

The explosion of the financial crisis came toward the end of the working lives of most Tea Party supporters. Everything they had earned, suddenly, was insecure. They would enter into a furious mobilization against those they felt were trying to take it away. Whereas, for many in the Occupy movement, the financial crisis came at the beginning of their working lives. Their prospects for housing, for adequate wages, for the mere opportunity to pay off their student loans—all this was bleak, and worse. They would mobilize against the skewed levels of inequality of wealth and income that had come to resemble 1920s levels. They would mobilize as the "99%" against the "1%."

Within short order, the Occupy movement's issues entered the national debate, reflecting or perhaps contributing to a significant shift in public opinion. In a *Time* magazine poll conducted in October 2011, 79 percent believed the gap between rich and poor has grown too large, and 68 percent agreed that the wealthy should pay more taxes.[12] As Robert Reich observed, "Not since the 1930s has a majority of Americans called for redistribution of income or wealth."[13]

The Occupy movement also mobilized around its profound disappointment with the Obama administration. There was a widespread sense among the movement's young people that they had only recently been part of a social movement—the 2008 Obama presidential campaign. But once in office, Obama seemed to abandon them in the name of a futile bipartisanship that they judge to have been wholly inadequate to the needs of the economic crisis that has gripped the nation for three years.

Running for reelection in 2012, candidate Obama seems to have discarded the bipartisan approach that has antagonized his progressive constituency in favor of an economic populism on the model of Theodore Roosevelt. In a December speech in Osawatomie, Kansas, the president described the debate over how to restore American prosperity as "the defining issue of our time"—a "make-or-break moment for the middle class, and for all those who are fighting to get into the middle class."[14] In his January State of the Union address, Obama repeatedly used the word *fair*—fair share, fair play, fair shot—when making the case for his economic proposals. The key concern of the Occupy movement—fairness—had now become the central theme of his domestic agenda and reelection campaign, just as Tea Party concerns (with "Obamacare," the free market, national debt, and taxes) have come to dominate the Romney campaign. In a way, the 2012 presidential campaign is shaping up as a tale of two movements.

Historians have noted that the United States underwent two "revolutions" between 1963 and 1990.[15] One was a cultural revolution, often called "the sixties." Another was a political-economic revolution, often called "the eighties," or the Reagan Revolution. Sexual mores, family life, religion, music, the use of intoxicants, all underwent radical transformation in the sixties revolution. With the "eighties revolution," majorities of American voters began supporting candidates whose policies represented sea changes from the liberal post-World War II consensus on fundamental economic matters like the welfare state, labor unions, and economic regulation.

These revolutions have undergone criticism and political attack, but both have weathered the decades intact. Christian conservatives, organizing around "social issues," have fought a relentless but losing battle to reverse the sixties revolution. Liberals have analyzed the political and economic forces that have arisen since the eighties, named them—neoliberalism and globalization—but mounted little in the way of political initiatives to roll them back. While both of the elected Democratic presidents in this period, Bill Clinton and Barack Obama, have been severely criticized by members of the left for their accession to the regime of the Reagan Revolution, no challenger emerged within the party when it came time for their reelection.

The financial crisis and ensuing recession, now three years running, have finally handed one of the revolutions, the Reagan Revolution, a challenge it might be hard-pressed to beat back. In its breakdown, the unfettered, "free-market" preserve at the heart of what this revolution most reveres has summoned forth two wholly unexpected social movements. One, the Tea Party, has insisted that the solution to the crisis is to double-down on free-market orthodoxy. The other, the Occupy movement, believes the free market has no tools available on its own terms to correct the damage it has wrought. True to its rightist roots, the Tea Party defines its identity by contrast to a reviled other. In this, its contradistinction could not be greater than to a movement that has taken on the most inclusive of identities, the 99%. In the realm of politics, and with these two movements playing leading roles, the future of the Reagan Revolution will be decided.

Lawrence Rosenthal
Christine Trost
March 2012

NOTES

1. This reprises, in much expanded form, one of the quirky dramas of the 2008 Republican primary battle. Then, there was a dissatisfaction with John McCain among conservative primary voters that resembled the current

dissatisfaction with Mitt Romney. Unhappiness with McCain's conservative credentials buoyed the candidacy of Mike Huckabee, but also led to a yearning for a conservative who seemed to have a possibility of winning the general election. This developed into the drama of waiting for Fred Thompson to enter the race. When he did, his inadequacies as a candidate came quickly to the fore and the "electable conservative" dream fizzled.

2. David Brooks, "Darkness at Dusk," *New York Times,* November 11, 2008, www.nytimes.com/2008/11/11/opinion/11brooks.html. In a similar vein and from a similar point of view in the Republican spectrum, see David Frum, "Why Rush is Wrong," thedailybeast.com, March 6, 2008, www.thedailybeast.com/newsweek/2009/03/06/why-rush-is-wrong.html.

3. David Brooks, "Darkness at Dusk."

4. See Chapter 2, "What They Believe: Ideas and Passions," in Theda Skocpol and Vanessa Williamson, *The Tea Party and the Remaking of Republican Conservatism* (New York: Oxford University Press, 2012).

5. OWS has adopted a tactic of occupation championed by the movements of the 2011 Arab Spring as well as youth movements (first in Spain and then in Israel) in the spring and summer of 2011, in which youth occupied public spaces to demand a change in what seem to be impossible economic odds against their chances for a decent living. On the domestic front, the drive by Wisconsin's newly elected Governor Scott Walker to take collective bargaining rights away from public unions led to the occupation of the State Capitol by hundreds of state employees and citizens in February 2011.

6. The OWS movement's slogan, "We are the 99%," echoes the title of Columbia economics professor Joseph Stiglitz's article "Of the 1%, for the 1%, and by the 1%," which was published in *Vanity Fair* in May ,2011 and widely circulated on the Internet in the fall of 2011. In the article, Stiglitz describes the growing income and wealth gaps in the United States. The article begins, "It's no use pretending that what has obviously happened has not in fact happened. The upper 1 percent of Americans are now taking in nearly a quarter of the nation's income every year. In terms of wealth rather than income, the top 1 percent control 40 percent. Their lot in life has improved considerably. Twenty-five years ago, the corresponding figures were 12 percent and 33 percent." See Joseph E. Stiglitz, "Of the 1%, by the 1%, for the 1%," *Vanity Fair,* May 2011, accessed on November 8, 2011, www.vanityfair.com/society/features/2011/05/top-one-percent-201105.

7. One Occupy Wall Street blogger writes, "Before the Occupy movement succeeds in turning the tide of the corporate state back toward communities and the common good, it needs a home. A place to put down roots and grow the movement. A place to reclaim the commons—and not just in theory but in actual, physically-manifested ways that say: 'Hey, we are here to stay. No more business and politics as usual. Now it's our turn to have self-determination and self-governance. Let the General Assembly begin (spirit fingers up in the air)! . . . [T]his movement is about a new way of being." See Jake Olzen, "Meeting Violence with Nonviolence: Why the Occupy Movement Will Succeed," NationofChange.org, October 27, 2011, accessed on November 8, 2011, http://wagingnonviolence.org/2011/10/meeting-violence-with-nonviolence

-why-the-occupy-movement-will-succeed/. There is also a global dimension to this movement that stands in sharp contrast to the national focus of the Tea Party movement. Soon after Occupy Wall Street was formed, a wave of "Occupy" protests swept across cities in Asia, Europe, and the Americas. See Cara Buckley and Rachel Donadio, "Buoyed by Wall St. Protests, Rallies Sweep the Globe," *New York Times,* October 15, 2011, accessed on November 8, 2011, www.nytimes.com/2011/10/16/world/occupy-wall-street-protests -worldwide.html?pagewanted=all.

8. Or "the Fordist deal." See Yiannis Gabriel and Tim Lang, "New Faces and New Masks of Today's Consumer," *Journal of Consumer Culture* 8 (2008): 321.

9. Robert Reich, *Supercapitalism: The Transformation of Business, Democracy and Everyday Life* (New York: Vintage, 2008).

10. Eva Pereira, "Wealth Inequality between Young and Old Generations Reaches Record High," *Forbes,* November 8, 2011, www.forbes.com/sites/ evapereira/2011/11/08/wealth-inequality-between-young-and-old-generations -reaches-record-high/.

11. Keith Naughton and Craig Trudell, "Ford Adds 12,000 Hourly Jobs in U.S. Plants under UAW Accord," Businessweek.com, October 4, 2011, accessed on November 10, 2011, www.businessweek.com/news/2011-10-04/ ford-adds-12-000-hourly-jobs-in-u-s-plants-under-uaw-accord.html. See also Louis Uchitelle, "Factory Jobs Gain, but Wages Retreat," *New York Times,* December 29, 2011.

12. There was also broad agreement on Wall Street: 71 percent of those surveyed thought "executives of financial institutions responsible for the financial meltdown in 2008 should be prosecuted," and 86 percent agreed that "Wall Street and its lobbyists have too much power in Washington." See "Topline Results of Oct. 9-10, 2011, TIME Poll," Swampland, Time.com, accessed on November 8, 2011, http://swampland.time.com/full-results-of-oct-9-10-2011-time-poll/.

13. Robert Reich, "The Occupiers' Responsive Chord," *Robert Reich* (blog), October 31, 2011, accessed on November 8, 2011, http://robertreich .org/post/12168464049.

14. A full text of President Obama's speech in Osawatomie, Kansas, on December 6, 2011, can be found at www.washingtonpost.com/politics/ president-obamas-economic-speech-in-osawatomie-kans/2011/12/06/ gIQAVhe6ZO_story.html.

15. See, for example, Mark Lilla, "A Tale of Two Reactions," *The New York Review of Books,* May 14, 1998, accessed on November 10, 2011, www.nybooks .com/articles/archives/1998/may/14/a-tale-of-two-reactions/.

About the Contributors

ALAN I. ABRAMOWITZ is the Alben W. Barkley Professor of Political Science at Emory University in Atlanta, Georgia, and a renowned expert on national politics and elections. His expertise includes election forecasting models, party realignment in the United States, congressional elections, and the effects of political campaigns on the electorate. He has authored or coauthored five books, dozens of contributions to edited volumes, and more than forty articles in political science journals dealing with political parties, elections, and voting behavior in the United States. His newest book, *The Polarized Public? Why American Government is So Dysfunctional*, will be published in 2012 by Pearson Longman. His other books include *The Disappearing Center: Engaged Citizens, Polarization and American Democracy* (Yale University Press, 2010); *Voice of the People: Elections and Voting in the United States* (McGraw Hill, 2004); *Senate Elections* (University of Michigan, 1992); and an edited volume, *The Life of the Parties: Activists in Presidential Politics* (with Ronald Rapoport and John McGlennon, University of Kentucky Press, 1986). He received his PhD from Stanford University.

CHIP BERLET has spent over thirty-five years investigating right-wing social movements and antidemocratic, authoritarian, and racist right-wing trends in the United States. From 1981 until 2011, he was senior analyst at Political Research Associates (PRA), an independent, nonprofit research center. He has written, edited, and coauthored numerous articles on right-wing activity and government repression for publications as varied as the *Boston Globe*, the *New York Times*, *The Progressive*, *The Nation*, *The Humanist*, and the *St. Louis Journalism Review*. Berlet is editor of *Eyes Right! Challenging the Right-Wing*

Backlash (South End Press, 1995), a popular primer on the right. He is also coauthor (with Matthew N. Lyons) of *Right-Wing Populism in America: Too Close for Comfort* (South End Press, 2000). Berlet warned reporters about the armed militia movement prior to the right-wing terrorist bombing in Oklahoma City, and quickly emerged as a leading authority on the nature and overlap of right-wing populism, the patriot movement, armed militias, and white suprema- cists and anti-Semites. He has been quoted as an expert on these and other right-wing movements in *Time*, *Newsweek*, the *Boston Globe*, the *New York Times*, *The Wall Street Journal*, and other national and international periodi- cals. He was interviewed widely, and retained by CNN as an on-camera expert. He has also appeared live on ABC's *Nightline*, NBC's *Today Show*, and *CBS This Morning*, and he has been interviewed on scores of other television and radio news programs and talk shows, national and local, including NPR's *All Things Considered*, David Barsamian's *Alternative Radio*, and Pacifica Radio's *Democracy Now*.

DEVIN BURGHART is vice president of the Institute for Research and Education on Human Rights and coordinates the Seattle office. He is an internationally recognized expert on far-right political and social movements. He has been researching and writing about the far right since 1992, including groundbreak- ing investigative work on the militia movement, white nationalism, and new nativism. He is author of *Guns & Gavels: Common Law Courts, Militias & White Supremacy* (1996) and coauthor (with Leonard Zeskind) of *Tea Party Nationalism: A Critical Examination of the Tea Party Movement and the Size, Strength and Focus of its National Factions* (2010). He is frequently quoted as an expert by the *New York Times*, *Wall Street Journal*, *Chicago Tribune*, *Los Angeles Times*, *Philadelphia Enquirer*, *Arizona Republic*, *Seattle Post-Intelligencer*, *The Nation*, and *Rolling Stone*. He has appeared on CNN, MSNBC, the CBS News, National Public Radio, and other broadcast media outlets. In 2007, he was awarded a Petra Foundation fellowship.

MARTIN COHEN is assistant professor of political science at James Madison University. He received his PhD from the University of California at Los Angeles. His dissertation, *Moral Victories: Cultural Conservatism and the Creation of a New Republican Congressional Majority*, addresses the growing electoral influ- ence of the religious right on the Republican Party. Specifically, it looks at how local, religiously conservative activists worked their way into the Republican Party and helped elect morally conservative candidates to the U.S. Congress. He is also coauthor (with David Karol, Hans Noel, and John Zaller) of *The Party Decides: Presidential Nominations Before and After Reform* (University of Chicago Press, 2008), which reexamines the role of parties in presidential nominations. He regularly teaches classes on the Christian right, as well as classes on political parties and interest groups.

MELISSA DECKMAN is Louis L. Goldstein Associate Professor of Public Affairs and Chair of the Political Science Department at Washington College in Chestertown, Maryland, where she teaches a variety of courses on American government and politics. She has written extensively about the role of evan- gelicals in American politics and women and politics. Among other works, she is the author of *School Board Battles: The Christian Right in Local Politics* (Georgetown University Press, 2004); coauthor (with Laura Olson and Sue Crawford) of *Women with a Mission: Religion, Gender, and the Politics of Women Clergy* (University of Alabama Press, 2005); and coauthor (with Julie Anne Dolan and Michele L. Swers) of the textbook *Women and Politics: Paths to Power and Political Influence*, now in its second edition (Pearson/Prentice Hall, 2010). She received her PhD in political science from American University.

LISA DISCH is professor of political science and women's studies at the University of Michigan, where she teaches courses in political theory and feminist theory. Her research interests also include gender and politics, political ecology, and theories of democracy in both the United States and France. She is the author of *Hannah Arendt and the Limits of Philosophy* (Cornell, 1994) and *The Tyranny of the Two-Party System* (Columbia, 2002). She has also published articles in *Political Theory, Signs, Hypatia, Parallax*, and *American Political Science Review*. She is currently at work on a book on political representation. She received her PhD in political science from Rutgers University.

CLARENCE Y. H. LO is associate professor and director of graduate studies in sociology at the University of Missouri at Columbia, where he teaches courses on political sociology, social movements, theory, urban sociology, and qualitative/historical methods. He is the author of numerous books and journal articles including *Small Property versus Big Government: Social Origins of the Tax Revolt* (2nd ed., revised and expanded paperback, University of California Press, 1995), which examines the property tax revolt that culminated in California's Proposition 13, and traces the formation of class alliances in suburban communities that led to the triumph of a pro-business program of tax reduction. He is coeditor and author (with Michael Schwartz) of *Social Policy and the Conservative Agenda* (Blackwell, 1998), which examines the consequences of conservative movements and politics for social policy issues. Currently, he is writing a book titled *The Politics of Justice for Corporate Wrongdoing: Equality, Market Fairness, and Retribution in Enron and Beyond*. He received his PhD in sociology from the University of California at Berkeley.

JOSEPH LOWNDES is associate professor of political science at the University of Oregon. His research interests include American political development, conservatism, political identity, and race. He is the author of *From the New Deal to the New Right: Race and the Southern Origins of Modern Conservatism* (Yale, 2008), and coeditor (with Julie Novkov and Dorian Warren) of *Race and American Political Development* (Routledge, 2008). He has been interviewed on NPR's *Morning Edition* and *C-Span Book TV*, and his essays on race and the right have appeared in the Portland *Oregonian*, and the blogs *Talking Points Memo* and *Huffington Post*. He earned a PhD in political science from the New School for Social Research in 2004.

PETER MONTGOMERY is senior fellow at People For the American Way Foundation in Washington, DC, where he previously served as vice president for research and communications. He has followed the religious right political movement for more than fifteen years and is a nationally recognized expert on the religious right in U.S. politics. He is the primary author for an ongoing series of "Right Wing Watch in Focus" reports and contributes to the *Right Wing Watch* blog. He is a member of the advisory council for the online magazine Religion Dispatches (RD), and is an occasional contributor to RD and to the Alternet news service.

CHARLES POSTEL is associate professor of history at San Francisco State University, where he teaches courses on U.S. political history. He has also taught at Sacramento State University and the University of California at Berkeley. A historian of American political thought, his research focuses on late nineteenth- and early twentieth-century social and political movements. His book *The Populist Vision* (Oxford, 2007), a history of the original Populists of the 1890s, won the 2008 Bancroft Prize, one of the most prestigious honors a work of American history can receive. His book also won the Frederick Jackson Turner Award from the Organization of American Historians. He earned a PhD in history from the University of California at Berkeley.

LAWRENCE ROSENTHAL is executive director and lead researcher of the Center for Right-Wing Studies at the University of California, Berkeley. Founded in 2009, the center is a research unit dedicated to the study of right-wing movements, ideology and politics in the twentieth and twenty-first centuries. He has taught at UC Berkeley in the sociology and Italian studies departments and was a Fulbright Professor at the University of Naples in Italy. He has studied the right in the United States and in Italy and is currently working on a study of the contemporary American right in comparison to movements of the right in twentieth-century Europe. His work has appeared in the *Nation*, the *International Herald Tribune*, the *San Francisco Chronicle*, the *Sacramento Bee*, *Foreign Policy*, and other venues. He received his PhD in sociology from the University of California at Berkeley.

CHRISTINE TROST is associate director of the Institute for the Study of Societal Issues and program director of the Center for Right-Wing Studies at the University of California, Berkeley. She has authored journal articles on a variety of topics related to political ethics, campaign practices, campaign finance reform, civic and political engagement, and immigrant political mobilization. She is coeditor (with Alison Gash) of *Conflicts of Interest and Public Life: Cross-National Perspectives* (Cambridge 2008); coauthor (with Matthew Grossmann) of *Win the Right Way: How to Run Effective Local Campaigns in California* (Berkeley Public Policy Press 2005); and coeditor (with Jonathan Bernstein and Adrienne Jamieson) of *Campaigning for Congress: Politicians at Home and in Washington* (Institute of Governmental Studies Press, UC Berkeley 1995). She has taught courses in American politics as a lecturer at UC Berkeley and as a visiting assistant professor at Mills College. She holds an MA in political science from the University of Wisconsin-Madison, and a PhD in political science from the University of California at Berkeley.

Index